Piano Repertoire Guide

Intermediate and Advanced Literature

Fifth Edition

Dr. Cathy Albergo
Professor of Music
Department of Music
University of North Carolina Wilmington
Wilmington, North Carolina

Dr. Reid Alexander
Professor of Music
School of Music
The University of Illinois
Urbana, Illinois

Published by

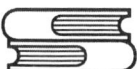

Stipes Publishing L.L.C.

ISBN 978-1-60904-049-9

© Copyright 2011
Stipes Publishing L.L.C.
All Rights Reserved
204 West University Avenue
Champaign, Illinois 61820
Printed in USA

Table of Contents

Foreword to the Fifth Edition..iv
Preface..vi
Introduction..viii

SOLO LITERATURE

The Baroque Period *circa* 1600–1750
    An Introduction to Baroque Keyboard Music..............................1
    Baroque Literature...8
    Baroque Collections and Anthologies...................................15

The Classical Period *circa* 1750–1820s
    An Introduction to Classical Piano Music..............................17
    Classical Literature..22
    Classical Collections and Anthologies.................................34

The Romantic Period *circa* 1820–1900
    An Introduction to Romantic Piano Music...............................37
    Romantic Literature...43
    Romantic Collections and Anthologies..................................68

The Contemporary Era *circa* 1900 to the Present
    An Introduction to Contemporary Piano Music...........................71
    Impressionism *circa* 1890–1920.......................................77
    Contemporary Literature from 1900.....................................84
    Contemporary Literature: Pedagogical Composers (Includes Jazz Selections)............117
    Contemporary and Jazz/Ragtime Collections and Anthologies............144

Multi-period Collections and Anthologies.......................................147

ENSEMBLE LITERATURE

Introduction to Piano Ensemble Music...151
Music for One Piano–Four Hands...153
Collections and Anthologies for One Piano–Four Hands...........................185
Music for One Piano–Six Hands..189
Music for Two Pianos–Four Hands..191
Music for Two Pianos–Eight Hands...211
Music for Multiple Pianos–Multiple Performers..................................215
Digital Keyboard Ensemble Music..217

OTHER CATEGORIES OF REPERTOIRE

Holiday Literature for Solo Piano..221
Holiday Literature for Piano Ensemble..225
Concerti for Young Pianists by James B. Lyke...................................229
Advanced Concerti for Skilled High School Students.............................233
Materials for Adult Instruction..237

APPENDICES

Appendix I: Listing of Publishers..239
Appendix II: Composer Catalogue Numbers..249
About the Authors..251

Foreword to the Fifth Edition

What is new and how is this Fifth Edition different from earlier versions? First, the title is not restrictive to intermediate. This edition, *Piano Repertoire Guide,* covers a wide variety of teaching literature, intermediate to advanced. Additionally, numerous changes in the publishing world have altered much of what is available in print. The official publisher listed for some works has changed as some large publishers have acquired other publishing firms or larger music publishing firms have become distributors globally for smaller firms.

These types of changes are mirrored in the publication of this text. The first two editions of the *Intermediate Piano Repertoire Guide* were published by the authors. The Third and Fourth editions were published by the Frederick Harris Music Company in Toronto, Canada. Stipes Publishing L.L.C., a publisher whose sole focus is texts, now publishes this important and greatly expanded Fifth Edition. The authors are appreciative to Stipes for the support and encouragement for taking on this substantial revision. We wish to single out Benjamin and Robert Watts for their combined efforts and encouragement as well as their expert design specialist, Brian McElwain, for his excellent work and attention to detail. It has been a pleasure to work with this publishing firm and exciting for us to see this new edition take shape.

We hope you will find this Fifth Edition of the *Piano Repertoire Guide* a useful and informative teaching reference for your independent music studio as well as for piano pedagogy, keyboard literature, and piano ensemble classes. We also include, at the end of this section, the informative *Foreword* to the Third Edition by Maurice Hinson that provides an excellent historical overview of texts in this area.

Reid Alexander
University of Illinois, Urbana

Cathy Albergo
University of North Carolina Wilmington

Foreword to the Third Edition

The piano teaching profession has been without a book for too long that focuses on the large body of intermediate level piano repertoire. We have to wait no longer—it is here in this volume: *Intermediate Piano Repertoire: A Guide for Teaching*.

Numerous books have partially addressed this subject. The Kern-Titus *Teacher's Guidebook to Piano Literature* (1954), aimed at the college non-keyboard major, was divided into eight semesters of study (four years of undergraduate study), and listed suggested repertoire for each semester. No annotations were included, only titles, composers, and publishers. Ernest Hutchinson's *The Literature of the Piano* (1948), revised by Rudolph Ganz (1964), touched on intermediate repertoire but only peripherally. The Friskin-Freundlich *Music for the Piano* (1954) included some of this repertoire but basically covered the period 1590–1952 and was organized by periods and style groupings. F.E. Kirby's *Short History of Keyboard Music* (1966) covered some of this material although it was musicologically oriented. My own *Guide to the Pianist's Repertoire* (1973), revised and enlarged edition (1987), looked at the important solo piano literature and answered the questions, What is it like? and Where can I get it? Some intermediate repertoire was included.

But now we have a book that concentrates entirely on this wonderful body of literature that provides the step to the great music written for our instrument. Many readers will be surprised to learn how much intermediate repertoire was composed by some of our 19th-century greats like Chopin and Liszt as well as by 20th-century educational composers. Both authors are authorities in the intermediate repertoire area; both teach piano pedagogy and practicum courses, and have worked with this body of repertoire for years.

The organization of the book by period is exemplary: Baroque, Classical, Romantic, and Contemporary. Also included are impressionistic literature, jazz literature, multi-period collections and anthologies, and holiday literature. An ensemble literature section (music for one piano–four hands, two pianos–four hands, and two pianos–eight hands), plus materials for adult study round out the thorough coverage. The volume is made even more useful by including suggested teaching orders plus the authors' designation of extremely successful teaching literature. The authors also grade the musical and technical difficulty of sets of pieces, e.g., Bach's Two-part Inventions, Debussy's Préludes, etc., a big asset for young and/or inexperienced teachers.

I cannot recommend this book too highly. It is a superb contribution all piano teachers will welcome with admiration and appreciation.

Maurice Hinson, Professor of Music
The Southern Baptist Theological Seminary
Louisville, Kentucky

Preface

This Fifth Edition has been re-titled *Piano Repertoire Guide: Intermediate and Advanced Literature*. Even though the primary focus is to overview piano teaching materials from the Early Intermediate through the Late Intermediate levels, in past editions we have listed selected Advanced repertoire in order to reflect the scope of a composer's works and to show the sequence of difficulty within a composer's output. In this edition, we have added more Advanced level compositions to further reflect that scope and to bring greater understanding about all levels or gradations of teaching literature. The works added are considered standard teaching literature, compositions that talented students often perform. We hope that this addition will give more support to those using the *Piano Repertoire Guide* as a text in undergraduate and graduate piano pedagogy and keyboard literature courses that focus on teaching literature.

The rapid expansion of contemporary pedagogical teaching materials has made updating the repertoire guide a necessity. To date, this is the only *Piano Repertoire Guide* in print that offers an overview of compositions written by pedagogical/educational piano composers. This is an important area of literature that should not be neglected when surveying teaching repertoire.

Along with revised and updated entries, new features of this text include the following:

- New essays introducing each of the major style periods: Baroque, Classical, Romantic and Contemporary.
- Updated listings for composers' birth and death dates.
- Brief composer biographies in the solo literature sections.
- Expanded annotations, commentary on especially significant collections.
- Additional listing of Early Advanced or Advanced materials to reflect the true scope of a composer's works.
- Update and expansion of recently published materials and contemporary pedagogical composers.
- Annotation of selected holiday music volumes.
- Updated teaching orders (denoted by * symbol).
- Revised listing of works (denoted by § symbol) that are deemed most important to the basic teaching literature and have been found to be very successful.
- Expanded one piano–four hands, one piano-six hands, two piano–four hands, and two piano–eight hands literature as well as the addition of multi-piano and digital piano ensemble materials.
- Expanded annotations for selected keyboard concerti including early advanced concerto possibilities.

We wish to thank those whose support, enthusiasm, and suggestions for new additions have made this revision possible. Special thanks are extended to our many colleagues who aided in proofreading and editing including: Dr. J. Stanley Ryberg, Dr. Barry D. Salwen, Dr. Tammie Walker, Dr. Soohyun Yun, Dr. Adrienne Wiley, Dr. Ronald Chioldi, Dr. Andrew Hisey, Professor Kathleen Theisen, and University of Illinois doctoral candidates, Chee Hyeon Choi and Kent Conrad. We appreciated the added insights that Drs. Yun, Salwen, and Walker provided on the music of Benjamin Lees, Rogers Sessions, and Amy Beach respectively. Continued thanks to Dr. Maurice Hinson for writing the supplementary Forewords to the earlier Third and Fourth editions and to the duo-piano teams—Dallas Weekley and Nancy Arganbright, Claire Aebersohl and Ralph Neiweem, and Cristina Perotti and Laurence Lynn Dutt—who took time from their busy schedules to read and make recommendations for the ensemble portions of the earlier editions. We also warmly thank the duet team of Marialena Fernandes (Professor of Piano and Chamber Music, University of Music and Performing Arts, Vienna, Austria) and Ranko Markovic (Artistic Director of the Conservatory of Vienna University) who carefully reviewed the ensemble manuscript for this Fifth Edition.

Key sources used in preparing this edition:

Resources and Bibliographical References:

Baker's Biographical Dictionary of 20th Century Classical Musicians 1997

Grove's Dictionary of Music and Musicians, Sadie, ed.

Grove Music Online

Oxford Music Online

The Oxford Companion to Music Teachers

The Oxford Dictionary of Music

ProQuest Digital Dissertations

The Music-in-Print Series Online

WorldCat Online

The Music and Performing Arts Library at the University of Illinois at Urbana-Champaign

Additional internet sources include:

classical.net

answers.com/library/Music+Encyclopedia

Bach-cantatas.com

classicalarchives.com

classical.composers.org

di-arezzo.com.uk/catalogue

essentialsofmusic.com

highbeam.com

music 44.com

Naxos.com

sheetmusicplus.com

On-line Publishers' Catalogs for composer biographies and current publications in print including, but not exclusive to:

- Alfred Music Publishing: Alfred, Kalmus, Warner, Belwin, Summy-Birchard, Myklas, Dover
- Carl Fischer Music: Carl Fischer, Theodore Presser, Universal–Wiener Urtext, Affiliated, Alphonse Leduc, Bärenreiter
- FJH Music Publishing Co.
- Frederick Harris Music Publishing Co.
- G. Schirmer Music Publishing Co.
- Hal Leonard Online: Hal Leonard, Willis, Durand, Schott, Ricordi, Schirmer, Henle, Marks, Associated, Boosey & Hawkes, Chester, Editio Musica Budapest
- Kjos Music Publishing Co.

Introduction

The intermediate level of piano study varies with each student according to age and ability. For our purposes, we define the intermediate level as music study following the completion of an elementary method or the mastery of the concepts needed to perform elementary level repertoire. During the intermediate level of study, the student becomes familiar with the wide variety of musical and technical elements required to perform the "classics" of the piano repertoire. The intermediate level is, therefore, a bridge to the more advanced repertoire such as Bach preludes and fugues; Haydn, Mozart, or Beethoven sonatas; character pieces of Chopin, Schubert, and Brahms; and more advanced contemporary and jazz compositions.

In our piano pedagogy and literature courses, we have found that young teachers are familiar with a narrow range of piano literature, which includes the compositions they are currently studying or have studied in the past, and maybe some of the better known standard repertoire. They usually are not aware of the wide range of intermediate level teaching literature in each period of musical history, the wealth of materials available from lesser-known composers, or the pedagogical literature of the contemporary period. In particular, students are unaware of the rich body of intermediate teaching repertoire for the instruction of their pupils. A broad spectrum of intermediate repertoire is necessary for our students, for it provides the musical stepping-stones to what we think of as "standard" repertoire. To be a flexible teacher, capable of working at a variety of levels and logically preparing students for advanced repertoire, one must be familiar with this middle, intermediate range of repertoire and the composers writing at this level.

In the context of our own degree programs, we each have taught piano practicum courses in which students are asked to observe model teaching, teach their own pupils, and through "composer projects" prepare overviews of both major and minor composers for weekly class discussion based on their own sight-reading and pedagogical analysis of repertoire outside of class. In this manner, students become intimately familiar with specific styles and with a wide variety of piano literature. This participatory role is crucial for both graduate and undergraduate students in order for them to substantially broaden their perspectives on useful teaching editions and understand the range of difficulty within a given composer's output. Through the sight-reading process, all teachers can discover areas that may present problems for their pupils as well as identify teaching concepts within a piece.

Through our teaching of piano pedagogy, practicum, and graduate literature courses, we continue to maintain and develop a bibliography of piano teaching literature, arranged by composer and style period, that we find useful as a reference tool for students as well as for teachers. Use of this *Piano Repertoire Guide* can help teachers avoid a "repertoire rut," i.e., continuous use of the same pieces, and can serve as a reminder of pieces which may have been taught in the past but since have been forgotten. The *Piano Repertoire Guide* also provides a look at lesser known or unfamiliar teaching pieces and composers. This Fifth Edition introduces many recently published editions and collections. Some advanced repertoire has been included to show the scope and range of difficulty within a given composer's writing. Much of this advanced literature is appropriate for quite skilled high school pianists and for undergraduate piano majors.

In the process of compiling this bibliography, we found an infinite number of possible listings. It is impossible to be totally comprehensive. Thus, we have streamlined the annotated bibliography to include what we would consider the central works of any given composer, especially those works that are representative of an early intermediate to early advanced level of teaching. Editions are included as a general guide, especially for lesser-known works, or for volumes available from only one publisher. When more than one edition or publisher is mentioned, citations occur in alphabetical order. Any Standard Edition (ASE) is used when there is not a preferred edition, or when several excellent editions are in print. Multiple sources (see partial listing in the Preface) were used to check availability and to obtain each composer's dates and country of birth when possible. Information on contemporary composers is often unavailable.

Important features of the *Piano Repertoire Guide* include grading the relative difficulty of the literature, a suggested teaching order for selected works, and the citation of works that we consider to be exceptional. Explanations of these features are as follows:

Grading (E – I – A)

In this bibliography, we have attempted to grade the relative musical and technical difficulty of each set, realizing that there are always gray areas between and within categories:

E (Early Intermediate)
Early intermediate literature (not elementary literature); entry-level pieces for the particular style; a composer's easiest writing; material appropriate for introducing the classics.

I (Intermediate)
Moderately difficult pieces; possible introductory pieces to the composer's style.

A (Advanced Intermediate to Advanced)
Difficult pieces that are possible for skilled, highly motivated high school students or undergraduate piano majors; a composer's more advanced compositions.

Teaching Order (*)

For selected publications, indicated by an asterisk (*), we have suggested a teaching order and thus have grouped pieces according to a general order of difficulty, beginning with the easiest. We find that this type of categorization is helpful for pedagogy students, less experienced teachers, and for those unfamiliar with a particular set of pieces. Examples of this feature are as follows:

1) Under the heading for Bach, J. S., in the Baroque solo literature section, you will find the following entry:

I-A §   *   Two-part Inventions (8, 1, 4, 13, 14)   Henle

The numbers in parentheses suggest that a teacher might consider teaching Invention no. 8 first, then no. 1, no. 4, etc. Within this set of numbers, the entries are arranged from easiest to more difficult with no. 14 (the B-flat Major Invention) being the most difficult of those listed. Depending on the student's background, we would teach one of these five inventions first and for a student with no background in playing the two-part inventions we would almost certainly select number 8 (F major) or 1 (C major). Why do we list Invention no. 8 first? The *Invention in F Major* has no ornaments to execute, which makes it slightly more accessible than the first invention.

2) Under the heading for Debussy, Claude, in the Impressionistic solo section, you will find the following entry:

I-A §   Children's Corner   Durand
    *   (The Little Shepherd, Doctor Gradus ad Parnassum, Golliwogg's Cakewalk)

Selected movements of Debussy's *Children's Corner* are taught to late intermediate and advanced students. Here, three of the most frequently taught movements are prioritized in order of difficulty. From this entry the reader can assume that introducing the *Children's Corner* with *The Little Shepherd* is preferable followed by *Doctor Gradus* and *Golliwogg*. Jumping to the more difficult *Golliwogg's Cakewalk* would depend on the preparedness of the student for a more advanced composition.

Citations (§)

Some selections are marked with the § symbol. These publications count among our favorite intermediate and early advanced to advanced level teaching pieces or collections and are usually annotated with some description. If you are looking for new literature and have not yet taught these works or used these editions, we highly recommend them to you. Again, these are general and subjective suggestions. We could have continued identifying works, but rather, have limited the § citations to include what we consider truly exceptional or unique editions based on editorial quality and/or musical value as well as less known repertoire deserving of greater recognition.

SOLO LITERATURE

The Baroque Period circa 1600—1750

An Introduction to Baroque Piano Music

The Baroque period in music history dates from approximately 1600 to 1750, between the late Renaissance and early Classical periods. The term *baroque* has a long and controversial history. Some say it is derived from a Portuguese word for a misshapen pearl and, until the late 19th century, the term was used mainly as a synonym for "absurd" or "grotesque". Others say that *baroque* is derived from the Italian term *barocco*, meaning bizarre. The use of this term originated in the 1860s to describe the highly decorated architectural style of religious and public buildings in Italy, Germany and Austria. Later, *baroque* was applied to music or art of the 17th and early 18th centuries. In current use, the term refers to the genre of music composed primarily between 1600 and 1750 although the dates are somewhat flexible since some composers were ahead of their time and some behind. The era of Baroque music was an age of significant progress with a new and vibrant intellectual, artistic and social atmosphere.

Unlike modern musicians who teach, compose, perform and live independently, Baroque musicians generally depended on the patronage of the church, the state or the aristocracy. Because of this complex patronage system, a great deal of Baroque music was written on demand for specific occasions at court, religious services or for the amusement or musical education of a royal family. Bach's music was influenced in his early years by several courts at which he was employed but most of his working life was spent as Cantor of St Thomas' Church in Leipzig where he composed an abundance of church cantatas. During his time in Leipzig, Bach also had a small ensemble that played music in a coffee house so there were also secular and purely instrumental works.

Many Baroque composers traveled throughout Europe and were aware of the works and styles of their colleagues. Through their travels and acquaintances, Vivaldi, Corelli, Scarlatti, Handel and many other composers met each other or were thoroughly conversant with one another's music. Bach owned and/or copied the music of many of his contemporary composers, often rewriting compositions for different instruments. Indeed, rewriting compositions during the Baroque period was a widely practiced method of study.

Music from the Baroque period includes a great diversity of Italian, French, English and German styles, both secular and sacred, as composers explored new musical ideas and styles. There were, however, several unifying elements in the Baroque period. One unifying theme was the exploration of forms such as fugue, canon, variations, dances, and concerto with the alternation of solo and *tutti* passages. Successive generations of composers have revisited these same forms. For example, Mendelssohn led a Baroque revival during the Romantic period, studying and playing Bach's works, writing fugues in the baroque style, adapting the works of Baroque composers and reintroducing Bach's *St. Matthew Passion* to the music public. Mozart, Schumann, Beethoven and many other composers wrote fugues, and dances (especially the minuet and trio), thus borrowing from the baroque style.

Other unifying themes included virtuosity, the use of counterpoint, and the *Doctrine of Affections*. In Baroque instrumental music, the emphasis was characteristically on virtuoso style. Both Bach and Handel were great virtuosi on the organ and harpsichord. There was an emphasis on developing counterpoint (imitative techniques) with strong rhythmic elements. Baroque thematic development, therefore, tends to be evolutionary as the themes are woven together using contrapuntal techniques rather than focusing on an interplay of contrasting materials as seen in the Classical period. At the same time, Baroque music generally focused on a central theme of evoking emotional states or affections by appealing to the senses. Each piece focuses not on reflecting the composer's emotions but on evoking a general emotion or affection.

An Introduction to Baroque Keyboard Music *continued*

I. Baroque Forms and Practice Suggestions

When learning Baroque music, pianists primarily study imitative works (inventions, sinfonias, and fugues) and preludes or dances that were originally written for the harpsichord.

Inventions and Sinfonias

J. S. Bach included *Inventions* and *Sinfonias* as well as eleven preludes from Book I of *The Well-Tempered Clavier* in the *Wilhelm Friedemann Bach Notebook* (*Clavierbüchlein*) for the instruction of his son. The *Inventions* (two-part inventions) and *Sinfonias* (three-part inventions) were sets of imitative pieces written in fifteen keys and arranged in the same order in each set. Written before the *Well-Tempered Clavier*, each *Invention* has a subject or theme and the *Sinfonias* have a subject and one or two countersubjects. Bach employs extraordinary creativity and craftsmanship using contrapuntal techniques to craft each invention.

Practice suggestions for *Inventions* and *Sinfonias*:

- Identify the subject and in some cases the parts (head and tail) of the subject. Bracket and label all presentations throughout the score using "S" for the subject, "H" for the head, and "T" for the tail.

- In the *Sinfonias*, identify the subject (x) and countersubjects (y and z). Map the use of x, y, and z throughout the invention. Discover how many times the subject (x) is in the top voice, middle voice, or bottom voice? Where then does Bach place y and z?

- Label all appearances of the subject in inversion.

- Find and label extensions of the subject and episode material.

- Find measures in the *Sinfonias* in which Bach changes from three to two voices creating variety of texture.

- Decide on the articulation for the subject or x and y themes using contrasting touches to highlight the themes. Write in your articulation decisions and any needed fingerings.

- Practice each voice separately. Then combine all voices practicing in sections.

Prelude and Fugues

In the early Baroque era, the Mean-tone tuning system for keyboard instruments used some acoustically pure intervals and others that were either compressed or stretched causing important harmonies in the key to sound intolerably out of tune. The newly developed *Wohltemperiert* tuning system (well-tempered—meaning that all keys were usable, though the remote keys were still fairly "active") employed slight modifications of the intervals and made it possible for composers to write in all keys. Bach celebrated this tuning system and showed how it could be used in *The Well-Tempered Clavier, Books I and II*. Each volume contains a prelude and fugue in each major and minor key (24 in each volume).

Each prelude or fugue in *The Well-Tempered Clavier* generally deals with one musical idea. Bach creates contrast within pieces by modulating to different keys and varying the texture. Analyzing the modulations and keys will help highlight the important new tonal centers and cadences.

Bach's extraordinary skill and craftsmanship are evident in the great variety and diversity of the forty-eight preludes and fugues. Pairing two contrasting movements, such as a prelude and fugue, was a standard practice in the Baroque period. Prelude literally means playing beforehand (to prepare for) as in a warm-up, setting the tonality for the music that follows. The prelude was generally a free, sometimes improvisatory piece usually in a through-composed form. Bach writes slow and fast preludes, free (fantasias) or strict preludes, and preludes that are *legato* and songlike (ariosos) as well as preludes that exhibit a joyful dance-like quality. Some preludes are more structured using imitative styles, such as two-part inventions or three-part sinfonias. Their variety is amazing. Bach used this free form as a natural partner for the contrasting fugue.

In contrast, Bach's fugues are in strict contrapuntal style written for a specific number of voices or parts. The term *fuga,* in Italian means flight. In many fugues you can imagine the "flight" as voices seem to chase each other. Before discussing or beginning to practice a fugue, become familiar with fugal terminology:

— *subject:* the theme on which the fugue is based

— *countersubject:* a contrasting melody to the subject, that rarely appears without the subject.

— *answer:* the second or fourth statement of the subject, in the dominant key

— *real answer:* a literal transposition of the subject in the dominant key

— *tonal answer:* a transposition with slight adjustments of intervals to accommodate the new key

— *episode:* a group of measures between presentations of the subject that are based on a fragment of the subject, countersubject, or new material.

— *stretto:* statements of the subject in two or more voices, each entry overlapping the previous one. All voices usually enter before the first voice has finished the subject.

— *invertible counterpoint:* reversing the subject and countersubjects among the registers or voices (i. e., upper, middle, or lower).

(It should be noted that other composers, like Handel, were far less strict in their fugal writing and use of contrapuntal techniques.)

When starting to practice a new fugue, it is helpful to determine the length of the subject and bracket each subject entrance. After completing this exercise, you will have a skeletal analysis of the fugue and can see how the composer presents the voices (soprano, alto, tenor, and bass). (Vocal ranges are not implied in this terminology.) By identifying the subject, you can more easily see features such as episodes and *strettos*.

Consider the following practice ideas when beginning a new fugue:

— Identify (find and bracket) the opening motive or subject and subsequent presentations or *episodes*. Decide how you will articulate the subject and make each voice clear. Write in your articulation decisions and any needed fingerings. Articulation is an important factor in establishing independence of each voice.

— Locate and label any countersubject and decide on the articulation. Because the subject and countersubject appear together, they usually require contrasting, independent articulation.

— Divide the fugue into practice units or sections and use a layered approach for practicing:

    1. Practice each voice separately with consistent articulation of the subject and countersubject.

    2. Combine pairs of voices, e.g., S and A, S and T, S and B, etc. Listen for the articulation and be consistent with fingering. Notice if the subject migrates from hand to hand or is shared by both hands.

    3. Combine all voices.

Dance Forms and Suites

Collections of instrumental dances date back to the early Renaissance period. Unlike the three movement classical sonata and sonatina where the middle movement occurs in a contrasting key center, the Baroque dance suite is a collection of dances in different tempos and moods, all in the same key, each movement in Binary form (A-B), with each section repeated. In general, the tempos of the dances follow a slow-fast-slow-fast pattern. The dances were often paired, a slower dance followed by a faster one. Contrast in the dance suite was achieved through the variety of dances, and their different meters, tempi and rhythmic formulae.

An Introduction to Baroque Keyboard Music *continued*

SOLO LITERATURE

Bach's six *French Suites*, six *English Suites*, and six *Partitas* are significant contributions to the keyboard literature. Bach formalized the Baroque dance suite to include a set of four standard dances: *allemande*, *courante/corrente*, *sarabande*, and *gigue/giga*. Newer, popular dances were inserted between the *sarabande* and *gigue* as optional dances. The most frequently used optional dances in the Bach suites are the *gavotte*, *minuet*, and *bourrée*. A prelude was an optional dance sometimes found at the beginning of the suite. The acronym ACSOG is a helpful tool that outlines the dances found in the standard dance suite of the late Baroque period.

Prelude The prelude could be in any form, free or strict, but would generally contrast with the *allemande* in mood and style. The prelude was optional. In the shorter *French Suites*, Bach begins with the *allemande*. In his *English Suites* and *Partitas*, Bach precedes the *allemande* with a large introductory movement.

A **Allemande** (French for "German") A stately and dignified dance in quadruple meter (4/4) of German origin, usually with an upbeat, in moderate tempo, and in binary form. (In the 18th century the *allemande* was often written in triple meter.)

C **Courante** (French) or **Corrente** (Italian) A 17th-century French dance characterized by running and gliding steps to an accompaniment in triple meter (3/4) in a quick tempo. The *courante*, the French form, is not overly fast, uses dotted rhythms to provide the character of the dance and was an important dance of the French court. The *corrente*, the Italian form and a lively courtship dance, often has a smoother, lighter texture and is comprised of a running upper line and supporting bass line. It is suitable for a faster tempo than the *courante*.

S **Sarabande** A slow, stately processional dance in triple meter (3/4) that originated in Spain in the 16th century as the *zarabanda*, a rather energetic and erotic dance. It was banned in Spain but developed in the Baroque era as a slow movement in the dance suite.

O **Optional:** One or more optional dances may be included.

Minuet or menuett A graceful dance in triple meter of French origin.

Gavotte An elegant and moderately fast court dance in 4/4 or 2/2 meter. It originated as a French folk or peasant dance and typically has an upbeat of two quarters or one half note.

Bourrée A brisk, lively French dance in duple meter usually beginning with an upbeat.

Passepied A lively French dance in triple meter, popular in France and England in the 17th and 18th centuries, resembling a minuet but in a faster tempo.

Polonaise A stately Polish processional dance in triple meter. Primarily a promenade by couples, this was a dignified ceremonial dance from the 17th to 19th century that often opened court balls and other royal functions. The couples according to their social positions, promenaded around the ballroom with gliding steps accented by bending the knees slightly on every third step.

Chaconne or **Ciaccona** A stately Spanish dance in triple meter (somewhat like a *sarabande*) with a series of variations on a melodic/harmonic sequence over a repeated bass (ground bass) or chord pattern.

Passacaglia A slow, stately Spanish or Italian dance in which there is a series of variations over a short repeating melodic figure usually found in the bass (bass-ostinato). Passacaglia and chaconne were virtually the same and the names sometimes seem to have been interchangeable.

G **Gigue** (French) or **Giga** (Italian) The final dance of the Baroque keyboard suite is fast and energetic. *Gigue* comes from jig, a Scottish or Irish dance. A French *Gigue* presents triplet figures in compound meters, frequently 6/8 or 12/8. In his suites, Bach usually adopts the imitative French *Gigue*, but on occasion also uses the Italian *Giga*, which is less imitative. A *gigue* usually starts with an eighth note up-beat.

Sonatas

Domenico Scarlatti, son of composer Alessandro Scarlatti, is most prominently known for his 555 keyboard sonatas, many written for his gifted pupil Maria Barbara. The earliest publication (1738) of thirty of Scarlatti's keyboard *Sonatas* was titled *Essercizi per gravicembalo,* literally meaning "Exercises for Harpsichord." In general, his sonatas are of one movement and in binary form with the two halves roughly equal in length. The first half modulates from the tonic or home key to a related key, usually the dominant or sometimes the relative minor or subdominant. The second half begins in the new key, modulates and ends in the original tonic key.

Several editors have catalogued the keyboard works of Scarlatti. In 1906, Alessandro Longo was the first to publish an ostensibly complete set of sonatas providing the first systematic ordering of the sonatas using Longo (L) numbers. In 1953, Ralph Kirkpatrick provided a revised numbering system for all of Scarlatti's sonatas using Kirkpatrick (K) numbers. Kirkpatrick's system was first published in his landmark book on Scarlatti and since has been widely adopted by musicians. Then in 1967, Giorgio Pestelli published the most recent edition of the 555 sonatas using an alternative third system of Pestelli (P) numbers. (See *Appendix II* for other catalog numbers.)

Longo and Kirkpatrick both believed that Scarlatti might have intended to group many of the sonatas, often in pairs and in some cases in sets of three. If grouped in a pair the two sonatas usually share the same tonal center but sometimes the pair may include one sonata in a minor key and the paired sonata in the related major key. Other than the tonal relationship, these sonata pairs either contrast (in tempos or compositional complexity) or complement (share stylistic agreement or harmonic palette) each other. Twelve sonatas form sets of three.

The sonatas exhibit a wide variety of moods, colors, and styles and often use effects to imitate other instruments such as guitars, trumpet fanfares, hunting horns, or castanets reflecting the influence of Iberian or Spanish folk music. Within these short keyboard works, Scarlatti often surprises us with his unusual key shifts, unexpected dissonances, gymnastic hand crossings, acciaccatura, chromatic passages, virtuosic technique and many other effects in these delightful pieces. When played on a modern piano, Scarlatti's sonatas require the same attention to articulation and rhythmic precision as compositions by Bach.

II. Performance Practice and Ornamentation

When discussing Baroque keyboard literature, it is important to consider the keyboard instruments (harpsichord, clavichord, organ and piano) of the time. The two primary keyboard instruments of the Baroque era were the harpsichord and the organ associated, respectively, with secular and sacred music. The harpsichord was a keyboard in which the strings were plucked by a quill and the player could not vary the tone through finger touch. Harpsichord construction and composition reached its high point during this period. The smaller clavichord was often either a practice instrument or a portable instrument and was capable of generating very soft, expressive playing by a tangent hitting the string. However, due to its size and construction it was certainly not loud enough for anything other than performance in a small setting. There is conflicting information about the exact date of the invention of the piano. It is generally agreed that a very early version of the Christofori piano existed by 1700 and that surviving instruments by this builder date from the 1720s. According to various accounts, Bach was not overly impressed with the early piano, having played on at least one of Gottfried Silbermann's instruments, which was a copy of an early Cristofori instrument. However, he played and praised Silbermann's organs, harpsichords, clavichords and his later (1747) pianofortes.

Most Baroque keyboard pieces were composed for the harpsichord. If possible, pianists should play Baroque compositions on a harpsichord to experience the unique touch and sound of that instrument. When playing these pieces on a modern piano, the primary challenges are tonal clarity, rhythmic precision, articulation and judicious pedaling, as pedal was unavailable on the harpsichord.

An Introduction to Baroque Keyboard Music *continued*

A harpsichord with double manuals (two keyboards with different "stops" to provide a variety of timbres) can provide a contrast of *forte* and *piano* colors. This is often imitated on the modern piano as the performer shifts between *forte* and *piano* dynamics in sections or passages using a technique termed "terraced dynamics".

Baroque works require special attention to touch and articulation, making effective use of detached and *staccato* articulations. In order to highlight each voice and bring out the musical themes, a contrasting mixture of *legato* and detached touches is highly desirable. Decide on the articulation of each musical idea, notate your decisions in the score and be consistent in your approach to phrasing and articulation. In general:

— Use a detached touch:

- to articulate skips, leaps and wider intervals.
- to imitate bass instruments (cello, bassoon, etc.).
- before emphasized notes: syncopations, downbeats, and *appoggiaturas*.
- for slower note values when contrasted with faster note values (i. e., eighth notes against sixteenth notes).
- to highlight energetic and joyful moods.

— Notes that move by step can be played *legato* while wider intervals are detached.

— Changes of direction, wide leaps, and changes of harmony were often highlighted by a detached touch.

— Slur pairs of quarters and eighths that descend or ascend by step.

— Slur LH descending arpeggios.

— Hold repeated half notes for full value then slightly detach.

— Observe the highest and lowest pitches in the score. These often represent peak moments of musical intensity.

— Identify the dynamic plan. Will you use terraced dynamics? How will your dynamic plan emphasize the contrasting textures (e.g., echo effects, solo and *tutti* effects)?

— "Short-short-long" phrase organization is frequently found. The "long" phrase moves forward to the cadence.

Ornamentation

Ornamentation is the embellishment of the musical line with trills, mordents, turns, *appoggiaturas* and grace notes. Baroque composers used ornamentation as a characteristic of their style derived from Renaissance music. Sometimes ornaments were not even indicated in the score, but were simply left to the discretion of the performer. However, Bach designated the ornaments he wanted in his keyboard music and in his organ works, he occasionally wrote out ornaments because he wanted to ensure that they were played a certain way. Bach provided a written "realization" of a few of the standard Baroque ornaments in his *Wilhelm Friedemann Bach Notebook*.

The following chart provides a written "realization" of a few of the standard Baroque ornaments:

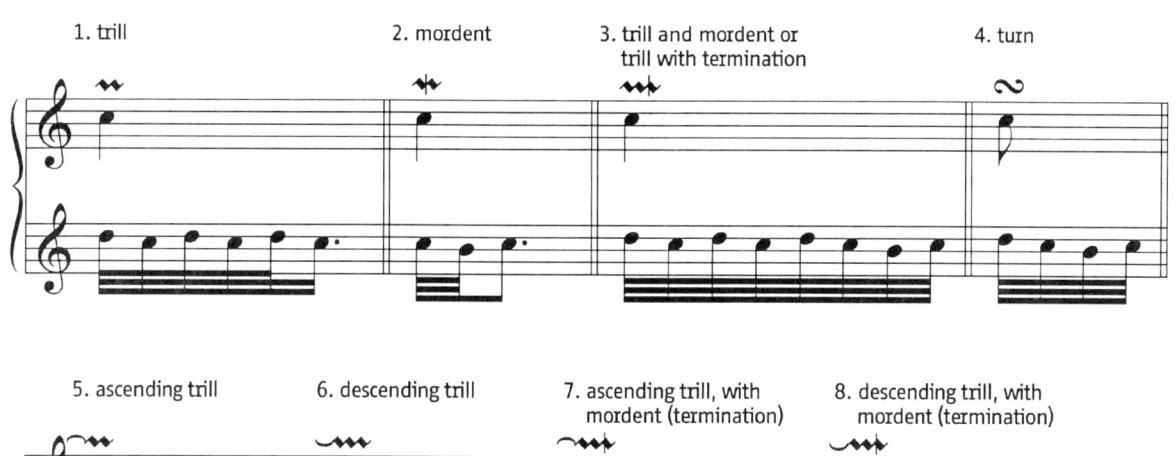

Recommended resources for further reading:

Badura-Skoda, Paul. 1993. *Interpreting Bach at the Keyboard.* Translated by Alfred Clayton. Oxford: Clarendon Press.

Burrows, Donald, ed. 1997. *The Cambridge Companion to Handel.* Cambridge: Cambridge University Press.

Kirkpatrick, Ralph. 1953. *Domenico Scarlatti.* Princeton, NJ: Princeton University Press.

Little, Meredith and Natalie Jenne. 2001. *Dance and the Music of J. S. Bach* (expanded edition). Bloomington: Indiana University Press.

Sutcliffe, W. Dean. 2003. *The Keyboard Sonatas of Domenico Scarlatti.* Cambridge: Cambridge University Press.

Baroque Literature

A. Characteristics

Students entering the intermediate level of piano instruction need to prepare carefully for the demands, both musical and technical, of this literature. The study of Baroque repertoire will lead the student to experience and understand several musical and technical elements of this literature:

- Hand and finger independence
- Contrapuntal voicing; polyphonic style
- Articulation—*legato*, detached, and *portato*
- Terrace dynamics
- Interpretation of phrasing (determining phrase groupings in the absence of slurs and expression markings)
- Phrasing across the bar line
- Use of subjects, motives, episodes, sequences, inverted motives, etc.
- Ornamentation
- Dance forms; ternary and binary; variations; prelude and fugue; invention
- Eighth, sixteenth, and triplet rhythms including triplets aligned with dotted figures; rhythmic augmentation and diminution of melodies
- Emphasis on strong beats and on upbeat patterns

B. Introducing the Baroque Style

Teachers should prepare students carefully before tackling some of the more complex Baroque literature. The following is a list of music that may be used to introduce the Baroque style. These pieces and collections are examples of the type of music that can serve as a valuable link between elementary method books and intermediate repertoire. They are listed in alphabetical order by composer or editor rather than in order of difficulty.

Blickenstaff, Marvin, ed.	Bach Dances	Carl Fischer
Gillock, William	Fanfare and Other Courtly Scenes in Baroque Style	Alfred
Hinson, Maurice, ed.	Dances for the Keyboard: 31 Short Pieces to Play Before the Two-Part Inventions	Alfred
Karp, David	Lady Margaret's Suite	Alfred
Palmer, Willard	Baroque Folk (Suite movements)	Alfred
Rollin, Catherine	Spotlight on Baroque Style	Alfred
Waxman, Donald, ed.	A Dance Pageant: Renaissance and Baroque Keyboard Dances	Galaxy Music

C. Gradation or Teaching Order

We suggest the following teaching order for Baroque literature:

Easier selections of Petzold, Bach, Handel, Purcell, Rameau, and Couperin
Selections from J. S. Bach's notebooks for Anna Magdalena and Wilhelm Friedemann
Selected easier suite movements (Bach, Handel)
Scarlatti — Easier sonatas
Bach — Kleine Präludien und Fughetten (Little Preludes and Fugues)
Bach — Two-part Inventions
Bach — Three-part Inventions (Sinfonias)
Bach — Well-Tempered Clavier (Book I)

| Composer | Title | Publisher |

Bach, Johann Sebastian (1685–1750) Germany

Bach was born into a family with a long history as fine musicians. His father (Johann Ambrosius) was a court trumpeter, his uncle (Johann Christoph) was a well-known organist, and his eldest brother (also named Johann Christoph) was an organist and teacher. J. S. Bach was a composer, organist, harpsichordist, violinist, and violist, *Kapellmeister* to the Court of Cöthen and later Cantor in the four principal Lutheran churches of Leipzig. One of the most renowned musicians in Germany and in music history, he fathered twenty children several of whom became composers and musicians: Wilhelm Freidemann Bach (eldest son), Carl Philipp Emanuel Bach (second son), Johann Christoph Friedrich Bach (ninth son), and Johann Christian Bach (youngest son).

E   First Bach Album (Bastien, ed.)   Kjos

E   The First Book for Young Pianists (Palmer, ed.)   Alfred

E   First Lessons in Bach, 28 Pieces (Tsitsaros, ed.)   Schirmer

         As part of the Schirmer performance editions, this volume is a revision of the earlier Schirmer publication of the same title. Content is drawn from Anna Magdalena's notebook and selected dances from the *English* and *French Suites*. Scores are lightly edited with dynamics and phrase markings. Informative performance notes and a performance CD are included.

E   §   Selections from the Notebook for Anna Magdalena Bach (Tsitsaros, ed.)   Hal Leonard

         With a Preface by Denise Taylor, this volume contains 12 of the most often played selections from this famous notebook in an *urtext* format. Informative performance notes and a performance CD are included.

E-I   An Introduction to His Keyboard Works (Palmer, ed.)   Alfred

E-I   Anna Magdalena Bach Notebook, BWV Anh. 113-132 (Langrish, ed.)   ABRSM

E-A   §   Celebrate Bach, Vols. 1, 2, 3 (Hisey, ed.)   Frederick Harris

         These three scholarly volumes comprehensively cover much of the important Bach keyboard repertoire ranging from the introductory Bach compositions in volume 1 to more advanced works like the *Italian Concerto, BWV 971* in volume 3. Volume 1 is devoted to revealing the best compositions from the two instructional notebooks: the *Klavierbüchlein für Anna Magdalena Bach* and the *Clavierbüchlein für Wilhelm Friedemann Bach*. Volume 2 addresses the *Two-Part* and *Three-Part (Sinfonias) Inventions*. Volume 3 is a compilation of frequently taught *Partitas*, *French* and *English Suites* and concludes with the *Italian Concerto*. All three volumes have extensive performance and study notes on sources and repertoire.

E-A   Klavierbüchlein für Anna Magdalena Bach, 1725 (Dadelsen, ed.)   Bärenreiter

         Teachers should consider owning the original and complete version of the 1725 second notebook for Anna Magdalena (the first dates from 1722), which contains forty-five compositions including contributions by composers such as Petzold and Couperin. These compositions are prefaced by two partitas (BWV 827 and 830) and followed with two sonatinas by C. P. E. Bach.

I   §   At the Piano with J. S. Bach (Hinson, ed.)   Alfred

         The collection includes Bach's early, less well-known programmatic work, *Capriccio on the Departure of his Beloved Brother, BWV 992*, which is sometimes difficult to obtain. The *Adagissimo* (third of the six movements) portrays extreme sorrow. Though not fully realized by Bach (he wrote only the bass line and melody), the movement consists of a four-measure ground bass. The frequent descending 2nds and two-note slurs imitate sobbing or sighing.

Baroque Literature *continued*

SOLO LITERATURE

I	Brandenburg Notebook (Kern, arr.) (Selections from Concerti 1-6)	Alfred
I	Dances for the Keyboard (31 Short Pieces to Play before the Two-Part Inventions)	Alfred
I	Easiest Piano Pieces	Peters
I	Eighteen Short Preludes (Palmer, ed.)	Alfred
I	First Lessons in Bach (Carroll/Palmer, eds.)	Alfred
I § *	Kleine Präludien und Fughetten (BWV 939, 927, 924, 999, 933)	Wiener Urtext

This edition of the *Little Preludes* contains an informative Foreword that outlines the origin of each prelude. It is one of the most scholarly and well-edited editions of these works.

I	Selections from The Anna Magdalena Notebook	Alfred
I-A	An Introduction to the Performance of Bach, Vols. I–III (Tureck, ed.)	Oxford
I-A §	Bach Dances (Blickenstaff, ed.)	Carl Fischer

A superb collection of dances selected from Bach's *English Suites*, *French Suites*, and *Partitas*. The editor points out that many students do not have the opportunity to learn an entire Bach suite and includes examples of all core dances in this collection. The volume is organized as one large suite, with several examples of each of the core dances (*Allemande, Corrente, Sarabande, Gigue*) and several optional dances (*Minuet, Gavotte, Bourrée*). General performance suggestions and specific notes on each piece are included at the end of the volume.

I-A	Inventions and Sinfonias (Palmer, ed.)	Alfred
I-A	J. S. Bach: Miscellaneous Keyboard Works	Dover
I-A	Notebook for Wilhelm Friedemann Bach	Kalmus

Not as well known as the *Anna Magdalena Notebook*, this notebook includes first drafts of the *Two-* and *Three-part Inventions*, several short preludes, and preludes which later were included in *The Well-Tempered Clavier* (Book I).

I-A	Selected Keyboard Works, (J. S. Bach) (Palmer/Schneider, eds.)	Alfred
I-A *	Sinfonias (1, 2, 9, 15)	Henle
I-A	Sinfonias (Three Part Inventions) (Palmer, ed.)	Alfred
I-A § *	Two-part Inventions (8, 1, 4, 13, 14)	Henle

Completed in 1723, the *Two-part Inventions* represent a musical milestone for the advancing intermediate student. In addition to the easier inventions listed above, teachers are urged to assign the less frequently taught, beautiful F minor invention (9) and the highly ornamented B minor invention (15).

I-A §	Two-Part Inventions (Carroll/Palmer, eds.) (Book or Book and CD)	Alfred
A §	Fantasia in C Minor, BWV 906 (Palmer, ed.)	Alfred

This edition includes detailed background about the *Fantasia* and a facsimile of the complete autograph.

A §	Italian Concerto (*Palmer, **Hisey, eds.)	*Alfred; **Frederick Harris

The *Allegro* movement is accessible to skilled teenage pianists. The concerto grosso concept allows the student to explore the range of sounds necessary to create the *tutti* versus *soli* effects. The second movement *Andante* requires a high degree of interpretive skill and musicality; the third movement *Presto* is technically challenging when played up to tempo. The concerto also is available in *Celebrate Bach, Vol. 3* (Harris).

A	J. S. Bach: Keyboard Music	Dover
A §	Partita in B-Flat (Palmer, ed.)	Alfred

This edition is recommended because the score includes a facsimile of the complete manuscript that is extremely interesting for student and teacher to examine. This partita is accessible for the skilled high school student. Particularly at-

E (Early Intermediate)   I (Intermediate)   A (Advanced Intermediate to Advanced)

tractive are the two minuets, which should be played in a *D.C. al Fine* manner, and the final *Giga* (Italian spelling rather than the traditional French *Gigue*).

A	*	Six English Suites (4)	Henle
A	*	Six French Suites (5)	Alfred; Henle
A	*	Six Partitas (1)	Alfred; Henle
A	*	The Well-Tempered Clavier: Book I (2, 16, 5, 21, 1), Book II (15, 1)	Henle

Bull, John (1562–1628) England

A composer, improviser, organist and virtuoso virginalist, Bull held positions as organist at Hereford cathedral in 1582 and in 1591 organist in Queen Elizabeth's chapel. He received a doctorate in music at Cambridge University in 1592 and became the first Professor of Music at Gresham College in London in 1596. In 1913, he moved to Brussels. Bull was noted as a keyboard performer on organ but little of his keyboard music was published. The British national anthem, *God Save the King* is often attributed to Bull and the Fitzwilliam Virginal-Book contains several of his pieces such as *The King's Hunting Jig*.

I-A	Compositions	Kalmus

Couperin, François (1668–1733) France

From a family of French musicians, he was a composer, organist and harpsichordist known as *Couperin le Grand* (Couperin the Great) to avoid confusion with his uncle of the same name. Couperin's best known work, *Piéces de clavecin* (1713-1730) in four volumes, includes 220 highly ornamented pieces including dance forms, character pieces and imitative pieces. He is also known for his treatise *L'art de toucher le clavecin* that includes short preludes as instructional pieces and describes performance practice, harpsichord style and ornamentation.

I-A		Album of Harpsichord Pieces	Kalmus
I-A		Couperin Complete Keyboard Works, Series I, II	Dover
I-A	§	L'art de toucher le Clavecin (Halford, ed.)	Alfred

This edition, translated from the French, highlights principles from the original treatise. Of particular interest to teachers will be Couperin's discussion on teaching students (e.g., provide more than one lesson a week so that students will not develop bad habits).

Daquin, Louis-Claude (1694–1772) France

A harpsichordist, organist, improviser and composer, Daquin was a child prodigy who performed for Louis XIV at age six. In 1727, Daquin became organist at the church of St. Paul in Paris until 1732. In 1755 he became organist at the Notre-Dame Cathedral in Paris. Known as a virtuoso performer and improviser, his concerts attracted large crowds and stories abound that police were called in on nights of his performances to maintain order. In 1735, Daquin published his *Premier livre de pièces de clavecin* (First Book of Pieces for the Clavichord). As a composer, he wrote harpsichord and organ music, chamber pieces, church music and a cantata, La rose.

I	§	Le Coucou	Frederick Harris; Promenade

This well-known composition in E minor is an important example of harpsichord music of this period that has survived into modern time. Written as a *rondeau* (repetitions of the theme separated by couplets), *Le Coucou* is representative of the French harpsichord style and is famous for its programmatic cuckoo motif of a falling third. This composition is also published in the Repertoire Album, volume 9 of the *Celebration Piano Series: Perspectives* edition.

Baroque Literature *continued*

Handel, George Frideric (1685–1759) England (b. Germany)

Handel was a composer, organist, harpsichordist, violinist, conductor and *Kappelmeister*. Born in Germany, he studied law briefly at the University of Halle, then became a church organist in 1702 and in 1706 left to study music (with Corelli) and new operatic trends in Italy. Handel returned to Germany in 1710 as court composer in Hanover with visits and finally a move in 1712 to England where he spent the rest of his life. Known as one of the leading composers of his day, his works include incidental keyboard music, 16 suites, 42 operas, 29 oratorios, 16 organ concerti, and a prolific number of cantatas, duets and trios. His most famous compositions include the *Harmonious Blacksmith Variations* (from Suite no. 5), the *Messiah (Hallelujah Chorus)* and his orchestral *Water Music* and *Royal Fireworks Music*.

I	§	An Introduction to His Keyboard Works (Lucktenberg, ed.)	Alfred

This volume contains many of the better-known one-page compositions of Handel including *Impertinence, HWV 494* and *Sonatina in B flat Major, HWV 585*, as well as lesser-known but deserving material. The Foreword by the Baroque specialist George Lucktenberg offers persuasive arguments for teaching (and not overlooking) the intermediate output of Handel.

I	§	Celebrate Handel (Hisey, ed.)	Frederick Harris

This edition contains many of the same one-page compositions as the Lucktenberg edition but also has selected movements from five of the most commonly played suites (HWV, 453, 441, 437, 432 430, and 431) including the famous Air with Variations, *The Harmonious Blacksmith* (Suite in E, HWV 430, fourth movement). Unlike Bach, Handel's suites do not always follow the standard dance suite format (Allemande, Courante, Sarabande, Optional dances, Gigue). In general, his suite movements are technically less complex than Bach. Detailed information about influences on Handel's keyboard style, stylistic interpretation, and performance notes round out this excellent collection.

I		Easier Favorites (Feldmann, ed.)	Heinrichshofen
I		Easiest Piano Pieces (Pfeiffer, ed.)	Peters
I		Six Little Fugues	Concordia
I-A		The First Book for Young Pianists (Lucktenberg, ed.)	Alfred
I-A	§	A Handel Anthology (Heath, ed.)	FJH

This recent collection of Handel's intermediate compositions for the keyboard contains twenty-one compositions including the famous *Harmonious Blacksmith Variations* and *Sonatina in B flat Major*. This *urtext* edition leaves all phrasing and dynamics to the performer.

I-A		Keyboard Works for Solo Instrument	Dover
I-A		Suites, Vols. I (1–8); II (9–17)	Henle
A	§	Air and Variations from Suite no. 5 (*Harmonious Blacksmith*) (Palmer, ed.)	Alfred

Purcell, Henry (1659–1695) England

One of England's most renowned composers, Purcell was the son of a court musician, studied briefly with John Blow and in 1680 became organist at Westminster Abbey succeeding Dr. Blow. After Purcell's death at the age of 36 of tuberculosis (Purcell was buried beneath the organ in Westminster Abbey), Blow returned to his post as organist and wrote an "Ode on the Death of Purcell." Purcell was a prolific composer writing church music, opera (*Dido and Aeneas*), dramatic works, songs, incidental music for theater (over 40 plays), chamber music and keyboard pieces.

E-I		Eighteen Easy Piano Pieces	Peters
I		Pieces for Klavier or Harpsichord	Schott
I-A	§	Keyboard Works (Squire, ed.)	Dover

E (Early Intermediate)   I (Intermediate)   A (Advanced Intermediate to Advanced)

This single volume contains all of Purcell's solo keyboard works. Overall, Purcell's writing is not as technically demanding as Bach and Scarlatti. There are many excellent one-page teaching pieces for study or sight-reading.

A		Keyboard Suites (Oesterle/Aldrich, eds.)	Schirmer

Rameau, Jean-Philippe (1683–1764) France

Rameau was a composer, organist, harpsichordist, teacher, conductor and music theorist known for his 1722 *Traité de l'harmonie* (Treatise on Harmony Reduced to Its Natural Principles). His treatise laid the foundation for 20th century theory asserting that harmony is the basis of music. His works include harpsichord music, operas and stage works of many genres including tragédie lyrique, comédie lyrique, opera and comédie ballet.

I-A		Complete Works for Solo Keyboard (Saint-Saëns, ed.)	Dover
I-A	§	The Graded Rameau (Motchane, ed.)	Alfred

These selections are organized by category: Lyric Pieces, Dances, Descriptive Pieces, and Dramatic Pieces. The collection includes interesting facsimiles of manuscript pages, and a Foreword with performance notes for each composition. Familiar titles such as *La Joyeuse* (The Joyful One) are included.

I-A		Pièces de Clavecin (Jacobi, ed.)	Bärenreiter

Scarlatti, (Giuseppe) Domenico (1685–1757) Italy

An organist, virtuoso harpsichordist, composer, and son of famous Italian composer and maestro di cappella, Alessandro Scarlatti, Domenico Scarlatti wrote over 550 harpsichord sonatas. In a famous competition instigated by Cardinal Ottoboni in Rome, Handel and Scarlatti were judged equal on the harpsichord, but Handel prevailed on the organ and a lifelong friendship was born. Scarlatti's most influential pupil was the Portuguese princess, Maria Magdalena Barbara, who later married Ferdinand VI and invited Scarlatti to the Spanish Court in Seville. In addition to his harpsichord sonatas, he composed 17 sinfonias, operas, cantatas and a harpsichord concerto.

E		The First Book for Young Pianists (Halford, ed.)	Alfred
E-I	§ *	An Introduction to His Keyboard Works (Halford, ed.) (K 73b, K 88d, K 83b)	Alfred

An exemplary collection of early intermediate sonatas and minuets. A unique feature of the collection is the inclusion of sonatas that contain figured bass.

E-I	§	Celebrate Scarlatti, Vols. 1, 2 (Hisey, ed.)	Frederick Harris

Volume 1 contains many of the easier, first taught Scarlatti Sonatas and comments on the musical language of the sonatas (e.g., large melodic leaps, repeated-note melodies, unusual harmonies). Understanding the sonatas through influences such as form (e.g., minuet, polonaise, gigue) and instrumental idioms (guitar music, concerto grosso), and musical imagery (the hunt, the procession, keyboard virtuosity), will elevate the teacher and students' understanding of this genre.

Volume 2 contains 16 of the popular but more difficult Scarlatti Sonatas. These include The *Sonata in G, L 387, K14; D minor, L 366, K. 1; D major, L 465, K96; and C major, L 52, K 420*. Detailed notes for study and performance and suggestions for further reading promote understanding of this important baroque genre of repertoire.

I		At the Piano with Scarlatti (Hinson, ed.)	Alfred
I-A		The Graded Scarlatti (Motchane, ed.)	Alfred
I-A		Great Keyboard Sonatas, Vols. I-IV	Dover
I-A		Scarlatti Sonatas, Books I, II (Kite, ed.)	Stainer and Bell
I-A		Selected Sonatas (Banowetz, ed.)	Kjos
I-A		Selected Sonatas, Vols. I, II (Hinson, ed.)	Alfred

Baroque Literature *continued*

SOLO LITERATURE

I-A	§	Sixty Sonatas in Two Volumes (Kirkpatrick, ed.)	Schirmer

* Volume I (K 3, L 378; K120, L 215; K 96, L 465; K 84, L 10; K 105, L 204; K 9, L 413)
* Volume II (K 426, L 128; K 263, L 321; K 420, L.S. 2)

The Preface to Volume I is essential reading for an understanding of performance practices of the time. Questions are posed to the performer concerning fingering, technical problems, ornamentation, phrasing, melodic inflection, harmonic inflection, tempo and rhythm, dynamics, and expressive character.

I-A	§	100 Sonatas in Three Volumes (Hashimoto, ed.)	Kalmus

This scholarly edition selects 100 of the 555 Scarlatti sonatas, presenting them according to Kirkpatrick's chronology, from K 6 at the beginning of Volume I to K 551 at the end of Volume III.

I-A		Twelve Easy Sonatas (Mirovitch, ed.)	Marks
A		The Five Fugues (Jones, ed.)	ABRSM

Soler (Ramos), Antonio (Francisco Javier José) (1729–1783) Spain

Known as Padre Soler, he was a composer, organist and teacher. He was also a priest, a monk (Hieronhymite), a mathematician and inventor. Little of his music was published during his lifetime except for his treatise on music theory, *Llave de la Modulación y Antiguedades de la Música* (1762). A prolific composer of over 400 compositions, Soler wrote over 200 harpsichord sonatas, 6 quintets for string quartet and organ, 9 masses, 5 Requiems, 60 Psalms, 13 Magnificats and a variety of other compositions in multiple genres. Scarlatti and Soler knew each other and scholars speculate whether Soler was a student of Scarlatti.

I-A		Sonata No. 84 in D Major (Palmer, ed.)	Alfred
I-A		Sonatas (in seven volumes)	Unión Musical Española

Soler composed well over 120 keyboard sonatas. In the Preface to his multi-volume sonata collection of Soler, the scholar Frederick Marvin, states that he has collected over 200 sonata manuscripts from the composer. Soler composed primarily one-movement sonatas though some later works are multi-movement with three or four movements. For the latter, he uses combinations of titles from *Allegro, Allegro Pastoral, Cantabile, Intento* (fugue), *Minuet, Presto,* and *Rondo*. Many of Soler's sonatas appear in anthologies and collections. This edition presents the majority of his keyboard sonatas with 10-20 per volume. F. Marvin has catalogued many of Soler's sonatas using "M" numbers, however, the numbering system has not been consistently adopted for this genre of keyboard sonatas.

A	§	Antonio Soler Sonatas for Piano (Marvin, ed.)	Continuo Music Press
A	§	Ausgewählte Klaviersonate (Selected Piano Sonatas) (Marvin, ed.)	Henle
A	*	8 Sonaten (8, 1)	Schott
A	*	14 Sonatas (Gilbert, ed.) (1, 7, 14)	Faber

Telemann, Georg Philipp (1681–1767) Germany

A well-known and celebrated composer who played multiple instruments, Telemann wrote his first opera by the age of 12. A prolific composer, he wrote over 3,000 compositions using French, German and Italian styles in his dance suites, fugues, motets, cantatas, passions, operas, overtures, concertos, and chamber works.

I		Easy Chorale Preludes	Peters
I		Easy Fugues and Short Pieces	International
I	§	Leichte Fugen mit kleinen Stücken (Ruf, ed.)	Schott

Approximately at the level of Bach's *Two-part Inventions*, this set contains six easy fugues, each fugue followed by three to four companion pieces using the same key signature, in a suite-like format. These fugues are excellent alternative material for the upper intermediate study of contrapuntal textures.

I-A	The 36 Fantasias for Keyboard (Seiffert, ed.)	Dover
A	Three Dozen Klavier Fantasias	Bärenreiter

E (Early Intermediate)   I (Intermediate)   A (Advanced Intermediate to Advanced)

Baroque Collections and Anthologies

	Title (editor)	**Publisher**
	A Dance Pageant: Renaissance and Baroque Keyboard Dances (Waxman, ed.)	Galaxy
	The Age of J. S. Bach (Herrmann, ed.)	Peters

       Includes solos for the intermediate student with original pieces by J. S. Bach, C. P. E. Bach, Handel, Krebs, Pergolesi, Rameau, Scarlatti and Telemann.

§   Anthology of Baroque Keyboard Music (Hinson, ed.)   Alfred

       This important Anthology is paired with a DVD on Baroque performance practices. Hinson performs music from the Anthology, and relates valuable formation on basic touches, articulations, dynamics and ornamentation that will help the performer create a more historically informed performance.

    Anthology of Piano Vol. 1: The Baroque Period   Music Sales

       Keyboard works by J. S. Bach, Handel, Couperin, Rameau, and Scarlatti highlight this volume of compositions by 54 baroque masters.

    Bach, Handel, Scarlatti: Their Greatest Solos for Piano   Music Sales

§   The Baroque Era: An Introduction to the Keyboard Music (Palmer/Halford, eds.)   Alfred

       This volume contains an interesting assortment of Baroque compositions evenly divided and categorized by country. The informative *Preface* has excellent suggestions for ornamentation.

§   Baroque Folk: Familiar Melodies Arranged in Baroque Style (Palmer, arr.)   Alfred

       This intermediate level volume is popular with students and teachers. Palmer uses familiar melodies and folk songs to create a Baroque Dance Suite complete with *Allemande* (Nick Nack, Paddy Wack), *Corrente* (Flow Gently, Sweet Afton), *Sarabande* (Gaudeamus Igitur), Optional Dances (*Minuet:* Lavender's Blue; *Passacaglia:* The House of the Rising Sun), and a *Gigue* (Old MacDonald). The volume also includes two two-part inventions (The Ash Grove, Streets of Laredo) that are excellent style introduction pieces. The arrangements help the student to enjoy dances written in the Baroque style and to understand a complete dance suite. Excellent for solo recital pieces or as an assignment for a class or studio to perform.

	The Baroque Period (Agay, ed.)	Music Sales
§	Early English Keyboard Music, Vols. I, II (Ferguson, ed.)	Oxford
§	Early French Keyboard Music, Vols. I, II (Ferguson, ed.)	Oxford
§	Early German Keyboard Music, Vols. I, II (Ferguson, ed.)	Oxford
§	Early Italian Keyboard Music, Vols. I, II (Ferguson, ed.)	Oxford

       These scholarly volumes, edited and annotated by Howard Ferguson are among the best available anthologies for their interesting compilation of repertoire based on difficult to find source material. For example, the English Keyboard volume contains early keyboard composers such as Blow, Byrd, and Gibbons.

	Easy Keyboard Music, Ancient to Modern (Palmer, ed.)	Alfred
	Early Keyboard Music, Vols. I, II (Oesterle, ed.)	Schirmer
§	Easy Solos by the Baroque Masters (Tucker, ed.)	Alfred

    (Piano Solos by Master Composers of the Period)

       Tucker's edition contains seventeen pieces that provide an introduction to the Baroque style. Composers include J. S. Bach, Clarke, Couperin, Handel, Purcell, and Rameau.

Baroque Collections and Anthologies *continued*

Title (editor)	Publisher
Eighteenth Century Women Composers, Vols. I, II (Harbach, ed.)	Vivace

These two volumes are billed as music written by women composers for the harpsichord. The selections are interesting, however, there is no doubt that some of the compositions written near the end of the century were intended for piano. Composers such as Cecilia Mari Barthélemon, Maríanne Martínez, and Elisabetta de Gambarini are presented.

English Piano Music for the Young Musician (György, ed.)	Editio Musica Budapest
Fitzwilliam Virginal Books 1, 2 (Maitland/Squire, eds.)	Dover
French Piano Music for the Young Musician (György, ed.)	Editio Musica Budapest
§ Harris Piano Classics: Baroque and Classical Repertoire, Vols. 1a–7a	Frederick Harris

These seven books progress in difficulty and include a wide range of Baroque and Classical composers. Each volume contains between 16 to 24 pages, and includes 9–16 piano compositions.

Henry Purcell and His Contemporaries (Hermann, ed.)	Hinrichsen

Includes 16 original pieces by masters of the 17th century such as Purcell, Blow, Clarke, Croft, Eccles, and Loeillet.

Italian Masters of the Baroque Period	Hal Leonard
The Joy of Baroque (Agay, ed.)	Music Sales
Masters before J. S. Bach (Herrmann, ed.)	Peters

Includes moderately difficult original pieces by Couperin, Frescobaldi, Froberger, Loeillet, Pachelbel, Purcell, Sweelinck, and Zipoli.

The Pianist's Book of Baroque Treasures (Banowetz, ed.)	Kjos

E (Early Intermediate)   I (Intermediate)   A (Advanced Intermediate to Advanced)

The Classical Period circa 1750–1820

An Introduction to Classical Piano Music

Historically, the Classical period (1750-1820s), represented essentially by Mozart's birth year of 1756 and Beethoven's death in 1827, is framed between the Baroque and Romantic style periods. For the purpose of this introductory essay, these questions are posed: How did the emergence of the *fortepiano* and the increased availability of print music affect keyboard music in the Classical period? How are classical piano scores different from Baroque? What compositional forms did classical composers prefer? What strategies assist in learning and performing piano music from this period? To what extent did Haydn, Mozart, and Beethoven use pedal markings and what are the implications for pedaling classical music on the modern grand piano?

The early piano of Bartolomeo Christofori, invented around 1699, came of age during the Classical period, becoming the preferred instrument to the harpsichord. The piano keyboard was gradually expanded and pedal mechanisms were improved by innovative craftsmen who, in part, were responding to the demands placed on the instrument by composers. For example, due to a limited keyboard range, the highest pitch in Beethoven's early *C Major Rondo, op. 51, no. 1* is F whereas in the third bagatelle of the *op. 119 Eleven Bagatelles*, it is a D, a full sixth higher. Beethoven's last piano, built by the English Broadwood piano manufacturer as a gift to the composer, had a range of six octaves. By contrast, the Baroque harpsichord had a range of slightly over four octaves (and no pedals). From the Baroque harpsichord to the early piano, composers often had to adjust thematic material because of a limited keyboard range.

During the transition from the harpsichord to the early *fortepiano*, composers often published works as written for either harpsichord or *fortepiano* to ensure that sales were not limited to one instrument or the other. It is reported that some of Mozart's early piano concerti were performed on either the *fortepiano* or harpsichord. References to harpsichord music even overlapped into Beethoven's time. The first two piano sonatas in op. 31 were initially (and incorrectly) published with the title *Repertoire des clavecinistes* (*clavecinistes* refers to the French harpsichord school of the 17th-18th centuries). Learning about the transition from the harpsichord to *fortepiano*, the general development of the piano, and differences between our modern instrument (the *pianoforte*) and the early *fortepiano* will help stimulate discussion and examination of interpretation and pedaling in music from the Classical period.

As the piano became commonplace, the appearance of the keyboard score also changed. Baroque keyboard scores show few slurs or dynamics (occasionally *f* and *p* to indicate a change of harpsichord manual) and the earliest classical dances often had no dynamic markings. This changed, however, as composers began to make full use of the early piano's capabilities. The dynamic markings in Haydn's sonatas, written throughout his long and productive career, mirror this transition of instruments. Perusing the scores of Haydn's 62 piano sonatas, using the Wiener *Urtext* numbering, reveals that the earliest sonatas had no dynamic markings. The remaining sonatas, beginning with the *Sonata in C Minor, Hob. XVI:20,* include dynamic markings. The piano manuscripts of Beethoven were, by comparison to Baroque scores and early Haydn, rich in detailed phrase markings, dynamic indications, and pedaling suggestions.

Early on, classical musicians adopted the *gallant* style, a term referring to the lighter Baroque dances that influenced classical musicians. Grace and clarity of melody supported by a light sounding accompaniment characterized the style, reflected in the many minuets and German dances penned by Mozart and Haydn. In these dances, the left hand often was an independent line that later became more pianistic with added harmonic tones in the accompaniment. Performers were expected to vary texture during the repeats in binary dances. This could include varying melodic fragments through ornamentation. We see this in written scores as well. Mozart frequently elaborated melodic figures upon repeat.

Gradually the contrapuntal complexity of Baroque music was discarded in favor of the simplicity of the lighter *gallant* style. Early classical composers also were influenced by the *Empfindsamer Stil* (sensitive style) of C. P. E. Bach that featured contrasting moods and textures within a composition unlike the Baroque

An Introduction to Classical Piano Music *continued*

Doctrine of Affections in which the same emotion or affect occurred throughout. Exploration of these new styles, combined with the growing popularity of the *fortepiano*, coincided with a society where printed music was becoming available and music was not just for the elite but also for the ever-expanding music audience. Steven Whiting states in *Keyboard Musicianship, vol. 2* (2010, Stipes Publishing L.L.C., page 242), "This new market is but one symptom of an age in which the advantages of parliamentary democracy were posing increasing challenges to absolute monarchies; hundreds of thousands of Europe's bourgeoisie had worked their way into a position to buy for themselves cultural prerequisites that had been the birthright of aristocracy." This market promoted the production of affordable pianos for the middle class which increased the demand for printed music. Even the classical musician and pianist Clementi played a dual role as composer and piano manufacturer.

Beyond the shorter dance forms, the two main forms used by Beethoven, Mozart, and Haydn for solo piano playing were the sonata (sonatina in miniature form) and theme and variations. It is important to recognize and explore how the sonatas of Haydn, Mozart, and Beethoven differ. Both Haydn and Mozart primarily relied on a three-movement structure, fast-slow-fast with a change of key for the middle movement. Even within this common structure there is great variety. Beethoven differs in that he expanded the sonata to four movements to raise the stature of the sonata to that of the string quartet and symphony. Indeed, Beethoven's first piano sonata, the *Sonata in F Minor, op. 2, no. 1*, dedicated to his teacher Haydn, has four movements, almost as if the composer was saying, "See what I can do that you did not."

The "standard" three-movement classical sonata form generally followed this design:

— A first movement *sonata-allegro* form containing an Exposition (A and B themes), Development, and Recapitulation
— A slow second movement, in contrasting key, often in ternary form
— Concluding fast movement, returning to the original key, often a Rondo (A-B-A-C-A, etc.)

This scheme, however, could vary. If the A thematic material of the Exposition dominates in the Development section of a first movement, the composer might begin the Recapitulation with the B theme, or an extended *Coda* may almost sound as a second Development section. Both Beethoven and Mozart occasionally used variations to replace the standard first movement *sonata-allegro* form and a Minuet-Trio could replace the middle slow movement. The slow first movement of Beethoven's *Sonata in C-Sharp Minor, op. 27, no. 2* ("Moonlight") is an example of departing from a typical fast tempo. Most classical composers, including Clementi, wrote a few two-movement sonatas. Indeed, there are so many variants to the so-called sonata form that in the larger picture no single scheme can be used to describe the many sonata and sonatina movements that were composed during the period. It is difficult to simplistically reduce the many features that comprise sonatas into one stereotypical form.

Part of the magic of hearing a classical sonata is the feeling of tension created by leaving the home key and the renewed stability of returning to the same key. This occurs at multiple levels. Hearing the middle movement in a different key creates anticipation for returning to the home key in the third movement. In a first movement, modulating to the dominant at the end of the Exposition and moving through other keys during the Development section creates expectation for returning to the home key in the Recapitulation. Composers became quite expert at deviating from this plan. A "false" Recapitulation teases listeners to think that they have returned to the home key when they have not. Clever modulations of thematic material in the first movement of Beethoven's *Sonata in F major, op. 10, no. 2*, and the *Rondo in C Major, op. 51, no. 1* demonstrate this vividly.

Practically speaking, we can identify three categories of classical repertoire for initial study, the easier dances (e.g., minuets, German dances), sonatinas, and shorter variation sets. Experiencing these forms is the first step in mastering music from the period and preparing for more advanced repertoire. Questions to ask when learning a sonata (the word sonata is derived from the Italian term, *suonare*, meaning to sound) or sonatina include:

- What is the general structure of the sonata (or sonatina)? Is the typical fast-slow-fast combination of movements adhered to or does the composer vary this arrangement by adding a fourth movement, altering a tempo, or substituting a different type of movement (e.g., Variations for an opening sonata-allegro)?
- How does the composer provide variety and contrast?
  - What are the key relationships among the various movements and within movements?
  - How is thematic contrast achieved within each movement and among movements? Also consider tempo, dynamics, silence (rests), and pedal usage.
- Identify phrase lengths. How are shorter phrase units organized into larger units? Where do cadences occur?
- Does the music resemble instrumental forms? [Consider the minuet and trio, string quartet, symphony, and concerto.]

In addition to the sonata, theme and variation sets were quite popular during the Classical period. Themes selected were often well-liked melodies of the time. Haydn, Mozart, and Beethoven each adopted the variation form in their composing. The variation structure allowed the composer to provide a wide range of compositional techniques within a compressed form. Listeners were challenged to detect the melody in each variation disguised by surrounding musical material. Beethoven, in particular, composed intermediate level variation sets such as his *Six Variations on a Swiss Folk Song,* WoO 64 and the *Six Variations on Nel cor più non mi sento,* WoO 70. By the late 1700s, a typical short set of variations included:

- A theme, often well known, comprised of longer rhythmic values.
- Sequential variations that give the illusion of increased momentum through shorter rhythmic values, though the underlying pulse remains constant.
- One parallel minor variation in a slower tempo and lower register.
- A longer, more demanding final variation to "show off" the performer's technique.

Questions to consider when studying a Classical period variation set:

- How are short and long phrases organized? Two bars, four bars, 2+2+4, etc.?
- Is the length of each variation the same as the theme?
- Does the composer base each variation on the same harmonic scheme?
- Within variations, does the melody shift from the right hand to the left hand?
- How is rhythm used to achieve variety?
- Does the composer use imitative counterpoint?
- To what extent does the composer write vocally or instrumentally? Does the composer "orchestrate" any of the textures (e.g., a flute, trombone)?
- To achieve variety, to what extent does the composer use touches such as *portato* (*staccato* under slur), two-note slurs, wedge *staccato* markings, regular *staccato* markings, unslurred notes, and longer slurs?
- In general, what musical elements either unify the entire set or provide contrast?

Considerations for phrasing and articulation

Awareness of classical style elements should include understanding form and phrasing, distinguishing between *legato* and non-*legato,* and implementing detailed touch articulations such as *staccato,* wedge marks, and two-note slurs to name a few. Slur markings indicate logical musical groups and the separation of musical ideas. Phrase marks are synonymous with playing *legato* and can mirror bowings for string players. Using the musical imagination to hear what a singer or string player might do with a passage is helpful when deciding on phrasing and touch.

The absence of slurs does not necessarily dictate a non-*legato* touch. In the absence of slur lines, Clementi argued that the best practice was first to adhere to a *legato* touch. Step-wise motion can be played *legato* and larger intervals non-*legato.* The amount of detachment depends on the tempo and musical context. Ultimately the production of sound expected from the fingers must match one's musical imagination for realizing the score.

An Introduction to Classical Piano Music *continued*

Ornamentation
Ornamentation is a form of improvisation and an embellishment of the musical line with trills, mordents, turns, *appoggiaturas* and grace notes. Ornaments might be changed or added to provide variety, especially in repeated passages in slow movements. *Appoggiaturas* (derived from the Italian term *appoggiare* meaning to lean upon) are normally played on the beat and take approximately half the value of the principal note. Trills should be played from above the principle note and on the beat. The turn is interpreted as a four-note figure beginning above the principal tone. Rolled chords can begin slightly before the beat and end with the top melodic tone.

Pedaling
From Haydn and Mozart to late Beethoven a pedaling evolution occurred, from the knee pedal to the foot damper pedal. Mozart did not notate pedal markings in his manuscripts though from correspondence we know he admired the knee pedal on the Stein piano and it can be presumed that he used this form of damper pedaling in his playing. Haydn only indicated pedal for one keyboard work, the *Sonata in C Major, Hob. XVI: 50,* whereas Beethoven frequently indicated pedal usage including the markings for soft pedal (*una corda*) and that pedal's release, *tre corda*. Beethoven was one of the first composers to notate the use of the soft pedal. Accounts of his playing report that he used both damper and soft pedals in his performances even more than the markings in his compositions.

Modern pianists must account for differences in the thinner, lighter sounding pianos (less substantial wooden frames and quicker decay of sound) of the Classical period compared to modern grand pianos with iron plates. A striking example is to try and play the entire first movement of Beethoven's *Sonata in C-Sharp Minor, op. 27, no. 2* without changing the damper pedal on the modern pedal (as indicated by the composer's directive *Si deve suonare tutto questo pezzo delicatissimamente e senza sordino*). It simply does not work. Yet, on his piano it did! When playing classical repertoire on modern instruments, pianists must use less pedal and change pedal more frequently especially in the lower registers. Especially with Mozart and Haydn, a judicious approach to damper pedaling will help avoid obscuring clarity of articulation and phrasing and if used properly provide greater resonance and color without blurring. Consideration also should be given to depth of pedaling, using partial pedals versus full pedals.

Considerations for selecting printed scores
Modern printed scores of music from the Classical period (and Baroque) raise the issue of keyboard editing and what are the best editions for students to own. For example, in the case of Haydn's early *Divertimenti*, is a younger student better served to play from a lightly edited score that includes some dynamic markings added by an editor? Or, should the less experienced student learn from an *urtext* edition with no such markings? It is known that Beethoven did not include dynamic markings in the first movement of his *Sonata in G Major, op. 49, no. 2*. Many editors of modern editions *add* dynamic markings to that particular movement to assist the performer. There are no clear cut answers to these questions, however, the age and experience of the student should be considered. Certainly, carefully prepared editions where the teacher and student can easily *discern the composer's intent* from whatever markings have been editorially added (e.g., phrasing, dynamics, fingerings, and pedaling) are highly preferred.

(The authors wish to clearly state that teachers should strictly avoid the use of any photocopied music. There are few instances where photocopying is legal and then for only short examples. In general, if one photocopies any part of a work in order to avoid purchasing a copy to own, it is illegal and prohibited.)

Recommended resources for further reading:

Harrison, Bernard. 1997. *Haydn's Keyboard Music: Studies in Performance Practice.* Oxford: Clarendon Press.

Forbes, Elliot, ed., 1967. *Thayer's Life of Beethoven,* Vols. 1, 2. 2nd ed. Princeton, NJ: Princeton University Press.

Ratner, Leonard. 1980. *Classic Music: Expression, Form, and Style.* New York: Schirmer Books.

Rosenblum, Sandra P. 1988. *Performance Practices in Classic Piano Music: Their Principles and Applications.* Bloomington: Indiana University Press.

Solomon, Maynard. 1995. *Mozart: a Life.* New York: Harper Collins.

Classical Literature

SOLO LITERATURE

A. Characteristics

Literature of the Classical Period presents different types of technique and musical forms for the intermediate student. Through the study of Classical literature, students will become familiar with the following elements of the period:

- Forms: sonata (including sonata-*allegro*); minuet and trio; rondo; variations; dances; concerto
- More detailed articulations such as slurs and *staccatos*
- Passagework including scales and arpeggios
- Dynamic contrasts
- Melody and accompaniment; balance between the hands
- Varied accompaniment patterns
- Greater rhythmic variety through the variation form
- Cadences and modulations
- Homophonic style—stronger tonal center
- Use of rests to achieve long silences

B. Introducing the Classical Style

Before beginning some of the more complex Classical literature, teachers should carefully prepare students for this level of repertoire. The following list of music can serve as a valuable link between elementary method books and more difficult classical repertoire and may be used to introduce the Classical style and test students' readiness for more challenging repertoire. Volumes are listed in alphabetical order by composer rather than in order of difficulty.

Bastien, James, ed.	First Sonatinas	Kjos
Bastien, Jane	Sonatina for the Seasons	Kjos
Czerny, Carl	Selected Piano Studies (Germer, ed.)	Boston Music
Frey, Martin, ed.	Das neue Sonatinen, Buch I	Schott
Gillock, William	Accent on Analytical Sonatinas	Willis
Gillock, William	Sonatina in Classic Style	Willis
Olson, Lynn F., ed.	Exploring Piano Literature	Carl Fischer
Olson, Lynn F., ed.	Exploring More Piano Literature	Carl Fischer
Olson/Bianchi/Blickenstaff, eds.	Music Pathways: Repertoire, Vols. 3A, 3B	Carl Fischer
Olson/Hilley, eds.	Essential Keyboard Sonatinas	Alfred
Palmer, Willard, ed.	The First Sonatina Book	Alfred
Rollin, Catherine	Spotlight on Classical Style	Alfred
Sheftel, Paul	Patterns for Fun, Books 1 and 2	Alfred
Sheftel, Paul	Etudes Brutus	Alfred

C. Gradation or Teaching Order

We suggest the following teaching order when introducing students to Classical literature:

Easier dances — Haydn, Beethoven, Mozart
Easier sonatinas — Clementi, Kuhlau, Haydn, Beethoven, Mozart
Haydn — early Sonatas/Sonatinas, Hob. XVI: 8, 9, 10
Beethoven — Bagatelles, op. 119 (no. 9 in A minor)
Mozart — Sonatas, K 545, K 283
Beethoven — Sonatas, op. 49, nos. 1, 2

| Composer | Title | Publisher |

André, (Johann) Anton (1775–1842) Germany

A composer and accomplished violinist whose father, Johann Andre, founded a music shop and printing press in 1774 that still exists as the Andre Company in Offenbach, Germany. Anton took over the music printing press after his father's death. He signed a contract with Constanze Mozart (Mozart's wife) to purchase the compositions left by Mozart and brought celebrity to the press. The Archive at Offenbach is an important research source of first editions of Mozart's works. André composed over 100 pieces in many genres.

E § * Sonatinas, op. 34 (1, 3) — Musicalion

These often played sonatinas are found in many collections such as the *Harris Piano Classics*. André's piano duets are even more widely published (see music for one piano-four hands).

Attwood, Thomas (1765–1838) England

Attwood studied composition with Mozart beginning in 1785. Some of his exercises are numbered as K 506a in the Köchel catalog of Mozart's works since they are works of an apprentice with additions and corrections supplied by Mozart. A notable English composer, Attwood was chamber musician for the Prince of Wales, music teacher for the Duchess of York and the Princess of Wales, and later organist for St. Paul's Cathedral.

E-I Easy Progressive Lessons, Four Sonatinas (Jones, ed.) — ABRSM

These four sonatinas are very melodic and among the easiest of the classical sonatina literature. The fourth is an easy set of variations. Selected movements of Attwood's sonatinas frequently appear in anthologies and collections.

E-I Four Sonatinas (House, ed.) — Carl Fischer

Bach, Carl Philipp Emanuel (1714–1788) Germany

The second son of J. S. Bach and Maria Barbara Bach (first wife) was for 28 years a pre-eminent harpsichordist for the court of the Crown Prince of Prussia (Frederick the Great). He moved to Hamburg in 1767 after the death of his godfather Telemann (the name Philipp is shared by both C. P. E. and Telemann), succeeding him as music director in Telemann's church. A leading composer of the early classical style, he wrote over 350 works for harpsichord, clavichord and piano. He is perhaps best known for his *Essay on the True Art of Playing Keyboard Instruments* (1753, later revised), an important treatise of the era.

E § Leichte Spielstücke für Klavier (six pieces) (Heilbut, ed.) — Hug Zürich

This volume is one of the most accessible collections for young pianists at the late elementary or early intermediate level. The final *Polonaise* (one page in length) is particularly attractive.

E-I § 23 Pièces Characteristiques (Hogwood, ed.) — Oxford

This volume serves as an excellent introduction to the early Classical style. The majority of the titles were first collected as a group by Johann Westphal and refer to individuals Bach knew during his lifetime (e. g., no. 22, *L'Ernestine*, no. 23, *La Caroline*). Many of the compositions contain dynamic marks, which suggest performance on the *fortepiano* or clavichord.

I § Solfeggietto — ASE, FJH

Also known as *Solfeggio*, this work is immensely popular with students. The arpeggiated texture suggests a goal of clean sounding technique.

A Six Sonatas, Vol. I — Hal Leonard

Classical Literature *continued*

A		Sonatas, Vols. I–III (Börner, ed.)	Henle

Bach, Johann Christoph Friedrich (1732–1795) Germany

"Friedrich" Bach was a keyboard virtuoso who wrote sonatas, symphonies, oratorios, operas, and a wide variety of vocal music. He was known as the Bückeburg Bach because he served as harpsichordist at the court in Bückeburg from 1750 until his death in 1795. He was the oldest surviving son of J. S. Bach and second wife Anna Magdalena.

E	§	Leichte Spielstücke für Klavier (Heilbut, ed.)	Hug Zürich
		Contains six early intermediate solos appropriate for middle school students, including an *Arioso* and *Menuet-Trio*.	
E		Sons of Bach (Easiest Piano Pieces) (Soldan, ed.)	Peters
I		The Sons of Bach (12 Original Pieces) (Hermann, ed.)	Peters
		Both these volumes include pieces by Wilhelm Friedemann, Carl Philipp Emanuel, Johann Christoph Friedrich, and Johann Christian.	

Bach, Wilhelm Friedemann (1710–1784) Germany

A gifted composer, organist and harpsichordist, Wilhelm Friedemann was the eldest son of J. S. and Maria Barbara Bach. His father composed the well-known instructional *Clavier-Büchlein* for Wilhelm when he was only nine years old. W. F. Bach composed keyboard works, church music, concertos, operas, symphonies, and vocal works.

E		Leichte Spielstücke für Klavier (Heilbut, ed.)	Hug Zürich
E	§	10 Easy Piano Pieces	Broekmans & Van Poppel B. V.
I-A		Nine Sonatas	Kalmus

Beethoven, Ludwig van (1770–1827) Germany

Beethoven studied organ, piano, and composition first with his father, a court musician, and later with Christian-Gottlob Neefe, his most influential teacher. Beethoven moved to Vienna when he was in his early twenties where he had the opportunity to study with Haydn while developing a reputation as a splendid pianist. In spite of later deafness, his prolific output includes 32 piano sonatas, piano duets, piano trios, nine symphonies, string quartets, concertos, opera, ballets, and chamber music in a musical career that spanned the transition from the Classical to the Romantic. At the time of Beethoven's death, his fame was such that over 10,000 people lined the streets in Vienna for his funeral.

E	§	An Introduction to His Piano Works (Palmer, ed.)	Alfred
		This thoughtful, well-edited collection includes many of the familiar intermediate compositions, including *Für Elise, Sonatina in G Major, Kinsky-Halm Anh. 5* and easier dances and bagatelles.	
E		German Dances	Peters
E		Sixteen of His Easiest Piano Selections	Alfred
E-I	§	Drei Variationenwerke für Klavier (Schmidt-Görg/Georgii, eds.)	Henle
		WoO 64, Variations on a Swiss Song	
		WoO 70, Variations on Nel cor più non mi sento	
		WoO 77, Six Easy Variations on an Original Theme	
		This edition includes three of the composer's landmark variation sets appropriate for intermediate study. *Nel cor più non mi sento*, translated "No longer do I feel youth sparkle in my heart," was a vocal duet from Giovanni Paisiello's opera *La molinara* (The Miller-Woman). Beethoven composed the set for a female friend to try and impress her.	

I		At the Piano with Beethoven (Hinson, ed.)	Alfred
I		Dances of Beethoven (Hinson, ed.)	Alfred
I		Easier Favorites	Heinrichshofen
I	§	Für Elise (Brendel, ed.)	Weiner Urtext

Often published in simplified versions, the original must be taught carefully, anticipating that the student can handle the thirty-second note passagework which must be played in the tempo of the principal theme. Originally published as *Bagatelle in A Minor,* the dedication to *Elise* most likely refers to the nickname for Therese Malfatti, the daughter of Beethoven's physician.

I		Rondo in C Major, op. 51, no. 1	Henle

Composed at about the same time as his op. 2 piano sonatas, this *Rondo* has a false restatement of the theme in A-flat major, and an extensive *Coda*. The use of an upbeat provides a graceful rhythmic feel that disguises the sense of true downbeat. The composer used the highest note on his piano, which at the time was F.

I	§ *	Seven Sonatinas (Hinson, ed.) (5, 6)	Alfred
I	§	Six Sonatinas for Pianoforte (Craxton, ed.)	ABRSM

This edition is unique because of the informative Foreword by Donald Francis Tovey. This edition includes the well-known *Sonatina in G Major, Kinsky-Halm Anh. 5,* attributed to Beethoven, that is in a compact two-movement structure rather than three; a must for the early intermediate pianist.

I		13 Most Popular Piano Pieces	Alfred
I	§	Two Short Sonatas, opus 49 (Taub, ed.)	Schirmer

Beethoven used the term *Leichte Sonate* (Easy Sonatas) to describe the two sonatas in op. 49, G minor (no. 1), followed by G major (no. 2). This edition is particularly attractive because of the supporting CD recording.

I-A	*	Bagatelles, op. 119 (9, 1, 3, 8, 10); op. 126 (3); op. 33 (1, 3, 4, 6)	Henle
I-A	§	Bagatelles, opp. 33, 119, 126 (Brendel, ed.)	Weiner Urtext

The term bagatelle was first used by Couperin and can be translated to mean a trifle or "little nothing". This edition, containing the three opus numbers of Bagatelles, includes an informative Preface by the editor. For those unfamiliar with Beethoven's Bagatelles, op. 119 is generally easier. The first bagatelles of op. 119 were completed around 1822 based on sketches from 1800-1804. No. 7-11 were composed later for publication in Friedrich Starke's piano method, *Wiener Pianoforte-Schule* (Viennese Pianoforte School).

I-A		Beethoven Bagatelles, Rondos, and Other Shorter Works	Dover
I-A		Beethoven: Piano Music From His Early Years (Hinson, ed.)	Alfred
I-A	§	Beethoven, Short Pieces (Blickenstaff, ed.)	Carl Fischer

This collection of fourteen pieces includes three bagatelles from op. 119, *Für Elise, WoO 59,* F and G Major *Sonatinas,* and the well-known set of *Six Variations on a Swiss Song, WoO 64.* Informative and detailed performance notes highlight important aspects of each piece as well as valuable background information.

I-A		Beethoven: Six Selected Sonatas (Taub, ed.; Book/CD pack)	Schirmer

Classical Literature *continued*

I-A	§	Celebrate Beethoven, Vols. I, II (Hisey, ed.)	Frederick Harris

Volume I is a virtual compendium of all the "starter" pieces teachers use to introduce Beethoven, ranging from short dances and *Für Elise* to sonatinas, bagatelles, and op. 49, no. 2. Vol. I concludes with the *Rondo in C Major, op. 51, no. 1*. Volume II is devoted to selected sonatas. As Beethoven's piano sonatas are usually published in two volumes, the compilers have placed in one volume some of the frequently played sonatas (op. 2, no. 1, op. 13, op. 79, etc.) that are normally not published together. Detailed performance notes accompany each sonata.

I-A		Complete Piano Sonatas, Vols. I, II (Schnabel, ed.)	Alfred

This is an interesting edition to examine because of the insights Schnabel provides through his editorial remarks.

I-A	§ *	Eleven Bagatelles, op. 119 (9, 1, 3, 8, 10) (Palmer, ed.)	Alfred
I-A		Pieces for Piano, Vols. I, II (Keller, ed.)	Peters

These volumes contain lesser-known works such as the *Fantasy in G Minor, op. 77* and *Andante favori, WoO 57*. Originally intended to be the middle movement of the famous *Waldstein* sonata, op. 53, Beethoven decided the *Andante* was too long and eventually published it separately. The title literally means "favored *Andante*", as the public liked the work and Beethoven often played the movement in public.

I-A		Selected Easiest Sonata Movements (Hinson, ed.)	Alfred
I-A	§ *	Sonatas (op. 49, nos. 1-2; op. 2, no. 1; op. 79; op. 14, no. 2, op. 10, no. 1, op. 13)	Henle

The lesser-known *Sonata in G Minor, op. 49, no. 1* is an entry-level sonata. The opening *Andante* is musically demanding but less difficult technically than the final *Rondo* which requires a facile technique to achieve the perpetual motion effect. The less difficult second sonata from this opus (G major) has sparse dynamic markings and students will need guidance on dynamic shaping. Evenness of passages and rhythmic accuracy of ties, especially at the beginning of the Development, challenge many students. Both the op. 49 sonatas feature a two-movement structure. Larger in scope, the first movement of op. 10, no. 1 epitomizes Beethoven's early period. The brisk dotted values, arpeggiated figures, and *sfz* indications make this an attractive movement.

I-A	*	Variations, Vols. I, II (WoO 64, 69, 70, 72)	Henle

Benda, Georg Anton (Jiří Antonin) (1722-1795) Bohemia

Benda was a Czech composer whose Bohemian name was Jiří Antonin Benda. He had a long career as a pianist, violinist and *Kapellmeister* in the chapel for Frederick III. He composed works for the theater and was known for his melodramas such as *Ariadne auf Naxos*, that was well received throughout Europe in 1775. Many of Benda's attractive sonatinas appear in collections and anthologies.

I		Sonatina in A minor (Lancaster/Renfrow, eds.)	Alfred
I	§	Twelve Sonatinas	ABRSM
I-A		Thirty-Five Sonatinas (Piano or Harpsichord)	Oxford

Cimarosa, Domenico (1749–1801) Italy

A talented singer, organist, keyboardist, and violinist, Cimarosa was a noted composer of the late eighteenth century. Cimarosa served at the court of empress Catherine the Great in St. Petersburg from 1788- 1791 and then in 1792 served as Kapellmeister at the court of Leopold II succeeding Salieri. He wrote over 65 operas including his most noted opera Il matrimonia segreto (1792).

I-A		32 Sonatas, Vols. 1–3 (Boghen, ed.)	Max Eschig

Several of the Cimarosa sonatas appear in multi-period anthologies including the Frederick Harris *Celebration Series*.

E (Early Intermediate) I (Intermediate) A (Advanced Intermediate to Advanced)

Clementi, Muzio (1752–1832) England (b. Italy)

A successful concert pianist, harpsichordist, composer, teacher, conductor, publisher, and piano manufacturer, Clementi was one of the first to compose for the *fortepiano*. His most notable works include over 60 piano sonatas, the collection of piano studies titled *Gradus ad Parnassum* (parodied by Debussy in the *Children's Corner*), and his important treatise, *Introduction to the Art of Playing on the Pianoforte* (1891). Beethoven had the highest regard for Clementi's compositions and signed a contract with Clementi's company to publish all of his music.

E-I		Clementi: First Book for Pianists	Alfred
I	§	Celebrate Clementi (Hisey, ed.)	Frederick Harris
		This excellent compilation of Clementi's intermediate works includes all of the op. 36 sonatinas and other musical gems including several preludes (from op. 43), selected Waltzes, and the *Prelude in the Style of Haydn* from Clementi's lesser known *Musical Characteristics*.	
I	§	Eight Waltzes for Piano, Triangle and Tambourine	Schirmer
		These curious pieces by Clementi reflect the late 18th century interest in adding percussive sounds to the piano as seen in Mozart's famous third sonata movement *Turkish March (Rondo alla Turca)* from K 331. These charming *Waltzes* are often found in collections and the piano part can be, if needed, played as a solo without the supplementary instrumentation.	
I	§	Preludes (from op. 43) (Bishop, ed.)	Carl Fischer
		These *Preludes*, excerpted from Clementi's *Introduction to the Art of Playing on the Pianoforte, op. 43*, are improvisatory in nature, often only eight to sixteen bars in length. They provide superb study material as sight-reading exercises, quick learn pieces, and models for improvisation in the style.	
I		Six Sonatinas (Palmer, ed.)	Alfred
I	§	Sonatinas, op. 36 (Linn, ed.)	Schirmer
		This is an excellent edition prepared by Jennifer Linn for the Schirmer performance editions. Book/CD pack.	
I		Sonatinen, opp. 36, 37, 38 (Taylor, ed.)	ABRSM; Peters
		(see the entry for Timm, Henry C. under Music for Two Pianos–Four Hands)	
	*	Six Sonatinas, op. 36 (1, 3, 2, 4)	
	*	Three Sonatinas, op. 37 (3, 2)	
	*	Three Sonatinas, op. 38 (3)	
I-A	§	Musical Characteristics	Presser
A		Gradus ad Parnassum	Hal Leonard; Schirmer
A		Preludes and Exercises	Ricordi
A		Rediscovered Masterworks, Vols. I–III	Marks
A	§ *	Clementi Sonaten, Vols. I–IV (Ruthardt, ed.)	Peters
	*	Vol. I contains seven sonatas. (op. 12, no. 1; op. 36, no. 2)	
	*	Vol. II contains five sonatas. (op. 47, no. 2)	
	*	Vol. III contains six sonatas. (op. 25, no. 2; op. 39, no. 3)	
	*	Vol. IV contains six sonatas. (op. 24, no. 3; op. 12, no. 2)	
		As with Haydn, there are conflicting numbering systems for Clementi's piano sonatas and some editions only publish a fraction of his output. Other editions number his famous sonatinas as part of the sonata writing. Beethoven greatly admired Clementi's sonata writing and Vladimir Horowitz, through his performances and recordings, brought Clementi's more advanced writing to the concert stage. Clementi's sonatas contain much variety and are	

Classical Literature continued

deserving of greater attention. He varies his approach to the "standard" sonata structure by occasionally writing two movement sonatas (e.g., op. 25, no. 2), using slow introductions to first movements (e.g., op. 36, no. 2) and substituting variation movements (e.g., op. 24, no. 3).

Czerny, Carl (1791–1857) Austria

A noted pianist, composer and teacher, Czerny was a child prodigy who studied with Hummel, Salieri, and Beethoven and later taught Liszt who dedicated his *Transcendental Etudes* to him. Czerny was a splendid pianist who premiered Beethoven's fifth piano concerto (*Emperor*) in 1812 at the age of 21. Czerny composed over 1,000 works including his studies and etudes, sonatas, symphonies, concertos, string quartets, choral works, and the treatises, *School of Extemporaneous Performance,* Opp. 200, 300 and *Complete Theoretical and Practical Pianoforte School,* op. 500 (1839).

E-I §	Czerny, The Young Pianist, op. 823 complete (Palmer, ed.)	Alfred

The *Young Pianist* represents Czerny's approach for teaching beginners. Divided into two sections or books, Book I focuses on the introduction of elementary reading material and the development of hand coordination, whereas Book II addresses more complex technical exercises in a greater range of tonal centers. From a historical perspective, it is particularly interesting to compare the opening of Book I with the development of contemporary piano methods.

E-I	Practical Method for Beginners, op. 599 (Ruthardt, ed.)	Peters
I	Selected Piano Studies (Palmer, ed.)	Alfred
I	6 Easy Sonatinas, op. 163	Cranz
I-A	100 Progressive Exercises without Octaves, op. 139	Alfred; Hal Leonard
I-A	125 Exercises for Passage-Playing, op. 261 (Martienssen, ed.)	Peters
I-A §	Selected Piano Studies, Books 1, 2 (Germer, ed.)	Boston Music

This is one of the best sequenced volumes of selected Czerny studies organized by his contemporary Heinrich Germer. The studies gradually increase in length and difficulty through the two volumes. Book 1 is appropriate for late elementary and early intermediate students beginning the study of sixteenth-note rhythms.

I-A	24 Studies for the Left Hand, op. 718	Alfred; Hal Leonard

Diabelli, Anton (1781–1858) Austria

A composer and teacher of piano and guitar, Diabelli is known today as the composer of the waltz on which Beethoven based his *Diabelli Variations, op. 120.* He was best known in his day as a music publisher and editor with partner Pietro Cappi primarily publishing music for the home amateur musician. He composed many works for piano, piano duets, and classical guitar.

E-I	25 Elementary Studies, op. 176 (Palmer, ed.)	Alfred
I	Eleven Sonatinas, opp. 151, 168 (Palmer, ed.)	Alfred; Kalmus
I-A §	Selected Piano Pieces (Hinson, ed.)	Alfred

This edition contains a wide variety of Diabelli's compositions, including the easier *10 Short Pieces*, and the waltz upon which Beethoven based his famous variations.

Dussek, Jan (Johann) Ladislav (1760-1812) Bohemia

Czech born, Dussek spent several years in England where he knew both Clementi and Haydn (shared concerts with Haydn) and worked with the English piano manufacturer Broadwood. He was considered a virtuoso pianist and is now viewed as an important composer in the London School of Pianoforte. He composed primarily for piano, writing several concerti, piano trios and sonatas. Comparisons have been made between Dussek's piano sonata writing and some of Beethoven's early piano sonatas. Dussek also wrote theoretical treatises such as his *Instructions on the Art of Playing the Piano-Forte or Harpsichord* (1796). Few of his solo compositions are performed today with the exception of these sonatinas.

I		Six Sonatinas, op. 20	Kalmus; ASE
I	§	Six Sonatinas, op. 19 (Salter, ed.)	ABRSM

        Dussek's sonatinas are excellent companion pieces to Clementi and Kuhlau.

Hässler, Johann Wilhelm (1747-1822) Germany

A German organist, pianist, teacher and composer, Hässler was held in high esteem in Germany. He competed against Mozart and Salieri in a competition for organists which he lost! Eventually he settled in Moscow (Russia) where he taught and composed in a wide variety of genres including sonatas, fantasies, and preludes. His easy piano sonatas (each in three movements) deserve greater attention.

E		Fifty Pieces for Beginners, op. 38	ABRSM
I	§	Easy Piano Sonatas (Doflein, ed.)	Peters

Haydn, Franz Joseph (1732–1809) Austria

Considered one of the great composers, Haydn was a pianist and violinist, who became *Kapellmeister* for the Hungarian Esterházy family in 1766 and served there for most of his life composing for a small group of chamber musicians for various palace functions. He wrote works in every genre including 106 symphonies, 68 string quartets, 14 masses, oratorios (*The Creation* and *The Seasons*), 62 piano sonatas (Wiener Urtext numbering) and other keyboard compositions. He visited London several times and received an honorary of Doctor of Music degree from Oxford University. Haydn was highly influential in the development of the classical style and was a teacher for Beethoven and friends with Mozart. (See Appendix II for an explanation of Hob. and Roman numeral catalog numbers.)

E		An Introduction to His Keyboard Works	Alfred
E		Haydn: Easiest Piano Pieces (Weitzmann, ed.)	Peters
E		Haydn: First Book for Pianists	Alfred
E		Twelve Short Piano Pieces (Palmer, ed.)	Alfred
E-I		Haydn: Easier Favorites (Feldmann, ed.)	Heinrichshofen
E-I		Pieces for Musical Clock (Salter, ed.)	ABRSM
I		At the Piano with Haydn (Hinson, ed.)	Alfred
I	§	Celebrate Haydn, Vols. I, II (Hisey, ed.)	Frederick Harris

        Volume I contains the most frequently taught Haydn compositions including early *Divertimenti* (sonatina level) and well-known German Dances perfect for introducing the composer's style. The compilers for the second volume have placed the frequently taught Haydn Sonatas into one collection that include the Sonatas in C, D, E minor, F, B minor, and E-flat; Hob. XVI: 35, 37, 34, 23, 32, and 49 respectively. Comprehensive notes for study and performance accompany each sonata.

I		The First Book for Young Pianists (Lucktenberg, ed.)	Alfred
I	§ *	Six Sonatinas (the early sonatas) (Hob. XVI:8, 4, 11, 7, 9, 10)	Alfred

        The early sonatas and divertimenti of Haydn were often excluded from editions until recent years. Haydn's first movements from these early works exhibit greater rhythmic variety when compared to the sonatinas of Clementi and Kuhlau. This collection features six of the frequently

Classical Literature *continued*

heard sonatinas, which are also included in Band 1a of the Wiener *Urtext* edition of the complete Haydn Sonatas and *Celebrate Haydn*, Vol. 1 (F. Harris). These *Divertimenti* serve as wonderful alternative teaching pieces to the popular Clementi op. 36 and Kuhlau op. 20. The *Scherzo* of Hob. XVI:9 and the opening movement of Hob. XVI:8 are especially noteworthy.

I		24 Minuets, Hob. IX: 8 & 10	ABRSM
A		Oxford Keyboard Classics: Haydn (Ferguson, ed.)	Oxford
A		Piano Sonatas (complete), Vols. I, II	Dover
A		Sonatas (complete), Vols. I–III (Hinson, ed.)	Alfred
	§	Sonatas (complete)	Wiener Urtext
I-A	*	Band 1a (Hob. XVI:8, 9, 10, 12)	
A	*	Band 1b (Hob. XVI:43)	
A	*	Band 2 (Hob. XVI:23, 35, 37)	
A	*	Band 3 (Hob. XVI:34, 49, 50, 51)	

The Wiener *Urtext* edition has the most complete numbering system for Haydn's 62 piano sonatas a few of which are incomplete sketches. Three Haydn sonatas are especially appropriate as an introduction to his style: Hob. XVI:12 (A major), 37 (D major), and 23 (F major). The A major first movement *Andante* has a lyrical scalar melody with arpeggiated chords in the development. It is a miniature first movement, only fifty-five measures long. The second movement is a delightful *Minuet* with triplet scalar passages. The *Trio* to the *Minuet* occurs in the parallel minor, with a rhythmically displaced melody over a chromatic descending bass. The perpetual motion third movement *Finale* is brief. Aspects of Haydn's humor are present in this movement, highlighted by the use of irregular phrase lengths and by ornamentation.

The *Allegro con brio*, from the Sonata in D major, is one of Haydn's most famous sonata movements and is appealing to students. The opening measures outline adjacent four-measure question and answer phrases. Technically, the movement contains unison scales and forceful left-hand passages under right-hand suspensions. It is followed by a short *Largo e sostenuto* and third movement *Finale*.

Dedicated to Haydn's patron Prince Esterházy, the more advanced *Sonata in F Major*, contains greater technical and rhythmic complexities. On a grander scale than earlier sonatas, the first movement fits the hand quite well and students enjoy playing the richly detailed sonata-*allegro* texture. The second movement, in binary form with repeats, echoes the structure and lyricism of a baroque *sicilienne* while the last movement is framed in a short variation-like structure.

Hook, James (1746-1827) England

Hook was a prominent English organist, harpsichordist, teacher and composer. He was a child prodigy who performed from the age of four. He composed many songs that were performed often in London as well as comic opera and over thirty works for stages such as Drury Lane and Vauxhall Gardens. His sonatinas appear in many collections and anthologies. The op. 12 collection is well known and published individually.

I	§	*	Twelve Sonatinas, op. 12 (no. 6)	ABRSM

E (Early Intermediate)   I (Intermediate)   A (Advanced Intermediate to Advanced)

Hummel, Johann Nepomuk (1778–1837) Austria

A composer and noted virtuoso pianist whose works bridge the transition from late classical to early romantic styles, Hummel lived with and was taught by Wolfgang Amadeus Mozart as a young boy and made his concert debut on one of Mozart's concerts. He also studied with Muzio Clementi, Haydn and Salieri and was friends with Beethoven and Schubert. His treatise, *A Complete Theoretical and Practical Course of Instruction on the Art of Playing the Piano Forte* (1828), influenced 19th century piano technique, fingering and ornamentation.

I		Sixteen Short Pieces	ABRSM
I-A		Sonatas, Rondos, Fantasies, and Other Works for Solo Piano (Bériot, ed.)	Dover

Kuhlau, Friedrich (Daniel Rudolph) (1786–1832) Denmark (b. Germany)

A German and Danish composer and concert pianist who fled from Germany to Denmark in order to avoid conscription into Napoleon's army, Kuhlau composed opera and dramatic works, sonatinas and duets. He produced over 200 works in a wide variety of genres bridging the transition from late classical to early romantic styles.

I	*	Sonatinas, Books 1, 2 (op. 55, nos. 1, 2, 3; op. 20, nos. 1, 2, 3	Schirmer
I	*	Sonatinas, Vols. I, II (op. 88, nos. 3, 2, 1, 4; op. 60, no. 1)	Kalmus
I		Sonatinen	Peters
I-A		Variations, op. 104	Presser

Mozart, (Johann Georg) Leopold (1719–1787) Austria (b. Germany)

A composer, teacher, theorist, and violinist, he is best known today as the father of Wolfgang Amadeus Mozart. He wrote an important violin textbook in 1756 titled *Versuch einer gründlichen Violinschule* dealing with violin technique and music theory. He was the primary keyboard and theory teacher of his two children Maria Anna (Nannerl) and Wolfgang whom he took on numerous concert tours.

E	§	Notenbuch für Nannerl (Schüngeler, ed.)	Schott
		Compiled for his daughter Nannerl in 1759, this notebook contains instructional pieces by anonymous composers of the period, as well as early compositions by Wolfgang Amadeus Mozart.	
E		Notebook for Wolfgang Amadeus Mozart (Keller, ed.)	Peters
E	§	Notebook for Wolfgang (Schüngeler, ed.)	Schott
		This edition highlights the simpler and more beautiful of the compositions contained in the original notebook.	

Mozart, (Johann Chrysostom) Wolfgang Amadeus (1756–1791) Austria

A child prodigy, harpsichordist, concert pianist, and composer, Mozart is considered a musical genius and one of the great composers. He gave his first public performances with his sister Maria Anna (Nannerl) at age five and toured throughout Europe (1763-73) with his father Leopold Mozart. After years of service (1773-1780) and a brief period as organist at the Salzburg cathedral in 1781, he became an independent composer and musician in Vienna achieving considerable musical success. A prolific composer, he wrote over 600 pieces in many genres and composed his first symphony at age eight. He is perhaps best known for his string serenade, Eine Kleine Nachtmusik (A Little Night Music), and operas, Don Giovanni, The Marriage of Figaro, Cosi fan tutte and Die Zauberflöte (The Magic Flute). His piano compositions are considered treasures of the core repertoire.

E	§	The First Book for Young Pianists (Palmer, ed.)	Alfred
E	§	15 Easy Piano Pieces and 15 Intermediate Piano Pieces (Abend, ed.)	Schirmer
		From the Schirmer Performance editions, these two beautifully prepared volumes stress phrasing and articulation in the style. Volume 2 provides more challenging music to prepare for the sonata level. Book/CD pack.	

Classical Literature continued

E-I	Mozart: Piano Music from His Early Years (Hinson, ed.)	Alfred
I	At the Piano with Mozart (Hinson, ed.)	Alfred
I	The Easiest Original Pieces for Piano	Hinrichsen
I	German Dances	Peters
I	An Introduction to His Keyboard Works (Palmer, ed.)	Alfred
I	The Joy of Mozart (Agay, ed.)	Music Sales
I	Klavierstücke	Henle
I	Mozart, Easier Favorites (Feldmann, ed.)	Heinrichshofen
I	Selected Piano Pieces	Peters
I § *	Six Viennese Sonatinas (1, 5, 4, 6) (Harding, ed.)	Schirmer

Mozart's six Viennese piano sonatinas are transcriptions from *Five Divertimenti, K 439b,* originally composed for a trio of wind instruments. The Viennese sonatinas provide excellent preparation for Mozart's solo piano sonatas. The textures challenge the pianist to imagine instrumental colors. Book/CD pack.

I	Sonata in C Major, K 545 (R. Faber, ed.)	FJH
I	The Young Mozart	Schott
I-A §	Celebrate Mozart, Vols. I, II (Hisey, ed.)	Frederick Harris

These two volumes are a compendium of the frequently taught piano works of Mozart. Volume I includes many of the easier and most often played pieces that Mozart wrote during his youth. It also includes more challenging and frequently performed works such as selected *Viennese Sonatinas,* the *Fantasy in D Minor, K 397; Sonatas, K 283* and *K 545; Rondo, K 485,* and the famous Variation set, *Ah, vous dirai-je, Maman.* Volume II is devoted to frequently played solo piano sonatas in E-flat, A, F, and C minor; K 282, 331, 332, and 457 respectively. Scholarly and detailed performance notes will benefit both students and teachers.

I-A	Selected Intermediate to Early Advanced Piano Sonata Movements	Alfred
I-A § *	Sonatas and Fantasies (K 545, 283, 280, 282, 332, 397)	ASE

Three excellent works for introducing the Mozart sonata and fantasy style are K 545 (C major), K 283 (G major), and K 397 (D minor). In the well-known K 545 sonata, the opening theme must be played in the same tempo of the remaining musical material. Note that the recapitulation begins in the subdominant. The middle *Andante* is an excellent study in balance between right-hand melody and left-hand accompaniment. The final *Rondo* is the most difficult of the three movements, though the shortest. Grieg wrote a second-piano part for this work (see annotation in Music for Two Pianos–Four Hands).

In K 283, all of the movements are in sonata-allegro form. The first movement *Allegro* uses short two- and three-note figures and Mozart elaborates melodic fragments in a variation-like manner. The second movement *Andante* is particularly beautiful, because of the manner in which Mozart varies thematic material in the right-hand when repeating a melodic idea. The *Presto* third movement requires care with the various sixteenth-note passages.

Teachers should use caution when assigning the *Fantasy in D minor,* K 397. An artistic performance requires a musically mature student capable of controlling contrasting tempi and textures. To publish the unfinished *Fantasy* after Mozart's death, the publisher added the final ten measures.

	12 Variations on Ah, vous dirai-je, Maman, K 300e (265)	Alfred

Based on the familiar theme of "Twinkle, Twinkle Little Star", the hands share technical difficulties throughout these variations. Mozart writes in a variety of styles, including some contrapuntal (VIII, IX) and coloratura (X) variations. The lack of dynamic markings in *urtext* editions requires guidance from the teacher. The entire variation set is challenging, but the final product is well worth the effort.

A	Variationen für Klavier, Vols. I-II (K 25, 300e/265)	Schott; Bärenreiter; Henle

Reinagle, Alexander (Robert) (1756–1809) USA (b. England)

An English and American composer, organist, concert organizer, theater musician and manager, Reinagle moved to New York in 1786 and later to Philadelphia. President George Washington was an admirer of his music and Reinagle composed several pieces honoring him. He wrote pieces dedicated to various American events such as the *Federal March, President Madison's March,* and *Mrs. Madison's Minuet* and composed four substantial sonatas known as the *Philadelphia Sonatas*.

E	24 Short and Easy Pieces, op. 2 (Hinson/Krauss, eds.)	Alfred
I	Theme with Variations (Hinson, ed.)	European American Music Corp.

Türk, Daniel Gottlob (1750–1813) Germany

A noted composer and organist, Turk was also a teacher and professor of music. He was appointed Director of Music at Halle University in Halle, Germany in 1709 and was the first professor of music theory and acoustics. His treatises, *Von den wichtigsten Pflichten eines Organisten* (On the Role of the Organist in Worship, 1787) and *Klavierschule* (Guide for Teaching Keyboard, 1789), and the two volumes of teaching pieces written to accompany the guide are influential contributions.

E	Easy Pieces for Piano	Schott
E	Little Piece	Nagel
E	Sixty Pieces for the Beginner	ABRSM; Litolff
E-I §	Sixty Pieces for Aspiring Players, Book II (Ferguson, ed.)	ABRSM

This collection is based on Türk's instructional manual, *120 Handstücke für angehende Klavierspieler,* Books I and II, published in 1792 and 1795 respectively.

Classical Collections and Anthologies

Title (editor)	Publisher
§ Anthology of Classical Piano Music (Hinson, ed.)	Alfred

This important Anthology is paired with a DVD on Classical performance practices. Hinson performs music from the Anthology and relates valuable information on musical characteristics, period instruments, and performance conventions not indicated in the manuscripts.

Anthology of Piano, Vol. 2: The Classical Period — Music Sales

Focuses on relatively unknown works by composers such as Kuhlau, Reichardt, Dittersdorf, and others.

At the Piano with the Sons of Bach (Hinson, ed.) — Alfred

Bärenreiter Sonatina Album for piano, Vol. 2. — Bärenreiter

The Classical Era — Hal Leonard

Includes 34 piano compositions and symphonic transcriptions by such composers as C. P. E. Bach, J. C. Bach, Beethoven, Benda, Cimarosa, Clementi, Diabelli, Haydn, and Mozart.

The Classical Era (Palmer/Halford, eds.) — Alfred

The Classical Masters (Lew, ed.) — Alfred

(Easy Piano Solos by Master Composers of the Period)
This volumes features authentic keyboard pieces exclusively from the Classical Period and serves as an excellent introduction to classical keyboard literature for late-elementary to early-intermediate level performers.

The Classical Period, Vol. II (Agay, ed.) — Music Sales

Classical Piano (Brisman, ed.) — Alfred

Das neue Sonatinen Buch, Books I, II (Frey, ed.) — Schott

Early Classical Sonatas, Vols. I, II (Smart, ed.) — Schirmer

First Sonatina Album (Bastien, ed.) — Kjos

The First Sonatina Book (Palmer, ed.) — Alfred

§ Für Elise (Heumann, ed.) — Schott

Contains 100 easier original works by composers of the classical era including Haydn, Cimarosa, Clementi, Mozart, and Beethoven.

§ Harris Piano Classics: Baroque and Classical Repertoire, Vols. 1a–7a — Frederick Harris

These seven books progress in difficulty and include a wide range of Baroque and Classical composers. Each volume contains between 16 to 24 pages, and includes 9–16 piano compositions.

Introduction to the Keyboard Sonatinas (Halford, ed.) — Alfred

Introduction to Theme and Variations (Halford, ed.) — Alfred

The Joy of Sonatinas (Agay, ed.) — Music Sales

Masters of the Sonatina, Vols. I–III (Hinson, ed.) — Alfred

§ The Pianist's Book of Classic Treasures (Banowetz, ed.) — Kjos

Piano Sonatinas, Vols. I–IV (Faber and Faber, eds.) — FJH

Selected Sonatinas, Vols. I–III — Schirmer

Sonatina Album (Kohler, ed.) — Schirmer

E (Early Intermediate)   I (Intermediate)   A (Advanced Intermediate to Advanced)

§ Sonatina Album (Small, ed.) — Alfred

This revised version of the Kohler *Sonatina Album*, a favorite of many teachers, includes newly revised fingerings by the editor and additional sonatinas by Beethoven and Diabelli. Other works include Clementi (op. 36 complete), Dussek, Haydn, Kuhlau (opus 20 and opus 55), and Mozart's *Sonata in C Major, K 545*. The spiral binding permits the book to lie flat.

Sonatina Album-27 Easy Sonatinas (Hofmann, ed.) — Editio Musica Budapest

Sonatinas and Easy Sonatas for Solo Piano. (Herder, ed.) — Dover

Sonatina Favorites, Vols. I–III (Bastien, ed.) — Kjos

Sonatinas for Piano, Vol. II, Classic Era (Herttrich/Kraus, eds.) — Henle

Includes works by Beethoven (op. 49), Clementi (op. 36), Dussek, Haydn (Hob. XVI:35, 37, 40), Kuhlau, and Mozart (K 545).

Sonatinen Album, Vol. I (Kohler/Ruthardt, eds.) — Peters

Sonatinen für Klavier, Vols. I, II — Henle

§ Style and Interpretation, Vol. III, Classical Piano Music (Ferguson, ed.) — Oxford

Style essays and performance notes accompany repertoire selected to demonstrate essential features of the period. Volumes I-II address baroque music and Vol. IV, romantic music.

World's Greatest Classical Sonatas, Vols. I, II (Hinson, ed.) — Alfred

The Romantic Period circa 1820—1900

An Introduction to Romantic Piano Music

The Romantic era of music, preceded by the Classical period and followed by the Contemporary period, developed roughly from the early 1800s and lasted for more than 100 years into the early 20th century. It is particularly difficult to pinpoint any specific year or event that launched the romantic era. Romanticism was an international movement in literature, art, music and philosophy; a period of great innovation and artistic freedom characterized by individualism and great intensity of feeling. Steven Whiting states (*Keyboard Musicianship, vol. 2*, Stipes Publishing L.L.C., 2010):

> The adjective *romantic* was derived from *roman* (French for "novel") and applied to flights of adventure or fancy likely to occur in novels but not in daily life. It was likewise applied to landscape paintings depicting scenes typical of novels-vast, distant perspectives and remote or otherwise exotic subjects. Indeed, the rejection of everyday reality in favor of the imaginative, the mysterious and the 'poetic' is a persistent theme of all art claiming to be romantic. (page 284)

While the Classical era in music was balanced and structured, the Romantic era moved away from that by encouraging more freedom and experimentation. The music of this time period was intensely expressive and melody became a dominant feature.

Social and Historical Influences

The years preceding and during the Romantic period coincide with what is referred to as the "age of revolutions", an age of tumult in the political, economic, and social spheres. Major cultural movements and developments in the arts are triggered and effected by the ideas, discoveries and historical events of society. Many of these "revolutions" involved expanding ideas of freedom and individual rights in the political sphere – very much analogous to the individualism of the artistic movements. During the Romantic era, the lives and fortunes of artists and composers were impacted by the disruptions of wars and revolutions such as the French revolutions (1789-99 and 1848), and the Spanish-American War (1898). Major conflicts at the outset of the 1900s effected late romantics such as Rachmaninoff, Paderewski, and Moskowski. [First World War (1914-1918), Russo-Polish War (1919-1920), and the German/Nazi invasion and occupation of Poland (1939) which began World War II (1939-1945)].

As pianists and composers traveled throughout Europe and the United States for concerts and performances, their lives were often governed by the political status of regions. Composers fled to other parts of Europe and the United States to avoid hostilities and possible imprisonment:

- Chopin, distressed by news of the capture of Warsaw by the Russians in the Russo-Polish war altered his travel plans and stayed in Paris and Vienna (1830-31), unable to return to his native Warsaw. He organized events for émigrés and supported them financially by giving charity concerts, and serving as a member of the Polish Literary Society.

- Richard Wagner, the Royal Saxton Court Conductor, wrote articles supporting political revolution in Germany, backing the insurgents. After the May Uprising in Dresden in 1849 he was forced to flee Germany to avoid arrest, enlisting the help of Franz Liszt who arranged for him to travel to Zürich.

- Enrique Granados (Spain) and his wife drowned in 1916, while returning from the New York premier of his opera *Goyescas* and performances of his works at the White House. The ocean liner Sussex on which they traveled, was torpedoed by a German U-boat while crossing the English Channel on route to Europe.

- Witold Lutoslawski's father and uncle were executed in the last days of WWI (Sept 1918) after being in the Butyrskaya prison in central Moscow, where Witold visited him as a 5 year old child.

- Ignace Paderewski was a successful touring piano virtuoso which helped him sponsor the Polish victims' relief fund in 1915. In 1919, he became the first Polish prime minister, signed the Versailles treaty and was considered a war hero. He was buried in Arlington, Virginia in the Arlington National

Solo Literature — The Romantic Period

An Introduction to Romantic Piano Music *continued*

Cemetery under the mast of the battleship Maine. According to his wishes, his body was returned to a free Poland for burial in St. John's Cathedral in 1992.

- Composers, such as Moskowski and Rachmaninoff, lost their fortunes or family estates during conflicts.

These world events influenced the themes and tenor of the music of the time and spurred the rise of *nationalism*, a major movement in the late Romantic period. Nationalist composers such as Dvořák, Gade, Gliere, Granados, Grieg, Janáček, Sibelius and Sinding used the folk melodies and dance rhythms of their homelands as the basis for their compositions and a source of support for their cultural identity and homelands.

At the same time, the Industrial Revolution, a century of gradual change from 1760 to approximately 1850, produced advanced technology and helped revolutionize economic and social traditions as well as the daily lives of people. As machines and manufacturing methods became more standardized and efficient allowing for mass production, the further development of the printing press, music publishing and piano manufacturing was possible. Pianos were available for individual homes and relatively inexpensive sheet music was accessible for purchase, bringing "classical" music out of the realm of the aristocracy (a trend that began in the Classical period) and closer to the lives of the general public.

The Romantic composer instead of writing primarily for aristocratic families or for special commissions now composed for public concerts and festivals. Liszt and Dussek are generally credited for heralding the modern recital in which the pianist performs with his profile to the audience. Clara Schumann's practice of performing by memory also influenced modern performance tradition. Exceptionally gifted performers (pianists, violinists, and singers) became enormously popular and virtuosic performers and stage personalities like Paganini and Liszt were idolized by large audiences of paying customers foreshadowing the popularity of the rock stars of today. These virtuosos, in turn, spurred the composition of more difficult music and the focus on individualism. Concert pianists traveled widely throughout Europe and the United States giving concerts to enthusiastic audiences. Included in this prestigious group were names such as Ignace Paderewski, Teresa Carreño, Clara Schumann, Felix Mendelssohn, Louis Gottschalk, Leopold Godowsky, Ignaz Moscheles, Theodor Leschetizky, Moriz Rosenthal, Moritz Moszkowski, and Ignaz Freidman. The birth of the 19th century piano virtuoso paralleled the rise of the subscription concert series for major orchestras as exemplified by the Gewandhaus Orchestra under the artistic direction of Felix Mendelssohn.

On a smaller scale, piano pieces also were composed for dancing or for refined evening salon concerts that became focal points for the gathering of musicians, their students, friends and supporters for performance and animated discussions about music, literature and the arts. With the lack of modern recordings and communications, music in the home at that time was used for evening entertainment and was supported by many smaller compositions written for the amateur musician. Indeed, the parlors of many middle-class families were arranged around their prized possession—the piano, and the composition and publication of piano music increased enormously. The piano was the most popular instrument during the Romantic period.

Influences of Technology

The Industrial Revolution influenced the music industry and there were improvements in the mechanical valves and keys of most wind and brass instruments. New, improved instruments could be played more easily and reliably, with a bigger, fuller, better-tuned sound. As wind instruments improved, more winds were added to the orchestra, and their musical parts became more difficult, interesting, and important. New instruments such as the tuba, saxophone and celesta were invented. The orchestra became increasingly large and powerful as these new instruments were added and composers explored new possibilities in timbre and sound.

The piano underwent major changes during the late Classical and Romantic periods in response to technology made possible by the Industrial Revolution and to demands made by composers and pianists (such as Liszt) for a more powerful and sustained sound. Changes such as high-quality steel for strings and precision casting for the production of iron frames along with the new double-escapement action created by Sébastien Érard, led to the modern instrument that we know today.

Advances in technology also influenced romantic composers. The chromaticism, thicker textures, and colorful pedaling that characterize Romantic keyboard music were possible, in part, because of improvements in piano construction. Greater string tension gave the piano a more brilliant sound. The range of the keyboard was extended. The availability of three pedals (*una corda, sostenuto*, damper) allowed musicians to try new and exciting effects to explore new sounds. The greater projection of the piano among instruments of the symphony orchestra offered new and exciting possibilities for the 19th century piano concerto.

Music Publishing and Music Criticism

The Industrial Revolution and the development of copyright agreements protecting the rights of composers made music publishing more viable. Inexpensive print materials and mass production, as well as the invention of lithography in Germany in 1798, led to further growth and development of the music publishing industry during the Romantic period. In Germany, Breitkopf (joined by Härtel in 1795) became one of the first music publishers to embark on the task of publishing the complete works of composers such as Beethoven, Haydn, Mozart, Schumann, Schubert, Chopin, Liszt and Wagner. Schott publishing (Stravinsky, Orff, Schönberg) was founded in 1770 and Simrock of Bonn and later Berlin was established in 1790.

Reading biographies of Romantic composers reveals interesting stories about the relationship between composers and their publishing houses, some of which still exist today. For example, Brahms' first *Piano Concerto* (D Minor, op. 15) was actually booed and hissed at its premiere and although he revised the work, he temporarily lost his publisher (Breitkopf & Härtel) and later changed to Simrock, who remained his major publisher. Brahms recognized opportunities in the rise of the public consumer and composed many works for amateur pianists. He published four-hand piano arrangements of his symphonies and arranged his popular requiem (*Ein deutsches Requiem, nach Worten der heiligen Schrift, op. 45*) for piano duet and choir.

Chopin became famous through his concert performances and attracted the interest of publishers. In 1832, he signed a contract with the Parisian publishing firm, Schlesinger, while at the same time, his compositions were published in Leipzig by Probst and then Breitkopf, and in London by Wessel. Music publisher Anton Diabelli, in a clever marketing promotion, sent a waltz theme to important Austrian composers, inviting them to write variations for inclusion in a patriotic anthology. Fifty composers responded, and Czerny wrote a *coda* for the 1824 set of "Diabelli Variations" (*Vaterländischer Künstlerverein*) that included the first published composition by Franz Liszt (age 11) as well as pieces by Schubert, the Archduke Rudolf, Pixis, Moscheles, and Kalkbrenner. This same waltz theme inspired Beethoven to compose a set of 33 variations, known as the *Diabelli Variations, op. 120*, one of the great masterpieces using variation form. As a publisher, Diabelli also experienced success by recognizing the talent of Franz Schubert, printing the song *Erlkönig* for the first time in 1821 and thus becoming Schubert's principle publisher.

Professional journals that heralded the opinions and descriptions of music by critics were created in this era. Robert Schumann's twice weekly periodical, *Neue Zeitschrift für Musik*, founded in 1834, played an important role in recognizing and supporting young composers of the time. Schumann, in his role as an editor and music critic, first brought Brahms to the notice of the German public, calling him a "young eagle." Lesser-known composers, such as Stephen Heller, were also recognized in this journal. Numerous reviews praised Liszt and his achievements, providing media attention to help develop his career. At the same time, articles and editorials produced controversial reactions, replies and feuds among these same composers.

Musical Language and Harmonic Expansions

Romantic composers increased emotional expression while preserving or even extending the formal structures from the classical period. They broadened the harmonic palette using musical elements such as:

An Introduction to Romantic Piano Music *continued*

- Adding chromatic notes to color the relationship of one harmony to another.
- Exploring new tonal relationships
- Using altered chords
- Using increased dissonance
- Exploring modulations to remote keys
- Composing with thicker textures
- Increased use of pedal markings

Romantic composers also marked their scores more precisely, indicating subtle variations of tone quality and dynamic range. The use of contrasts and extremes of dynamics added to the intense expressivity of this music. The enhanced tone quality and harmonies were blended with the subtle and varied use of pedaling, which was an important aspect of the development of pianism in the 19th century. The expansion of the tonal language by composers like Liszt and Wagner, would eventually lead to atonal compositions, music that shattered traditional tonality altogether.

Looking at a broad overview of the century of Romanticism, we see a variety of approaches and schools of composers or lines of development in the area of piano composition:

1. Early Romanticism, roughly 1820-1850 or around the death of Schumann in 1856 – Some composers chose to stay closer to the classical traditions while exploring Romantic style and feeling. Beethoven, Schubert, Schumann, Mendelssohn and Brahms are in this category (composers active during Beethoven's lifetime). These composers created a style that blended the lyrical and intellectual and served as a contrast to the progressive style of the New German School.

2. Late Romanticism – Composers born near to or after Beethoven's death in 1827, felt more comfortable creating new styles and pushing the boundaries. Berlioz, Liszt, Bruckner, and Wagner were more innovative composers whose music challenged the audiences of their day.

3. Folk-lore nationalism – Nationalist composers sought to incorporate elements of folk music, song and dance into their works. Dvořák included Bohemian elements in his *Slavonic Dances*, Gliere and Tchaikovsky drew on Russian elements, Granados used Spanish elements, while the music of Gade (Denmark), Grieg and Sinding (Norway) and Sibelius (Finland) reflected Scandinavian influences.

There is, of course, overlap among these three categories. One can view Brahms, for example, with his deep artistic attachment to German folklore and older music, as a German nationalist or Chopin with his fondness for native dances, a Polish nationalist.

Musical Forms

Composers of the Romantic era continued to write symphonies, concertos, operas and sonatas, forms that already existed. The main difference between Classical and Romantic music came from attitudes toward the traditions or rules of these forms. The Romantic composers did not feel constrained by form. Experimenting with the length of compositions produced short piano character pieces, the symphonic poem (a single continuous movement or work with multiple interior sections), and large, expansive symphonies reaching 90 minutes. They used classical forms as a starting point, and began focusing on new melodic styles, richer harmonies, and ever more dissonance. Composers turned their attention to the expression of intense feelings in their music in the pursuit of moving their audiences

In piano repertoire, prominent 19th-century composers wrote sonatas and works with larger forms, but they favored short, expressive piano miniatures. As a simple comparison, Haydn composed 62 sonatas and Beethoven 32, while both Chopin and Schumann each wrote only three. Many composers focused on music of a programmatic nature, pieces that represented ideas, scenes, dramatic events, or themes found in literature. These piano miniatures attempted to express or represent a character or extra-musical theme and evolved into several different forms including:

Character Pieces: Expression, mood, and color, rather than extensive thematic development, are at the heart of these short pieces that were a lyrical, intimate contrast to the dramatic and virtuosic sonata. Most character pieces are in ternary (ABA) form, focus on one motive and emphasize an expressive melody and harmony. Although they may feature elaborate keyboard figurations, especially in Chopin's case, many resemble an instrumental song much like the German *Lied*. Examples of character pieces include Schumann's *An Important Event* (from *Kinderszenen, op. 15*) or Mendelssohn's *Duetto, op. 38, no. 6* (from his *Songs without Words*). Other titles composers used for piano miniatures as well as larger structures, included nocturne, ballade, rhapsody, intermezzo, impromptu, *moments musicaux*, barcarolle, capriccio, scherzo, and song without words.

In an effort to create compositions larger in scope, some composers linked shorter character pieces together to form larger works. Examples would be Schumann's *Fantasiestücke, op. 12*, and *Carnaval, op. 9*, the latter of which has an underlying four note theme, ASCH (A, E-flat, C, B). The linking of individual movements developed into another significant form that paralleled the symphonic poem. It was the development of a continuous one-movement hybrid sonata form that had interior sections linked without pause. This is reflected in works such as Schubert's *Fantasie in C major (Wanderer), Op. 15 (D760)*, Schumann's *Fantasy in C Major, op. 17*, and Liszt's *Sonata in B Minor*, S. 178.

Nocturne: The nocturne deserves special mention because it was an important contribution to romantic piano music. The title refers to a composition evocative of the night or of music played in the evening as in a serenade. Although the nocturne is generally credited to John Field, an Irish composer and pianist, who published his first three nocturnes in 1814, Chopin wrote 21 nocturnes throughout his career many of which are among his most beloved works. In ABA form, they served as a vehicle for Chopin to explore melody, harmony, range of expression, and an astonishing variety of left hand accompaniment patterns under adorned right hand melody. Late Romantic and early 20th century composers such as Fauré, Scriabin, Satie, Poulenc and Samuel Barber also borrowed the nocturne style.

Études: The étude was a study that showed off the performer's technical ability often focusing on one technical element such as projecting a melodic line from its surrounding texture, or successfully playing textures that featured scales, arpeggios, octaves, chords, etc. Shorter etudes were often framed as character pieces (e.g., music by composers such as Stephen Heller and Johann Friedric Burgmüller) and, at a more advanced level, true concert etudes were composed by Chopin (e.g., opp. 10 and 25) and Liszt (e.g., *Transcendental Etudes*).

Theme and Variations: This form includes a theme that is then modified through changes of rhythm, meter, harmonies and musical texture. Popular in both the 18th and 19th centuries, composers often used well-known tunes as the theme for the pleasure of the audience. Two romantic examples include Mendelssohn's *Variations sérieuses, op. 54* and Schumann's *Variations on the name Abegg, op. 1*.

Stylized Dances: Stylized dances were popular dance forms such as the waltz, mazurka, polka and gallop that were not meant to be danced, but were composed in the spirit and mood of the original dance form. Chopin's *Mazurkas* and *Waltzes* epitomize a composer transforming dance styles into a musical art form.

Looking to the Future

The final decades of the nineteenth century and the first decades of the twentieth are often called the post-Romantic era. After years of exploration and pushing at the limits of form and tonality, the Romantic era left composers with the question of what to explore or challenge next. Perhaps because there were many possible answers, a variety of things were happening in music by the end of the Romantic era. Composers, such as Sibelius, Bartók, and Vaughan-Williams, were writing strongly nationalistic music. Others, such as Mahler and Strauss, were expanding Romantic musical techniques to their utmost reasonable limits. Impressionism and some other -isms such as Stravinsky's primitivism still had some basis in tonality, but others, such as serialism, rejected tonality. Though the sounds and ideals of Romanticism continued to inspire some composers, the Romantic period was essentially over by about 1910, the outset of the twentieth century.

An Introduction to Romantic Piano Music *continued*

Recommended resources for further reading:

Eigeldinger, Jean-Jacques. 1986. *Chopin, Pianist and Teacher: as seen by his Pupils.* 3rd English ed. Translated by Naomi Shohet with Krysia Osostowicz and Roy Howat. New York: Cambridge University Press.

Schonberg, Harold C. 1963. *The Great Pianists from Mozart to the Present.* New York: Simon and Schuster.

Todd. R. Larry, ed. 1990. *Nineteenth-Century Piano Music.* New York: Schirmer Books.

Romantic Literature

A. Characteristics

Students entering the intermediate level of piano instruction will experience increased demands, both musical and technical (i.e., expanded vocabulary of accompaniment patterns and of textural balance), in Romantic literature. Through the study of Romantic literature, students will encounter the following elements:

Style considerations:
- Character and descriptive pieces
- Singing lines, *cantabile* playing
- Varied phrase lengths
- Syncopation, and more difficult rhythmic demands
- Chromatic harmonies, thick textures, chord doublings
- Expanded use of secondary dominants, diminished 7ths, and altered chords
- Increased use of the pedals for coloring of sound

Technical experiences:
- Expansion and contraction of the hand
- Complex inner voicings
- Octave stretching and octave fill-in
- Balance between hands and within the hand
- Voicing of melodic lines
- Wider reading range due to expanded range of keyboard

B. Introducing the Romantic Style

Teachers should prepare students carefully before beginning more complex or advanced Romantic repertoire. The following is a list of music that may be used to introduce the Romantic style. These pieces and collections can serve as a valuable link between late elementary method books and more difficult repertoire. The listing is alphabetical, not in order of difficulty.

Collection	Title	Publisher
Burgmüller, Johann	25 Progressive Pieces, op. 100	Alfred
Gillock, William	Lyric Preludes in Romantic Style	Alfred
Grill, Joyce	In Style, Book 2	Alfred
Grill, Joyce	Preludes	Alfred
Olson, Lynn F.	Adventures in Style	Carl Fischer
Rocherolle, Eugenie	Six Moods for Piano	Kjos
Rollin, Catherine	Preludes for Piano (Vols. I, II)	Alfred
Rollin, Catherine	Spotlight on Romantic Style	Alfred
Sheftel, Paul	Patterns for Fun (Vol. II)	Douglas
Vandall, Robert	Preludes (Vols. I, II)	Alfred

C. Gradation or Teaching Order

We suggest the following teaching order when introducing students to Romantic literature:

Gurlitt and Burgmüller – easier pieces and studies
Heller – Studies
Schumann and Tchaikovsky – each composer's Album for the Young
Grieg – selected Lyric Pieces
Chopin – easier Preludes, Waltzes, and Mazurkas
Mendelssohn – selected Songs without Words

Romantic Literature *continued*

Composer	Title	Publisher

Albéniz, Isaac (1860–1909) Spain

Along with de Falla and Granados, Albéniz is revered as one of Spain's most important composers. A pianist, teacher and nationalistic composer from Catalonia, he was a child prodigy who first performed at age four. He developed a reputation as a virtuoso pianist and was compared to Liszt and Anton Rubinstein as he toured England, Belgium, France, Germany and Austria. His compositions reflect a synthesis of Spanish styles and evoke images of Spain and the Iberian Peninsula. His major work for piano, *Ibéria* (in four books), depicts 12 scenes from his native land.

I-A   España, op. 165 (6 pieces)   Henle; Unión Musical Ediciones
     España describes a journey through the Spanish countryside and includes *Zortzico*, using dance rhythms, *Serenata*, a folk melody, and the famous *Tango*.

I-A §   Malagueña, op. 165, no. 3 (Hinson, ed.)   Alfred
     The title mirrors the dance from the Spanish province Málaga. This is the third movement of the *España, op. 165*, and is often published separately because of the movement's popularity.

I-A   Songs of Spain, op. 232   Kalmus

A   Best of Isaac Albéniz, The   Salabert

A   Iberia (12 pieces) and España (6 pieces) Suites   Dover
     Both suites are presented in their entirety.

A   Mallorca, op. 202   International; ASE

A   Piano Album   Schirmer
     This collection includes: *Azulejos, Cordoba, El Puerto, En la playa, Evocation, Granada, Malagueña, Minuetto del gallo, Preludio, Cantos de España, España, Seguidillas, Sevilla* and *Tango*.

A   Piano Solos   Salabert
     This book includes *Chants d'españa, Suite Española, Iberia*, and more.

A   Serenade Españole, op. 181   Kalmus

A §   Suite Española, op. 47   Henle; Kalmus; ASE
     One of his most popular works, this suite of eight movements (*Granada, Cataluña, Sevilla, Cádiz, Asturias, Aragón, Castillas, Cuba*) reflects the rhythms and melodies of different Spanish regions.

A   Travel Impressions (Recuredos de viaji)   International; ASE

Arensky, Anton (Antony) Stepanovich (1861–1906) Russia

A Russian pianist, composer, teacher, and conductor, Arensky studied with Rimsky-Korsakov at the St. Petersburg Conservatory. He later taught harmony and counterpoint at the Moscow Conservatory to students such as Rachmaninoff, Scriabin, and Gliére. He was Music Director at the Imperial Chapel of St. Petersburg from 1895 to 1901 and wrote two symphonies, a violin concerto, piano trios, string quartets and other chamber music. His compositions reflect the influence of Tchaikovsky who gave Arensky encouragement and support. Arensky traveled and toured widely as a pianist and conductor.

I-A §   Twenty-four Morceau Characteristiques (Character Pieces), op. 36   Kalmus
     (includes *Nocturne* and *Consolation*)

A   Arabesques, op. 67   Peters

A   Twelve Etudes for Piano, op. 74   Marks

A   Twelve Preludes, op. 63   Peters

E (Early Intermediate)   I (Intermediate)   A (Advanced Intermediate to Advanced)

Beach, Amy Marcy Cheney (1867–1944) USA (New Hampshire)

A virtuoso pianist and composer, also known as Mrs. H. H. A. Beach (husband and amateur musician Henry Harris Aubrey Beach, M.D.), she was a child prodigy and one of the first major female American composers. She was a prolific composer who wrote in a wide variety of genres (i.e., choral, chamber, keyboard) including over 120 songs, an opera, and her large *Gaelic Symphony*. Additionally, Beach was an active participant and leader in national musical organizations such as Music Teachers National Association, Music Educators National Conference, and the Society of American Women composers.

E-I	Young People's Carnival, op. 25 (*Hinson, **Glickman, eds.)	*Alfred;**Hildegard
	A suite of six pieces reflecting pantomime characters.	
I	Young People's Album, op. 36 (1897) (*Hinson, ed.)	*Alfred; Schmidt
	Five dances, written in treble clef, form a suite with a *Minuet, Gavotte, Waltz, March,* and *Polka*.	
I-A §	A Hermit Thrush at Eve, op. 92, no. 1	Hildegard
I-A §	A Hermit Thrush at Morn, op. 92, no. 2	Hildegard
	Both of the "Thrush" pieces can be found in *Beach: Music For Piano, Vol. 2* published by Hildegard. Beach, not unlike Messiaen, was an avid ornithologist. Some right hand figurations in this beautiful composition relate to birdcalls.	
I-A	From Grandmother's Garden, op. 97	Hildegard
	Available in *Beach: Music For Piano, Vol. 1*, the five pieces in this set (*Morning Glories, Heartease, Mignonette, Rosemary and Rue, Honeysuckle*) are all charming and trickier than they sound. Students can select one or more of these highly characterized pieces to study as they do not have to be learned as a set.	
I-A	Sketches, op. 15	Masters Music
I-A §	The Life and Music of Amy Beach: The First Woman Composer of America	Mel Bay
	Compiled and edited by Gail Smith, and published by Mel Bay in conjunction with *Creative Keyboard Publications* (see *Appendix* on publishers), this beautiful book and collection features a biography, 22 photos and 25 piano compositions dating from the early *Mamma's Waltz* (written at age 4) to the collection *Summer Dreams, op. 47* (six duets). Other titles include *Scottish Legend, Canoeing* as well as compositions from opp. 25, 26, 28, 36, 54, 64 and 119.	
I-A	Three Pieces, op. 28	Masters Music
A	Five Improvisations for Piano, op. 148	Composers Press
A	Variations on Balkan Themes, op. 60	Hildegard
	Available in *Beach: Music For Piano, Vol. 2*, this is Beach's longest and most difficult solo piano work. The theme is hauntingly beautiful and the text of folk songs is included in the Hildegard edition. The folk songs Beach uses were obtained by missionaries to the region. She starts and ends this major work with a slow, meaningful theme, much as Bach does in his *Goldberg Variations*.	

Berens, (Johann) Hermann (1826–1880) (b. Germany, d. Stockholm, Sweden)

A German-Swedish pianist and composer, Berens was the son of Karl Berens, a German flutist. After a move to Sweden in 1847, he was appointed professor of composition and orchestration at Stockholm Conservatory where he was noted for his chamber performances.

E	Fifty Pieces without Octaves, op. 70 (Complete)	Schirmer
I §	Twenty Children's Studies, op. 79	Schirmer

Romantic Literature *continued*

Bertini, Henri Jérôme (1798–1876) (b. England, d. France)

Bertini was a French pianist, teacher, composer and arranger whose early music study was with his brother (a Clementi student). Recognized as a child prodigy and piano virtuoso, he toured with his father at age 12 in England, Holland, and Germany. He later settled in France and gave a concert with Liszt in 1828 that included his own transcription of Beethoven's *Symphony no. 7* for two-pianos, eight-hands (performed with Liszt, Sowinsky, and Schunke). Bertini authored a piano method, *Le Rudiment du pianiste*, and many piano studies.

I-A	Forty-eight Studies, opp. 29, 32	Kalmus; ASE
I-A	Forty-nine Etudes, opp. 101, 166	Kalmus; ASE

Brahms, Johannes (1833–1897) Germany

A pianist, accompanist, conductor and composer, Brahms is considered one of the great composers. He began his early study of music (cello and horn) with his father who was a double bassist in the Hamburg Philharmonic Society. Later, he helped support his family by playing in taverns, dancehalls and brothels, and arranging music for his father's orchestra. At twenty he began touring as an accompanist for the accomplished violinists Eduard Reményi and Joseph Joachim. His closest friends and supporters, however, were Robert and Clara Schumann. Schumann published an article praising Brahms and their admiration was mutual. After Schumann's death, Brahms supported the Schumann household so Clara could tour as a concert pianist. Brahms made significant contributions in many genres including his four symphonies, piano and violin concertos, choral and vocal works, chamber music, and piano works. His piano works include the important *Variations on themes of Schumann* (1854*)*, *Handel* (1861), and *Paganini* (1862-1863) as well as numerous ballades, intermezzi and rhapsodies. These works are essential in the standard piano repertoire of the nineteenth century.

I	§	Dances of Brahms (Hinson, ed.)	Alfred
I-A		Brahms: The Composer and His Music (Banowetz, ed.)	Kjos
I-A	§	Celebrate Brahms (Hisey, ed.)	Frederick Harris

> This volume is devoted to the core solo piano repertoire that teachers use to introduce Brahms to advancing students: the complete *Waltzes, op. 39*, all of the *Klavierstücke, op. 118*, and the two great *Rhapsodies, op. 79* (B minor and G minor) which cap off the volume. Selected works from opp. 10, 76, and 117 also are present.

I-A		Complete Shorter Works (Mandyczewski, ed.)	Dover
I-A	§ *	Waltzes, op. 39 (3, 5, 9, 15, 1)	Henle
I-A		The Young Pianist's Brahms (Dexter, ed.)	Hansen
A	§ *	Ballades, op. 10 (no. 1) (*Hinson, ed.)	*Alfred; Henle

> These four *Ballades* are in D minor (subtitled "Edward"), D major, B minor (subtitled "Intermezzo"), and B major. Of the four, no. 1 is the most accessible. The volume includes a thorough Foreword, which outlines the historical background of the *Ballades*, and includes performance notes on each piece. The programmatic "Edward" ballade musically portrays the events in a Scottish ballad in which the mother questions her son about killing his father.

A		Complete Works for Piano Solo, Vols. I-III (Mandyczewski, ed.)	Schirmer
A	*	Eight Piano Pieces, op. 76 (2)	Henle
A	*	Four Piano Pieces, op. 119 (3)	Henle
A		Sarabandes and Gigues	Peters
A		Selected Works (Levine, ed.)	Alfred
A	*	Seven Fantasies, op. 116 (3, 6)	Henle
A	§	Shorter Piano Pieces, The (Hinson, ed.)	Alfred

E (Early Intermediate) I (Intermediate) A (Advanced Intermediate to Advanced)

  This valuable edition includes the complete opp. 76, 79, 116, 117, 118, and 119, with performance notes and stylistic commentary on each opus.

A		*	Six Piano Pieces, op. 118 (1, 2)	Henle
A			3 Intermezzi, op. 117 (Palmer, ed.)	Alfred
A	§	*	Two Rhapsodies, op. 79 (no. 2) (*Hinson, ed.)	*Alfred; Henle
A			Variations and Fugue on a Theme by Handel, op. 24	Breitkopf & Härtel; ASE

  Of Brahms' most advanced piano works (e.g., three sonatas and several variation sets) this work stands out as an exemplar of the romantic variation set. Handel's theme is presented in 25 variations ending with a large, complex fugue.

Burgmüller, (Johann) Friedrich Franz (1806–1874) Germany

Born into a musical family, Burgmüller's father (Johann August Franz) was an organist and theater conductor and his younger brother (Norbert) was a composer and pianist greatly admired by musicians such as Mendelssohn. During his life, Friedrich was best known for his ballet music. Because he was a recluse, much of his music was lost, however, numerous piano studies have survived which now are part of the standard intermediate teaching literature. Much of Burgmüller's piano music is intended for young students with small hands.

E-I	Burgmüller: 25 Progressive Studies, op. 100	Alfred; ASE

  Burgmüller's music is especially appropriate for introducing the Romantic style. These early intermediate studies are particularly useful with late elementary and middle school students. Throughout, the composer presents a variety of technical demands. Familiar titles include *Ballade*, *The Chase*, and *Arabesque*. In the last composition (no. 25), *The Knight Errant*, Burgmüller musically summarizes by including snippets of technical passages from earlier studies. Several very fine editions of the op. 100 studies are in print by editors such as Orwell (Hal Leonard) and Palmer (Alfred).

E-A		Collected Studies for Piano, opp. 100, 105, 109 (Oesterle, ed.)	Schirmer
I	§	Celebrate Burgmüller (Hisey, ed.)	Frederick Harris

  One of the most comprehensive collections of Burgmüller's music in print, this volume consists of the complete op. 100, *25 Easy and Progressive Studies* (see above annotation), and the harder op. 105 (*18 Characteristic Studies*) and op. 109 (*12 Brilliant and Melodious Studies for the Piano*). The delightful *Rondo alla Turca, op. 68, no. 3* (rarely published), based on the famous Mozart sonata movement of the same title, concludes the collection.

I-A	Burgmüller: 18 Characteristic Studies, op. 109 (Westney, ed.) Book & CD	Hal Leonard
I-A	18 Characteristic Studies, op. 109 (Hinson, ed.)	Alfred
A	12 Brilliant and Melodious Studies, op. 105 (*Hinson, ed.)	*Alfred; Schirmer

Chopin, Frédéric François [Fryderyk Franciszek] (1810–1849) Poland

A virtuoso pianist, composer and teacher, Chopin was a child prodigy who began composing and performing in aristocratic settings at age 7. He studied music first at the Warsaw Lyceum and later in 1826 at the University of Warsaw. Chopin concertized in Vienna and throughout Germany and Austria, settling in Paris in 1831. He was eagerly accepted and admired in Paris counting among his friends Liszt and Mendelssohn. Chopin had a close relationship with French writer George Sand (Aurore Dupin) from 1838 until 1847. They spent summer vacations in Sand's house in Central France where Chopin composed his 24 Preludes and many other piano masterpieces. His works, written almost entirely for piano, reflect his love of Polish folk music and include rhythmic dances (mazurkas, and polonaises) as well as waltzes, nocturnes, preludes and etudes.

Romantic Literature *continued*

**Chopin Institute Publications: The *NIFC Fryderyk Chopin National Institute* is a state cultural institution established by an act of the Polish Parliament in 2001 and dedicated to preserving the Fryderyk Chopin cultural legacy. The IFC was created in 1934 and focused primarily on editorial work for *The Complete Works of Frederic Chopin* edited by Ignacy Jan Paderewski, Ludwik Bronarski and Józef Tuczyński.

E-I §	An Introduction to His Piano Works (includes the posthumous *Waltz in A Minor*)	Alfred
E §	First Book for Pianists (Palmer, ed.)	Alfred
E-I §	Selected Easy Pieces	**Chopin Institute
I	Four Preludes, op. 28, nos. 4, 6, 7, 20 (Palmer, ed.)	Alfred
I §	Three Easier Waltzes (Faber, ed.) * (posth. Waltz in A Minor; op. 69, no. 2; op. 69, no. 1)	Hal Leonard
I § *	Three Mazurkas (Faber, ed.) (op. 68, no. 3; op. 67, no. 2; op. 7, no. 1)	Hal Leonard
I-A	At the Piano with Chopin (Hinson, ed.)	Alfred
I-A §	Celebrate Chopin, Vols. I, II (Hisey, ed.)	Frederick Harris

Volume I contains introductory Chopin compositions such as the *A Minor Waltz* (*KK IVb, no. 1, op. posth.*) and the beautiful, but hard to find one-page *Cantabile in B-Flat, KK IVb, no. 6, op. posth.*), a perfect composition to introduce Chopin's nocturne style. Both volumes present selected *Preludes, Waltzes, Nocturnes,* and *Mazurkas* in a progressive order of difficulty. Care is taken to provide both the autograph and Fontana versions for selected compositions. Informative study and performance notes accompany each volume. Volume II contains slightly more difficult repertoire.

I-A	Chopin: Piano Music from His Early Years (Hinson, ed.)	Alfred
I-A	Chopin: Preludes (Ganz, ed.) Book & CD	Schirmer
I-A	Chopin Selected Works for Piano, Vols. I, II (Schnell, ed.)	Kjos
I-A	Complete Preludes, Nocturnes & Waltzes	Schirmer
I-A	Dances of Chopin (Hinson, ed.)	Alfred
I-A	Joy of Chopin, The (Agay, ed.)	Yorktown
I-A §	Mazurkas * (op. 68, no. 3; op. 7, nos. 1, 2; op. 67, no. 2; op. 17, no. 2; op. 33, no. 2)	Chopin Institute
I-A § *	Preludes (op. 28, nos. 4, 6, 7, 9, 15, 20, 22)	Chopin Institute

When playing Chopin preludes (note the above ordering of difficulty), notice the key relationship that he used for the entire set (circle of 5ths alternating major and minor; C, A minor, G, E minor, etc.).

I-A	Selected Favorites (Palmer, ed.)	Alfred
I-A § *	Waltzes Chopin Institute (op. 69, nos. 1, 2; op. 34, no. 2; op. 64, nos. 1, 2; op. 70, no. 2)	
A	Barcarolle in F-Sharp Major, op. 60 (Timbrell, ed.)	Alfred
A § *	Etudes (op. 10, nos. 3, 6, 9; op. 25, nos. 1, 2, 7)	Chopin Institute

The Chopin *Études* represent an advanced level of study (note the suggested order [*] above). The *Étude in E Major*, op. 10, no. 3 is an excellent introduction to Chopin's etude style. With melody over accompaniment, the opening texture requires careful voicing and *legato* projection of top tones. The B section, comprised of contrary motion tritones and 6ths, will challenge most pianists.

A §	Fantaisie-Impromptu, op. 66 (*Palmer, ed.)	*Alfred; ASE

One of the most frequently performed of Chopin's freestanding works, it is a rhythmic masterpiece of playing three against four in the outer A sections (ABA-Coda). The Hinson edition includes both the standard and Fontana versions.

E (Early Intermediate) I (Intermediate) A (Advanced Intermediate to Advanced)

A	§ *	Nocturnes	Chopin Institute
	*	(KK IVb/6; KK Iva/16 op. posth.; op. 9, no. 2; op. 72, no. 1 posth.)	

Chopin's nocturnes can be approached incrementally through these four pieces. Thought not listed as a *Nocturne*, the one-page, beautiful *Cantabile in B-flat, KK IVb/6* (available in *Celebrate Chopin, vol. 1*, Frederick Harris), contains a florid operatic melody over a nocturne-like accompaniment. A step up in difficulty, the *posth. Lento in C-Sharp minor, KK Iva/16* quotes musical material from the composer's second piano concerto. The slightly more difficult *Nocturne in E-flat Major, op. 9, no. 2* requires careful attention to pedaling and right hand detailed phrasing. This can then be followed by the *posth. Nocturne in E minor, op. 72, no. 1*. Chopin's 21 *Nocturnes* (ABA format) require careful tonal balance. The variety of left hand accompaniments Chopin draws upon is simply astounding.

A	*	Polonaises (op. 26, no. 1; op. 40, no.1; op. 32, no. 1)	Chopin Institute
A		Prelude in D flat Major "Raindrop," op. 28, no. 15 (R. Faber, ed.)	Hal Leonard
A	*	Scherzos (no. 3), Impromptus (no. 1), and Ballades (no. 3)	Chopin Institute

Without question, the *Ballades, Impromptus,* and *Scherzos* frame Chopin's most advanced writing (not including the three sonatas). Chopin wrote four compositions in each of the above genres. The *Impromptus* (the term *Impromptu* suggests improvisation) and *Scherzos* all fall into an ABA ternary structure. The fourth *Impromptu in C-Sharp minor* (op. 66) was not published during Chopin's lifetime.

Dvořák, Antonín (Leopold) (1841–1904) Czechoslovakia

An organist, violist and violinist, Dvořák is considered a leading Czech composer who wrote in a nationalistic style combining folk melodies and Classical forms in a wide variety of genres. His *Symphony no. 9 (New World* – based on Longfellow's poem *Hiawatha)* is perhaps his best-known work along with his landmark *Cello Concerto in B Minor*. A professor at Prague University, he was invited to the United States as Artistic Director and Professor of Composition at the National Conservatory of Music in New York (1892-1895) and incorporated American influences into some of his music. His best-known piano works are the *Humoresque in G flat major, op. 101, no. 7,* and the *Slavonic Dances* for piano duet.

I	§	Humoresque, op. 101, no. 7	Hal Leonard
I-A		Easy Original Pieces for Piano (Roggenkamp, ed.)	Universal
I-A		Dances for Piano	Schirmer
		Includes ten dances: 3 *Waltzes*, 2 *Mazurkas*, a *Polka, Slavic Dance, Goblin Dance, Furiante* and his well-known *Humoresque*, op. 101, no. 7.	
I-A		Humoresques and Other Works for Solo Piano	Dover
I-A		Silhouettes, op. 8	Kalmus; Masters Music
A		Dvořák Selected Works	Schott
A		Eight Waltzes, op. 54	Masters Music; Presser
A		Poetical Tone Pictures, op. 85	Henle: Kalmus
A		Waltzes, op. 54 and Mazurkas, op. 56 (Döge, arr.)	Hal Leonard

Fauré, Gabriel (Urbain) (1845–1924) France

An organist, pianist, professor, composer and music critic with *Le Figaro* (1903-1921), Fauré is viewed as one of the great French composers. He studied with Camile Saint-Saëns at the *École Niedermeyer* in Paris and was a professor of composition at the Paris *Conservatoire* (1896-1920) teaching such noted students as Maurice Ravel and Nadia Boulanger. A prominent composer of French art song, his *Requiem* is one of his most important works. His piano works include the popular *Dolly Suite, op. 56* for piano duet.

Romantic Literature *continued*

I-A	Berceuse, op. 56, no. 1	Hamelle
I-A	Complete Préludes, Impromptus, and Valses-Caprices	Dover
I-A	Romances sans paroles (Romances without Words), op. 17	International
I-A	13 Nocturnes	International
A	Fauré: Album of Piano Pieces (Philipp, ed.)	Schirmer
A	Impromptu no. 2 in F Minor, op. 31	International
A	Nocturnes and Barcarolles for Solo Piano	Dover
A	Selected Piano Works (Bricard, ed.)	Alfred
A § *	Six Barcarolles (4)	Kalmus

Field, John (1782–1837) b. Ireland

An Irish born composer, teacher, violinist and pianist, Field was the son of Robert Field, a violinist. He made his piano debut at the age of nine and after his family moved to London became an apprentice and pupil of Muzio Clementi, a composer and piano manufacturer. Field toured and performed as a piano soloist throughout Europe and eventually settled in Russia for the rest of his life. His expressive keyboard style influenced numerous Romantic composers and many recognize Field as the creator of the Nocturne.

I	Nocturne no. 5 (Hinson, ed.)	Alfred
I-A	Favorite Nocturnes and Other Works (Smith, ed.)	Dover
I-A	Selected Piano Works	Carl Fischer
A § *	Eighteen Nocturnes (B flat Major)	Peters
A	Eighteen Nocturnes (Liszt, ed.)	Schirmer/Masters

Franck, César (-Auguste-Jean-Guillaume-Hubert) (1822–1890) France (b. Belgium)

A touring piano virtuoso at an early age, Franck later became a church organist and choirmaster. He was also a noted organist recognized by Liszt and others for his organ improvisations. In 1872, he became a professor of organ at the Paris *Conservatoire* where he composed symphonies, chamber music, organ and piano music. His noted works are the *Prélude, Chorale et Fugue, Symphonic Variations* for piano and orchestra and *Symphony in D minor*.

E-I §	18 Short Selected Pieces	Peters
I	7 Traditional French Noëls	Werner-Curwen
I-A	46 Short Pieces for Piano (Agay, ed.)	Presser
I-A	Selected Piano Compositions (d'Indy, ed.)	Dover
	This edition is an excellent overview of Franck's output for piano.	
I-A	Twenty-five Short Pieces from L'Organiste	ABRSM
A §	Prélude, Chorale et Fugue	Kalmus; Peters; ASE
	Approximately 18 minutes in length, this may be Franck's best-known piano solo. The single broken figuration of the opening prelude is reminiscent of the Baroque style as is the concluding fugue. The middle *Chorale* serves as a transition to connect the outer sections.	

Gade, Niels Wilhelm (1817–1890) Denmark

Gade was a Danish nationalistic composer, organist, and teacher who began his career as a violinist with the Danish Royal Orchestra. Championed by his friends Schumann and Mendelssohn, he taught at the Leipzig Conservatory and served as assistant conductor of the Gewandhaus Orchestra in Leipzig (Mendelssohn was principal conductor). He became the director of the Copenhagen Academy of Music in 1866, teaching composition and music history. His pupils included Edvard Grieg and Carl Nielsen. His piano output, in addition to smaller pieces, includes a piano sonata, *Fantasy Pieces* and *Akvareller* (Water Colors).

I		Children's Christmas Eve, op. 36	Kalmus; ASE
		Clearly at an intermediate level, this set is excellent preparation for Chopin. The *Little Girls' Dance* is an easier waltz.	
I-A		Aquarellen, op. 19 (10 character pieces)	Kalmus; Peters
I-A		Folkedanse for Piano, op. 31	Music Sales
I-A		Pieces: Aquarellen, op. 19; Idylles, op. 34; Noëls, op. 36	Masters Music
I-A		Selected Piano Pieces (Johnsson, ed.)	Henle

Gliere, Reinhold (1875–1956) Russia

A Russian Romantic and nationalistic composer, Gliere studied composition and harmony at the Moscow Conservatory and was awarded the gold medal in composition in 1900. In 1913, he was named director of the Kiev Conservatory of Music, and in 1920 was appointed a professor of music at the Moscow Conservatory where he taught Prokofiev, Khachaturian and Mossolov.

I	*	Eight Easy Pieces, op. 43 (1. Prelude in D-Flat) (Jones, ed.)	ABRSM
		Originally published in 1910, these attractive pieces represent the 19th-century Russian Romantic tradition.	
I	§	Prelude in D-flat Major, op. 43, no. 1 (Lancaster, ed.)	Alfred
		This *Prelude* is Gliere's most frequently played piano solo. With its lush, beautiful harmonies, it is composed in the romantic tradition but also has hints of impressionism. The flowing eighth notes fit comfortably under the fingers and the entire piece is at the late intermediate level.	

Gottschalk, Louis Moreau (1829–1869) USA (New Orleans)

Born in New Orleans (died in Brazil), Gottschalk was a child prodigy and virtuoso pianist. He left the U.S., studied in Paris and was a prolific composer whose music reflects elements of his Creole heritage (Creole, Latin American and African-Caribbean rhythms and melodies). He toured widely throughout Europe, the United States and Canada and lived for extended periods of time in the Caribbean and South American.

I-A	§	A Compendium of Piano Music (List, ed.)	Carl Fischer
		Eugene List (1918-1985) was a long time member of the Eastman School of Music piano faculty who specialized in the music of both Gottschalk and Edward MacDowell.	
I-A		Gottschalk Album	Kalmus
		Contains *Le Banjo, Pasquinade, Pastorella, Scherzo Romantique, Tremolo,* and *Valse Poetique.*	
I-A		Gottschalk: Collected Works for Piano	Schirmer
A		Piano Music of Louis Moreau Gottschalk (Jackson, ed.)	Dover

Granados, Enrique (1867–1916) Spain

One of Spain's most important composers, Granados is known for his solo piano works and guitar transcriptions that reflect Catalan and Spanish folk melodies. In addition to being a teacher and pianist, he also was known for his collaborative performances with musicians such as Pablo Casals, Isaac Albéniz, and Saint-Saëns. When deciding whether to think of Granados as a romantic or modern composer, his music is essentially Romantic and nationalistic. His death was tragic in that he and his wife sailed to New York in 1916 for the premier of his opera, *Goyescas*, and several concerts including a performance at the White House. On the return trip by way of England, a German U-boat torpedoed the ship, Sussex, in the English Channel and both Granados and his wife drowned. *Goyescas*, his suite originally for piano, is a set of ten pieces based on the paintings of Goya, and is perhaps his most famous work.

Romantic Literature *continued*

E-I	§ *	Stories of the Young, op. 1 (no. 1, *Dedicatoria*) (Johnson, ed.) (Cuentos de la Juventud)	ABRSM

This is the most accessible Granados set and represents his own "Album for the Young" so to speak. The ten titles translated are *Dedicatoria* (Dedication), *La mendiga* (The Beggar Woman), *Canción de mayo* (May Song), *Cuento viejo* (Old Man's Tale), *Viniendo de la fuente* (Coming from the Fountain), Untitled (*Lento con ternura*), *Recuerdos de la infancia* (Childhood Memories), *El fantasma* (The Phantom), *La huérfana* (The Orphan Girl), and *Marcha* (March).

I		Sketches	Masters
I-A	§ *	Escenas Poéticas, Bks. 1 (no. 3), II (no. 3)	Kalmus, Dover, ASE

Book one consists of three pieces (*Berceuse, Eva y Walter, Dance of the Rose*), that are more late intermediate than advanced and quite romantic sounding in approach. Book II is more advanced and contains *Recuerdo de paises lejanos, El angel de los claustros, Cancion de Margarita,* and *Suenos del poeta*.

I-A		6 Estudios Expresivos (6 Expressive Studies)	Masters

Contains *Tema y variaciones, Allegro moderato, El caminante* (The Traveler), *Pastoral, La última pavana* (The Final Pavane), and *María: Romanza sin palabras* (María: Romance without Words).

I-A		7 Valses Poéticos	Salabert; ASE

Framed by a more advanced *Prelude* and ending *Presto* (Postlude), the interior 7 *Waltzes* are less difficult: *Melodioso, Valse noble, Valse lente, Allegro humoristico, Allegretto, Quasi ad libitum,* and *Vivo*.

A		Album for Piano	Schirmer

An excellent Granados compilation.

A		Bocetos (Colección de obras fáciles)	Masters Music
A		Collected Works	Salabert

Includes *Danzas Espanolas, Goyescas, Valses Poeticos, Allegro de Concierto* and *Escenaas Romanticas*.

A		Goyescas, Spanish Dances, and Other Works	Dover
A		My First Granados (five miscellaneous advanced works)	Ricordi
A	§	Spanish Dance (*Playera*, op. 5, no. 5) (Hinson, ed.)	Alfred
A	§ *	Twelve Spanish Dances, op. 5 (no. 1, Minuetto)	Dover; International; ASE

Grieg, Edvard (Hagerup) (1843–1907) Norway

Norway's most famous composer, Grieg was a pianist, teacher, and conductor. He studied composition with Reinecke at the Leipzig Conservatory and with Gade in Copenhagen. His most notable works are the *Piano Concerto in A Minor, op. 16* (see annotation in concerto section) and the *Peer Gynt* orchestral suite reflecting elements of Norwegian folk music. His ten volumes of *Lyric Pieces* and the *Norwegian Dances* for piano duet are standards in the piano teaching literature.

I		An Introduction to His Piano Works (Halford, ed.)	Alfred
I		Four Lyric Pieces (Waltz, Watchman's Song, Puck, Sailor's Song)	FJH
I	§	Poetic Tone Pictures, op. 3	Peters
I-A	§	Celebrate Grieg (Hisey, ed.)	Frederick Harris

In addition to offering a panoramic overview of the most important selections from Grieg's monumental collection of *Lyric Pieces* (e.g., *Puck, Weddingday at Troldhaugen, Elfin Dance, Little Bird, Notturno,* etc.), other segments of Grieg's lesser-known piano writing are presented which will interest both teachers and students. These include the *Poetic Tone Pictures, op. 3* and selections from his *Norwegian Folk-Songs and Dances, Opp. 17/66,* such as *Song of the Alpine Cowherd* and *Tomorrow You Shall Marry Her*.

I-A	First Book for Pianists (Halford, ed.)	Alfred
I-A	Grieg: Easier Favorites (Feldmann, ed.)	Peters
I-A	Grieg Selected Lyric Pieces (Schnell, ed.)	Kjos
I-A §	Grieg: Short Pieces (Blickenstaff, ed.)	Carl Fischer
I-A	Joy of Grieg, The (Duro, ed.)	Music Sales
I-A § *	Lyric Pieces, complete (66 pieces in ten opus numbers)	Dover; Schirmer

        op. 12 (Waltz, National Song, Arietta, Elfin Dance)
        op. 38 (Norwegian Dance)
        op. 43 (To Spring)
        op. 47 (Norwegian Dance)
        op. 54 (March of the Dwarfs, Notturno)
        op. 57 (Illusion)
        op. 62 (Home-ward)
        op. 65 (Peasant's Song, Wedding-Day at Troldhaugen)
        op. 68 (Sailor's Song)
        op. 71 (Puck)

The Grieg *Lyric Pieces* rival Mendelssohn's *Songs without Words* as one of the most important collections of Romantic character pieces. After the study of such composers as Burgmüller, Heller, and easier Schumann, Grieg's music is the next stepping-stone to prepare for the more difficult music of Chopin and Brahms. The pieces cover a wide range of difficulty levels. Opus 12 tends to be the technically easiest of the collection. The *Lyric Pieces* can serve a wide variety of teaching purposes. For example, the op. 12 *Waltz* is excellent for teaching off-beat pedaling and double sharps, while *Wedding-Day at Troldhaugen* is a fine "pupil saver" high school piece with brilliant sounding textures in the outer sections (ABA form). Its rhythmic left-hand accompaniment under a spirited right-hand melody make it one of Grieg's most famous piano solos. *Sailor's Song* is excellent for left-hand octave technique and is popular with middle school students. The more difficult *Puck* is ideal for introducing the key of E flat minor.

I-A	Lyric Pieces, opp. 12, 38 (Hinson, ed.)	Alfred
I-A	Norwegian Dances and Songs, op. 17	Peters
I-A	Piano Album	Schirmer

    Includes *Poetic Tone Picture, op. 3, nos. 4, 5*; *Humoreske, op. 6, nos. 2, 3*; *Norwegian Bridal Procession, op. 19, no. 2*; *Album-leaves, op. 28* (nos. 1, 2, 3, 4) and *The Last Spring, op. 34, no. 2*.

I-A	Selected Works for the Piano (Levine, ed.)	Alfred
A	Sonata in E Minor, op. 7 (Hinson, ed.)	Alfred
A	Wedding-Day at Troldhaugen (Olson, ed.)	Alfred

Gurlitt, Cornelius (1820–1901) Germany

Born in Altona, Prussia, Gurlitt was an organist, pianist, military bandmaster and conductor. He taught at the Hamburg School of Music and was a friend of Norwegian composer Niels Gade. He was a prolific composer in many genres including songs, operas, symphonies and piano teaching pieces. His charming piano miniatures are at the Burgmüller level or easier.

E	A First Book	Kalmus
E	First Lessons, op. 117	Kalmus
E §	Gurlitt: Album Leaves for the Young, op. 101 (Otwell, ed.)	Hal Leonard
E §	I Remember Gurlitt, Vols. I, II (F. Clark, ed.)	Alfred

Romantic Literature *continued*

From the Frances Clark Library and republished by Alfred, this is one of the definitive collections of Gurlitt's best-loved miniatures.

E	Twenty-four Easy Melodious Studies, op. 50	Schirmer
E-I	Der Neue Gurlitt, Vols. I, II (Rebberg, ed.)	Schott
E-I	First Steps of the Young Pianist, op. 82	Schirmer: ASE
E-I	Little Flowers (*Kleine Blumen*), op. 205	ABRSM
I *	Album for the Young, op. 140 (twenty pieces) (nos. 3, 15) (Palmer, ed.)	Alfred
I	Gurlitt: Album Leaves for the Young, op. 101 Book & CD	Schirmer
I	Six Sonatinas, op. 54 (Palmer, ed.)	Alfred
I-A	Buds and Blossoms, op. 107	Kalmus

Heller, Stephen (1813–1888) France (b. Hungary)

A pianist and composer who was born in Hungary, Heller lived and worked in Paris teaching, arranging and writing as a music critic. Schumann greatly admired Heller's compositions and Heller was a music critic for Schumann's *Neue Zeitschrift für Musik* (New Chronicle for Music).

E-I	Selected Progressive Etudes (Olson, ed.)	Alfred

19 selected studies arranged in progressive order of difficulty.

I	Heller: Selected Piano Studies, opp. 45 and 46 (Westney, ed.)	Hal Leonard
I-A	Album for the Young, op. 138	Kalmus
I-A §	Celebrate Heller (Hisey, ed.)	Frederick Harris

Heller's piano writing is an excellent stepping-stone to slightly more difficult compositions by Schumann, Mendelssohn, and Chopin. One of the newer editions of Heller's character pieces, *Celebrate Heller* picks up where many do not. In addition to the best known compositions from opp. 45, 46, and 47 (e.g., *Avalanche, Warrior's Song, Grief*, etc.), a much broader musical portrait of the composer is presented with compositions such as *Barcarole, op. 138, no. 5*; *Prelude in C-Sharp Minor, op. 81, no. 10* (mirrored after Chopin's *Préludes, op. 28*); and *Dream Picture, op. 79, no. 4*. Detailed notes about the composer and music offer much hard to find information. This volume is a "must" for any Heller enthusiast.

I-A *	Fifty Selected Studies from opp. 45, 46, 47 (3, 6, 13, 16)	Schirmer
I-A	Flower, Fruit and Thorn Pieces, op. 82 (*Nuits blanches*)	Schirmer
I-A §	Heller Collection, The (Hinson, ed.)	Universal

As with *Celebrate Heller* (see above annotation), this collection reveals lesser-known, attractive studies composed by Heller.

I-A	L'art de phraser, op. 16, Bks. I, II	Schirmer
	(Twenty-Six Melodious Studies for the Piano)	
I-A	Selected Piano Works: Character Pieces	Henle
I-A	Thirty Progressive Studies, op. 46 (Wager, ed.)	Schirmer
I-A	25 Melodious Studies, op. 45 (Palmer, ed.)	Alfred
I-A	Twenty-five Studies, op. 47 (Wager, ed.)	Schirmer
A § *	(24) Preludes, op. 81 (3, 6, 7, 17)	Schirmer; ASE

These very fine but little known preludes were modeled after Chopin's op. 28 key organization and deserve greater attention. Some could be paired with selections form Chopin's op. 28 in student recitals.

Hensel, Fanny (Cécilie) Mendelssohn (1805–1847) Germany

The older sister of Felix Mendelssohn and an accomplished composer and pianist herself, Fanny's works include chamber music, lieder, oratorios and a large body of piano works. Some theorists speculate that Fanny may actually have composed a few of Mendelssohn's *Songs without Words*.

E (Early Intermediate)   I (Intermediate)   A (Advanced Intermediate to Advanced)

I-A	Piano Music (Todd, ed.)	Dover
A	Lieder für das Pianoforte	Boosey & Hawkes
A	Piano Book in E Minor	Breitkopf & Härtel

Consists of six pieces which can be excerpted individually or played as a group: *Praeludio, Fuga, Allegro di molto, Largo, Praeludio,* and *Toccata.*

A	Selected Piano Works	Henle

Janáček, Leoš (1854–1928) Czechoslovakia

A composer, teacher, and conductor, Janáček founded the Brno Conservatory and served as Director of the Czech Philharmonic Orchestra. He composed opera, vocal and instrumental works that reflect the elements and rhythms of Moravian folk music.

I-A		Danze Popolari Della Moravia	Ricordi
I-A		Fifteen Moravian Folksongs (1922)	Masters Music
I-A	§	In the Mist (1912)	Kalmus

Composed in four parts (*I. Andante, II. Molto adagio, III. Andantino, IV. Presto*), this is probably the composer's best writing and features the use of flat keys and impressionistic colors.

A	On an Overgrown Path (Bks. I, II)	Bärenreiter; Masters

Assembled over a period of approximately 10 years, these are beautiful pieces, earlier and less adventuresome than *In the Mist*. The set is deserving of greater attention.

Kirchner, (Fürchtegott) Theodor (1823–1903) Germany

A pianist, organist, composer, arranger, teacher and accompanist, Kirchner was organist at Winterthur in Switzerland for nearly twenty years, after which he traveled and held a variety of musical positions having difficulty maintaining a stable life. He studied with Mendelssohn in Leipzig and counted as his friends Brahms and Robert and Clara Schumann, as well as supporters Gade, Grieg, Liszt and Wagner. He composed over 1,000 miniatures or character pieces for piano and was sought after as an arranger.

I		Miniatures, op. 62	ABRSM
I	§	New Album Leaves: 20 Character Pieces, op. 49	Schott
I	§	New Scenes from Childhood, op. 55	ABRSM
I-A		Night Scenes, op. 25	Breitkopf and Härtel
I-A		Selected Piano Works (Hoffman, ed.)	Henle
I-A		Spielsachen 14 Leichte Clavierstücke, op. 35 (Goebels, ed.)	Schott
A		Preludes, op. 9	Schott
A		Skizzen, op. 11	Heugel

Köhler, (Christian) Louis (Heinrich) (1820–1886) Germany

A pianist, composer, arranger, music critic and teacher, Köhler wrote operas and ballet music, but his primary works were pedagogical miniatures and arrangements for piano. His writings on piano and piano pedagogy were widely recognized and influential. His graded collections and books focus on technique, exercises and student teaching pieces.

E	Children's Album, op. 210	Schirmer
E	Easiest Studies, op. 151	Kalmus
E	The Very Easiest Studies, op. 190	Kalmus
E	12 Easy Studies, op. 157 (Palmer, ed.)	Alfred
E-I	The Little Pianist, op. 189	Kalmus
I	The Children's Friend, op. 243	Schirmer
I	First Studies for the Piano, op. 50	Schirmer

Romantic Literature *continued*

Kullak, Theodor (1818–1882) Germany

A pianist and composer, Kullak studied with Czerny in Vienna and composed primarily for piano. He was considered a great piano teacher of his time working with students such as Hans Bischoff, Xaver Scharwenka, Moritz Moszkowski, and Nikolai Rubinstein. In 1851, he founded the *Neue Akademie der Tonkunst* which became one of the largest and most important private music schools in Germany. His 1848 work, *Schule des Oktavenspiels* (School of Octave Playing), reflects the technical facility that he sought to impart to others.

E-I		Scenes from Childhood, opp. 62, 81 (12 pieces in each opus) (Klauser, ed.)	Schirmer

These early intermediate pieces, deserving of greater attention, are very attractive, have descriptive titles, and are at the same level as easy Burgmüller and Gurlitt.

Lichner, Heinrich (1829–1898) Germany

A pianist, organist, director and composer, Lichner was cantor and organist for the Church of the 11,000 Virgins in Breslau and directed the choral festival (Sangerbund) in Breslau. He wrote psalms and choral works but is best known for his educational piano pieces including *Gypsy Dance* (1914), three *Sonatinas*, op. 4, *Scherzo*, op. 24 and *La Cascatelle*, op. 19.

I	§	Nine Sonatinas, opp. 4, 49, 66	Carl Fischer; Schirmer
I		Sonatinas, op. 66	Schirmer
I		Three Sonatinas, op. 4	Schirmer
I		Three Sonatinas, op. 49	Schirmer
I-A		Kleine Blumen - Kleine Blätter, op. 64	Schott

Liszt, Franz (1811–1886) Hungary

A child prodigy, Liszt was a virtuoso concert pianist, conductor, piano teacher, improviser and composer. He studied piano with Czerny and composition with Salieri in Vienna and in 1823 moved with his family to Paris. In 1848, he settled in Weimar as *Director of Music Extraordinary*. Liszt was greatly influenced by the great violinist Paganini, emulating his technical facility and stage presence in his piano concerts and is still known as a virtuoso performer with unrivaled technical facility and a talent for showmanship. He composed hundreds of piano pieces characterized by technical demands that pushed the performers and the piano of that time to their limits. By playing to larger audiences and not just for the aristocracy, Liszt brought music to the general public. He also developed the tradition of playing by memory and, like Dussek, having audiences view the profile of the pianist on stage, thus establishing the format of the modern piano recital.

I-A	§	An Introduction to the Composer and His Music (Banowetz, ed.)	Kjos

This volume contains some of the well-known "late" works including *En rêve* (Nocturne or Dreaming), *S 207*, The *Shepherds at the Manger* (from *Christmas Tree*), *S 186*, and *Four Small Piano Pieces, S 192*.

I-A		At the Piano with Liszt (Hinson, ed.)	Alfred
I-A	§	Celebrate Liszt (Hisey, ed.)	Frederick Harris

A recent contribution to Liszt anthologies, this volume covers much of the commonly taught repertoire including lesser-known late works: *Consolations: Six pensées poetiques* (Six poetic thoughts) *S 172*, *En rêve* (Nocturne or Dreaming), *S 207*, *Weihnachtsbaum* (The Christmas-Tree), *S 186*, *La lugubre gondola* (The Mournful Gondola), *S 200/2*, *Liebestraum-O lieb, so lang du lieben kannst!* (O Love, as Long as You Can Love!), *S 541/3*, *Valse oubliée no. 1* (Forgotten Waltz), *S 215*, *Hungarian Rhapsody no. 3, S 244/3*, and the famous *Concert Etude, no. 3* (*Un sospiro*) *S 144/3*.

I-A	§	Liszt: Forgotten Masterpieces (Banowetz, ed.)	Kjos

This volume is an excellent collection of lesser-known works, primarily from his later period but also dating as early as 1827. The *Liebeslied* (Dedication) is useful for teaching balance and for controlling moving eighth notes shared between the hands. The majority of the writing in this volume is at an intermediate level, not advanced.

I-A		Liszt: Piano Music from His Early Years (Hinson, ed.)	Alfred
I-A		Liszt: 21 Selected Piano Works (Banowetz, ed.) CD included	Alfred
I-A		Liszt: Very Best for Piano	Creative Concepts

Includes 25 pieces : *By the Lake of Wallenstadt, Consolation* (nos. 1, 2, 3, 4, 5), *Dance of the Gnomes, Farewell, La Regatta Venetiana, Liebestraum* (nos. 1, 2, 3), *Mephisto Waltz, Nocturne in B, Nuages Gris* and more.

I-A		Piano Works, Vols. I-XII	Peters
I-A	§	Selected Intermediate to Early Advanced Piano Solos (Hinson, ed.)	Alfred

An interesting feature of this collection is the inclusion of seven of Liszt's harmonizations of well-known hymn tunes. These chorales (S 50), written around 1879, were intended for Liszt's friend, Cardinal Gustav Hohenlohe. These chorales are ideal for the intermediate student developing four-part reading skills.

A	Christmas Tree, S 186, Vols. I, II	Peters

(See annotation in Selected Holiday Music for Piano Ensemble.)

A	Consolations and Liebesträume (Joseffy, ed.)	Schirmer
A	Six Consolations, S 172 (*Hinson, ed.)	*Alfred; ASE
A	Sonata in B Minor, S 178	Peters; Schirmer; ASE

Of Liszt's advanced masterpieces (e.g., *Années de Pèlerinage* [3 volumes], *S 160-161, 163*; *Harmonies poétiques et religieuses, S 173*; *12 Etudes d'exécution transcendante, S 139*; the many *Hungarian Rhapsodies*; and multiple versions of the *Mephisto Waltz*), the *Sonata in B minor* stands out as a singular outstanding example of the one movement romantic hybrid sonata. Any pianist, remotely interested in romantic piano music and the output of Liszt should listen to and eventually study this work.

Lynes, Frank (1858–1913) USA (b. New Hampshire)

An organist, composer, and piano teacher, Lynes studied at the New England Conservatory and later at the Leipzig Conservatory. He served as a church organist and piano teacher in Boston. His works include songs and church anthems, organ and chamber works as well as piano pieces. His *Sonatinas* remain a staple of the early intermediate repertoire.

E	§	Analytical Sonatinas, op. 39 (Olson, ed.)	Alfred

Although Lynes' dates bridge the late Romantic to the Contemporary periods, these sonatinas exhibit style characteristics of the Classical period and are excellent preparation for the sonatinas of Clementi and Kuhlau.

E	Four Sonatinas, op. 39 (Schnell, ed.)	Kjos

MacDowell, Edward (Alexander) (1860–1908) USA (New York)

An American pianist, teacher and composer of English and Irish heritage, MacDowell left the U.S. to study music at the Paris *Conservatoire* in 1877 and later traveled to Germany (Frankfurt) to study and teach piano. He returned to Boston in 1888 to perform and compose and soon after served as head of the music department at Columbia University from 1896-1904. MacDowell wrote many songs but primarily composed for piano and wrote many of his early pieces under the pseudonym of Edgar Thorne.

I	*	Six Fancies, op. 7 (Summer Song, Bluette, To a Humming-Bird) (Hinson, ed.)	Alfred
I-A		(Eight) Sea Pieces, op. 55 (*Olson, ed.)	*Alfred; Elkan-Vogel
I-A		Fireside Tales, op. 61 (Hinson, ed.)	Alfred

Romantic Literature *continued*

I-A	MacDowell Selected Works for Piano (Schnell, ed.)	Kjos
I-A	MacDowell the World Loves	Willis
I-A	Piano Works	Dover
I-A § *	Woodland Sketches, op. 51 (To A Wild Rose, To a Water Lily)	FJH

   This is a thoroughly researched volume edited by Gary Busch. MacDowell's op. 51 includes some of the composer's most familiar titles.

A	Four Little Poems, op. 32	Schirmer
A	Four Pieces, op. 24	Schirmer
A	Praeludium (First Modern Suite)	Shawnee
A	Two Fantastic Dances, op. 17	Presser
A *	Twelve Studies, op. 39 (Busch, ed.)	FJH

   (*Alla Tarantella, Hungarian, Shadow Dance, Romanze)

Mendelssohn (-Bartholdy), (Jakob Ludwig) Felix (1809–1847) Germany

A remarkably talented pianist, conductor, and composer, Mendelssohn was a musical prodigy along with his older sister Fanny. They both studied piano and composition at the Berlin *Singakademie*. Mendelssohn championed the revival of the music of J. S. Bach. In 1835, he became artistic director of the Gewandhaus Orchestra and also founded the Leipzig Conservatory which is now a major European Conservatory. Robert Schumann was an inaugural member of the faculty as was his wife Clara. Mendelssohn composed orchestral works, concertos, oratorios, and the famous collection of character pieces, *Songs Without Words*, for piano solo.

I-A	Album of 25 Piano Favorites	Schirmer
I-A	An Introduction to His Piano Works (Halford, ed.)	Alfred
I-A §	Celebrate Mendelssohn (Hisey, ed.)	Frederick Harris

   The volume is a compendium of the most important Mendelssohn solo compositions including 16 frequently performed selections from his *Songs without Words* (e.g., the three *Venetian Boat Songs, Consolation, Spinning Song, Duetto*), selections from the *Six Children's Pieces, op. 72*, and the *Scherzo in E Minor, op. 16, no. 2*. The frequently performed *Rondo Capriccioso, op. 14* completes the collection. Strengths of this edition include the in-depth performance notes and care with fingerings and pagination.

I-A	Complete Works for Pianoforte Solo, Vols. I, II (Rietz, ed.)	Dover
I-A	Six Children's Pieces, op. 72 (Christmas Pieces)	Kalmus; ASE
I-A § *	Songs without Words, Complete (*Hinson, ed.)	*Alfred; Schirmer

   (*in general order of difficulty)

      op. 30, no. 3 (Consolation)
      op. 62, no. 4 (Morning Song)
      op. 85, no. 1 (Reverie)
      op. 102, no. 6 (Faith)
      op. 19, no. 4 (Confidence)
      op. 19, no. 6 (Venetian Boat Song no. 1)
      op. 30, no. 6 (Venetian Boat Song no. 2)
      op. 19, no. 1 (Sweet Remembrance)
      op. 19, no. 2 (Regrets)
      op. 102, no. 3 (Tarantella)

   Mendelssohn's *Songs without Words* were written in eight opus numbers with six compositions contained in each opus, most of which were published during his lifetime. Mendelssohn gave titles to only five (the three *Venetian Boat Songs, Duet*, and *Folk Song*) with a few additional titles supplied by his circle of friends, but the majority of titles were added by editors of later editions. The songs can be organized by four compositional types: solo song, accompanied duet, choral song, and instrumental. The excellent Hinson edition includes thorough performance notes on each piece. The cover for the volume depicts an original painting by the composer.

A	Fantasy on the Last Rose of Summer, op. 15	Novato
A	Rondo Capriccioso, op. 14 (Klauser, ed.)	Schirmer
A	Scherzo in E Minor, op. 16, no. 2 (Palmer, ed.)	Alfred; Editio Musica Budapest
A	(6) Preludes and Fugues, op. 35	Peters; ASE
A	Variations sérieuses, op. 54 (Hinson, ed.)	Alfred; ASE

Consisting of 17 variations, this is Mendelssohn's exemplary writing for piano solo.

Moszkowski, Moritz (1854–1925) Germany

A virtuoso pianist, teacher, and conductor, Moszkowski entered the Dresden Conservatory at age 11 and later studied piano with Kullak in Berlin. He became a teacher at Kullak's *Neue Akademie der Tonkunst* at age 17 and was recognized as a virtuoso pianist throughout Europe. His compositions are primarily piano solos and duets.

I	Étincelles, op. 36, no. 6	Schirmer
A	15 Etudes, op. 72 (Hinson, ed.)	Alfred
A	Spanish Dances, op. 12	Kalmus; Peters
A	20 Short Studies, op. 91 (Hinson, ed.)	Alfred

Paderewski, Ignace Jan (1860–1941) Poland

A concert pianist, teacher, and composer, Paderewski began his music studies at the Warsaw Music Institute at age 12. He later studied with the famous Polish pianist and pedagogue, Theodor Leschetizky (1830-1915), and was active in a circle of famous composers and pianists of the day including Moszkowski, Strauss and Anton Rubinstein. A compelling pianist and public figure, he toured throughout the United States and Canada as well as South America, Australia, New Zealand, South Africa and Europe. In 1919 he became Poland's first prime minister and was later an active fund-raiser for the support of the Polish people after the Nazi invasion in 1939. Paderewski also was an editor for the complete works of Chopin (see annotation under Chopin). He died in 1941 in New York and was given a hero's burial at Arlington National Cemetery. It should be noted that Dover publishes *The Leschetizky Method* (ed. Bree), the legendary teacher who taught both Paderewski and Schnabel.

I		Melodie, op. 8, no. 3	Willis
I-A		Nocturne, op. 16, no. 4	Willis
I-A		Selected Compositions of Moderate Difficulty	Boosey & Hawkes

Includes: *Menuet in G, op. 14*; *Sarabande, op. 14*; *Au Soir, op. 10*; *Mélodie in B-Flat, op. 8*; *Un Moment Musical, op. 16*; and *Mazurka, op. 9, no. 2*.

A		Album for Piano	PWM
A	§	Minuet in G Major, op. 14, no. 1 (Menuet à l'antique) (Palmer. ed.)	Alfred

The *Minuet in G Major* remains a very popular composition frequently seen in piano anthologies.

Poldini, Ede (Eduard) (1869–1957) Hungary

Eduard (nicknamed Ede) was a late Romantic pianist and composer who studied first at the National Conservatory in Budapest and later in Vienna. He is known for his operas as well as his works for piano such as Poupée valsante (The Dancing Doll).

Romantic Literature *continued*

E		Little Musical Moments, op. 150 (a suite of five pieces)	Ricordi
I		Album for the Young, op. 122	Universal
I		Springtime Pictures, op. 151	Schmidt
I-A		Poupée valsante (The Dancing Doll) (*Hinson, ed.)	*Alfred; Schirmer

Rachmaninoff, Sergey (Vasilyevich) (1873–1943) Russia
(Rakhmaninov, Sergey) (b. Oneg, near Semyonovo, Russia; d. Beverly Hills, CA)

A virtuoso concert pianist and recording artist, conductor, teacher and composer, Rachmaninoff studied piano with Nikolai Zverev and composition with Anton Arensky at the Moscow conservatory. Rachmaninoff was one of the last great composers connecting 19th century Russian romanticism with modern times. Born into an aristocratic family, he suffered personal tragedies. Through mismanagement his father lost one of the family estates, his sister died of diphtheria, his parents divorced and later in 1917, the Leninist regime seized Rachmaninoff's estate near Tambov. He moved with his wife and daughters to Denmark and then to New York, later criticizing the Soviet government in a March 1931 letter to the New York Times, after which his music was banned from performance throughout the USSR. Rachmaninoff was a renowned virtuoso who toured continuously and made numerous recordings with RCA Victor as pianist and conductor. He is compared to pianists such as Ignace Paderewski, Artur Rubinstein, Francis Planté, and Alfred Cortot in preserving the 19th century romantic virtuoso tradition. He is known for his piano concerti, pieces for solo piano and his work for piano and orchestra titled *Rhapsody on a Theme of Paganini, op. 43*.

A		Etude, op. 39, no. 2	Boosey & Hawkes
A	§	Humoreske, op. 10, no. 5 (Oesterle, ed.)	Schirmer
A	§	Polichinelle, op. 3, no. 4 (Oesterle, ed.)	Schirmer
A	§ *	Preludes, op. 3, no. 2; op. 23; op. 32	Boosey & Hawkes

(Prelude in C-Sharp Minor, op. 3, no. 2; Prelude in G Minor, op. 23, no. 5)
> These two preludes are accessible to skilled students. An early work, the immensely popular C-Sharp minor is one of the most often performed works in the entire piano literature. Care must be taken to achieve *forte* colors without attacking the keyboard and to achieve technical fluency in the contrasting middle section. The more complex G minor texture is more challenging than it appears because of the arpeggios and subtle voicing required in the B section. Beyond these two preludes, consider the witty *Humoresque, op. 10, no. 5* listed above.

A	*	Ten Preludes, op. 23 (5, 10)	Boosey & Hawkes
A	*	Thirteen Preludes, op. 32 (5, 7, 10, 12)	Boosey & Hawkes

Reger, (Johann Baptist Joseph) Max (Maximilian) (1873–1916) Germany

A concert pianist and organist, violinist, teacher and composer, Reger became a professor and director of music at Leipzig University in 1907 and in 1911 was appointed conductor of the Meiningen Orchestra. His unique compositional style combined Baroque elements and forms with the characteristics of Romantic music. His compositions include major organ works, nine sonatas for violin and piano, choral works, orchestral works, chamber pieces and compositions for piano.

I	Album for Young People, op. 17, Bks. 1, 2	Schott
I-A	Leichte Spielstücke für Klavier	Hug
I-A	Selection of Easy Pieces	Breitkopf and Härtel
I-A	Sonatinas, op. 89	Henle
A	Dreaming at the Fireside, op. 143	Peters
A	Ten Little Instructional Pieces, op. 44	Henle; Universal
A	Ten Pieces for Piano, op. 79a	Sikorski

Reinecke, Carl (Heinrich Carsten) (1824–1910) Germany

Pianist, accompanist, teacher, conductor and composer, his father (J. P. Rudolf Reinecke) was a noted music text author and piano teacher. Reinecke was appointed court pianist at the Danish Royal Court in 1846 and became a faculty member of the Leipzig Conservatory in 1860 and director in 1897. He was also conductor of the Gewandhaus Orchestra until 1895. He composed pieces for orchestra and opera but is primarily known for his piano works.

E	Six Miniature Sonatinas, op. 136	Breitkopf and Härtel
E-I	Five Serenades for the Young, op. 183	ABRSM; Peters
I-A	Suite à la Rococo, op. 173	Breitkopf and Härtel
A	Three Sonatinas, op. 47	Breitkopf and Härtel; Schirmer

Reinhold, Hugo (1854–1935) Austria

A pianist, piano teacher and composer, Reinhold entered the *Conservatorium der Musikfreunde*, where he studied composition with Anton Bruckner, Felix Dessoff and Julius Epstein. He taught piano at the *Akademie der Tonkunst* in Vienna. He was a prolific and popular composer whose works were performed by the Vienna Philharmonic Orchestra and the Hellmesberger Quartet.

I	Miniatures, op. 39	Schirmer
A	Impromptus, op. 28	Schirmer

Rossini, Gioachino (Antonio) (1792–1868) Italy

A noted and influential Italian composer of the early nineteenth century, Rossini was born into a musical family. His father (Giuseppe Antonio Rossini) was a horn player and teacher at the *Accademia Filarmonica* in Bologna. His mother (Anna Guidarini) was a soprano. He was musically trained at the *Liceo Musicale* in Bologna and lived and worked in Naples, Milan and Paris. Rossini was a highly respected and successful composer. He is best known for his 32 operas including *Guillaume Tell* (William Tell), *Il barbiere di Siviglia* (The Barber of Seville), *L'Italiana in Algeri* (The Italian in Algiers) and *La cenerentola* (Cinderella). He also composed two symphonies, chamber works, cantatas, songs and piano miniatures.

I-A	Album for Lively Children, Parts, I, II (Cafaro, ed.)	Masters Music
A	Piano Works, Vols. I, II	Kalmus
A	Rossini: Original Piano Pieces (Zeitlin, ed.)	Presser

Saint-Saëns, Camille (1835–1921) France

A pianist, organist, teacher, composer, poet and playwright, Saint-Saëns was a child prodigy who began piano study with his aunt around age two and composed his first piece at age three. By age ten he performed a concert that included Beethoven's *Third Piano Concerto* (C minor, op. 37) and Mozart's *Concerto in B flat, K 460*. He held church organist positions, taught at the École Neidermeyer and toured in the United States, Africa and Egypt. He composed in almost every genre. Some of his best known works include the *Piano Concerto no. 2*, *Symphony no. 3* ("Organ"), the symphonic poem *Danse macabre*, the opera *Samson et Dalila*, and probably his most widely performed work, *The Carnival of The Animals,* written for chamber orchestra and two pianos.

I	Two Little Piano Pieces	Morning Star Music
I-A	Six Etudes, op. 52	Kalmus
A	Album, op. 72	Masters Music
A	Dance Macabre (Liszt, transcriber) and Other Works for Piano	Dover
A	Les cloches du soir, op. 85	Peters
A	Six Bagatelles, op. 3	Peters
A	Three Waltzes, opp. 104, 120, 139	Masters Music

Romantic Literature *continued*

Schubert, Franz (Peter) (1797–1828) Austria

A Viennese pianist, teacher, and prolific composer by the age of 20, he worked briefly as a schoolteacher and later for a short time as a private music teacher to the Esterházy family. He composed in almost every genre using a rich romantic harmonic palette in traditional classical forms. Although he did not achieve recognition and fame during his short lifetime, Schubert is now recognized as one of the great composers. He wrote hundreds of art songs such as *An die Musik, Gretchen am Spinnrade* and *Erlkonig* and is credited with developing the song cycle with works such as *Die Schöne Müllerin,* and *Die Winterreise.* His solo piano and piano duet compositions are today considered a mainstay of the standard repertoire.

E-A	First Book for Young Pianists (Halford, ed.)	Alfred
E-A	An Introduction to His Works (Halford, ed.)	Alfred
I-A §	Celebrate Schubert (Hisey, ed.)	Frederick Harris

This edition merges Schubert's shorter, best known *German Dances* and *Waltzes* with the more advanced, frequently played *Moments Musicaux, D 780/op. 94* and *Impromptus* (opp. 90 and 142). All of his *12 Ländler, D 790/ op. 171* are presented. Unlike many dance sets, Schubert conceived of these *Ländler* as an uninterrupted set for public performance. This volume provides a valuable cross section of Schubert's piano compositions.

I-A §	Dances of Schubert (Hinson, ed.)	Alfred
I-A	Dances for Piano (Zeitlin, ed.)	Presser
I-A	Dances, Vols. I, II (D 844, 841, 681, 421)	Henle
I-A	Joy of Schubert, The (Duro, ed.)	Yorktown
I-A	Franz Schubert: Shorter Works	Dover
I-A §	Moments Musicaux and Impromptus, opp. 90, 94, 142 (Baylor, ed.)	Alfred
I-A	Piano Works (Banowetz, ed.) Book and CD	Belwin
I-A §	Sämtliche Tänze, Bands I, II (Mies/Theopold, eds.)	Henle

This complete set includes the *Ecossaisen, Ländler, Walzer,* and *Deutsche Tänze* that are excerpted for various collections. It is a useful collection to have as a teaching resource, as well as for sight-reading material with more advanced students.

I-A	Selected Piano Pieces (Clara Wieck-Schumann, ed.)	Henle
A	Shorter Works	Dover
I-A	Sixteen German Dances and Three Ecossaises, op. 33	Henle
I-A §	Sonata in A Major, op. 120 (Hinson, ed.)	Alfred

Hinson notes that Schubert composed this work in the summer of 1819 for pianist, Josefine von Kohler.

I-A	3 Kleine Klavierstücke	Doblinger
I-A	Waltzes (Maier, ed.)	Belwin
A *	Complete Sonatas (Epstein, ed.)	Dover

(Sonata in E Minor [1817]; Sonata in A Minor, op. 164; Sonata in A Major, op. 120)

A *	Four Impromptus, op. 90 (3, 2, 4)	Henle
A *	Four Impromptus, op. 142 (2, 3)	Henle
A	Impromptus, Moments Musicaux, Drei Klavierstücke	Wiener Urtext
A	Moments Musicaux, op. 94, D. 780 (with CD)	Music Sales
A	Preludes and Fugues for Piano, op. 16	Vivace
A §	Schubert: Four Impromptus, D. 899 (op. 90) (Gruenberg, ed.)	Hal Leonard

This edition contains excellent performance notes and is based on the autograph manuscript.

A § *	Six Moments Musicaux, op. 94 (2, 3)	Henle

Schumann, Clara Josephine Wieck (1819–1896) Germany

A concert pianist, composer, wife of Robert Schumann and mother of eight children, Clara Schumann wrote meaningful piano and vocal compositions. She began her piano studies with her father (Friedrich Wieck), a noted piano teacher and performer. Clara toured Europe with her father and was recognized as perhaps the greatest female pianist of her time. After marrying Robert, they lived in Leipzig and both taught at the University of Leipzig. After Robert's death in 1856, she moved to Berlin to teach at the Frankfurt *Hochschule für Musik* and continue her performance career.

I-A	At the Piano with Robert and Clara Schumann (Hinson, ed.)	Alfred
I-A	Clara Schumann Piano Music (Reich, ed.)	Dover
I-A § *	Quatre Polonaises, op. 1 (no. 4) (Hierholzer, ed.)	Carl Fischer
I-A	Selected Piano Works (Klassen, ed.)	Henle
A	Clara Schumann: Romantische Klaviermusik, Bks. 1, 2	Muller
A	Larghetto, op. 15	Novello

Schumann, Robert (Alexander) (1810–1856) Germany

A pianist, composer, conductor and music critic, Schumann wrote in almost every genre but is best known for his vocal and piano works. He studied piano with Friedrich Wieck and married his daughter Clara in 1840. He founded and edited the periodical *Neue Zeitschrift für Musik*. In his writings and compositions Schumann referred to two personalities: Florestan for his impetuous self and Eusebius for his contemplative, reserved side. Schumann suffered a mental breakdown in 1854 and tried to commit suicide by throwing himself into the Rhine river. He survived but was institutionalized in a private asylum where he lived for two more years. He is considered one of the great Romantic period piano composers and was innovative by adding descriptive titles to short character pieces and linking character pieces into larger works, e.g., *Fantasiestücke, op. 12* (Fantastic Pieces) and *Kinderszenen, op. 15* (Scenes from Childhood).

E-I § * Album for the Young, op. 68 — Schirmer; ASE
   *(Melody, Chorale, Soldier's March, Happy Farmer, Wild Horseman,
   Little Etude, First Loss, Knecht Ruprecht)
   > Schumann divided this album, composed in 1848, into two parts, for younger people and older people. Many of his most celebrated teaching pieces are from this set.

E-I § An Introduction to His Piano Works (Palmer, ed.) — Alfred
I * Album-Leaves, op. 124 (Fantastic Dance) — Peters
   > Opus 124 is a collection of 20 short pieces that Schumann wrote throughout his life but assembled under this opus number for publication later in his life. A few pieces (*Elfe* and *Waltz in A minor*), that he rejected from the *Carnaval, op. 9*, are included in this collection. Each composition exhibits the ASCH theme of A, E-Flat, C, B.

I Arabesque, op. 18 (Herttrich, ed.) — Henle
   > A favorite among professionals and amateurs, the *Arabesque* has a Rondo-like organization with quite contrasting thematic material.

I Colored Leaves, op. 99 — Henle
I * Forest Scenes, op. 82 (The Prophetic Bird) — Henle
I § * Kinderszenen (Scenes from Childhood), op. 15 — Peters
   (From Foreign Lands and People, The Poet Speaks, Important Event,
   Frightening, Reverie)
   > The *Scenes from Childhood* are artistic musical reflections on childhood. To play the entire set requires mature pianism. The set is not for children. However, selected movements can be taught to aspiring student pianists.

Romantic Literature *continued*

A descending melodic tetrachord fragment links the set. *The Poet Speaks* is made more difficult by the improvisatory middle section. In this movement, Schumann reveals that he is the poet speaking by musically self-quoting the opening theme from *Aufschwung* (op. 12).

I-A	At the Piano with Robert and Clara Schumann (Hinson, ed.)	Alfred
I-A §	Celebrate Schumann (Hisey, ed.)	Frederick Harris

As with other introductory volumes in the *Celebrate Composer* series, this volume is an excellent collection of virtually all the pieces teachers use to introduce Schumann's music. Selections range from the best of the *Album for the Young, op. 68* to the complete *Scenes from Childhood, op. 15,* and highlights from *Forest Scenes, op. 82,* and *Album Leaves, op. 124.* At a more advanced level, the beautiful *Romance in F sharp, op. 28, no. 2,* and three selections (*Grillen, Why?, Aufschwung*) from *Fantasiestücke, op. 12,* conclude the volume. A special feature is the inclusion of difficult to find unpublished pieces from the original *Album for the Young.* Of particular interest is the variant of the *Wild Horseman,* which ends quite differently in the repeat of the A section, *Playing Tag* with its Kabalevsky-like feel, and the brilliant, quite surprising Bartók-like *Bear Dance.*

I-A	Complete Piano Works, Vols. 1–6 (Herttrich, ed.)	Henle
I-A	Hits & Rarities (Péteri, ed.)	Editio Musica Budapest

This collection includes selections from *Forest Scenes, op. 82, Scenes from Childhood, op. 15, Album Leaves, op. 124,* and *Novelletten, op. 21.*

I-A §	Papillons, op. 2 (Hinson, ed.)	Alfred

Papillons foreshadows the *Carnaval,* op. 9 but lacks descriptive titles of individual movements and is not as complex technically nor as long. *Papillons* is an excellent set for the secondary pianist or undergraduate major who has never studied Schumann's music.

I-A	Piano Music of Robert Schumann, Series I–III	Dover
I-A	Piano Works (Banowetz, ed.) Book and CD	Belwin
I-A	Scenes from Childhood (Busch, ed.)	FJH
I-A	Schumann, Easier Favorites (Feldmann, ed.)	Peters
I-A §	Schumann: Scenes from Childhood, op. 15 (Linn, ed.)	Hal Leonard

This carefully prepared edition has excellent background information. Selected movements of the *Kinderszenen,* such as *About Strange Lands and People* and *An Important Event,* may be individually taught to students. Because of musical and technical demands, including large intervallic reaches, these pieces are not written for children to play, but are descriptive pieces about elements of childhood.

I-A § *	Three Romances, op. 28 (no. 2)	Peters

The "romance" element of no. 2 in F sharp major is characterized by beautiful *legato* duet playing between the thumbs.

A § *	Fantasiestücke, op. 12 (Warum?, Grillen, Aufschwung)	Henle

These three compositions are superb pieces for the skilled high school student. *Warum* (Why?) is lyrical and shorter in scope. Both *Grillen* and *Aufschwung* are demanding technically—the former contains chordal writing, the latter more intricate passagework.

A	Three Piano Sonatas for the Young, op. 118	Breitkopf and Härtel; Henle
A *	Carnaval, op. 9 (Chopin)	Peters; Presser; ASE

Of Schumann's most advanced keyboard works (*Etudes en forme de variations, op. 13, Davidsbündlertänze, op. 6* [second version], *Kreisleriana, op.*

E (Early Intermediate)   I (Intermediate)   A (Advanced Intermediate to Advanced)

16, Fantasia, op. 17, Toccata, op. 7 and *sonatas*), the *Carnaval* probably is the most accessible and certainly a large work where single movements, such as *Chopin*, are excerpted for study and performance. Teaching single movements to a talented student is recommended. Based on a single four-note theme (ASCH; A, E-Flat, C, B), some movements of the *Carnaval* are musical portraits of musicians from the period, e.g., *Paganini, Chopin.*

A	Fantasie in C, op. 17 (*Hinson, ed.)	*Alfred; ASE
A	Symphonic Etudes, op. 13 (*Hinson, ed.)	*Alfred; ASE

Scriabin, Alexander (Nikolayevich) (1872–1915) Russia (b. and d. Moscow, Russia)

(See Scriabin entry in Contemporary Solo Literature.)

Sibelius, Jean [Johan] (Christian Julius) (1865–1957) Finland

A violinist, teacher and conductor, Sibelius enrolled in 1885 in Helsinki University as a law student but left after one year to enroll in the Helsinki Music Institute to study violin. He primarily performed chamber and ensemble music and is perhaps the most important Finnish nationalistic composer. His works were mostly symphonic and were often based on elements from the Finnish-language folk legend, *Kalevala,* evoking characteristic moods or the mysteries of folk myths and landscapes. Finland regarded him as a national hero and its most renowned artist.

A	Five Pieces, op. 75	Masters Music
A	Jean Sibelius Piano Album	Chester
A	Piano Music	Dover
	Includes *Finlandia, Valse Triste, Romance in D-Flat* and more.	
A	Ten Pieces, op. 58 (Book I, nos. 1–4; Book II, nos. 5–10)	Masters Music
A	Ten Pieces, op. 58	Kalmus
A	Two Rondinos, op. 68	Masters Music

Sinding, Christian (August) (1856–1941) Norway

A Norwegian violinist and composer, he attended the Leipzig Conservatory in 1874 studying violin and composition. He lived and worked in Germany for many years, but also taught theory and composition at the Eastman School of Music in Rochester, New York from 1920-1921 before returning to Oslo, Norway to live. A prolific composer, he wrote over 250 songs, four symphonies, concertos and chamber works incorporating Norwegian elements in his works. *Rustles of Spring* is one of the few pieces by Sinding still in print for contemporary use.

I-A §	Rustles of Spring, op. 32, no. 3 (Hinson, ed.)	Alfred

Smetana, (Friedrich) Bedřich (1824–1884) Bohemia

A Czech pianist, violinist, conductor, teacher, nationalistic composer and music critic, Smetana began music study with his father who was an amateur violinist. He supported himself for a short time as a music teacher for the family of Count Leopold Thun in Prague. Franz Liszt knew and supported Smetana who founded a new piano school. He wrote eight operas including his most famous opera *Prodaná nevěsta* (The Bartered Bride) and composed piano miniatures.

I-A	Easier Pieces	Masters Music
I-A	Selected Works for Piano	Schott
A	Polkas (ten compositions)	Peters
A	Six Bohemian Dances	Kalmus
A	Smetana (Schwerdtner, ed.)	Schott

Romantic Literature *continued*

Streabbog, Jean-Louis [Jean Louis Gobbaerts] (1835–1886) Belgium

By reversing the spelling of his last name, Jean-Louis Gobbaerts composed and published under the pseudonym Louis Streabbog. A noted pianist, piano teacher and composer, he wrote a great number of piano compositions popular with teachers and students.

E	Twelve Melodious Pieces, op. 63, Book 1	Kalmus; Masters Music, Schirmer
I	Streabbog Album	Schott

Tchaikovsky, Pyotr Il'yich (1840–1893) Russia

A remarkably talented pianist, conductor, teacher and composer, Tchaikovsky began piano lessons at age four. In 1850 he was sent to study at the School of Jurisprudence in St. Petersburg and in 1859 took a position as a clerk in the Ministry of Justice. However, he yearned for a musical career and in 1862 enrolled in the St. Petersburg Conservatory studying orchestration and composition with Anton Rubinstein and teaching private piano and theory lessons to support himself. He accepted a professorship in harmony at the Moscow Conservatory in 1865. He completed a successful 1891 American tour and in 1893 Cambridge University awarded him an honorary doctorate. Some of his best-known works include his *Piano Concerto no. 1 in B-flat minor, op. 23*, his ballets *The Nutcracker* and *Swan Lake*, the *1812 Overture* and his symphonies.

E-I	Easiest Piano Pieces from Album for the Young, op. 39 (Niemann, ed.)	Peters
E-I § *	Tchaikovsky: Album for the Young, op. 39 (Dossin, Schnell, eds.)	Kjos; Schirmer

For the intermediate student, the 24 selections from Tchaikovsky's *Album for the Young* are a *must*. Similar to Schumann's *Album for the Young*, this is a landmark collection of short romantic character pieces. The *Mazurka* is excellent preparation for the easier *Mazurkas* of Chopin. *Hobby Horse* could be "teamed" with Schumann's *Hobby Horse* from *Kinderszenen* or Pinto's *Scenas Infantis*. The chordal hymn-style writing in *Morning Prayer* and *In Church* is useful for teaching finger *legato* and syncopated pedaling. Book with CD.

I	Chanson Triste in G Minor, op. 40, no. 2	Henle
I	Humoresque in G Major, op. 10, no. 2	Schirmer
I-A	At the Piano with Tchaikovsky (Hinson, ed.)	Alfred
I-A	Seasons and Other Works for Solo Piano, The	Dover

Includes *Album for the Young, op. 39* and *18 Characteristic Pieces, op. 72*. The *Characteristic Pieces* are not as well known as his *Album for the Young* and *The Seasons*, but are deserving of greater attention. Composed near the end of his life, they contain short salon type pieces including dances, pieces with descriptive titles and tributes to both Chopin and Schumann.

I-A §	Tchaikovsky: The Seasons, op. 37a (*Hinson, **Dossin, eds.)	*Alfred; **Schirmer

The Seasons consist of 12 piano pieces, each representing a single month of the year. No. 6, *June* (*Barcarole*) is a frequently performed "season".

I-A	Tchaikovsky: 12 Pieces of Medium Difficulty	Schott
I-A	Tschaikowsky Album for Piano	Editio Musica Budapest
I-A	Tschaikovsky: Selected Works, Vols. I, II	Kalmus
A	The Nutcracker Suite (Tchaikovsky, arr.; Hinson, ed.)	Alfred

Tomášek, Václav Jan Křtitel [Tomaschek, Wenzel Johann] (1774–1850) Bohemia

A composer, pianist and respected piano teacher, he received violin and vocal instruction as a boy and attended Charles University where he studied math, history, philosophy and law among other subjects, but he was largely self-taught in music. He held the position of music tutor and composer for Count Georg Buquoy which enabled him to travel and meet composers such as Haydn and Beethoven. He is primarily known for his songs and dances and piano miniatures including 42 eclogues, 15 rhapsodies and 3 dithyrambs.

I		Sonatina for Piano	Editio Baerenreiter Praha
I-A		Ausgewählte Klavierwerke (Zahn, ed.)	Henle

Includes: *6 Eglogues, op. 35*; *3 Ditirambi, op. 65*; *3 Allegri Capricciosi di Bravura, op. 84.*

Weber, Carl Maria (Friedrich Ernst) von (1786–1826) Germany

A virtuoso pianist, conductor, composer and music critic, Weber was an early romantic period composer. He was appointed *Kapellmeister* at Breslau in 1804 and *Director* of the Prague Opera in 1813. Known for his successful opera *Der Freischütz* (1821) and works for woodwinds, he made important contributions to lieder, choral music, and opera.

I	§	(20) Easy Dances	Peters

This is an excellent collection of shorter German dances, Waltzes, and Écossaises.

I-A		Complete Piano Works (in three volumes)	Peters

The core of Weber's advanced solo output consists of four sonatas, several sets of Variations, shorter dances, and miscellaneous works such as the op. 65 *Invitation to the Dance*.

I-A		Complete Sonatas, Invitation to the Dance and Other Piano Works	Dover
I-A		Selected Piano Works (Concert Pieces, Variations) (Viertel/Gerlach, eds.)	Henle
A	§	Invitation to the Dance, op. 65	Peters; ASE

Weber's most often played piano solo; a Rondo with a mixture of various themes.

Romantic Collections and Anthologies

	Title (editor)	Publisher
§	Anthology of Romantic Piano Music (Hinson, ed.)	Alfred

This important Anthology is paired with a DVD on Romantic performance practices. Hinson performs music from the Anthology, and shares interesting historical anecdotes about the composers represented therein and the writers and artists who influenced them.

	Contemporaries of Schumann (Hermann, ed.)	Hinrichsen
	Early Romantic Treasures (Banowetz, ed.)	Kjos
	Late Romantic Treasures (Banowetz, ed.)	Kjos
	Easy Piano Music from the period of Romanticism	Editio Musica Budapest
§	Harris Piano Classics: Romantic and 20th Century Repertoire, Vols. 1b–7b	Frederick Harris

These seven books progress in difficulty and include a wide range of Romantic and Contemporary composers. Each volume contains between 16 to 24 pages, and includes 9–12 piano compositions.

	The Joy of Romantic Piano, Vols. I, II (Agay, ed.)	Music Sales
	Masters of French Piano Music (Hinson, ed.)	Alfred
	Nineteenth-Century American Piano Music (Gillespie, ed.)	Dover

Unfamiliar works such as etudes, toccatas, polkas, impromptus, and waltzes by 23 composers, including Albéniz, Bizet, Chabrier, Fauré, Smetana, and Wagner.

	The Pianist's Book of Early Romantic Treasures (Banowetz, ed.)	Kjos
	The Pianist's Book of Late Romantic Treasures (Banowetz, ed.)	Kjos
§	Rare Masterpieces of Russian Piano Music (Feofanov, ed.)	Dover

Feofanov, a native of Russia, assembled this collection of eleven pieces by composers such as Glinka, Balakirev, and Glazunov. Difficulty levels range from late intermediate to advanced.

	The Romantic Era	Hal Leonard
	Romantic Masters (Kobler, ed.)	Peters

This volume contains twenty-four early intermediate pieces by nine 19th-century composers such as Schubert, Chopin, Smetana, Brahms, and Grieg.

	The Romantic Masters	Alfred

Subtitled, *Piano Masters Series: The Romantic Masters Piano Solos by Master Composers of the Period*, this edition contains sixteen pieces by Burgmüller, Chopin, Ellmenreich, Grieg, Gurlitt, MacDowell, Schubert, Schumann, and Tchaikovsky.

	The Romantic Period, Vol. III (Agay, ed.)	Music Sales
	Romantic Piano Anthology, Vols. 1-4 (Franke, ed.)	Schott
	The Romantic Period-Intermediate Piano Book	Peters

Includes easy to moderately difficulty pieces by Brahms, Chopin, Dvorak, Grieg, Liszt, Schubert, Schumann, Tchaikovsky and Wagner.

E (Early Intermediate)   I (Intermediate)   A (Advanced Intermediate to Advanced)

§ The Romantic Pianist, Vols. I–IV (Johnson, ed.)   Peters
    These volumes are interesting because of the relatively unknown composers who are featured. For example, volume III includes eight compositions by Raff, Bennett, Reger, Sjogren, Nicode, Reinecke, Severac, and Scharwenka.

§ The Romantic Spirit, 1790–1910, Book I (Bachus, ed.)   Alfred
    This volume contains twenty-three intermediate compositions including interesting pieces by lesser-known composers such as Joseph Lanner (1801–1843) and Francisco Tárrega (1852–1909).

The Russian Romantics   Schirmer

Schubert to Shostakovich (Anthony, ed.)   Presser

§ Style and Interpretation, Vol. IV (Ferguson, ed.)   Oxford
    Style essays and performance notes accompany repertoire selected to demonstrate essential features of the romantic period. Volumes I-III address baroque and classical music.

The Contemporary Era circa 1890 to the Present

An Introduction to Contemporary Piano Music

Music composed from the 1890s forward, beginning with early impressionism, is generally referred to as contemporary music. As we noticed in the Romantic era (see *An Introduction to Romantic Piano Music*), at the outset of the 20th century, some composers such as Paul Hindemith and Béla Bartók were "classicists," staying closer to the traditions and forms of earlier periods while incorporating their personal musical vocabulary. Others, such as Claude Debussy, Arnold Schönberg, and John Cage stretched the musical language of the time and proved to be more innovators than traditionalists.

We now have moved well into the 21st century. Current composers, by definition, can be called *contemporary* and from that group, individuals who truly are breaking new ground, the *Avant-garde*. Is there a point at which the present contemporary period is considered over and another period begins? Only time will help us further define and refine the labels we use to describe the music of the 20th and 21st centuries.

Looking back, cataclysmic events of the 20th century, particularly World Wars I and II, shaped composers' lives and the music they wrote. Composers throughout Europe suffered life-changing experiences from events surrounding the wars:

- Claude Debussy and Maurice Ravel were so moved by the loss of friends in World War I (1914-1918) that they wrote compositions dedicated to victims of that war (i.e., Debussy's *En blanc et noir* and Ravel's *Le tombeau de Couperin*). Ravel, who served in the French army, wrote his *Piano Concerto for the Left Hand* for pianist Paul Wittgenstein who lost his right arm after a gunshot to the elbow in the First World War.

- Olivier Messiaen (France) was held in a World War II (1939-1945) German prison camp from 1940-41 and wrote the famous *Quartet for the End of Time*, performed by Messiaen and three fellow professional musicians who were prisoners. The instrument combination of Bb clarinet, violin, cello and piano is unusual, but those were the instruments available in the prison camp at the time.

- Dmitri Shostakovich served as a firefighter and survived the Siege of Leningrad (1941-44) in Russia.

- Anton Webern's only son was drafted by the German army and was killed in a troop train. This tragedy affected Webern to the point that he had difficulty composing. Then mere days after World War II ended in 1945, Webern, an Austrian, was shot and killed by an American soldier in Mittersill, Austria in a tragic accident. During the Allied occupation, Webern, breaking curfew, was smoking on his front porch when the soldier mistook the flame as a weapon.

A remarkable number of talented European composers immigrated to the United States to avoid war-torn Europe, some to escape the disastrous anti-Semitic practices of the Nazi regime. Béla Bartók, in 1940, gave a farewell two-piano concert with his wife, Ditta Pásztory, at the Budapest Conservatory and departed soon after for the United States, settling in New York City. Arnold Schönberg traveled in 1933 from Austria to Boston and later Los Angeles where he taught at both UCLA and USC and played tennis with George Gershwin! The influx of European musicians to their newly adopted country influenced music composition in the United States, not least by serving on the faculties of major music schools and teaching the aspiring young composers who would make their mark in the following decades.

An Introduction to Contemporary Piano Music *continued*

Post-Romantic Trends and Late Romanticism

The final decades of the nineteenth century and the first decades of the twentieth are often referred to as the post-Romantic era. After years of exploration and pushing at the limits of form and tonality, the Romantic era left composers with the question of what to explore or challenge next. Perhaps because there were many possible answers, a variety of things were happening in music:

- Composers such as Jean Sibelius, Béla Bartók, and Ralph Vaughan Williams, were writing strongly nationalistic music.

- Gustav Mahler and Richard Wagner were expanding Romantic chromaticism and forms to their utmost limits.

- Claude Debussy and Maurice Ravel were composing impressionistic compositions that made use of non-typical scale forms and forward looking harmonic extensions.

- Igor Stravinsky's primitivism still had some basis in tonality, but other -isms, such as serialism (twelve-tone), rejected tonality.

- In the United States (St. Louis and Memphis), the "blues" style was taking hold just as syncopated ragtime was becoming popular in Sedalia, Missouri.

Late romantic piano music is represented in the music of Sergei Rachmaninoff, Alexander Scriabin, and Americans like Edward McDowell and Amy Beach. Scriabin's chromaticism is most closely tied to Chopin. Rachmaninoff's lyricism, instrumental textures, and rich harmonies are more reflective of the 19th century (his model was Tchaikovsky) than modernistic trends. Rachmaninoff composed works which continue to be popular with pianists and audiences. How many aspiring pianists want to learn Rachmaninoff's *Prelude in C-Sharp Minor, op. 3, no. 2* after one hearing? Pedagogical composers writing in the late 20th and 21st centuries draw upon the tonal framework and sonorities of romanticism and make frequent use of the popular idiom of the character piece. One only has to play Catherine Rollin's *Preludes for Piano* to hear the link.

Impressionism

If 18th century composers such as J. S. Bach and Wolfgang Amadeus Mozart are, musically speaking, the "old masters," then surely Debussy represents the "new guard." The sounds he created by breaking many of the so-called rules of traditional composition, opened up a new world of sound. These groundbreaking developments in piano sonority and streams of parallel chords for which the composer is famous had not been heard before. He used modes, whole-tone and pentatonic scales (e.g., *Voiles*) and was influenced by gamelan music and far Eastern sounds (e.g., *Estampes*). Debussy's *24 Préludes*, published in two books of twelve in 1910 and 1913 respectively, are at the core of 20th century impressionism and are a seminal set of piano compositions. The sounds are evocative and the placement of each "title" after the final measure suggests an ephemeral image, almost an afterthought. Prominent performers and historians like Chick Corea, Pierre Boulez, William Austin and others believe that modern music begins with Debussy.

Ravel also is referred to as an *impressionistic* composer, though neither Debussy nor Ravel liked this visual arts label. Ravel was, however, more of a neo-classic traditionalist. Unlike Debussy, Ravel never received the prestigious *Prix de Rome*, but he was well-known for his orchestrations, not only of his own works, which he sometimes sketched first for the piano, e.g., *Ma Mere l'Oye* (Mother Goose Suite), but for orchestrations of other composers' works such as Mussorgsky's *Pictures at an Exhibition*. Compared to Debussy, Ravel's solo piano compositions reach a higher level of technical difficulty as in *Gaspard de la nuit*. As with Debussy, Ravel was drawn to the music of Spain and we see this influence in popular works such as *Boléro*. He was also influenced by American jazz styles in his *Piano Concerto in G* and other works.

Les Six

Moving in a rather different direction, a group of six French composers (Georges Auric, Louis Durey, Arthur Honegger, Darius Milhaud, Francis Poulenc, and Germaine Tailleferre, the only female member) collaborated on a collection of pieces, *L'album des six* in 1920, which included one composition by each composer: *Prélude* (1919) by Auric; *Romance sans paroles*, op. 21 (1917) by Durey; *Sarabande*, H 26 (1920) by Honegger; *Mazurka* (1914) by Milhaud; *Valse en ut*, FP 17 (1919) by Poulenc; and *Pastorale* (1919) by Tailleferre. Each composer made his or her artistic mark in modern composition partly as a reaction to late Germanic romanticism and impressionistic styles. They gave concerts together, often at the studio of the painter Emile Lejeune, and used Parisian popular elements for their inspiration. Referred to as the *Groupe des Six* in 1920 by French critic Henri Collet in a review of a concert featuring all of them, these young composers explored un-conventional styles and were united by strong friendship.

Neo-classicism

Simultaneous with the impressionistic movement, some composers followed a more neo-classical approach (see Ravel above), as they borrowed structural forms from the past but within those forms created their own musical language. Igor Stravinsky is thought of as a neoclassicist. His two piano sonatas are idiomatic, borrowing from past styles. Sergei Prokofiev's nine sonatas represent one of the largest collection of contemporary piano sonatas by a major composer. Single sonatas by Samuel Barber, Béla Bartók, and Aaron Copland also have gained a lasting place in the repertoire. Other composers, like Paul Hindemith, crafted their own highly stylized version of tonal music within standard forms. His monumental set of sonatas for piano and each orchestral instrument is at the heart of the term *neo-classic*.

Folk Music and Nationalism

Folk music also is at the heart of much contemporary music. Perhaps the greatest exponent during the modern era was Béla Bartók, pianist, teacher, composer and ethnomusicologist who recorded native folk tunes in rural Eastern Europe and Northern Africa and then penned original musical settings for many of the melodies he discovered. In a letter to his sister, Bartók indicated that through his arrangements of native folk tunes he wanted to raise them to a new level of art music. He achieved this goal in piano compositions like *Roumanian Folk Dances* and the two-volume set, *For Children*, the latter based entirely on Hungarian and Slovakian folk melodies. Other examples include Alberto Ginastera's *Rondo on Argentine Children's Folk Tunes* and Dianne Goolkasian Rahbee's *Concertino No. 1*, titled *Peasant Folk Dance*.

Serialism, Aleatoric or Chance Music (Indeterminacy) and Minimalism

The peak of romanticism from Richard Wagner to Alban Berg's *Sonata, op. 1*, saw tonality stretched to the breaking point. The advent of impressionism, particularly the use of whole tone and pentatonic scales, lessened the pull of a tonal center and led to a weaker sense of key. The final break with tonality occurred with the advent of atonal and serial styles as seen in the music of Arnold Schönberg and his followers, known as the second Viennese school (the first being Mozart, Haydn, Beethoven, and Schubert). Schönberg, Alban Berg, Anton Webern, and others used expressive chromaticism that evolved into twelve-tone serial writing, where a tone row (12 tones of the chromatic scale) is created and no single pitch can be repeated until all have been heard. The row may then be manipulated by playing it backward (retrograde) or upside down (inverted), to mention just two possibilities. Other composers such as Olivier Messiaen and his students, Pierre Boulez, Karlheinz Stockhausen, etc. "serialized" not only pitches but rhythm and dynamics, some of which were determined by computer calculations.

As a reaction against the total control and predetermination of all musical elements in serial music, Serialism was followed by "indeterminacy," which removed control from the composer and placed it in the domain of the performer. "Chance" or aleatoric music, as seen in the works of composers like Henry Cowell, John Cage, and Earle Brown left the performer to decide the final sequence of events within a composition, thus ensuring that no single performance of a work is ever the same. Such works are often not based on a traditional music score, but upon charts and graphs where the performer selects events at random.

An Introduction to Contemporary Piano Music *continued*

If serialism and indeterminate music has a limited audience, *Minimalism* has appealed to larger audiences. Philip Glass and Steve Reich are two names among current composers who are known as minimalists, composing music that is based on a few melodic and rhythmic fragments and is highly repetitive in nature. Glass's music has garnered wide appeal with numerous film scores to his credit such as *The Fog of War*.

Prepared Piano and the *Avant-Garde*

The idea of playing "inside the piano" originated with the music of Henry Cowell. Like Robert Schumann did in the 1830s, Cowell founded a journal—*New Music*— in 1927, which promoted music of the time. His *Aeolian Harp* and *The Banshee* were landmark compositions which used the piano in a non-traditional manner, the pianist striking or strumming the strings inside the piano. Cowell's innovative tactics foreshadowed John Cage's *Sonatas and Interludes,* which make use of a "prepared" piano. Cage instructs the performer to place rubber, metal nuts and bolts, plastic, and other objects on and between the strings to change the sound of the instrument.

John Cage, who had a profound and positive influence on the direction of contemporary music was and is, nevertheless, a controversial figure. His music provokes questions about the artistic goal of the music itself. What is music? Can any sound, even water drops in a glass, be considered music? Is the performer's total inactivity in Cage's *4'33" really* music or the clever product of the composer? Does it matter if there is an audience? Does any composer, from any period, write solely for self-defined artistic goals or for an audience (or both)? These questions are not easily answered. However, since the audience riots at the premiere of Stravinsky's *Le sacre du printemps* (The Rite of Spring), there sometimes has been a decidedly uncomfortable relationship between modern composers and contemporary audiences.

Unlike romantic composers, who indeed composed with the audience in mind, contemporary composers have bridged the gap between the very abstract and the practical by writing music that appeals to a broader audience. Copland's esoteric set of *Piano Variations* (Leonard Bernstein described it as "hard as nails" and music which would end any social party) is not for every listener, but his *Appalachian Spring* has wide appeal and enduring popularity. Similarly, Bartók's percussive sounding *1926 Piano Sonata* may be too abrasive for some ears, but his *Concerto for Orchestra* is routinely programmed by major orchestras. Some modernists have sought the practical solution of balancing their own artistic interests with those of their potential audiences.

Jazz, Blues and Ragtime

On the American scene, another popular style began developing in the early 1900s. Jazz is an original art form rooted in the African-American culture that combines both African and European musical traditions. It includes blue notes, improvisation, swing, syncopation and polyrhythms in a variety of styles such as ragtime, blues, boogie-woogie, swing, big band, Dixieland, stride and bebop. Certainly the blues scale (i.e., F, A-flat, B-flat, B-natural, C, E-flat, F) is an essential element that should be understood by all pianists. The blues scale is at the core of understanding the style and is equal in importance to understanding other scales, e.g., major, minor, whole tone, pentatonic, octatonic as well as modes. Jazz and blues sounds appealed to and influenced composers like Aaron Copland (*Four Piano Blues*), Samuel Barber (*Excursions*) and Ravel (*Piano Concerto in G*).

At the heart of jazz sounds are harmonic extensions (9th, 11th and 13th) to various types of 7th chords. Studying jazz harmony and arranging is essential to mastering chord voicings, chord substitutions, and transpositions. We are fortunate to have publications in which we can see, note for note, transcriptions of piano solos by greats such as Oscar Peterson and Bill Evans and study how they applied jazz voicings in performance.

A sister to jazz, the influence of ragtime cannot be underestimated. Piano rags, originally sold as sheet music solos, are usually in duple meter, syncopated with a stride bass, and comprised of contrasting 16-bar "choruses." Though Scott Joplin (1867-1917) and others (Eubie Blake [1883-1938], for example) are viewed as the primary representatives of ragtime, it is not difficult to see the influence of ragtime in standard 20th century piano literature such as the cakewalk piano pieces of Debussy (e.g., *Golliwogg's Cakewalk*), Stravinsky's *Piano-Rag-Music*, and more recently William Bolcom's ragtime compositions, e.g., *Three Ghost Rags*.

The ageless melodies and lyrics of songwriters such as Cole Porter, Irving Berlin and George Gershwin are also part of 20th-century American music and should be mentioned here. Their music and tuneful melodies remain popular worldwide and contemporary arrangers such as James Lyke have helped keep this genre of music alive in the piano studio through superior arrangements for solo piano and piano four-hands.

The Modern Piano and Technology

The modern grand piano matured to its current state in the mid-1800s. There have been few changes since, except for the number of keys added in the bass register for some concert instruments. The most important innovation from some manufacturers of acoustic pianos has been the development of the digital piano or synthesizer. The electronic or digital piano is always in tune, easy to transport, lower in cost, and includes the convenience of recording (including sequencing) and playback capabilities, ease of transposition and possible access to hundreds of voices and timbres. The digital piano is an inventive practice resource, a tool for sequencing and recording and an excellent portable instrument for exploring sounds and entertainment. However, the sound, touch, and pedaling of the digital keyboard, despite modern refinements, do not compare with a high quality, beautiful, acoustic piano with sounds produced by vibrating strings and not electronic chips. The digital piano has evolved as a practical and useful teaching tool in the piano classroom, however, for most pianists and teachers it is not an adequate substitute for the modern grand piano when performing art music.

Advances in technology, recording and the personal computer have had a profound impact on all areas of music, from serious *avant-garde* compositions, including prepared piano, chance and minimalistic compositions, to film scores. From the development of electronic soundtracks to the use of synthesizers to create "artificial" sounds, the very essence of what we often hear is not sounds made by instruments being played, but by artificially produced pitches and colors. The ability to create artificial sounds through the synthesizer and related computer technology led to works for piano and computer, piano and tape, as well as piano and supporting disk. Composers such as Pierre Boulez, Karlheinz Stockhausen, Mario Davidovsky and Lejaren Hiller were very influential in this genre of composition. As a benefit of this technology, many current composers package recorded performances of their works along with the score and provide ancillary accompaniment disks supporting student compositions.

Another key factor to consider is whether we listen to recorded music or live musicians. Now, large audiences comprised of thousands can hear performances through amplification, a feat unheard of not that long ago. However, because of advances in technology, live music is no longer the only source for performances. One only has to go to a circus to realize that the pit orchestra of live musicians has been largely replaced by "canned" music as is the case at wedding receptions and other entertainment functions which use DJs (disc jockeys) and recorded music instead of live musicians.

Who would have imagined, even twenty years ago, that samples of both amateur and professional piano performances could be seen and heard at the convenience of the consumer on *You Tube,* CDs, iPods and iTunes or that mp3 files could be downloaded. Computers, amplification and quicker forms of communication have impacted music performance throughout society. The listener can select any piece to hear (if desired, repeatedly) and also truncate the experience by skipping sections (moving forward or backward in the performance) or simply turning the music off.

The Future

Returning to the opening definition of contemporary and *Avant-Garde*, we are now in the 21st century with an array of talented living composers (see the many names in the contemporary and pedagogical solo literature sections) exploring new sounds for art music, jazz styles, and compositions for students. What styles, forms and musical experiences will current composers bring us in the years to come? Whose works will stand the test of time? Is there a new "master" composer whose works have not yet gained international attention? Finally, what new young composers will appear whose music attracts our attention?

An Introduction to Contemporary Piano Music *continued*

We are too close to the "contemporary" sounds of the present to gain the musical and artistic perspective to adequately evaluate current music. However, just as it was important to support the *avant-garde*, forward looking composers of the past, such as Beethoven, Liszt, Debussy, and Messiaen, it is important for musicians and teachers to perform, teach, and support the music of our current contemporary composers. Whatever direction music performance takes for pianists, the role of the teacher and pianist in being an engaged advocate of music study, performance, and funding for the arts, will be a crucial element in keeping music and the arts at the forefront of society.

Recommended resources for further reading:

Debussy, Claude. 1948 (c1928). *Monsieur Croche, the Dilettante Hater.* Translated by B. N. L. Davies. New York: Lear.

Simms, Bryan R., ed. 1999. *Composers on Modern Musical Culture, an Anthology of Readings on Twentieth-century Music.* New York. Schirmer Books.

Strickland, Edward. 1991. *American Composers: Dialogues on Contemporary Music.* Bloomington, IN: Indiana University Press.

Impressionism circa 1890—1920

A. Characteristics

Through the study of Impressionistic literature, students will become familiar with the following musical characteristics of the period:

- Imagery
- Pedal effects
- Layering of sounds
- Pentatonic and whole tone colors
- Expressive and evocative writing
- Use of harmonic extensions such as 7ths, 9ths, 11ths, 13ths
- Use of quartal and quintal chords

B. Introducing the Impressionistic Style

The following is a list of music that may be used to introduce the Impressionistic style and is listed in alphabetical order by composer rather than in order of difficulty. These pieces and collections are examples of literature that can serve as a valuable link between volumes that conclude a piano method and the more advanced impressionistic repertoire.

Bloch, Ernest	Enfantines	Carl Fischer
Debussy, Claude	Le petit nègre	Alfred
Ibert, Jacques	Histoires	Alfred
Karp, David	Seasons: Six Impressionistic Solos	Warner
Rebikov, Vladimir	Silhouettes, op. 31	Alfred
Rollin, Catherine	Spotlight on Impressionist Style	Alfred
Satie, Eric	Three Gymnopédies	Alfred

C. Gradation or Teaching Order

We recommend the following order for introducing the music of Debussy:

- The Little Shepherd from Children's Corner
- Le petit nègre
- Page d'album
- First Arabesque
- Valse Romantique
- Mazurka
- Reverie
- La fille aux cheveux de lin (Préludes, Book 1)
- Des pas sur la neige (Préludes, Book 1)
- Canope (Préludes, Book 2)

Impressionistic Literature

Composer	Title	Publisher

Bloch, Ernest (1880–1959) USA (b. Switzerland)

Born in Geneva, Bloch studied composition with Jaques-Dalcroze and Eugène Ysaÿe and is known for his expressive, emotional works. He moved to the United States in 1916, became a citizen in 1924 and was Director of the Cleveland Institute of Music and later the San Francisco Conservatory of Music. Former students include Roger Sessions.

E-I § *   Enfantines (1923), Ten Pieces for Children — Carl Fischer
         (1. Lullaby, 4. Elves, 10. Dream)
A   Five Sketches in Sepia (1925) — Schirmer
A   In the Night — Schirmer
A   Poems of the Sea (1922) — Schirmer
> These three poems, inspired by writings from Walt Whitman, include *Waves, Chanty,* and *At Sea.*

Debussy, (Achille-) Claude (1862–1918) France

Perhaps more than any other composer, the influence of Claude Debussy on the modern era is incredibly profound. Born in 1862, Debussy died in 1918 from cancer. Musicians from Chick Corea to Pierre Boulez proclaim the impact of his music. Debussy entered the Paris Conservatory with only a piano background and proceeded to create new sounds that had never before been imagined, eventually winning the *Prix de Rome*. The sounds he created not only impacted piano sonorities but other musical genres as well. William Austin maintains that music of our modern time, from the cabaret to the concert hall, was influenced by Debussy.

I §   Children's Corner — Durand
  *   (The Little Shepherd, Doctor Gradus ad Parnassum, Golliwogg's Cakewalk)
> Debussy dedicated this set to his daughter, Chouchou, though the set is not for young children to play. *Doctor Gradus ad Parnassum* is a musical and technical parody of Clementi's *Gradus ad Parnassum*. *The Little Shepherd* contains a few difficult dotted rhythms but may be the most accessible of Debussy's piano solos. It is an excellent movement to introduce his style to the intermediate pianist.

I   Danse — Durand
I §   Le petit nègre — Alfred
> *Le petit nègre* is the easiest of Debussy's cakewalk pieces (the others being *Golliwogg's Cake-walk, Minstrels, General Lavine - eccentric*) and one of his most accessible solos. Two repeating themes reduce the amount of material to be learned.

I §   Page d'album (Howat, ed.) — Presser
> One of the last piano solos Debussy composed (1915), *Page d'album* was written to raise money for the French Red Cross during World War I. Debussy inscribed the manuscript with the words, *Le Vêtement du Blessé* (The Dressing of the Wounded). A stunningly beautiful slow waltz of only one page, it is an ideal piece for introducing Debussy's music.

I   Rêverie — Peters
I-A   At the Piano with Debussy (Hinson, ed.) — Alfred
I-A *   Dances of Debussy (Hinson, ed.) (Doll's Dance I) — Alfred
I-A   Debussy: An Introduction to His Piano Music (includes CD) (Halford, ed.) — Alfred
I-A   Deux Arabesques for the Piano (Olson, ed.) — Alfred
I-A *   Deux Arabesques (no. 1) — Durand
> An arabesque refers to a repeating figure or design. The first *Arabesque* is more challenging than it appears and should not be taught until a student

E (Early Intermediate)   I (Intermediate)   A (Advanced Intermediate to Advanced)

has experienced Debussy's music through shorter less complex textures and has learned to play 2 against 3 in an easier work! Striking melodic (right hand) and harmonic similarities occur between Liszt's *Sposalizio* (*Années de Pèlerinage,* second book) and this composition. The scherzo-like second arabesque, in G major, deserves greater attention.

I-A	Easier Favorites (Feldmann, ed.)	Peters
I-A	Etudes, Children's Corner, Images Book 2, Other Works	Dover
I-A	The Great Piano Works of Claude Debussy (Tucker, ed.) (Artistic Preparation and Performance Series)	Alfred
I-A §	Piano Music (1888–1905)	Dover
I-A §	Préludes, Books I, II (Stegemann/Béroff, eds.)	Durand

* Selected préludes from Books I and II in general order of difficulty:

Book I: La fille aux cheveux de lin

La fille aux cheveux de lin contains beautiful pentatonic sounds and streams of parallel chords for which Debussy is famous. Four presentations of the melodic theme mirror the four verses of the poem of the same title (written by de Lisle) on which the composer based the music.

Minstrels

Jazz cakewalk rhythms influence this ending prelude to book I.

Voiles

In an ABA format, *Voiles*, translated as Sails or Veils uses a whole tone scale in the outer sections and a pentatonic scale in the middle. Debussy's student, Robert Schmitz maintains that the low B-flat could musically represent an anchor under the floating musical texture above.

Des pas sur la neige

Ideal for exploring Debussy's prélude style, the technically less difficult *Des pas sur la neige* is an excellent choice for introducing Debussy's early advanced *prélude* style, with its vague atmosphere, *ostinato*-like left hand and gentle hand crossings. The score reveals subtle voicing challenges along with triplet and sixteenth cross rhythms.

La cathédrale engloutie

This prelude is a favorite among aspiring pianists. The musical imagery paints a dynamically varied sound picture. The parallel chords convey musical pillars as does the score visually through the outer register treble and bass chords. The marking *doux et fluide* should be interpreted as the half note pulse equal to the opening quarter note pulse. Organ-like pedal points under ringing bell sounds make the piece irresistible to students.

Book II: Canope

The technically less challenging *Canope*, refers to the Egyptian city of Canopus and a type of funerary urn. Stately opening chords recall the ancient world of Egypt and the majesty of the city, with sad, intensely mournful melodies heard throughout.

Feuilles mortes

More than likely this piece was inspired by an Arthur Rackham illustration of children kicking fallen leaves. This lament, calls to mind Debussy's own observation about the season of autumn, as he lingered "in autumn-filled landscapes, bound by the spell of ancient forests." Slowly falling melodic lines, which zigzag back and forth, are at the forefront of the musical landscape.

Impressionistic Literature *continued*

    Brúyeres
        Through its lyric simplicity and opening melody, this *prélude* recalls *La fille aux cheveux de lin* (The girl with the flaxen hair) from the first book of *Préludes*. *Bruyères* is the French word for heather, a lavender colored bush that grows close to the earth. The dynamic level never exceeds *mf*.

    La Puerta del Vino
        This *prélude* was inspired by a postcard sent by Manuel de Falla to Debussy. The pulsating rhythm of the Spanish *habanera* style is heard throughout.

A	§	At the Piano with Debussy (Hinson, ed.)	Alfred
A	§	Celebrate Debussy, Vols. I, II (Hisey, ed.)	Frederick Harris

        Volume I contains all the "starter" pieces for introducing Debussy's music including *Page d'album*, *The Little Shepherd*, *Le petit nègre*, the first *Arabesque*, and lesser known works such as *La plus que lente*. *Jardins sous la pluie* is the capstone work in volume I. The informative *Preface* is written by the well-known Debussy scholar, James R. Briscoe.

A	*	Estampes (Jardins sous la pluie)	Durand

        The term *Estampes* refers to woodcut prints. These three compositions (*Pagodes, La soirée dans Grenade, Jardins sous la pluie*) were inspired by the paintings of artist Jacques-Emile Blanche. The third *Estampe*, *Jardins sous la pluie* (Gardens in the Rain) is a favorite. Based upon two French folk songs, *Dodo, l'enfant do* (Sleep, child, sleep) and *Nous n'irons plus au bois* (We'll not return to the woods), the stormy E minor texture of this make-believe garden eventually evolves into a bright, cloudless and sunshine filled E major at the end.

A	*	Images (Reflets dans l'eau)	Durand

        Of the three movements, *Reflets dans l'eau* (Reflections in the water), *Hommage à Rameau*, and *Mouvement*, the first is frequently taught individually. The shimmering texture falls into an A-T(transition)-B-A1-T-B1-*Coda* structure. Be aware of the variety of soft dynamic markings and how musical material in the A and B sections is manifested in the final *Coda*.

A	*	Suite Bergamasque (Prélude, Clair de lune)	Peters

        Debussy draws from the baroque suite with titles such as prélude, menuet and passepied. *Clair de lune*, probably the most popular of Debussy's keyboard music, could be thought of as a slow sarabande because of the long rhythmic values on the second and third beats. The work was inspired by Paul Verlaine's 1869 poem of the same name

A	*	Suite pour le Piano (Sarabande)	Durand

        Consisting of a *Prélude*, *Sarabande* and *Toccata*, the ending toccata is the more challenging movement.

A	*	12 Études (no. 1: pour les "cinq doigts")	Durand

Griffes, Charles Tomlinson (1884–1920) USA

One of the most important American composers in the early 20th Century, he was born in New York, and in 1903 moved to Berlin where he studied piano and composition (with Humperdinck) at the Stern Conservatory. He returned to the U.S. in 1907 and was Director of the Music Department at Hackley School in New York until his early death at age 35. Much of his music reflects the French Impressionistic style.

I-A	Lake at Evening Op. 5, No. 1	Schirmer

I-A		Three Preludes	Peters

These intermediate level short preludes are an excellent introduction to Griffes' music and to the impressionistic style.

A	*	Four Roman Sketches, op. 7	Schirmer

(The White Peacock, The Fountain of Acqua Paolo)
Composed between 1915-16 and inspired by the poetry of William Sharp, the first sketch, *The White Peacock,* is best known for the chordal, arpeggiated texture which musically depicts the Peacock's fan. *The Fountain of Acqua Paolo* reveals Ravel's influence. The second and fourth movements are *Nightfall: Al Far della Notte* and *Clouds*.

A		The White Peacock (Hinson, ed.)	Alfred
A	*	Three Tone Poems, op. 5 (1. The Lake at Evening)	Schirmer

Includes 1. Lake at Evening, 2. Vale of Dreams and 3. Night Winds

Ibert, Jacques (Jacques-François-Antoine) (1890–1962) France

Ibert, a pupil of Fauré, won the *Prix de Rome* at the Paris Conservatoire in 1919 and was Director of the French Academy in Rome from 1937 until 1960. He was a prolific composer who wrote vocal and instrumental works, operas, ballets and music for theatre, radio, and cinema including *Circus* from Gene Kelly's film, *Invitation to the Dance* (1952).

I		Petite Suite en Quinze Images (fifteen pieces) (1943)	Foetisch
I-A	§ *	Histoires (ten pieces) (Hinson/Nelson, ed.)	Alfred; Alphonse Leduc

(Le petit âne blanc, A Giddy Girl)
Ibert's writing offers an excellent companion to the easier music of Debussy in terms of introducing the impressionistic style. His piano suite, *Histoires* (Stories), is one of his most popular works.

Ravel, Joseph Maurice (1875–1937) France

Ravel studied composition with Gabriel Fauré and was a friend Igor Stravinsky. A contemporary of Debussy, the two composers influenced and respected each other. Unlike Debussy, Ravel was never able to win the prestigious *Prix de Rome* in composition. He composed in almost every genre and is best known for his ballet *Daphnis et Chloé*, the orchestral *La Valse* and *Boléro*, his *Piano Concerto in G Major*, and the important piano work, *Jeux d'Eau*.

I	§	Prélude (1913)	Alfred; Durand

This two-page miniature in ternary form (ABA^1 *Coda*) may be the only solo piano composition by Ravel accessible to the late intermediate student. Originally, it was written as a sight-reading piece for Paris conservatory auditions. The exquisite writing mixes elegant melody with interesting harmonies throughout.

I-A	§	At the Piano with Ravel (Hinson, ed.)	Alfred
I-A		Pavane pour une Infante défunte (1899)	Alfred; Schirmer

(Pavane for a Dead Princess) Ravel wrote the music while still a student and studying composition with Gabriel Fauré. The music has a decidedly Spanish flair and, as the composer notes, does not commemorate a death but rather a petite princess dancing in a Spanish court of olden times.

I-A		Ravel: Selected Favorites (Hinson, ed.)	Alfred
I-A	§	Valses Nobles et Sentimentales (1911)	Durand

Inspired by Schubert's many waltzes, this set of eight waltzes by Ravel foreshadows his later *La Valse*. Tempo markings for the eight are: *Modéré, Assez lent, Modéré, Assez animé, Presque lent, Vif, Moins vif,* and *Epilogue: lent*.

A		Menuet antique (1895)	International

Impressionistic Literature *continued*

A		Menuet sur le nom de Haydn (1909)	Durand
A		Piano Masterpieces of Maurice Ravel	Dover

      Includes *Pavane pour une infante défunte, Jeux d'eau, Sonatine, Miroirs, Menuet antique, Gaspard de la nuit.*

A   Gaspard de la Nuit   Henle

      Based on poems of Louis Bertrand, *Gaspard* represents one of the most challenging works in the entire piano repertoire. It is comprised of three movements, *Ondine, Le gibet,* and *Scarbo.*

A   Jeux d'Eau   Henle

      Inspired by Liszt, *Jeux d'Eau* is often interpreted as water fountains. Composed when still a student of Fauré, the work is full of imagery and is a must work for advancing pianists. Ravel inscribed the manuscript, *Dieu fluvial riant de l'eau qui le chatouille* (a quote from Henri de Régnier) which can be translated as "River god laughing as the water tickles him".

A   Le Tombeau de Couperin   Durand

      Comprised of six movements (*Prélude, Fugue, Forlane, Rigaudon, Menuet,* and *Toccata*) and imitating the Baroque suite, each movement is dedicated to a friend of the composer killed in WWI.

A § *   Sonatine (1905) (I: *Modéré*)   Durand

      Much of Ravel's piano music is accessible only to quite advanced pianists. The *Modéré* movement to the *Sonatine* is a notable exception and represents a rare example of the sonata form in an impressionistic style. The use of the term *sonatina* refers more to the brevity of the work than a simplistic level of difficulty. The opening *Modéré* is followed by *Mouvement de Menuet* and *Animé.*

Rebikov, Vladimir Ivanovich (1866–1920) Russia

Known as the father of Russian impressionism, Rebikov's use of whole tone and pentatonic colors prepares younger students for impressionism. He studied at the Moscow Conservatory with a student of Tchaikovsky. He is best known for his piano miniatures, his ballet, *The Christmas Tree,* children's choruses and songs, and his works for musical theater.

E   Pictures for Children, op. 37 (Gretchaninoff, ed.)   International

      These pictures represent seven early intermediate impressionistic pieces.

I   The Christmas Gift   ASE

I §   Nine Silhouettes, op. 31 (Palmer, ed.)   Alfred

      Familiar titles from this intermediate set include *Shepherd Playing On His Pipe* and *Playing Soldiers.*

Satie, Eric (Alfred Leslie) (1866–1925) France

Although considered an eccentric composer, Satie's creativity and ideas influenced his contemporaries Debussy, Ravel, and Stravinsky as well as later composers like Poulenc. He was an independent and rebellious figure whose pieces have interesting titles (*Three Pieces in the Shape of a Pear* and *The Dreamy Fish*) and unusual written directions to the performer.

E   Menus Propos Enfantines (Three sets of children's pieces)(1913)   Durand

E-I §   3 Gymnopédies (1888) and 3 Gnossiennes (1890) (Baylor, ed.)   Alfred

E-A §   The Satie Collection (Hinson, ed.)   Schott

      A comprehensive collection which includes the *Trois Gymnopédies,* the lesser-known *Bureaucratic Sonatina* (composed in 1917 as a parody on Clementi's op. 36, no. 1), as well as the late work *Sports et Divertissements.* Hinson's

	particular selection of repertoire is an excellent exploration of the range of difficulty in Satie's writing.	
I	Easy Pieces and Dances (Töpel, ed.)	Bärenreiter
I	Trois Gymnopédies (1888)	Salabert
	These three forward looking compositions, which share thematic material, have a unique, distinctive sound and should be remembered as possible teaching material. Each requires careful voicing and pedaling.	
I-A	Gymnopédies, Gnossiennes and Other Works for Piano	Dover
I-A	Piano Solo Album (complete solo piano music)	Salabert
I-A	Selected Piano Works (Ohmen, ed.)	Schott
I-A	Seven Gnossiennes	Salabert
I-A	Sports et Divertissements (1914) (twenty Brief Sketches)	Dover
A	Cinq Nocturnes (published in two volumes)	Masters Music

Contemporary Literature from 1900

Composer/Title   **Publisher**

Adler, Samuel (b. 1928) USA (b. Mannheim, Germany)

Adler is the son of cantor-composer Hugo Adler, who moved the family to the U.S. in 1939. Samuel composed over 400 works, including five operas, six symphonies, twelve concerti, eight string quartets, four oratorios and many other instrumental and choral works and songs, which have been performed globally. He studied composition with Aaron Copland, Paul Hindemith, and Koussevitzky (Tanglewood in 1949). He has received several honorary doctorates including Southern Methodist University and Wake Forest University. He taught at the Eastman School of Music from 1966-95, where he served as chair of the composition department from 1974-95 and retired as professor *emeritus*. He has taught at the Juilliard School since 1997.

E-I	Gradus 60 Studies, Vols. I–III	Oxford
I	The Sense of Touch	Presser
A	The Road to Terpsichore	Schirmer

Albright, William (Hugh) (1944-1998) (USA) (b. Gary, IN; d. Ann Arbor, MI)

A composer, organist and pianist, Albright studied at the University of Michigan where his primary composition teachers included Ross Lee Finney and Leslie Bassett. He excelled at the organ and later composed organ rags. In 1970, he received a D.M.A. in composition and joined the faculty at the University of Michigan where he directed the electronic music studio. As a Fulbright recipient, he spent time at the Paris *Conservatoire*, where he studied with Olivier Messiaen. Albright concertized as an organist and pianist specializing in contemporary music and ragtime, a style that attracted and influenced both him and his colleague, William Bolcom.

I	§	The Machine Age: A Set of Six Short Piano Pieces for Our Time	Peters
		No. III. *Computer's Revenge* uses alternative notation.	

Arnold, Malcolm (1921-2006) Great Britain (b. Northampton; d. Norwich, England)

Principal Trumpet with the London Philharmonic Orchestra, Arnold was acknowledged as one of the finest players of his generation. He has a remarkable catalogue of major concert works including nine symphonies, seven ballets, two operas, one musical, over twenty concertos, two string quartets, and music for brass-band and wind ensemble. He wrote widely praised film scores including *Bridge on the River Kwai* (winning an Oscar in 1958) and *Inn of the Sixth Happiness*. Arnold helped establish and support the National Youth Orchestra of Great Britain. All of Arnold's output for solo piano fits on one CD. Virtually all the solo piano works are miniatures.

E	§	Children's Suite, op. 16 (1948) (six pieces)	Lengnick
		Subtitled *Six Little Studies,* these intermediate pieces focus primarily on intervallic and rhythmic studies. Titles: *Prelude, Carol, Shepherd's Lament, Trumpet Tune, Blue Tune,* and *Folk-Song.*	
E		Eight Children's Pieces (1952)	Lengnick
		Contents: *Tired Bagpipes, Two Sad Hands, Across the Plains, Strolling Tune, Dancing Tune, Giants, The Duke,* and *The Buccaneer.*	
I-A		Two Bagatelles for Solo Piano (1947)	Paterson/Chester
A		Variations on a Ukrainian Folk-Song (1946) (10 variations)	Lengnick

Barber, Samuel (Osborne) (1910–1981) USA (b. West Chester, PA; d. New York, NY)

An Irish-American organist, pianist and composer, Barber is known for his orchestral, opera, choral and piano music. At age 14, he entered the Curtis Institute in Philadelphia, where he studied piano, composition, and voice. His *Adagio for Strings*, performed by the NBC Symphony Orchestra under the direction of Arturo Toscanini in 1938, is perhaps his most popular composition along with *Knoxville: Summer of 1915*, for soprano and orchestra. He received the Pulitzer Prize twice for music, for his opera *Vanessa* and the *Concerto for Piano and Orchestra, op. 38*. Barber's lifelong personal and professional partner Gian Carlo Menotti, whom he met at Curtis, supplied the libretto for *Vanessa*. Barber's *Sonata for Piano, op. 26*, has maintained a prominent position in the contemporary piano repertoire.

I	§	Love Song (1924) (Hinson, ed.)	Alfred

The most accessible of Barber's solo compositions, this little known gem is in spirit a song without words at the late intermediate level.

I-A	§	Souvenirs	Schirmer

Though originally written for one piano, four-hands, Barber's solo version contains six movements which emphasize dance music including a waltz, pas de deux, and tango.

A			Ballade, op. 46	Schirmer
A			Complete Piano Music (includes the composer's *Sonata, op. 26*)	Schirmer
A	§	*	Excursions, op. 20 (1942-1944) (1, 4)	Schirmer

The four *Excursions* present jazz-like, advanced textures feasible for the skilled pianist. The first, written in a rondo format, is very appealing because of the left hand perpetual motion *ostinato* imitating the boogie-woogie style. The fourth, a Hoedown in duple meter, is also recommended.

A	Nocturne, op. 33	Schirmer

The composer offers a tribute to John Field in this romantic texture using a contemporary harmonic palette.

A	Sonata, op. 26	Schirmer

Bartók, Béla (Viktor János) (1881–1945) Hungary (b. Hungary; d. New York, NY)

Bartók is considered one of the important composers of the 20th century and certainly the greatest Hungarian composer since Franz Liszt. A composer, concert pianist, teacher, and ethnomusicologist, he transcribed thousands of folk tunes from his native country and surrounding regions. In 1907, he became a piano instructor at the Budapest Academy, a post he held for more than twenty-five years. From 1912-1914, he devoted himself to the collection, arrangement and study of folk music and in 1916 was introduced to Kodály, who collected recordings of Hungarian folk music, and became Bartók's closest friend. Bartók moved to the U.S. in 1940 to escape Nazi Germany, and succumbed to leukemia in 1945. His most notable contributions are his large body of pedagogical piano compositions, orchestral works and string quartets.

E			Fifteen Hungarian Peasant Songs and Dances, Sz. 71	Universal
E	§		The First Term (at the Piano), Sz. 71 (1911)	Kalmus

A set of 18 selected pieces that the composer excerpted from the five-volume piano method (Zongoraiskola) co-authored with Sándor Reschofsky. *Folksong* and *Minuet* are particularly well known from this collection.

E-I	§	*	For Children, Vols. I, II, Sz. 42	Boosey & Hawkes

Originally published (between 1908 and 1911) in four volumes, they included a total of 85 pieces based on Hungarian and Slovakian folk tunes. After Bartók immigrated to the United States he revised and published 79 pieces in two volumes for Boosey & Hawkes. Minor modifications included a few rhythmic changes and title changes. For example, the well known *Play* or *Play Song* was titled *Kitty-Kitty* in the original edition. The main difference in the revision is that the text for each folk song was omitted. The compositions in *For Children* deserve greater attention. They often are

Contemporary Literature from 1900 *continued*

overshadowed by other sets such as the *Mikrokosmos*. Unfortunately, many collections and anthologies include selections from *For Children* without properly identifying the source. A few recommended compositions from each volume include: Vol. I (based on Hungarian tunes): *I Lost My Young Couple, Play* (alternate title *Kitty-Kitty*), *A Lad Was Killed, My Little Graceful Girl,* and *The Sun Shines into the Church*. Vol. II (based on Slovakian tunes): *Allegretto, Round Dance I* (alternate title *Rondo*), *Frisky,* and *Revelry*.

E-I § * Ten Easy Piano Pieces, Sz. 39 (Evening at the Village) — Editio Musica Budapest
Some of the composer's most well known miniatures are included in this set—titles such as *Evening at the Village* and the famous *Bear Dance,* which concludes the set.

E-A §   Celebrate Bartók (Hisey, ed.) — Frederick Harris
This volume includes a wide range of difficulty levels so that students can explore Bartók's piano music for several years. Background information on the composer and performance notes accompany commonly played works such as selections from *For Children* and the *Bagatelles,* as well as the complete *Sonatina* and *Six Romanian Folk Dances*. *Allegro Barbaro* caps off the edition.

E-A § * Mikrokosmos, Sz. 107 — Boosey & Hawkes
The *Mikrokosmos* is a monumental set of graded piano pieces in six volumes (153 progressive piano pieces) intended to assist the student's technical and reading development and introduce many 20th-century compositional techniques. For example, the *Six Dances in Bulgarian Rhythms* (contained in Volume VI) demonstrate additive meter. A few recommended compositions from each volume include: Vol. I. *Question and Answer, Imitation and Inversion*; II. *Staccato and Legato, Buzzing*; III. *Chord Study, Tale*; IV. *Notturno, Harmonics*; V. *Boating, Village Joke*; VI. *From the Diary of a Fly, Minor Seconds, Major Sevenths*. MIDI disks are available from the publisher for albums I–IV.

I   §   An Introduction to His Piano Works (Palmer, ed.) — Alfred
I   §   The Joy of Bartók (Agay, ed.) — Yorktown
I   § * Rumanian Folk Dances, Sz. 56 (2, 4, 1, 3, 5, 6) — Boosey & Hawkes
Translated titles: Dance with Sticks (*Joc cu bâtă*), Sash Dance (*Brâul*), Stamping Dance (*Pe Loc*), Horn Dance (*Buciumeana*), Romanian Polka (*Poarga Românească*), and Quick Dance (*Mărunțel*). These six dances, composed in 1915, provide an excellent introduction to Bartók's music. Individual dances can be studied or the set can be taught in its entirety (approximately 5 minutes in length). The last two dances in quick tempo are noticeably more difficult than the first four. Transcriptions for piano and violin as well as string orchestra popularized the work.

I   § * Three Rondos on Folk Tunes, Sz. 84 (no. 1) — Boosey & Hawkes
These rondos are based on Slovakian folk tunes.

I-A § * Fourteen Bagatelles, op. 6, Sz. 38 (1, 3, 4, 6) — Kalmus
Composed in 1908, some of these pieces are excerpted for inclusion in multi-period anthologies. Busoni commented, upon hearing Bartók play the *Bagatelles* in June of 1908, "At last!, something *really* new." These textures reveal contemporary compositional techniques such as bitonality and quartal harmonies and show Bartók's personal compositional style taking shape. Most are one to two pages in length.

E (Early Intermediate)   I (Intermediate)   A (Advanced Intermediate to Advanced)

I-A		9 Kleine Klavierstücke, Sz. 82 (9 Little Pieces for Piano)	Boosey & Hawkes

These little known pieces are organized in three groups: I: no. 1-4 (*4 Dialogues*), II: no. 5-8 (*Menuetto, Chanson, Marcia delle Bestie, Tambour de Basque*), III: no. 9 (*Preludio*).

I-A		Piano Music of Béla Bartók, Series I, II	Dover

This edition is unique in that it includes hard to find lyrics of each folk song Bartók used in *For Children*.

A		Allegro Barbaro, Sz. 49	Universal

The primitive percussiveness of this work foreshadows the composer's 1926 *Sonata*. In Italian *Barbaro* means barbaric. The title was Bartók's witty response to a French critic who characterized his music as sounding barbaric.

A		Out of Doors, Sz. 81	Boosey & Hawkes

A suite comprised of five movements: *With Drums and Pipes, Barcarolla, Musettes, The Night's Music, The Chase*.

A	§ *	Sonatina, Sz. 55 (II movement)	Schirmer

This sonatina is a very effective piece to team with a Classical period sonatina. Bartók's *Sonatina* comprises three movements (*Bagpipers, Bear Dance, Finale*) and is closer in difficulty to Ravel's *Sonatine* than easier sonatinas. The work was fashioned on five Hungarian folk tunes distributed throughout the movements. The *Finale* is the most challenging musically and technically.

A	*	Sonata, 1926, Sz. 80 (II movement: *Sostenuto e pesante*)	Schirmer
A	§	Suite, op. 14, Sz. 62 (in four movements)	Universal

Next to his *Sonata*, this may be the composer's most significant advanced solo piano work. The four movements are: *Allegretto, Scherzo, Allegro molto,* and *Sostenuto*. Originally Bartók composed five movements but discarded the second movement *Andante* and published it separately.

Bernstein, Leonard (1918–1990) USA (b. Lawrence, MA; d. New York, NY)

A gifted conductor, composer, pianist, and teacher, Bernstein was appointed in 1943 as Assistant Conductor of the New York Philharmonic Orchestra and in 1945 became Music Director of the New York City Symphony Orchestra, a post he held until 1947. In 1958, Bernstein became *Music and Artistic Director* of the New York Philharmonic. He toured worldwide as a conductor and was a leading advocate of American composers, particularly Aaron Copland. His televised concert and lecture series started with the *Omnibus* program in 1954, and was followed in 1958 by the *Young People's Concerts*. Bernstein substantially contributed to the Broadway musical stage including collaborations for *On The Town* (1944), *Wonderful Town* (1953), *Candide* (1956), and the landmark musical, *West Side Story* (1957).

I-A		Five Anniversaries (1949-51)	Schirmer
I-A		Four Anniversaries (1948)	Schirmer
I-A		Seven Anniversaries (1943)	Schirmer
I-A	§	Thirteen Anniversaries (1990)	Schirmer

Bernstein wrote these groups of anniversaries to celebrate and honor friends, relatives and follow musicians. Most were written before he became artistic director for the New York Philharmonic, with exception of the last group of 13. Some of the names he pays homage to include, Aaron Copland, For My Sister Shirley, Lukas Foss, and Susanna Kyle (daughter of Bernstein's colleague Betty Comden).

Contemporary Literature from 1900 *continued*

Binkerd, Gordon (1916-2003) USA (b. Lynch, NE, d. Urbana, IL)

Professor (theorist and composer) at the University of Illinois (1947-71), he was a prolific composer whose works are written in a distinctive compositional style characterized by clever yet tonal writing. He is best known for his choral music but also wrote symphonies, piano sonatas, string quartets, sonatas for wind and string instruments, and a large quantity of chamber, choral and vocal music.

E-I §		The Young Pianist	Boosey & Hawkes
		These pieces are really not for young students as they represent a more advanced level of difficulty rhythmically and technically.	
I		Entertainments for Piano	Boosey & Hawkes
I		Piano Miscellany	Boosey & Hawkes
A	*	Concert Set (Etude, Mice)	Boosey & Hawkes
A		Sonata (1955)	Boosey & Hawkes
A		Suite for Piano (5 Fantasies)	Boosey & Hawkes

Bolcom, William (Eldon) (b. 1938) USA (b. Seattle, WA)

A noted pianist and composer, Bolcom has received the National Medal of Arts, a Pulitzer Prize and two Grammy Awards. He studied with Milhaud at Mills College while working on his M.A. degree, with Leland Smith at Stanford University (D.M.A.), and with Messiaen and Milhaud at the Paris *Conservatoire*, where he received the *2éme Prix de Composition*. He served on the faculty at the University of Michigan from 1973 to 2008 and was named the *Ross Lee Finney Distinguished University Professor of Composition* in 1994. Bolcom has performed and recorded his works frequently in collaboration with his wife and musical partner, mezzo-soprano Joan Morris, specializing in cabaret songs, show tunes, and popular songs from the early 20th century. He is well known for his piano rags composing over 20 rags since 1967. He employs syncopations, stride, and cakewalk style, in his ragtime writing. The *Graceful Ghost Rag* is a favorite among students and teachers.

E §		Monster Pieces (and Others)	Marks
		An adventure in contemporary music for the piano student, these 10 short pieces are excellent for introducing contemporary sounds.	
I-A §		Piano Rags	Marks
I-A		Three Dance Portraits	Marks
I-A §		Three Ghost Rags	Marks
		These three rags represent some of Bolcom's most popular titles including *Graceful Ghost Rag, The Poltergeist,* and *Dream Shadows*.	
A		Complete Rags for Piano	Marks
		This important edition includes every piano rag written by William Bolcom. The composer provides a Foreword and commentary.	
A	*	Nine Bagatelles (VII. Andante)	Hal Leonard
		(commissioned for the Tenth 2005 Van Cliburn International Piano Competition)	
A		Seabiscuits Rag	Marks

Britten, (Edward) Benjamin (1913–1976) England
(b. Lowestoft, Suffolk, England; d. Aldeburgh, Suffolk, England)

A renowned English composer, conductor and pianist, Britten entered the Royal College of Music in London in 1930 and studied composition with John Ireland and piano with Arthur Benjamin. From 1935 until the beginning of World War II, Britten composed for the GPO (government post office) Film Unit, for BBC Radio, and for small theater groups. He is well known for his operas, such as *Paul Bunyan* (1941), *Peter Grimes* (1945), and *The Rape of Lucretia* (1946), as well as his orchestral works.

I §		Walztes [sic], op. 3	Faber
		Five waltzes of which the last is in a variation structure.	

E (Early Intermediate)   I (Intermediate)   A (Advanced Intermediate to Advanced)

A	Three Character Pieces (1930)	Faber
A	Moderato and Nocturne (1940)	Faber

These two movements are the posthumously published first and second movements of Britten's self-rejected (never published) four-movement *Sonatina Romantica*.

Cage, John (Milton) (Jr.) (1912-1992) USA (b. Los Angeles, CA; d. New York, NY)

A composer, philosopher, poet and music theorist, Cage is considered one of the most influential American composers of the 20th century. He studied at UCLA with composer Arthur Schönberg and explored new sounds and ways of creating music including "chance" or aleatoric music and music for prepared pianos. Two of his most important collaborators were dancer Merce Cunningham and painter Robert Rauschenberg.

E		A Valentine Out of Season (1944)	Peters
E	§	4' 33" (1952)	Peters

With no pitches to be played, this very well may be the most famous "composition" of the modern era and certainly of Cage's output. The score itself is very interesting to see. The performer(s) does not produce any sound from the instrument. Through this composition, Cage broke all traditions of classical music. Through musical silence, both the performer and audience are engaged in listening without an instrument being touched. *4' 33"* can work as a novelty piece on a recital.

I	Prelude for Meditation (1944)	Peters
I	Suite for Toy Piano (or piano)	Peters

Consists of five short movements based on a limited number of tones. It was originally written to support dance choreography. A curious aspect of the piece is that the wide dynamic range could never be achieved on a true toy piano with a limited register.

A	Sonatas and Interludes (1946-48)	Peters

This work, which explores far Eastern sounds, is the composer's signature work for prepared piano.

Casadesus, Robert (1899–1972) France (b. and d. Paris, France)

Casadesus was a composer and concert pianist who toured throughout Europe and the United States. He met Ravel in 1922 and they became friends and colleagues. Casadesus traveled and studied with Ravel and was a leading proponent of his music. Casadesus became head of the piano department of the American Conservatory at Fontainebleau, France in 1935. His works include seven symphonies, concertos for one, two and three pianos, as well as numerous instrumental concerti and chamber works.

I	Six Enfantines, op. 48 (1955)	Durand
I-A	24 Préludes, op. 5 (1924), Vols. I–IV	Max Eschig

Casella, Alfredo (1883–1947) Italy (b. Turin, Italy; d. Rome, Italy)

Casella went to the Paris Conservatory in 1896 to study piano under Louis Diémer and composition under Gabriel Fauré. He was a noted piano virtuoso and performed with Arturo Bonucci (cello) and Alberto Poltronieri (violin), as the *Trio Italiano*, touring to acclaim in Europe and the U.S. He also made player piano rolls for the Aeolian Duo-Art system, which can still be heard today. His compositional style was influenced by late romanticism and early 20th century modernism embracing jazz and mildly dissonant harmonic clashes.

I	11 Pièces enfantines, op. 35 (1920)	Universal
I	Inezie, op. 32 (1918)	Masters Music
A	Sonatina, op. 28 (1916)	Masters Music

Contemporary Literature from 1900 *continued*

Chávez, Carlos (Antonio de Padua Cháves y Ramírez) (1899–1978) Mexico (b. Popotla, near Mexico City, Mexico; d. Coyoacán, Mexico City, Mexico)

A noted composer, conductor, teacher and music critic, early in his career Chávez was Director of the National Conservatory in Mexico (1928-1934). Later, in 1958-59 he was appointed to the Charles Eliot Norton Professorial Chair at Harvard. His music reflects Mexican, Indian, and Spanish-Mexican influences and includes five ballets, seven symphonies, four concertos, a cantata and opera, and pieces for voice, piano, and chamber ensemble. His book, *Toward A New Music: Music and Electricity*, is considered a significant contribution to the literature.

I-A	Sonatina (four movements)	Boosey & Hawkes
I-A	Waltzes and Other Dances for Piano (1919-1925) (Lifchitz, ed.)	Schirmer

These early works include: *Valses Intimos* (I, II, III, IV), *Vals Elegia, Valses Moderato, A Fox Trot,* and *Cakewalk*.

A	Ten Preludes	Schirmer

Copland, Aaron (1900–1990) USA (b. New York, NY; d. Tarrytown, NY)

A highly respected American pianist, conductor, teacher, writer and composer, Copland went to Paris in 1921-24 as a student at the American Conservatory at Fontainebleau, France where he studied with Nadia Boulanger. His music includes works that reflect American jazz and folk elements, *Billy the Kid* (1938) and *Rodeo* (1942), as well as the film scores for *Of Mice and Men* (1938), *Our Town* (1940) and *The Heiress* (1948). He won the Pulitzer Prize for his ballet *Appalachian Spring* (1944). Along with his friend Roger Sessions, he founded the Copland-Sessions concert series presenting works of young composers. His many awards include the Presidential Medal of Freedom in 1964.

E	Down a Country Lane (1962)	Boosey & Hawkes
E	In Evening Air	Boosey & Hawkes
E	Midsummer Nocturne	Boosey & Hawkes
E	Three Moods (1921)	Boosey & Hawkes
E	Two Children's Pieces	Carl Fischer

(Sunday Afternoon Music, The Young Pioneers)

I	Scherzo Humoristique (The Cat and the Mouse) (1920)	Durand

One of Copland's most successful piano solos, this piece was written very early in his career when he studied with Nadia Boulanger. The musical imagery and programmatic story line make the work incredibly popular with students.

I-A § *	Four Piano Blues (1, 3)	Boosey & Hawkes

The movements are subtitled 1. *Freely Poetic,* 2. *Soft and the Languid,* 3. *Muted and Sensuous,* and 4. *With Bounce.* Freely Poetic is most accessible and achieves an improvisational feel through the use of mixed meter. The wide left-hand stretches can be redistributed for smaller hands.

A §	Passacaglia (1922)	Salabert

Passacaglia is an early work written during Copland's student days under the supervision of Nadia Boulanger, to whom he dedicated the work.

A §	Piano Album	Boosey & Hawkes

This superb collection includes many early pieces by Copland which are otherwise either out of print or difficult to locate. Contents include: *Petit Portrait, Down a Country Lane, Midsummer Nocturne, In Evening Air, Four Piano Blues* (numbers 1 and 4), *Saturday Night Waltz, Sentimental Melody, The Resting-Place on the Hill, The Young Pioneers,* and *Sunday Afternoon Music.*

E (Early Intermediate)   I (Intermediate)   A (Advanced Intermediate to Advanced)

A		Variations (1930)	Boosey & Hawkes

        Consisting of a theme, 20 variations and *coda*, this work represents a musical pinnacle in 20th century variation writing. Mixed meter, austere serial-like writing using four notes, and interesting effects (overtones from silently depressed keys) characterize the writing.

Cowell, Henry (1897–1965) USA (b. Menlo Park, CA; d. Shady, NY)

A pianist, violinist, teacher and composer, Cowell was noted for his new compositional techniques including tone clusters and "string piano" (strumming or plucking inside the piano). He taught at the New School for Social Research in New York as well as Peabody Conservatory and Columbia University. Many of his late works were based on American folk music.

I	Bounce Dance	Merion
I	The Irishman Dances	Carl Fischer
I	The Irish Minstrel Sings	Carl Fischer
I	Sway Dance	Presser
I-A	Piano Works, Vol. I	Associated

        Includes some of Cowell's most famous works including *The Tides of Manaunaun, The Banshee,* and *Aeolian Harp.*

Creston, Paul (Giuseppe Guttoveggio) (1906–1985) USA (b. New York, NY; d. Poway, CA)

Born of Italian heritage, Creston studied piano and organ but was largely a self-taught composer studying works of great composers. He Americanized his name and found work as a theater organist for silent movies and later as organist for St. Malachy's Church in New York. He received two Guggenheim Fellowships and taught at the Cummington School of the Arts in Massachusetts. He wrote numerous scores for radio and television, five symphonies, concertos for violin, piano, saxophone, and marimba, as well as choral, chamber, and instrumental pieces.

I	Five Little Dances, op. 24	Schirmer

        Contents: *Festive Dance, Languid Dance, Pastoral Dance, Rustic Dance,* and *Toy Dance.*

Dello Joio, Norman (1913-2008) USA (b. New York, NY; d. East Hampton, NY)

A church organist, pianist and composer, Dello Joio first studied piano with his father and organ with his godfather, Pietro Yon, who was organist at St. Patrick's Cathedral. He studied composition first at the Juilliard School and later with Hindemith at Yale. He received numerous awards and grants including two Guggenheim Fellowships. He won the New York Music Critics' Circle Award twice (1948 and 1962), the Pulitzer Prize in 1957 for *Meditations on Ecclesiastes* for string orchestra and an Emmy Award for his music in the television special *Scenes from the Louvre*. Dello Joio was a prolific composer who taught at Sarah Lawrence College, the Mannes College of Music, and Boston University. He helped establish a program sponsored by the Ford Foundation that placed young composers in high school residencies.

E	§	Suite for the Young (ten easy pieces)	Schirmer

        Represents Dello Joio's easiest writing. The well-known *Lullaby* is very lyrical, uses *legato* double note thirds in the right hand, and touches of damper pedal.

I	§ *	Lyric Pieces for the Young (*Prayer of the Matador, Street Cries*)	Marks

        A superior and frequently heard collection of six late intermediate pieces, *Prayer of the Matador* uses a Habanera rhythm similar to Debussy's *La Puerta del Vino*. The other titles are *Boat Song, Night Song, Village Church,* and *Russian Dancer.*

I	Prelude: To a Young Dancer (1945)	Schirmer

Contemporary Literature from 1900 *continued*

I	§	Prelude: To a Young Musician (1944)	Schirmer
I-A	§	Diversions (5 pieces)	Hal Leonard

Consists of a *Preludio, Arietta, Caccia, Chorale,* and *Giga.* This is an overlooked set which is deserving of greater attention. The *Chorale* is based on the tune, "Good Christian Men, Rejoice."

I-A		Norman Dello Joio Piano Music (selections)	Associated Music/Hal Leonard
I-A		Salute to Scarlatti-A Suite of Sonatas (for piano or harpsichord)	Schirmer
A		Short Intervallic Etudes (for Well Tempered Pianists)	Schirmer
A		Suite for Piano	Schirmer

Of the four movements, the fourth toccata-like movement (*Fast, with ferocity*) is the most challenging.

Dett, Nathaniel, R. (Robert) USA (1882–1943) Canada
(b. Drummondville (Niagara Falls), Ontario; d. Battle Creek, Michigan)

Dett was a composer, pianist, teacher and choral director and the first African-American musician to earn an undergraduate music degree in piano and composition from Oberlin Conservatory. During his career, he taught at several colleges and universities including Northwestern University. His best-known piano composition is the *Juba-Dance* which appears in various anthologies.

I-A	*	Desert Interlude (no. 2 from *Eight Bible Vignettes*)	Mills

Each Vignette in the *Eight Bible Vignettes* is published separately. Titles include: *Father Abraham, As His Own Soul, Barcarolle of Tears, I Am the True Vine, Martha Complained, Other Sheep,* and *Madrigal Divine. Desert Interlude* is appealing with its Satie-like colors.

I-A	§	In the Bottoms (Suite caractéristique)	Masters Music

A suite in five movements, *Prelude (Night), His Song, Honey (Humoresque), Barcarolle (Morning), Dance (Juba),* this is Dett's best-known piano work.

A		The Collected Piano Works (Gowe, ed.)	Alfred

Though currently out of print, this is an excellent "find" for enthusiasts of Dett's music.

A	§	Juba-Dance from the Suite In the Bottoms (Gowe, ed.)	Alfred

Diamond, David (1915-2005) USA (b. Rochester, NY; d. Brighton, New York)

Diamond began his violin and composition studies at the Cleveland Institute of Music and later at the Eastman School of Music. He also tutored with Roger Sessions and Nadia Boulanger. As an up and coming American composer, he received numerous grants and awards including three Guggenheim Fellowships, the *Prix de Rome*, and a National Academy of Arts and Letters Grant. From 1952-1965 he lived and worked in Europe as a Fulbright Professor settling in Florence, Italy. On his return to the U.S., he taught at the Manhattan School of Music from 1965 to 1967 and received the Rheta Sosland Chamber Music prize for his String Quartet no. 8, the Stravinsky ASCAP award, and election to the National Institute of Arts and Letters. He became Professor of Composition at the Juilliard School in 1973 where he taught for more than two decades. Other significant honors include the William Schuman Lifetime Achievement Award, the Edward MacDowell Gold Medal for Lifetime Achievement and, in 1995, the National Medal of Arts in a ceremony at the White House. Diamond is best known for his numerous works for orchestra, chamber music and songs for voice and piano.

E	Album for the Young (ten pieces) (1946)	Presser
E	Eight Piano Pieces (based on nursery rhymes)	Schirmer

(*Pease-porridge hot, Jumping jacks, The old Mr. Turtle, Handy-spandy jack-a-dandy, Jack and Jill, Rock-a-bye, baby, Little jumping Joan,* and *Lullaby*)

I		Sonatina for Piano (1935)	Presser
		(*Largo assai, Allegretto, Allegro Vivace*)	
I		Then and Now (11 short contemporary sounding pieces)	Presser

Donhányi, Ernst von (1877-1960) Hungary (b. Bragislava, Hungary; d. Tallahassee, FL)

Donhnányi is known as a great Hungarian pianist, composer, and conductor and is ranked by some as the country's most versatile Hungarian musician next to Liszt and Bartók. He served on the faculty of the Berlin *Hochschule* (1905-1915) and then returned to Budapest to take a more active part in his homeland's musical development, supporting Hungarian composers such as Bartók and Kodály. He served as conductor for the Budapest Philharmonic Society (1919-1944), and later the New York State Symphony Orchestra. In 1949, he accepted a position at Florida State College in Tallahassee where he continued to teach, perform and conduct until his death in 1960. Donhnányi wrote in virtually every genre including three operas and two symphonies, three string quartets and two piano quintets, but is best-known for his *Variations on a Nursery Song*, a work for piano and orchestra based on Twinkle, Twinkle, Little Star.

E-I	§	Albumleaf (1899)	Editio Musica Budapest
		This work is a two-page short character piece.	
I-A		Complete Rhapsodies and other works for solo piano	Dover
		This volume contains Donhányi's most important piano solos.	

Dring, Madeleine (Winefride Isabelle) (1923–1977) Great Britain

A composer, pianist and actress, Dring combined her love of theatre and music, composing incidental music for stage and television. She studied at the Royal College of Music from the age of nine where her composition teachers included Ralph Vaughan Williams, Herbert Howells, and Gordon Jacob. She composed solo piano and chamber music as well as works for oboe (*Dances* for solo oboe) written for her husband Roger Lord, principal oboist with the London Symphony Orchestra. She also wrote a one-act opera, *Cupboard Love*, and a dance drama, *The Fair Queen of Wu*.

E	Twelve Pieces in the Form of Studies	Marks
I	A Colour Suite	Arcadia
I	Three Dances: Mazurka, Pavane, and Ländler	Cambria

Dutkiewicz, Andrzej (b. 1942) USA (b. Staszów, Poland)

A composer, pianist and professor, Dutkiewicz studied at the Chopin National Music Academy in Warsaw in both piano and composition. He earned the D.M.A. at the Eastman School of Music in 1976 studying with Samuel Adler and George Crumb in composition and with Eugene List in piano. He began his teaching career at the Chopin National Music Academy in Warsaw in 1972 becoming full professor in 1991. From 1999-2005 he served as Dean of the Department of Piano, Harpsichord and Organ. He then became Head of the Contemporary Music Studies program. He is known as a pianist specializing in contemporary music performance and has given guest lectures at over 50 American universities. Dutkiewicz has performed throughout Europe, Asia and North and South America. His compositions include works for orchestra, chamber music and piano.

E	§	The Puppet Suite (15 early intermediate pieces)	Kjos
		This is an outstanding collection of easy contemporary compositions.	
I		Seascapes (11 pieces)	Kjos

Evans, Bill (1929–1980) USA (b. Plainfield, NJ; d. New York, NY)

Bill Evans' music and enduring sensitive, lyrical jazz piano style have influenced musicians and composers for several decades, in particular serving as an iconic model for aspiring jazz pianists. As a child, Evans studied piano, flute and violin, exploring composers such as Debussy, Stravinsky and

Contemporary Literature from 1900 *continued*

Milhaud. He graduated from Southeastern Louisiana University in 1950 and also studied composition at Mannes College of Music in New York. Evans performed with many jazz greats and recorded over fifty albums receiving five Grammy awards. Many of his original tunes, such as *Waltz for Debby*, have become "standards" for jazz pianists. Considered by many to be the most important jazz pianist since 1950, his style has influenced current jazz pianists such as Chick Corea and Herbie Hancock.

A	The Artistry of Bill Evans, Vols. I, II (Esposito, ed.)	Alfred
	These two volumes include transcriptions of famous Evans' transcriptions including *Seascape*, *The Summer Knows* (theme from the movie, Summer of 42), *A Time of Love*, and *Here's That Rainy Day*.	
A	Solo Transcriptions (five volumes)	TRO

Fernandez, Oscar Lorenzo (1897–1948) Brazil (b. and d. Rio de Janeiro, Brazil)

Fernandez was a nationalist composer inspired by Brazilian folk music. He studied and later taught at the *Instituto Nacional de Música* and served on the faculty of the *Conservatório Nacional de Canto Orfeônico*. His works include a ballet, an opera, orchestral music, concertos for piano and violin, chamber music, choral music, songs and many compositions for piano.

I		Children's Visions (three pieces)	Peer International
I		Dolls (five pieces)	Peer International
I	§	Suite das 5 Notas (eight short pieces)	Peer International
I		Yaya, The Doll	Peer International

Finney, Ross Lee (1906–1997) USA (b. Wells, MN; d. Carmel, CA)

Finney began his musical studies by playing jazz guitar and piano. He received a B.A. from Carleton College in 1927 and later traveled to Paris to study composition with Nadia Boulanger. He also studied at Harvard, with Alban Berg in Vienna, and lifelong friend, Roger Sessions. He received many awards throughout his career including two Guggenheim Fellowships, a Pulitzer Prize in 1927, the Boston Symphony Award, the Brandeis Medal, and an appointment to the American Academy of Arts and Sciences. From 1949 until 1974 he was Professor of Music and Composer-in-Residence at the University of Michigan, heading both the Composition Department and a graduate program in composition with students including William Albright, Leslie Bassett, and George Crumb.

E	§	32 Piano Games (1969)	Peters
		This innovative set, very forward looking at the time it was published, explores wide keyboard registers and forms of alternate, non-traditional notation in pieces for less advanced pupils. Techniques include bar-less and cluster writing, mirror writing, and innovative use of repeating patterns.	
I		Inventions (twenty-four pieces)	Peters
I-A		Youth's Companion (Five Short Pieces, Riddle Song) (1981)	Peters
		(*Hawk over the Prairie*, *Pasque Flowers on the Hill*, *Jack Rabbit*, *The Town Dump*, and *Riddle Song*)	
A	*	Nostalgic Waltzes (five waltzes) (no. 1)	Mercury

Floyd, Carlisle (b. 1926) USA (b. Latta, SC)

Floyd served as *Distinguished Professor* on the Florida State University music faculty for many years teaching first piano and then composition. He is best known for his operatic writing of which *Susannah* is best known. His many recognitions include a Guggenheim Fellowship, the National Medal of Arts from the White House, (2004) and lifetime Opera Honoree from the National Endowment for the Arts (2008)

| I-A § | Episodes, Vols. I, II | Boosey & Hawkes |

* Vol. I (13 pieces; Chorale); II (12 pieces; Impromptu)

The *Episodes* are effective intermediate contemporary pieces and an important pedagogical collection. Vol. II is slightly more difficult. Vol. I titles: *First Lyric Piece, Second Lyric Piece, Scherzino, Third Lyric Piece, Fourth Lyric Piece, Marching Hymn, An Ancient Air, Arietta, Lullaby, Chorale, Ballad, Pavane,* and *Serenade.*

Gershwin, George (1898–1937) USA (b. Brooklyn, NY; d. Beverly Hills, CA)

Born Jacob Gershowitz into a Russian-Jewish immigrant family, Gershwin composed, with lyricist Irving Ceaser, his first hit song *Swanee* in 1919. *Swanee* went on to sell over a million copies. In later years and throughout the rest of his life, he collaborated with his brother, lyricist Ira Gershwin, on a series of hits including the musical comedy *Lady Be Good* with songs such as "Fascinating Rhythm" and "The Man I Love" and the musicals *Oh Kay!* and *Funny Face*. He also composed major works merging elements of jazz with classical forms including the landmark *Rhapsody in Blue,* the *Piano Concerto in F,* and *An American in Paris*. Gershwin died suddenly at the young age of 38 of a brain tumor. A brilliant pianist and composer, Gershwin is considered one of America's most noted and influential musicians.

| I | George Gershwin for Piano | Hal Leonard |
| A | The Complete Gershwin Keyboard Works (Zizzo, ed.) | Alfred |

The title of this volume is misleading because it does not include all the Gershwin keyboard works, however, it does include his three preludes and unfinished drafts of other preludes as prepared by the composer.

| A | George Gershwin for Piano | Alfred |
| A § * | Gershwin Transcriptions for Piano (Hinson, ed.) | Alfred |

(18 Song Hits Arranged by the Composer)

This recent edition replaces the former Warner edition of the Gershwin song transcriptions for piano. Many teachers are familiar with Gershwin's *Preludes* but not the *Songs*. Most of the song arrangements, which are piano solo transcriptions based on the vocal tunes, are two to three pages in length and sound improvisational. Aside from their attractive melodies and rhythmic excitement, they are excellent study material for any skilled student interested in arranging. Two of the most challenging are the *The Man I Love* and *I Got Rhythm.*

| A | Impromptu in Two Keys | Schott |
| A § * | Preludes (2, 1, 3) | New World |

Every pianist and teacher should know these three preludes. They are commonly performed and accepted as part of the standard teaching and piano literature. The second prelude is a beautiful 12-bar blues with soulful melody over engaging harmonies.

| A | Two Waltzes in C | Schott |

Ginastera, Alberto (Evaristo) (1916–1983) Argentina (b. Buenos Aires; d. Geneva, Switzerland)

One of Argentina's most important composers, Ginastera was a nationalistic composer who combined Argentine folk elements with contemporary techniques. He visited the United States in 1945 on a Guggenheim grant. He served as Dean of the School of Music, Sciences and Arts at the Argentine Catholic University, and Professor at the La Plata University. In 1968, Yale University awarded him an honorary doctorate. His output includes music for opera, ballet, orchestra, choir, and concertos for several instruments, as well as music for theater and film.

Contemporary Literature from 1900 *continued*

I		Rondo on Argentine Children's Folk Tunes	Boosey & Hawkes
I-A	§ *	12 American Preludes (Vol. I: 2, 4, 5, 3, 6; Vol. II: 8, 10, 12, 7, 9, 11)	Carl Fischer

Ginastera made a lasting contribution to the teaching literature with these preludes. Long published in two separate volumes of six preludes each, they now are available in one volume. The *American Preludes* focus on a variety of textures and sounds and range in difficulty from intermediate to early advanced. *For Accents* and *Sadness* introduce the set nicely. *Creole Dance* and *Tribute to Roberto Garcia Morillo* are perfect as a climax for any student recital. Some of the preludes are tributes to other composers such as Aaron Copland (no. 9), and Villa-Lobos (no. 11). This is a collection well worth studying and teaching.

A	§ *	Danzas Argentinas (three dances; 2, 1, 3)	Durand

The beautiful slow middle movement, *Danza de la moza donosa* (Dance of the Beautiful Maiden), with a climatic middle section is recommended for introducing the set. The outer movements are *Danza del viejo boyero* (Dance of the Old Herdsman) and the more challenging, *Danza del gaucho matrero* (Dance of the Arrogant Cowboy).

A	Sonata No. 1, op. 22 (1952)	Hal Leonard

Of the composer's three sonatas, with numbers two and three composed in the early 1980s, no. 1 is an established sonata of the modern repertoire along with singular works such as the piano sonatas by Béla Bartók and Samuel Barber. Not that long (ca 15') when compared to larger sonatas from the Classical and Romantic periods, the four movements are, *Allegro marcato, Presto misterioso, Adagio molto appassionato,* and *Ruvido ed ostinato.*

Grainger, (George) Percy (Aldridge) (1882–1961) USA
(b. Brighton/Melbourne, Australia; d. White Plains, NY)

A virtuoso pianist, music teacher, composer and arranger, Grainger was born in Australia but moved to Frankfurt in 1895 at the age of 13 to study music. He lived in London from 1901 to 1914 where he became friends with and performed the music of Grieg. At the start of World War I, Grainger returned to the United States and joined the U.S. Army Band in 1917 playing oboe and saxophone. He became a U.S. citizen in 1918 and taught in Chicago and New York. Grainger experimented with contemporary idioms including "string piano", electronic music and a new style of orchestration called "elastic orchestrations." His *Country Gardens* is his best-known composition which has been arranged for many instrumental combinations.

I	§	Country Gardens	Schirmer
I		Young Pianist Grainger (Stevenson, ed.)	Scott

This volume contains 15 compositions some of which are original and others simplified arrangements.

A	A Percy Grainger Piano Album	Schirmer

Gretchaninoff (Grechaninov), Alexander Tikhonovich (1864–1956) Russia
(b. Moscow, Russia; d. New York, NY)

Gretchaninov began his studies at the Moscow Conservatory in 1881 with Sergei Taneyev and Anton Arensky later moving to St. Petersburg to study composition and orchestration with Nikolai Rimsky-Korsakov. After the Revolution, he immigrated to France in 1925 and then to the United States in 1939 where he became an American citizen. He was a prolific composer who wrote symphonies, string quartets, piano solos, piano trios, sonatas for violin, cello, clarinet, and balalaika, operas and a song cycle *Les Fleurs du Mal.*

E	§	Children's Book, op. 98	Schott
E		Five Miniatures for Piano, op. 196	Marks
E		Grandfather's Book, op. 119 (seventeen pieces)	Kalmus, Schott
I		Eight Pastels, op. 61	Kalmus
I		Glass Beads, op. 123 (twelve pieces) (*Palmer, ed.)	*Alfred; Kalmus; Schott
I-A		Five Little Pieces, op. 3	Kalmus
I	§	The Gretchaninoff Collection (20 pieces) (Hinson, ed.)	Schott

Hanson, Howard (1896–1981) USA (b. Wahoo, NE; d. Rochester, NY)

Hanson was an influential and prominent American composer, conductor and educator. He began his musical studies at Luther College in Nebraska later studying at Northwestern University in Illinois. He taught theory and composition at the College of the Pacific in San Jose, California and became Dean of the Conservatory of Fine Arts in 1919. His works combine elements of his Scandinavian heritage with American influences in a neo-Romantic style. From 1924 to 1964, Hanson held the position of *Director* of the Eastman School of Music in Rochester, New York. In 1935, Hanson was elected to membership in the National Institute of Arts and Letters. He received the Pulitzer Prize in 1944 for his *Symphony no. 4* (Requiem).

I-A		The Bell	Carl Fischer

Other late intermediate solos published by Fischer include *Clog Dance, Dance of the Warriors,* and *Enchantment.*

I-A	§	For the First Time: Twelve Impressions in a Child's Day	Carl Fischer
I-A		Three Miniatures, op. 12 (Reminiscence, Lullaby, Longing)	Carl Fischer

Harris, Roy (1898–1979) USA (b. Chandler, OK; d. Santa Monica, CA)

A noted American composer and conductor, Harris studied in Paris with Nadia Boulanger on a Guggenheim Fellowship. As a cultural ambassador for the U.S. State Department, he was the first American composer to conduct his own works with the Leningrad Philharmonic in Russia. He received numerous awards and honors including election to the American Institute and Academy of Arts and Letters, and the title of *Composer Laureate* of the State of California. Harris and his wife, concert piano virtuoso, Johana Harris, were guests during the administrations of several presidents, including John Kennedy. Harris taught at Princeton, Cornell, Peabody College for Teachers in Nashville, TN, Indiana University, and UCLA.

I-A	American Ballads (original settings of 5 American folk tunes)	Carl Fischer

(*Streets of Laredo, Wayfaring stranger, The bird, Black is the color of my true love's hair, Cod liver ile*)

I-A	Little Suite for Piano	Schirmer

Hindemith, Paul (1895–1963) Germany (b. and d. Frankfurt, Germany)

A violist, violinist, teacher, conductor, and composer, Hindemith is regarded by many as one of Germany's most important contemporary composers. He served as Professor of Composition at the *Hochschule für Musik* in Berlin. His beliefs about music and its social purpose brought him into conflict with the National Socialist Party from 1933-1947 which led to many of his works being banned by the Nazi party. Hindemith resigned from his teaching post in Berlin in 1938, later immigrating to America in 1940 and attaining citizenship in 1946. He taught at Yale University and Tanglewood (where his pupils included Leonard Bernstein). Hindemith resigned from Yale in 1953 and returned to Europe to teach at the University of Zurich in Switzerland. One of the major composers of the 20th century, Hindemith discusses his musical philosophy in *The Craft of Musical Composition*. He is best known for his many chamber sonatas composed for each instrument of the orchestra and piano.

Contemporary Literature from 1900 *continued*

E	§	Wir bauen eine Stadt (Let's Build a City)	Schott
I		Kleine Klaviermusik (12 pieces)	Schott
I-A	§	The Hindemith Collection (Hinson, ed.)	Schott

For those unfamiliar with Hindemith's output, this is a superior introductory collection which includes 10 compositions organized by level of difficulty.

I-A	Ludus Tonalis	Schott

(Studies in Counterpoint, Tonal Organization and Piano Playing) (1943)

This collection is a contemporary version of Bach's Well-Tempered Clavier. It represents 25 piano pieces consisting of 12 fugues, each separated by an *Interludium*, with the entire work framed by an opening *Praludium* and closing *Postludium*.

A	Sonata no. 2	Schott

Hindemith wrote three solo piano sonatas. Each composed in 1936, no. 2 is the most accessible. It comprises three movements, the opening *sonata-allegro* and final *Rondo* with *Scherzo* interspersed.

Honegger, Arthur (1892–1955) Switzerland (b. Le Havre, France; d. Paris, France)

Born in Le Havre, of Swiss heritage, Honegger maintained his Swiss nationality throughout his life. Violinist and composer, he was a member of a French group of young composers known as "Les Six" along with Poulenc and Milhaud. He wrote five symphonies, choral works, chamber music and works for solo piano.

I	§	Souvenir de Chopin	Choudens
I-A		Piano Album	Hal Leonard

An excellent compilation of Honegger's piano writing including the *Souvenir de Chopin*.

Hovhaness, Alan (Chakmakjian, Alan Hovhaness) (1911-2000) USA (Armenian heritage) (b. Somerville [Boston], MA; d. Seattle, WA)

An American organist and composer, Hovahaness' father was Armenian and his mother of Scottish ancestry. In 1940, he became organist at Boston's Armenian Cathedral. His awards include a 1959 Fulbright grant to study the Carnatic system of music in South India and a Rockefeller grant in 1962 to study music of the Far East. His music reflects elements of his Armenian heritage and Indian and Asian cultures, but always within a tonal or modal context.

E		Sketchbook of Mr. Purple Poverty, Vols. I, II	Broude

There are 13 selections in each book. Vol. I does not use key signatures.

I		Mountain Idylls (Moon Lullaby, Moon Dance, Mountain Lullaby)	Associated
I		Mystic Flute, op. 22	Peters
I		Slumber Song, Siris' Dance, op. 52, nos. 2, 3	MCA
I	§	Twelve Armenian Folk Songs, op. 43	Peters
I		Two Ghazals, op. 36	Peters
A	§	Komachi, op. 240 (7 character pieces)	Peters

Joplin, Scott (1868–1917) USA (b. Texas; d. Manhattan, NY)

A pianist, cornet player, violinist, teacher, conductor and composer, Joplin was born near Linden, Texas. His father was a former slave and the records of Joplin's birth are not exact. He eventually settled and grew up in Sedalia, Missouri, later playing cornet in the Queen City Band and forming his own band. He traveled and performed throughout the United States and in Sedalia at the famous

"Maple Leaf" club. He is most famous for his piano rags. During his lifetime he received modest recognition and success. It was not until more than 50 years later, after a revival of ragtime music partially inspired by the use of Joplin's music in the movie *The Sting*, which won an academy award for its film score, that he received proper recognition for his significant achievements. Joplin was given a *posthumous* Pulitzer Prize award in 1976 for his contribution to American music and for his opera *Treemonisha*.

A	At the Piano with Joplin (Hinson, ed.)	Alfred
A	Celebrate Joplin (Hisey, ed.)	Frederick Harris

Students benefit technically and musically by studying the compositions of this talented American composer. This excellent edition includes the composer's instructions on how to play ragtime (School of Ragtime) and favorites such as *Maple Leaf Rag* as well as lesser-known titles deserving of more attention.

A	Collected Piano Works	Schott
A	Complete Piano Rags	Alfred

Contains 38 Joplin piano rags including six collaborations.

Kabalevsky, Dmitri Borisovich (1904–1987) (b. St. Petersburg, Russia; d. Moscow, Russia)

A pianist, teacher, composer, and writer, Kabalevsky first studied at the Scriabin Musical Institute and in 1925 began his training at the Moscow Conservatory in composition and piano. He became a professor at the Moscow Conservatory in 1932 and was a founding member and official of the Union of Composers. Kabalevsky joined the Communist Party in 1940 and later received the Medal of Honor from the Soviet government in recognition of his musical contributions. He had an important influence on Soviet music education and was elected Head of the Commission of Musical Esthetic Education of Children in 1962 and President of the Scientific Council of Educational Esthetics in the Academy of Pedagogical Sciences of the USSR in 1969. He composed cantatas, operas and orchestral music as well as music for the stage and radio. Though he composed advanced works for many genres including piano, he is most noted for his large body of piano music for children.

E	28 Piano Pieces (Kabalevskaya [Kabalevsky's daughter], ed.)	Hal Leonard
E-I §	Children's Pieces, op. 27	Boosey & Hawkes

Kabalevsky's most well-known early intermediate pieces are in this collection of thirty compositions including *Étude in A Minor*, *Toccatina*, *Scherzo*, and *Novelette*.

E-I §	Twenty-four Pieces for Children, op. 39 (Palmer, ed.)	Alfred

Unfortunately, many Kabalevsky collections mix and match pieces from opp. 27 and 39 without distinguishing the difference. Familiar titles from op. 39 include *A Little Joke, March, Scherzo, Waltz,* and the well-known *Clowns*.

I	At the Piano with Kabalevsky (Hinson, ed.)	Alfred
I §	Five Easy Sets of Variations, op. 51	Schirmer

Generally, these variation sets are easier and superior to the two variation sets in op. 40. Each variation set is based on a different folk song, Russian (1 and 2), Slovak (3), and Ukrainian (4 and 5).

I	Four Little Pieces, op. 14	MCA
I	Four Preludes, op. 5	MCA
I	Sonatinas, op. 13, no. 1, 2	Boosey & Hawkes

These two sonatinas are part of the core of important contemporary sonatinas.

Contemporary Literature from 1900 *continued*

I	§	Toccatina	MCA
I-A	§	Twenty-Four Preludes, op. 38 (1, 15)	Peters

Kabalevsky is best known for his many elementary and early intermediate teaching pieces such as *Clowns* (op. 39, no. 20) and *Toccatina* (op. 27, no. 12). Composed during WWII, this set of *Preludes* represents Kabalevsky's more advanced, abstract writing and borrows the key arrangement used by Chopin in his preludes. The preludes are based on Russian folksongs from the Rimsky-Korsakov collection and were often performed by Vladimir Horowitz.

I-A		Variations, op. 40 (two sets)	MCA
A	§	Four Rondos, op. 60	Schirmer

This edition, based on the Library of Russian-Soviet Music, contains these early advanced Rondos, each two to three pages in length, of which no. III is the easiest. The four rondos are subtitled *March, Dance, Song,* and *Toccata*.

A		6 Preludes and Fugues, op. 61	Hal Leonard

Kadosa, Pál (1903–1983) Hungary (b. Levice, Czech Republic; d. Budapest, Hungary)

A noted concert pianist and composer, Kadosa studied composition with Kodály and later taught piano at the Budapest (Franz Liszt) Academy from 1921 to 1927. He also served as vice-president of the Hungarian Arts Council (1945 - 1949), a member of the Hungarian Composers' Union (1949 - 1953), and as president of the nation's performing rights bureau. He received many awards and honors in Hungary and an honorary membership in the Royal Academy of Music, London, in 1967.

E	Kaleidoscopes, op. 61	Boosey & Hawkes
E-I	55 Small Piano Pieces, Books I, II	Boosey & Hawkes
I	Six Little Preludes	Universal
I	24 Easy Technical Studies	Boosey & Hawkes
A	Sonatina, op. 11/b	Boosey & Hawkes

Kennan, Kent (1913-2003) USA (b. Milwaukee, WI; d. Austin, TX)

Kennan first studied at the University of Michigan and later received his B.M. and M.M. from the Eastman School of Music. He is well known to college music students as the author of two important music theory texts, *Technique of Orchestration* and *Counterpoint*. He served as Professor of Music at the University of Texas in Austin for the majority of his teaching career. His many awards include the prestigious *Prix de Rome* award in composition (1936).

I-A		Retrospectives	Schirmer
A	§	Three Preludes for the Piano (1938)	Schirmer

Though not as well known as the Gershwin Preludes, this set, comprised of two fast outer movements with a chorale-like texture for the middle prelude, has received deserved recognition.

Khachaturian, Aram Il'yich (1903–1978) (b. Tbilisi, Georgia, Russia; d. Moscow, Russia)

An Armenian cellist, teacher, composer and author, Khachaturian began his studies at the Gnessin Institute in 1925, transferring in 1929 to the Moscow National Conservatory while also completing a degree in biology at Moscow State University. His awards and honors included being elected as a member of the Armenian Soviet Republic's Academy of Sciences and designated an honorary member of the Italian Music Academy "Santa Cecilia" (1960) as well as an honorary professor of the Mexican Conservatory (1960). His works feature elements of Armenian folk-music and his "Sabre Dance" from the ballet *Gayaneh* is one of the most well-known compositions of our time. (See the annotation on the *Sabre Dance* in the Two-Piano, Eight-Hands section.)

E		Album for Young People, Vol. I (Palmer, ed.)	Alfred
E-I	§	Adventures of Ivan (contained in Children's Album, Vol. I)	ASE

The pieces that comprise the *Adventures of Ivan* are included as part of the ten pieces in his Children's Album, Vol. I., however, several publishers print the *Adventures of Ivan* as a separate publication.

I		Children's Album, Vols. I, II	Peters
I	§	Sonatina (1959)	Alfred

In three movements, this is one of Khachaturian's best-known works, and an excellent piece to team with a more advanced Classical sonatina or easier sonata. The first movement (*Allegro giocoso*), with its left-hand octaves under right-hand passagework, is probably the best known. The second and third movements deserve greater attention.

A	§	Toccata (1932)	MCA

A virtual warhorse of the preparatory repertoire, the *Toccata* appeals to secondary students because of the energetic rhythms, repeating technical patterns, and brilliant *forte* colors. Specific attention must be given to the complex rhythms in the middle section.

Kodály, Zoltán (1882–1967) Hungary (b. Kecskemét, Hungary; d. Budapest, Hungary)

A composer, violinist, ethnomusicologist and educator, Kodály studied languages at the University of Budapest and composition and teaching at the Budapest Academy of Music. His study of folk music led him, along with his lifelong friend, Bartók, to travel across Hungary collecting and making phonograph recordings of folksongs, thus becoming one of the important early figures in ethnomusicology. Kodály was influential in music education, writing copious material on music education as well as composing for children. His research and writings became the basis for what we now know as the "Kodály Method" of music education including his well known "hand signs" which helped revolutionize the teaching of music singing and sight-reading.

E	Twenty-four Little Canons on the Black Keys	Boosey & Hawkes
I	Gyermektáncok (Children's Dances)	Boosey & Hawkes

Lecuona, Ernesto (1895–1963) Cuba
(b. Guanabacoa, Havana, Cuba; d. Santa Cruz de Tenerife, Canary Islands, Spain)

Arguably Cuba's greatest composer, Lecuono is well-known for both his guitar and piano compositions with *Malagueña* at the top of the list in terms of recognition and transcription for several instrumental combinations. He also composed for stage and screen receiving an Oscar nomination for *Always in my heart* (*Siempre en mi Corazon*). The Cuban actor, Desi Arnaz, was influential in bringing attention to Lecuona's music. Lecuona fled Cuba under Castro's rule and settled in Tampa, Florida during his last years. Many suggest that Lecuona was the "George Gershwin" of Cuba.

I	Malagueña (six pieces)	Hal Leonard
I-A	Lecuona, Ernesto-Piano Music	Hal Leonard

This is the definitive collection of Lecuona's piano solos.

I-A	Suite Espagnole (six pieces)	Hal Leonard

Contains: *Cordoba, Andalucia, Alhambra, Gitanerias, Guadalquivir,* and *Malagueña.*

Contemporary Literature from 1900 *continued*

SOLO LITERATURE

La Montaine, John (b. 1920) USA (b. Oak Park, IL)

A student of Nadia Boulanger and Howard Hanson, La Montaine won a Pulitzer prize in 1958 for his *Piano Concerto, op. 9*.

E		Copycats, op. 26 (canons in five finger positions)	Broude Brothers
		Almost all the canons are at the octave.	
I	§ *	A Child's Picture Book (5 pieces) (Story for a Rainy Day)	Broude Brothers
A	§	Toccata, op. 1 (1957)	Broude Brothers

Perhaps not as well known as the Khachaturian *Toccata*, this work is similar in scope and is seen on many festival lists.

Lees, Benjamin (Benjamin George Lisniansky) (1924–2010) USA (b. Harbin, Manchuria, China; d. New York, NY)

Lees was born to a Russian family in China but raised in San Francisco. A student of George Antheil, Lees was a recipient of many honors including two Guggenheim Awards, a Fulbright Award, and a Grammy nomination (2004). Guggenheim support allowed Lees to live in Europe and compose before returning to the U.S. in 1961 to pursue a career of teaching and composing. After teaching at Peabody Conservatory, the Manhattan School of Music, and the Juilliard School, Lees, in his later years, focused on composing while living in Palm Springs, CA. Lees' piano output includes thirteen compositions for piano solo, two for two pianos and three piano trios. His piano works reveal a very individualistic style--a clear formal structure (e.g., ABA), rejection of atonality in favor of a tonal center, and frequent meter changes and use of irregular rhythmic patterns. Influenced by Surrealism in Arts, dramatic intensity and unexpected surprises characterize his writing such as extreme dynamic contrasts (*ppp* to *fff*) and sudden accents.

I		Kaleidoscopes (1958)	Boosey & Hawkes

Approximately 10 min. in length and comprised of ten short pieces, this work is dedicated to the composer's daughter Janet. Each movement has its own character and unique *ostinato* patterns. The set is an excellent introduction to Lees' piano writing.

I-A		3 Preludes (1962)	Boosey & Hawkes
I-A		Toccata (1947)	Boosey & Hawkes
A	§	Fantasia (1954)	Boosey & Hawkes

A work that is seen on many festival repertoire lists for secondary students, *Fantasia* reveals Lees' early compositional style which was influenced by Bartók, Prokofiev and Stravinsky. Dramatic intensity is reinforced by a use of a wide register, sweeping unison passages and octaves.

A	Mirrors (1992-2003)	Boosey & Hawkes

It took twelve years to complete all twelve movements. Written for and premiered by Ian Hobson in 1992, 1997 and 2003, *Mirrors* is a reflection of personal musical ideas personified in each movement as a compact form. Using dotted rhythms, octaves, arpeggios and sweeping scale passages, each movement projects its own atmosphere. English expression markings are presented at the beginning of each movement: *I. Intense, II. Calmly, III. Steady, IV. Easy, Unhurried, V. Quick, precise, VI. Mysterious, probing, VII. Gentle, langorous, VIII. Quickly, IX. Steady, quiet, X. Turbulent, restless, XI. Heavy, grotesque, XII. Clangorous, turbulent.*

A	Six Ornamental Etudes (1957)	Boosey & Hawkes

These six etudes have identifiable tonal centers as focal points. The last pitch of each etude is the first pitch of the following etude. *Ostinato* patterns provide an underlying musical structure for the right hand melody.

Lutoslawski, Witold (1913–1994) Poland (b. and d. Warsaw, Poland)

A child prodigy, Lutoslawski was a pianist, conductor and composer. He studied piano and composition at the Warsaw Conservatory and mathematics at the University of Warsaw. His life, studies and career developed during a difficult political time in Poland during which he completed military training and was a prisoner–of–war in 1939, escaping to play his own piano music and transcriptions in Warsaw cafés from 1940 to 1945. During this time, he had to bow to political restrictions on composing. Even after the war, his first symphony was banned until 1947. Eventually, Lutoslawski developed his own 20th century composition style including 12–note chords (different from Schönberg's), aleatory or chance elements and various *ostinato* and harmonic patterns. Lutosławski lived in Warsaw but was active as a guest lecturer and conductor throughout Europe and the United States. He received many honors including the UNESCO Prize twice, the French order of *Commandeur des Arts et des Lettres*, and the Inamori Foundation Prize, Kyoto, for his contribution to contemporary European music. Most of his works were written for orchestra although there are important compositions for voice and chamber ensembles.

I	Popular Melodies of Poland (twelve easy pieces)	PWM
I-A	Three Pieces for the Young (1953)	PWM

Menotti, Gian Carlo (1911-2007) USA (b. Cadegliano, Italy; d. Monte Carlo, Monaco)

An Italian-American composer, director and librettist, Menotti entered the Milan Conservatory at age 13 already having composed two operas. He moved to the United States and studied at the Curtis Institute in Philadelphia (1928–33) where he became a close friend and partner with Samuel Barber. Menotti taught at the Curtis Institute from 1948 to 1955. Known primarily as an opera composer, he wrote the first radio and television operas and achieved international fame with *The Medium* (1946), *The Telephone* (1947), *The Consul* (1950) and the television opera *Amahl and the Night Visitors* (1951). Menotti wrote the librettos for his own operas and for Barber's *Vanessa*. He also wrote works for Beverly Sills (opera *La loca*, 1979) and Placido Domingo (opera *Goya,* 1986). In 1958 he founded the Festival of Two Worlds summer festival in Spoleto and later in Charleston, S.C. His first full-length opera, *The Consul*, received a Pulitzer Prize. In 1984, Menotti was awarded a Kennedy Center Honor for lifetime achievement in the arts.

I § * Poemetti (1937) (twelve pieces; The Brook) (Lew, ed.) Alfred
> Shows romantic and impressionistic influences. Use of mixed meter raises the level of difficulty. Titles include: *Giga, Ninna-Nanna, Bells at Dawn, The Spinner, The Bagpipers, The Brook, The Shepherd, Untitled, The Stranger's Dance, Winter Wind, Manger,* and *War Song.*

Messiaen, Olivier (Eugène Prosper Charles) (1908–1992) France (b. Avignon, France; d. Paris, France)

An organist, composer and teacher, Messiaen was a unique musician who taught many famous composers including Boulez and Stockhausen who influenced the *avant-garde* styles of the 20th Century. Messiaen studied at the Paris *Conservatoire* and developed a distinctive musical style which reflected early influences of Debussy and Ravel and evolved to focus on elements of his life including his unique modal system, a focus on patterns and rhythms, his fascination with birdsong and devotion to the Catholic faith. He held positions as organist of *La Trinité* in Paris and taught at the *École Normale de Musique* and the *Schola Cantorum*. He was later appointed Professor of Harmony at the Paris *Conservatoire* where he published his *Technique de mon langage musical* explaining the rhythmic and harmonic principles of his music and finally, in 1966, was Professor of Composition at the Paris *Conservatoire*. He spent his life teaching, composing, and traveling to hear performances of his music and to research and record exotic birdsong. He recorded his *Visions de l'Amen* for two pianos with his wife, Yvonne Loriod.

Contemporary Literature from 1900 *continued*

A	§ *	Préludes (no. 7) (1928)	Durand

This two-page *prélude* is definitely approachable by secondary students and useful for introducing this French composer's style. Not nearly as complex and dissonant as his later piano works, the highly expressive writing uses repeating material and demonstrates the use of mixed meter.

A	*	Vingt Regards sur l'enfant Jésus (1944) (II. Regard de l'étoile)	Durand

Messiaen was heavily influenced by Catholicism. The *Vingt Regards sur l'enfant Jésus* (Twenty Reflections on the Infant Jesus) represent his mature pianistic writing. It is based on three themes: the star and cross, God, and harmony. A few of the reflections are accessible to capable secondary students or undergraduate majors, particularly no. II, *Regard de l'étoile* (View of the Star). It features both complex chords and single-line unison writing between the hands, based on the theme of the star.

Milhaud, Darius (1892–1974) France (b. Marseilles, France; d. Geneva, Switzerland)

A violinist, pianist, composer, orchestrator and conductor, Milhaud began his studies at the Paris Conservatory in 1909. He was a member of *Les Six* along with Poulenc and Honegger. A prolific composer, his works included 12 symphonies, concertos, chamber works, choral works, songs, film and ballet scores, and operas. His music includes polytonality, jazz, aleatoric and percussive elements. Milhaud visited the United States and taught at Mills College, California from 1940-1947 and later served as Professor of Composition at the Paris Conservatory. Jazz pianist Dave Brubeck was one of his many successful students.

I	Accueil amical: Pièces enfantines	Heugel
I-A	Saudades do Brasil, op. 67 (Suite of Dances, Books I, II)	Max Eschig

Mompou, Federico (1893–1987) Spain (b. and d. Barcelona, Spain)

A Catalan pianist and composer, Mompou studied at the Barcelona Conservatory and then with Philipp in Paris. His works were primarily piano miniatures and songs in what he referred to as *primitivista* style (no bar divisions, key signatures, or cadences). His music reflects his Catalan heritage with elements of folk music and modal elements.

I	Charmes	Max Eschig
I	Quatre Préludes	Heugel
I	Scènes d'Enfants (1915)	Salabert
I-A	Canciones y danzas (Spanish Songs and Dances)	See annotation

This is a remarkable collection of 12 dances that is published in three separate volumes. Numbers 1-4 are in *Musica para Piano* published by Music Sales; numbers 5-8 are published separately by Marks as *Canciones y danzas 5-6-7-8* (Hal Leonard distributor); and numbers 9-12 are in the *Frederic Mompou Piano Album* published by Salabert.

A	Suite, op. 13	Schirmer

Muczynski, Robert (1929-2010) USA (b. Chicago, IL; d. Tucson, AZ)

A pianist and composer, Muczynski studied composition with Tcherepnin at DePaul University in Chicago. He was on the faculty of Loras College in Iowa and later served as Professor of Composition and Composer in Residence at the University of Arizona, Tucson. His awards and honors included a Pulitzer Prize nomination for his *Concerto for Alto Saxophone and Orchestra, op. 41*, two Ford Foundation fellowships, and numerous ASCAP merit awards.

E	Fables	Schirmer
I	Diversions, op. 23	Schirmer
I-A	A Summer Journal, op. 19	Schirmer

I-A	Collected Piano Pieces	Schirmer

This is a useful collection as it includes all of Muczynski's piano works under one cover with the exception of the sonatas.

A § *	Six Preludes, op. 6 (I, VI)	Schirmer

One of the best known of Muczynski's works, no. I has a bright ascending melody over left-hand *staccato* and accented chords. No. VI is a brilliant *forte* study incorporating right-hand chromatic melodies over left-hand syncopated octave accents.

Nazareth, Ernesto Júlio (1863–1934) (Brazil) (b. and d. Rio de Janeiro)

A pianist and composer, Nazareth was particularly well known for his tango compositions and other dances including polkas, waltzes, and marches. He merged different cultural influences into his compositions including ragtime and Western music traditions. His untimely death by drowning followed a period of mental illness.

I-A § *	Brazilian Tangos and Dances (Brejeiro) (Appleby, ed.)	Alfred

Appleby is perhaps *the* foremost scholar on Brazilian music. He compares Nazareth's place in Brazilian art music to that of Scott Joplin in the U.S. Nazareth's piano compositions appear in selected anthologies featuring composers from South America. This particular collection presents the highlights of his pianistic output including two well-known tangos, *Brejerio* and *Odeon*, among other popular dances.

Paderewski, Ignace (Ignacy) Jan (1860–1941) Poland (b. Kurylowka, Podolia, Poland; d. New York, NY)

A concert pianist, teacher, and composer, Paderewski began his music studies at the Warsaw Music Institute at age 12. He later studied with the famous Polish pianist and pedagogue Theodor Leschetizky (1830-1915) and was active in a circle of famous composers and pianists of the day including Moszkowski, Strauss and Anton Rubinstein. A compelling pianist and public figure, he toured throughout the United States and Canada as well as South America, Australia, New Zealand, South Africa and Europe. In 1919 he became Poland's first prime minister and was later an active fund-raiser for the support of the Polish people after the Nazi invasion in 1939. He died in 1941 in New York and was given a hero's burial at Arlington National Cemetery (later reburied in Poland in 1992 as per his wish to be reburied when Poland was free).

I	Melodie, op. 8, no. 3	Willis
I-A §	Minuet in G Major, op. 14, no. 1 (Menuet à l'antique) (Palmer, ed.)	Alfred

The *Minuet in G Major* remains a very popular composition frequently seen in piano anthologies.

I-A	Nocturne, op. 16, no. 4	Willis
I-A	Selected Compositions of Moderate Difficulty	Boosey & Hawkes

Includes: *Menuet in G, op. 14, Sarabande, op. 14, Au Soir, op. 10, Mélodie in Bb, op. 8, Un Moment Musical, op. 16,* and *Mazurka, op. 9, no. 2.*

A	Album for Piano	PWM

Peeters, Flor (1903–1986) Belgium (b. Thielen (Antwerp); d. Antwerp, Belgium)

Organist, teacher and composer, Peeters served as Professor of Organ at the Lemmens Institute, the Royal Conservatory in Ghent and the Royal Flemish conservatory in Antwerp. Active as an organ recitalist in Europe, South Africa, the Philippines and United States, Peeters composed chamber music, songs, choral music and piano music but is mainly known for his organ compositions including a widely used beginning organ method.

Contemporary Literature from 1900 *continued*

I	§ *	Ten Bagatelles, op. 88 (no. 2, Minuet)	Peters

This collection includes very attractive pieces, some of which imitate Baroque and Romantic styles.

Persichetti, Vincent (1915–1987) USA (b. and d. Philadelphia, PA)

A pianist, organist, double bass player, conductor, teacher, publisher and composer, Persichetti received his degrees from the Combs Conservatory in Philadelphia (B.M.) and the Philadelphia Conservatory (M.M., D.M.A.). He taught at the Philadelphia Conservatory, the Julliard School of Music, and also was *Director of Publications* for the Elkan-Vogel Publishing Company. He wrote an impressive number of works ranging from simpler pieces written for children to larger symphonic and choral works.

E	§	Little Piano Book, op. 60 (fourteen short pieces)	Elkan-Vogel
E	§	Parades, op. 57 (March, Canter, Pomp)	Elkan-Vogel

Tonal pieces at the early intermediate level with a mild contemporary sound.

E		Serenade no. 7, op. 55	Elkan-Vogel
I		Little Mirror Book, op. 139	Elkan-Vogel

Intervallic writing and fingerings that are mirrored.

I		Six Sonatinas, Vols. I, II	Elkan-Vogel
I-A		Poems, op. 4; op. 5, Vols. I, II	Elkan-Vogel

Pinto, Octavio (1890–1950) Brazil (b. and d. Sao Paulo, Brazil)

Pinto was a successful Brazilian architect who was also a pianist and composer and known for his marriage to Guiomar Novaes, a famous Brazilian pianist and Bartók specialist. He took piano lessons from Isidore Philipp and wrote many piano miniatures and character pieces. *Scenas Infantis* is his most well-known piano work.

E		Festa de Crianças (Children's Festival)	Schirmer
I		Marcha do Pequeña Polegar (Tom Thumb's March)	Schirmer
I	§	Scenas Infantis (five descriptive scenes)	Schirmer

These five superb solos are worth mentioning by name: *Run, run!; Ring around the rosy!; March, little soldier; Sleeping Time;* and *Hobby-horse.* The set encompasses both technical and musical challenges ranging from the triadic structures in *Run, run!,* excellent for wrist *staccato,* to the final brilliant texture of *Hobby-horse,* which stresses various shifting technical patterns and clusters. Each solo is two to three pages in length.

Piston, Walter (1894–1976) USA (b. Rockland, ME; d. Belmont, MA.)

A violinist, saxophone player, teacher, author and composer, Piston studied music at Harvard University and later in Paris at the *Ecole Normale de Musique* with Boulanger, Dukas and Enescu. Piston taught at Harvard University with students including Leonard Bernstein, Leroy Anderson, Gordon Binkerd, Daniel Pinkham and Elliott Carter. He is known to a generation of American Musicians as the author of four important music textbooks, *Principles of Harmonic Analysis, Harmony, Counterpoint* and *Orchestration.* Piston received a Pulitzer Prize, A Naumburg Award, the New York Music Critics' Circle award, and a Guggenheim Fellowship.

I	Improvisation	MCA
A	Passacaglia	Mercury

Poulenc, Francis (Jean Marcel) (1899–1963) France (b. and d. Paris, France)

A member of the French group of young composers known as *Les Six,* Poulenc composed and performed his own works and those of friends such as Milhaud, Honegger, Auric, Tailleferre and Durey. Active as a concert pianist and composer, his works include compositions written both in secular and sacred traditions. He toured frequently in the United States from 1948 through 1960 and presented broadcasts for national radio shows in France. His works for piano present a focus on lyrical, charming melodies and subtle use of the pedal combining romanticism with 20th century elements.

E-I	§	Villageoises (1933) (Petites pièces enfantines)	Salabert
		Contains six less difficult compositions: *Valse Tyrolienne, Staccato, Rustique, Polka, Petite Ronde,* and *Coda*.	
I		Feuillets d'album (Ariette, Rêve, Gigue) (1933)	Salabert
I		Pastourelle	Heugel
I-A	*	Five Impromptus (II, IV)	Chester
I-A	§	Mouvements perpétuels (1918) (three pieces, II) (1918)	Chester
		Mouvements perpétuels is a very attractive set for the advancing student pianist. Charming yet slightly dissonant melodies and an *ostinato* accompaniment highlight the first movement. The second movement is technically the easiest, with the final movement the most challenging.	
I-A		Suite (1920)	Durand
A		15 Improvisations	Salabert
A		Suite française d'après Claude Gervaise (1935)	Durand
A		Trois novelettes (C major, B flat minor, E minor on a theme by de Falla)	Chester
A	§	Trois pièces (Pastorale, Toccata, Hymne)	Heugel

Previn, Sir André (George) [Priwin, Andreas Ludwig] (b. 1929) USA (b. Berlin, Germany)

An American pianist, conductor and composer, of Russian-Jewish heritage, Previn was born in Berlin and began his studies at the *Hochschule für Musik* in Berlin at age six. His family immigrated to the United States in 1939 and Previn became a U.S. citizen in 1943 using Los Angeles, California, as his professional base. He played piano for silent films and movie houses, later working as a pianist, composer and arranger in Hollywood. He received four Academy awards for his adaptations of film scores for *Gigi, Porgy and Bess, Irma la Douce* and *My Fair Lady*. He also served as artistic director and conductor for major orchestras in St. Louis, Houston, Los Angeles, Pittsburgh, and England. His compositions include works for orchestra, piano, and chamber ensemble as well as compositions written specifically for artists such as Ashkenazy (piano) and Yo-Yo Ma (cello). He received the Kennedy Center Honor for lifetime achievement in 1998 and The Recording Academy's Lifetime Achievement Award in January 2010.

I		Birthday Party	Robbins
I	§	Impressions for Piano	ASE
		This is an excellent collection of twenty intermediate-level compositions. *Promenade in the Park, In Perpetual Motion,* and *Roundup* are particularly attractive for students and teachers	
A		The André Previn Collection	Hal Leonard
		Nine piano transcriptions of jazz standards as performed by Previn.	

Prokofiev, Sergei (Sergeyevich) (1891–1953) Russia (b. Sontsovka, Ukraine; d. Moscow, Russia)

An accomplished pianist, conductor and composer, Prokofiev was a child prodigy who wrote his first opera at age 8. He was tutored by Reinhold Glière and attended the St. Petersburg Conservatory from 1904 to 1914, where, playing his own composition, he won the Anton Rubinstein prize for best student pianist. He traveled and toured for many years in Europe and the United States, moved to the United States in 1918 but relocated to Europe in 1921. After a comparative lack of success in Europe and the United States, he returned to Russia permanently in 1932 and was celebrated and honored in his homeland. He wrote for a wide range of musical genres, including symphonies, concerti, film music, operas, and ballets.

Contemporary Literature from 1900 *continued*

E-I	§ *	Music for Children, op. 65	Boosey & Hawkes

This landmark set of twelve early intermediate solos exhibits wonderful imagery. For example, in *The Rain and the Rainbow* the left hand shifts physically outline rainbows in the air. The opening left-hand voicing of the *Waltz* is similar to Grieg's *Waltz in A Minor*, op. 12, though major, not minor. The *Tarantella* is a well-known technical piece.

I		Sonatine Pastorale (from op. 59)	Boosey & Hawkes
I		Tales of the Old Grandmother, op. 31	Leeds
I-A	§	Peter and the Wolf, op. 67	Hal Leonard

This symphonic tale for children is, in this volume, reduced by the composer and includes descriptive text of the story in English, French, and Spanish.

I-A		Selected Works (Baylor, ed.)	Alfred
I-A	§	Shorter Piano Works (Feofanov, ed.)	Dover

Feofanov's collection includes: *Four Pieces, op. 3*; *Sarcasms*, *Fugitive Visions*, *Children's Music*, and *Two Sonatinas*.

I-A	§ *	Visions fugitives, op. 22 (1, 2, 16)	ASE
A		Four Pieces, op. 4	Leeds
A	*	Sonatas (no. 3)	ASE

Rachmaninoff, Sergey (Vasilyevich) (1873–1943) Russia
(Rakhmaninov, Sergey) (b. Oneg, near Semyonovo, Russia; d. Beverly Hills, CA)

(See entry in the Romantic Literature section)

Rochberg, George (1918-2005) USA (b. Paterson, NJ; d. Bryn Mawr, PA)

An American composer who was influenced by George Szell and Menotti, Rochberg taught composition at the University of Pennsylvania for many years and also chaired the music area. Rochberg gravitated between serialism and writing tonally. He also served as a senior editor for the Theodore Presser Publishing House. Rochberg is best known for his string quartet writing though his composing spanned virtually all genres (chamber ensembles, symphonies, instrumental pieces, songs, opera). Subtitled *The candid, insightful memoir of a maverick American composer and publisher*, The University of Illinois press recently published his memoirs, *Five Lines, Four Spaces, The World of My Music*.

I		Arioso (1956) (two page solo)	Presser
I-A		Two Preludes and Fughettas (1946)	Presser

Early tonal writing, the fugues are in three voices.

A	§	Twelve Bagatelles (1952) (atonal writing)	Presser

Rorem, Ned (b. 1923) USA (b. Richmond, IN)

An American pianist, author and composer, Rorem studied at Northwestern University in Illinois, Curtis Institute in Philadelphia and at the Julliard School of Music in New York where he completed his B.A. and M.M. degrees. He later studied composition with Honegger in Paris. He taught at the University of Buffalo, University of Utah and the Curtis Institute. He wrote works for piano and orchestra but is most noted for his songs (approximately 400). He authored several books and several autobiographical "Diaries" beginning with *The Paris Diary of Ned Rorem* (1966). Rorem received the Pulitzer Prize in 1976 for his orchestral suite, *Air Music*.

I	§	A Quiet Afternoon	Peer International
I-A		Three Barcarolles	Peters

Rowley, Alec (1892–1958) Great Britain (b. London, England; d. Weybridge, England)

Born in London, Rowley was a pianist, organist, teacher and composer. He studied at the Royal Academy of Music and was a professor at Trinity college. He was also a piano duet performer known for his BBC radio broadcasts with partner Edgar Moy in 1933-1943. He wrote two piano concertos, orchestral works, chamber music, songs, choral music and works for organ and strings as well as many piano works including miniatures, piano duets and pieces for children.

E		Elves and Fairies	Peters

Though intended as easy pieces, these fourteen compositions based on five-finger patterns involve rather intricate rhythmic patterns which challenge hand coordination.

E	§	Erholung, op. 37 (Recreation)	Peters

The collection contains thirteen pieces, each hand in a five-finger position. The most challenging use sixteenth-note rhythms, achieving an early intermediate level.

E	§	Five Miniature Preludes and Fugues	Chester

This collection is at the early intermediate level and written with the small hand in mind. The fugues contain two-part writing.

E-I	§	Four Sonatinas, op. 40	Peters

These four sonatinas are titled after the seasons: *Spring, Summer, Autumn,* and *Winter*. The writing is quite tonal, folk-like in nature, and technically very accessible to the late elementary or middle school student. These sonatinas are excellent transition material into the intermediate level. Though listed in one opus, these sonatinas are published separately in pairs, *Summer/Spring* and *Autumn/Winter*. Most movements replicate traditional sonata movement structures. The last movement of the *Winter* sonatina incorporates the tunes "The Mulberry Bush" and "The First Noël."

E-I		30 melodische und rhythmische Studien, op. 42	Peters

Published in two volumes, Book I contains nos. 1–18, and Book II, nos. 19–30. The studies tap into style period titles such as Invention, *Romance, Toccatina, Caprice,* and *Blues*. The etude-like aspects are reinforced by an index of various technical skills emphasized in each study (e.g., hands crossing, trill, fourth and fifth fingers, clarity of finger work, etc.). Most are one or two pages, though a few are longer. No. 28, *Blues*, is particularly attractive.

Schickele, Peter (Johann) (b. 1935) USA (b. Ames, IA)

An American composer, arranger, educator, performer and satirist, Schickele studied music at Swarthmore College and later received a master's degree in composition from the Julliard School of Music. Influenced by teachers such as Roy Harris and Vincent Persichetti, Schickele's compositions span the serious classical side to jazz and contemporary elements. Through recordings and live concerts, Schickele is internationally known for his spoofs of Baroque music through the fictitious composer P.D.Q. Bach. A prolific composer and performer, Schickele has written for television, films, musicals, and received Grammy awards.

E	§	In My Nine Lives (based on musical themes about cats)	Elkan-Vogel
I		Hollers, Hymns and Dirges	Elkan-Vogel
I		Little Suite for Susan (7 pieces; composed for his wife)	Elkan-Vogel
I		Small Serenade	Elkan-Vogel
I-A		Epitaphs	Elkan-Vogel

Late intermediate style imitation pieces patterned after five selected composers including D. Scarlatti and Chopin.

I-A		Razzle-Dazzle Triptych	Elkan-Vogel

Contemporary Literature from 1900 *continued*

Schönberg, [Schoenberg] Arnold (Franz Walter) (1874–1951) Germany (b. Vienna, Austria; d. Los Angeles, CA)

Schönberg was a violinist, teacher, music theorist, painter and composer who taught in Vienna. Together with Alban Berg and Anton Webern, the group of three represent the so called Second Viennese school (the first being Haydn, Mozart, and Beethoven). Other pupils include names such as John Cage. Like so many composers and artists of the time, Schönberg immigrated to the U.S. to escape Nazi Germany, later teaching at both UCLA and USC (University of Southern CA). He was held in such esteem that both campuses named structures after him. Acknowledged for developing 12-tone compositional techniques, Schonberg was a pioneer in exploring atonality and 20th century compositional techniques using serialism. He is considered one of the most influential composers of the modern era.

I	§ *	Sechs kleine Klavierstücke, op. 19, (nos. 2, 6)	Universal

Suitable for the serious secondary student, this opus represents the least difficult pieces of Schönberg's piano output. Though musically abstract, numbers 2 and 6 are quite easy technically and best for introducing the opus.

I-A	Drei Klavierstücke (1894)	Universal

After, op. 19, the next most accessible of the composer's piano sets.

A	Five Piano Pieces, op. 23 (1923)	Wilhelm Hansen
A	3 Klavierstücke, op. 11 (1908)	Universal

Schuman, William Howard (1910–1992) USA (b. and d. New York, NY)

It is reported that Schuman became inspired to be a composer after hearing the New York Philharmonic in 1930. He went on to study at Columbia Teachers College and privately with names such as Roy Harris. Schuman's academic career began at Sarah Lawrence College followed by the Juilliard School where he served as President (1945-1962) and founded the Juilliard String Quartet. He left Juilliard to become the first President of Lincoln Center (1962-68). He is recipient of a Pulitzer Prize (1943) and the National Medal of Arts. Schuman wrote for all musical genres and is probably best known for his symphonic writing and violin concerto (1947, rev. 1957). His output for piano is relatively small though the two works listed below are important contributions.

I	§	Three Score Set (1943)	Schirmer

Though short, this is an important intermediate set that appears in contemporary anthologies.

I-A	Three Moods	Presser

The three Moods are *Lyrical, Pensive,* and *Dynamic.*

Scriabin, Alexander (Nikolayevich) (1872–1915) Russia (b. and d. Moscow, Russia)

A virtuoso pianist and composer, Scriabin studied composition at the Moscow Conservatory with Arensky and later became a professor at the Conservatory. He studied with the same piano teacher (Zverev) as Rachmaninoff and they formed a lifelong friendship. He toured Europe and the United States as a concert pianist performing his own works and met an early death at age 43 of blood poisoning and pleurisy. Greatly influenced by the piano music of Chopin and Liszt, Scriabin studied mysticism and astrology and experimented with new harmonies and means of musical expression. He was the first composer to notate music for light and color, creating the first color keyboard, and his new 'Prometheus' chord' and music were often used in science-fiction movies. He wrote technically demanding preludes, études and ten sonatas for the piano that are considered masterpieces of 20th century pianism.

I-A	§ *	Twenty-four Preludes, op. 11 (4, 15, 22)	Peters

Written early in his career, while a student, these *Preludes* replicate Chopin's key arrangement of moving around the circle of fifths. They can be excerpted individually for study and performance.

A	Prelude and Nocturne for Left Hand, op. 9 (Hinson, ed.)	Alfred; ASE

Comparable in difficulty to a slow Chopin etude (e.g., E-flat minor, op. 10), the *Prelude* (C-Sharp minor) is much shorter (*ca* 3 min.) and can be played separately from the *Nocturne*. It requires excellent sensitivity to sound and balance. This could be a repertoire choice for exploring new technical challenges with an advancing student.

A	Preludes and Poems	Peters
A	Selected Works (Baylor, ed.)	Alfred

The volume is an excellent representation of Scriabin's output including *preludes, poems, études,* and the fourth *sonata*.

Sessions, Roger (Huntington) (1896–1985) USA (b. Brooklyn, NY; d. Princeton, NJ)

An American composer, teacher and writer, the often-complex music of Sessions is characterized by motivic cohesion, rhythmic dynamism and long melody. He graduated from Harvard (B.A.) and Yale Universities (B.M.) and studied privately with Ernst Bloch, who was his major composition teacher. Eight years spent in Europe helped create Sessions' cosmopolitan worldview; during this period he co-sponsored the influential Copland-Sessions concerts in New York. His teaching career of fifty years included posts at Smith College, Princeton University, the University of California Berkeley, and the Juilliard School. His primary piano works are three sonatas, which span his stylistic development. Other music includes nine symphonies, two string quartets, two operas, and the lyrical masterpiece *When Lilacs last in the Dooryard Bloom'd*. He received numerous awards and honors including two Guggenheim Fellowships, the *Prix de Rome*, a Carnegie grant, two Pulitzer Prizes and fourteen honorary doctorates.

I	March	Carl Fischer
I	Scherzino	Carl Fischer

Short, attractive, and fairly tonal.

A	From my Diary (1937-1940)	Marks

Four character pieces, widely varied in mood. The first is meditative, calling for extended phrasing; the second is the longest and most difficult digitally, with irregular technical patterns and a lyrical middle section. The third is a short, sustained tone-poem, and the fourth, an energetic march. Mainly dissonant, though key signatures are used in the first and third pieces. Performance time is 9 minutes total.

Shostakovich, Dmitri (Dmitriyevich) (1906–1975) Russia (b. St. Petersburg (Leningrad), Russia; d. Moscow, Russia)

Shostakovich was a leading 20th Century Russian concert pianist and composer who spent his entire life in Russia. He studied composition with Glazunov at the St. Petersburg Conservatory. His life and works were influenced by communism, the rise of Stalin and the restrictions and political scrutiny of the times. His music is more traditional and more accessible than much 20th Century music and include 15 symphonies, 15 string quartets, chamber works, song cycles, operas, ballets, film scores, and piano works.

E	§	Six Children's Pieces (Palmer, ed.)	Alfred

Written for his daughter Galya (1936), these six pieces are most attractive miniatures: 1. *March,* 2. *Waltz,* 3. *The Bear,* 4. *A Funny Story,* 5. *A Sad Story,* and 6. *The Mechanical Doll*. Two-part writing prevails throughout, with the last piece, The Mechanical Doll, being the most difficult rhythmically and technically.

I	Doll's Dances (seven easy pieces)	MCA

Contemporary Literature from 1900 *continued*

I-A		Preludes and Fugues for Piano	Dover

This set includes the *Five Preludes* (1920–21), *Twenty-four Preludes*, op. 34 (1932–33), and the later *Twenty-four Preludes and Fugues*, op. 87 (1950–51). The 1932 set is mirrored after Chopin's key order, and includes some intermediate writing. No. 15 is particularly attractive for its waltz-like character. Unlike Bach's chromatic key order in the WTC, the 1950 set uses Chopin's major-relative minor order around the circle of 5ths.

A	§	Three Fantastic Dances, op. 5	Boosey & Hawkes

Composed when Shostakovich was still a teenager, these three early advanced dances, arranged in a fast-slow-fast order, provide much variety. No. I (*Allegretto*) introduces the set with its rhythmic melody and left hand jumping bass all in a march-like texture and ABA structure. The second movement is a waltz and the latter resembles a lively polka incorporating clever harmonies.

Stevens, Halsey (1908–1988) USA (b. Scott, NY; d. Long Beach, CA)

A pianist, writer and composer, Stevens studied at Syracuse University (B.M., M.M.) and at the University of California Berkeley. He taught at Syracuse University, Dakota Wesleyan University, Bradley University, the University of Redlands and the University of Southern California, Los Angeles. He received many awards and honors including two Guggenheim Fellowships, a National Institute of Arts and Letters Grant and the Abraham Lincoln Award. He is a noted Bartók scholar and composed works for many genres including orchestral, choral, and chamber.

E		Five Little Five Finger Exercises	Helios
E		Six Russian Folktunes	ACA
E		Ten French Folksongs	ACA
E		Ten Short Pieces	ACA
I		Five Swedish Folk Tunes	Helios
I		Jumping Colts	Helios
I-A		17 Piano Pieces	Westwood
A		5 Portuguese Folksongs	Peer International

Stravinsky, Igor (Fyodorovich) (1882–1971) (b. Lomonosov, Russia; d. New York, NY)

Stravinsky is regarded as one of the most influential composers of the 20th century. He studied with Rimsky Korsakov in St Petersburg. His works reflect a variety of styles as his compositional techniques evolved through elements of French impressionism (Debussy and Ravel), nationalism, modernism and neo-classicism to more contemporary serialism. At the start of the Second World War he moved to the United States, settling in Los Angeles, California. His ballet scores are among the most significant contributions to the genre.

E	§	Les Cinq Doigts (8 easy pieces based on five finger patterns)	MMB Music
I		Tango	Schott; Presser
I		Valse pour les enfants	Alphonse Leduc; Presser
I-A	§	Short Piano Pieces (Soulima Stravinsky, ed.)	Boosey & Hawkes

This is a valuable compendium of Stravinsky's piano solos which includes informative comments from his son, Soulima.

A	§	Piano Rag-Music (1919)	Masters Music

Stravinsky, Soulima (1910–1994) USA (b. Lausanne, Switzerland; d. Sarasota, FL)

Soulima was the youngest son of the famous Igor Stravinsky. A noted pianist, teacher and composer, Soulima studied with Isadore Philipp and Nadia Boulanger. He served on the piano faculty of the University of Illinois for his entire teaching career and most of his compositional projects for piano developed during his Illinois tenure. He wrote orchestra works, chamber works and educational pieces for children.

E-I	§	Piano Music for Children, Vols. I (nineteen pieces), II (11 pieces)	Peters
I	§	6 Easy Sonatinas for Young Pianists, Vol. I (nos. 1–3), Vol. II (nos. 4–6)	Peters
I		6 Sonatinas	Peters
I-A		Art of Fingering, The (12 short preludes)	Peters
I-A		15 Character Pieces	Peters

Sumera, Lepo (1950-2000) Estonia (b. and d. Tallinn, Estonia)

Sumera parallels Paderewski, in that Sumera, like Paderewski served as an official in his country's government as *Minister of Culture.* Highly regarded as a composer in his native country and surrounding regions, he studied at the Estonian Academy of Music and Theatre and later did graduate work at the Moscow Conservatory. His symphonic works have been widely performed. Later in his career he was a pioneer in the area of electro-acoustic music.

I	Drei Klavierstücke für Kinder	Hans Sikorski

It is challenging to find current music from composers from Eastern Europe. Frederick Harris Music publishes an entire series (see Souvenirs' entries in the contemporary pedagogical section) devoted to pedagogical compositions by Eastern European composers. In this attractive set the titles are *The One Who Is Wiser Concedes, The Sad Toreador,* and *The Butterfly Who Woke Up in Winter.*

A	Fughetta und Postludium für Klavier	Edition 49 GmbH

Tailleferre, Germaine (Marcelle) (1892–1983) France (b. Saint-Maur-des-Fossés, Val-de-Marne [Paris]; d. Paris, France)

A French pianist, teacher, painter and composer, she studied with Ravel at the Paris Conservatory where she won several musical prizes and was the only female member of a group of French composers known as *Les Six* (Poulenc, Honegger, Milhaud, Auric and Durey). She was married twice, first in 1925 to New York caricaturist Ralph Barton (a close friend of Charlie Chaplin) and after a divorce, to French lawyer Jean Lageat which also ended in divorce. Both husbands were critical of her work as a musician and composer but Tailleferre remained active as a composer throughout. Her works include operas, ballets, film scores, chamber music, and songs as well as works for piano.

E	§	3 Sonatines pour piano	Lemoine

Three excellent sonatinas, of which the second is shorter with fewer tempo indications. The writing is tuneful, slightly contemporary, but most appealing. Each movement is one page in length. The third movement of the first sonatina is based on "A Tisket A Tasket." The *Andantino* of the third sonatina is very attractive with its drone-sounding bass. The final *Allegro* is Clementi-like.

A	§	Sicilienne	Heugel

An early advanced piece, this short *Sicilienne* requires large stretches, but is attractive because of its slightly jazz-like harmonies and *cadenza*-like right-hand improvisatory figures.

Tajčević, Marko (1900–1984) Yugoslavia (b. Osijek, Croatia; d. Belgrade, Serbia [Yugoslavia])

A Czech violinist, teacher, choral conductor, writer, music critic and composer, Tajčević helped found the Lisinski Music School in Zagreb and was active as a choral conductor. He was a professor at the Belgrade Academy of Music where he composed and wrote texts on music theory and harmony. Teaching was the main focus of his life. His compositions have been widely published in Yugoslavia, Germany, the former Soviet Union, and more recently the U.S. Famous pianists such as Artur Rubinstein have included Tajčević's compositions in their recital repertoire.

Contemporary Literature from 1900 *continued*

E-I	Lieder von der Mur-Insel (Tajcevic/Georgii, eds.)	Henle
I	Serbian Dances (five movements)	Broude Brothers
I-A	Seven Balkan Dances	Schott

Takács, Jenö [Eugene] (1902–2005) Hungary (b. Cinfalva, Hungary; d. Eisenstadt Austria)

An Austrian pianist, teacher, composer and ethnomusicologist, Takács studied composition in Vienna and taught at the Cairo Conservatory and the University of the Philippines in Manila. Influenced by his friend Bartók, he had a keen interest in the folk music of Hungary and later in Arabic music and music of the tribes and cultures of the Philippines. As a concert pianist he toured Europe, the United States, the Middle East and East Asia. He was appointed to the faculty of the University of Cincinnati, Ohio from 1952 to 1970. He was a multi-nationalist composer who used Hungarian folk music and music of several cultures combining atonal and aleatoric styles with tonal. His centennial birthday was celebrated with 300 concerts, a *Festschrift*, and new editions and recordings of his music.

I	Doubledozen for Small Fingers	Universal
I	From Far Away Places, op. 111	Universal
I	Little Sonata, op. 51	Doblinger
I	Something New for You	Doblinger
I	Sounds and Colors, op. 95	Doblinger

Tansman, Alexandre [Aleksander] (1897–1986) France (b. Łódź, Poland; d. Paris, France)

Tansman was a pianist, conductor and composer who studied at the Łódź Conservatory and completed his doctorate in law at the University of Warsaw. He later moved to Paris and became friends with Ravel and Stravinsky. As a concert pianist he toured Europe, Asia, Palestine, India and the United States and his works were performed internationally. He lived in Los Angeles from 1941-1946 renewing friendships with Milhaud and Stravinsky and composing several film scores. His works include eight symphonies, orchestral pieces, ballets, operas, and choral works. Tansman authored the book, *Igor Stravinsky: The Man and his Music* (New York: Putnam, 1949).

E-I	Pour les Enfants	Max Eschig
	(in four progressively difficult books, 10–12 pieces each)	
E-I §	Ten Diversions for the Young Pianist	Associated
	The easiest of Tansman's writing, excellent for late elementary and middle school students.	
I-A	Piano Album	Salabert
	A comprehensive collection including *Vingt Piéces Faciles*, *Etude-Scherzo*, *Quatre Danses Miniatures* (*Gavotte*, *Menuet*, *Mazurka "a la Chopin,"* *Petite Marche*), *Trois Etudes* and *Sonatine pour Piano*.	
I-A §	Tansman Collection, The (Hinson, ed.)	Universal
	The fifteen pieces for this collection were excerpted from the sets *Ten Easy Pieces* and *Suite Variée* (both Universal publications). An excellent sampling of Tansman's style, the collection is arranged by level of difficulty.	

Tcherepnin, Alexander (Nikolayevich) (1899–1977) USA (b. Saint Petersburg, Russia; d. Paris, France)

Born in Russia, Tcherepnin moved to France because of the revolution and eventually immigrated to the U.S. to teach at DePaul University in the 1950s. The op. 5 *Bagatelles* represent his early period in Russia. He composed in many genres including four symphonies and six piano concerti. Some of his writing reflects Asian influences as he lived in China for a period of his life. Several of Tcherepnin's elementary compositions appear in the Frances Clark *Contemporary Piano Literature* six-volume series.

I	Bagatelles Chinoises, op. 51, no. 3	Heugel
I	Episodes (twelve sketches)	Heugel

I		Pour Petits et Grands, Vols. I, II	Durand
I-A	§	Bagatelles, op. 5 (Olson, ed.)	Alfred

Firmly entrenched in the 20th century late intermediate repertoire, these ten bagatelles individually can serve as contrasting recital material to earlier bagatelles by Beethoven. No. 1 (*Allegro marciale*) is best known for the *forte* martial-like texture, dissonant intervals, and brilliant octave texture.

I-A		8 Preludes, op. 9	Presser
I-A		Expressions, op. 81 (10 pieces)	Leeds

In approach and musical substance, these are often compared to the early *Bagatelles, op. 5*.

I-A		Songs without Words, op. 82 (five pieces)	Peters

Thompson, Randall (1899–1984) USA (b. New York, NY; d. Boston, MA)

An organist, teacher and composer, Thompson completed his degrees (A.B. and M.A.) at Harvard University and studied privately with Ernest Bloch in New York. He served as organist and teacher at Wellesley College and went on to teach at the Curtis Institute of Music (where Bernstein was one of his students), the University of Virginia, Princeton University, the University of California at Berkeley, and Harvard. His three-year research in music education commissioned by the Association of American Colleges resulted in the important report, *College Music* (New York, 1935), which emphasized a liberal arts approach to music education. He composed symphonies, songs, operas and instrumental works, but is best known for his numerous choral compositions.

I	§	Little Prelude (two-page miniature)	Carl Fischer
I-A		Suite for Piano	E. C. Schirmer

Toch, Ernst (1887–1964) Austria (b. Vienna, Austria; d. Los Angeles, CA) (naturalized American)

An Austrian-American pianist and composer, Toch first studied medicine in Vienna and then music at the Frankfurt Conservatory. He was a Professor of Composition at the Mannheim *Musikhochschule* and in 1934 moved to Los Angeles, California where he composed music for Hollywood films. Composer of operas, symphonies and works for voice and orchestra, he was nominated for two Academy Awards for Best Music, Scoring of a Dramatic or Comedy Picture for *Ladies in Retirement* (1941) and *Address Unknown* (1944).

E-A		Five Times Ten Studies for Piano (*Fünfmal zehn Etüden für Klavier*)	Schott
A	*	Burlesken, op. 31, no. 3 (The Juggler)	Schott

Turina, Joaquín (y Perez Turina) (1882–1949) Spain (b. Seville, Spain; d. Madrid, Spain)

A Spanish pianist, nationalistic composer, conductor, music critic, teacher and musicologist, Turina studied first in Madrid and Seville and later in Paris at the *Schola Cantorum*. He was friends with Isaac Albeniz and Manuel de Falla and became a Professor of Composition at the Madrid Conservatory in 1931. His works include operas, chamber music, orchestral works, songs, and numerous works for guitar and piano.

I		Miniatures	Schott
I-A		Album de Viaje (five Travel Impressions)	Warner
I-A		Danzas Gitanas, op. 55, Vols. I, II (five pieces in each volume)	Salabert
I-A	§	Turina Collection, The (twenty pieces) (Hinson, ed.)	Schott

This comprehensive set includes selections from *Miniatures*, *The Circus*, and *Postcards*. *The Circus* (1932) is the best-known of Turina's output, and this volume includes, among others, *Jugglers* (alternating hands texture), and *Clowns* (*Allegro burlesco*). The volume organizes the twenty compositions in two parts by increasing order of difficulty.

A	§	The Circus (Clowns) (1932)	Schott

Contemporary Literature from 1900 *continued*

Villa-Lobos, Heitor (1887–1959) Brazil (b. and d. Rio de Janeiro)

A guitarist, cellist and composer, Villa-Lobos was a leading figure in 20th century Brazilian music. He achieved an international reputation as a composer and founded the Brazilian Academy of Music in 1945. He toured throughout Brazil collecting and notating folk songs and themes from the regions and using these as inspiration for future compositions. He was largely self-taught, studying repertoire from great composers such as Bach's *Well Tempered Clavier.* He became friends with Artur Rubinstein in Rio de Janeiro who encouraged him to compose piano music and who brought the composer's piano compositions to the concert stage.

I	Petizado	Peer International
I	Ten Pieces on Popular Children's Folk Tunes	Mercury
I	The Three Maries (Alnitah, Alnilam, Mintika)	Carl Fischer
I-A §	A Prole do bebê no. 1 (The Baby's Family) (Appleby, ed.)	Alfred
	This authoritative edition, with commentary by the Villa-Lobos scholar David Appleby, is highly recommended. Through performances by Artur Rubinstein, this set of eight compositions has become Villa-Lobos' most famous piano composition, and includes the well-known *O Polichinello.*	
I-A	Piano Music	Dover

E (Early Intermediate)   I (Intermediate)   A (Advanced Intermediate to Advanced)

Contemporary Literature: Pedagogical Composers

Who are the *Contemporary pedagogical piano composers* and how are their works different? Whether composers' names were placed in the "regular" or "pedagogical" contemporary category in this text depended largely on a sense of each individual's place in history and whether the composer wrote widely recognized works, not only for piano but other genres as well. For example, both Aaron Copland and Béla Bartók composed piano miniatures which we immediately think of as pedagogical, for less advanced students to play or sight-read, but both composers also wrote widely recognized concert works (e.g., orchestral, string quartets, etc.). Both of these composers were placed in the Contemporary listing while William Gillock, who is considered a leading composer of educational piano compositions, is cited in the Pedagogical listing. Gillock's works are considered important and essential teaching repertoire but his overall body of work does not reflect the same breadth as Copland or Bartók.

To date, this is the only *Piano Repertoire Guide* in print that offers an overview of compositions written by pedagogical/educational piano composers. This is not an easy task because pedagogical compositions and collections tend to move in and out of print much more quickly than the "standard" literature such as Chopin's *Nocturnes* or Bartók's *Mikrokosmos*. Even so, we should not dismiss the important role that many of our vital pedagogical composers (William Gillock and Lynn Freeman Olson, etc.) play just because they did not, for example, write string quartets for the concert stage. Their compositions are quite special. As pedagogical composers' compositions stand the test of time, some names may later be viewed as significant composers of the 20th and 21st centuries; we simply are too close to make that determination at this time.

Indeed, so much valuable piano music (pedagogical or introductory literature) has been composed and published by "piano educators" to prepare students for the more difficult standard literature, that it would seem unfair, if not dismissive, to avoid including such teaching literature in this *Piano Repertoire Guide*. Undoubtedly, thousands of young pianists, in their musical journey, have been greatly inspired to learn how to play and experience successful performances early on because of this important body of teaching literature.

Thus, this edition of the *Piano Repertoire Guide* updates what is a rather significant body of literature and offers insights into composers' backgrounds and their music, focusing on the highlights of each individual's compositional efforts. This annotated listing cannot and does not list all works by any given composer, or even all composers' names, nor does it replace seeking out any composer's entire body of compositions. (That can be accomplished through perusal of publishers' catalogues.) The purpose here is to offer a focused overview of selected collections at the intermediate and more advanced levels (not elementary level compositions or sheet music solos) by contemporary pedagogical composers. Certainly, the best way to experience this repertoire is to teach and play the music. It is just as meaningful to teach Eugenie Rocherolle's lovely *Downstream* (from *Six Moods for Piano*; Kjos) as it is to teach Chopin's *Prelude in E Minor, op. 28, no. 4,* and, it is equally satisfying to hear a pupil play either composition well.

We hope this overview is a helpful resource for experienced and new teachers, individuals responsible for making excellent matches between their pupils' many gifts and talents and the excellent body of pedagogical literature available to our piano teaching profession.

Composer/Title   **Publisher**

Agay, Denes (1911-2007) USA (b. near Budapest, Hungary; d. Los Altos, CA)

While attending law school at the University of Budapest, Agay concurrently earned his Doctorate in piano composition and performance from the Liszt Academy. After moving to the United States in 1939 to escape Nazi Germany, he served in the U.S. army during WWII and later used New York as a base for his editing, arranging, and composing. He is best known for his many editions of standard teaching literature including one of the first multi-period anthologies, *Easy Classics to Moderns* and its several ensuing volumes. He also composed for film scores. In addition to the items cited below, Agay has numerous sheet music solos published through Schirmer/Hal Leonard.

Contemporary Literature: Pedagogical Composers *continued*

I		Denes Agay Songs to Remember (collection of Agay's sheet piano solos)	Yorktown
I	§	Four Dance Impressions	Presser
		Includes: *Night Music, Vibrations, Ballad Without Words,* and *Hommage à Joplin.*	
I		Four Popular Diversions for Piano	Presser
		Includes: *Little Prelude in Waltz Time, Baroque Bounce, Echoes of the Blues,* and *Ragtime Doll.*	
I		Sonatina Hungarica	MCA
I		Sonatina no. 3	Alfred
		Attractive late intermediate sonatina in three movements.	
I		3 Recital Dances (Parade Polka, Waltz Serenade, Mardi Gras Bolero)	Presser
I		Two Improvisations on Hungarian Folk Songs	Presser

Alcon, Susan (b. 1953) USA (b. Greensboro, NC)

Alcon writes lyrically with lush, romantic colors, often using pedal indications for the performer and occasionally exploring jazz sounds. Educated at Salem College in Winston-Salem, NC, Alcon has received awards for her compositions including the North Carolina Federation of Music Clubs' *Mabel Doggett Composition Award.*

E	§	Wildflowers (13 solos)	Frederick Harris
		This set is an excellent representative of Alcon's style. The musical textures feature jazz, popular, and lyrical styles that offer opportunities for the student to work with issues such as rhythm, voicing, and pedaling.	
I	§	Carefree Days (13 solos)	Frederick Harris
I		Enchantment (6 lyric solos)	Frederick Harris
I		Lyric Sketches (9 solos)	Frederick Harris
I		Reflections (10 lyric solos)	Frederick Harris

Alexander, Dennis USA (b. Kansas)

A University of Kansas graduate, and former piano faculty member at the University of Montana, Alexander has established himself as one of the leading educational composers in North America. He has presented and/or performed throughout the U.S. (including Carnegie Recital Hall) and in other countries including Australia and the Far East. His compositions are on contest and festival lists nationally and internationally.

E		Best of Dennis Alexander, The, Vol. II	Alfred
E		Magic of Music, The	Alfred
E-I		Dennis Alexander's Favorite Solos, Vols. II, III	Alfred
E-I	§	Performing in Style	Alfred
		This volume contains descriptions of each style period (e.g., discussions of instruments, performance style, principal composers, musical form, period terminology), followed by original pieces composed in the particular style (five Baroque, two three-movement Classical sonatinas, two Romantic, two Contemporary).	
I		***Intermediate Level Collections***	Alfred
	§	A Splash of Color, Vols. I, II; Especially in Jazz Style; Simply Sensational; Especially in Romantic Style; Just for You; Simply Sonatinas.	
I-A		Planet Earth	Alfred
I-A	§	24 Character Preludes (book and CD)	Alfred
		In the spirit of Gillock's *Lyric Preludes in Romantic Style* and following Chopin's key order, these preludes are stylistically modeled on composers from different style periods-Bach to Gershwin. The *Preludes* are performed by the composer on a companion CD.	

E (Early Intermediate)   I (Intermediate)   A (Advanced Intermediate to Advanced)

Applebaum, Stan (b. 1922) USA

Applebaum is best known for his instrumental arrangements. He has composed for various U.S. military bands and leading symphonic orchestras such as the New York Philharmonic and the London Philharmonic.

E-A §	Sound World, Vols. I , II		FJH
	Originally published by Schroeder & Gunther and reissued by FJH, these are effective compositions that inspire the musical imagination and embrace modern idioms including dissonance. They may be played individually or in miscellaneous groups.		

Barratt, Carol (b. 1945) USA

A piano teacher, specialist in music education and composer, Barratt graduated from the Royal College of Music. She has won awards from the Music Industry Association and the Composers' Guild for her works for beginning pianists and also writes vocal and instrumental works. She is active in the United Kingdom as a lecturer and clinician.

E	Play It Again, Vols. 1, 2	Chester
I	At the Piano (Homage to Bartók for Children and Adults)	Boosey & Hawkes
I-A	Fantasy Preludes	Boosey & Hawkes
I-A	Pattern Preludes	Boosey & Hawkes

Beard, Katherine USA

An independent piano teacher and composer, Beard studied at Julliard. Her works include pieces for elementary and intermediate piano students.

I		All That Stuff!	Willis
I		Fantasie in F Major	Willis
I	§	Seven Two-Part Inventions on Borrowed Themes	Boston
		(for the development of expressive performance in contrapuntal style)	
I		Ten Two-Part Inventions	Boston
I		Twelve times twelve: 12 short pieces in the 12-tone style	Boston
I-A		Etudes on Intervals – 5 Studies in Sound	Willis
I-A		Sonata in C Major	Willis

Berkowitz, Sol USA

Author of the text *A New Approach to Sight Singing* (5th ed., Norton), Berkowitz was a faculty member at Queens College, City University of New York.

E-I	Jazzettes	ECS Publishing
E-I	Nine Folk Song Preludes	Frank

Berlin, Boris (1907-2001) Canada (b. Kharkov, Russia; d. Toronto, Canada)

A faculty member at the University of Toronto and Royal Conservatory of Music, Berlin was a leader in piano education in Canada, developing widely used teaching materials (e.g., *Four Star Sight Reading and Ear Tests* and *Technical Requirements for Piano*) still in current use. He was a teacher, examiner for the Royal Conservatory and a festival adjudicator.

E-I	§	Legacy Collection (includes well-known solos by Berlin)	Frederick Harris

Contemporary Literature: Pedagogical Composers *continued*

SOLO LITERATURE

Berr, Bruce USA

With music degrees from Washington University in St. Louis and Northwestern University, Berr is based in Chicago, Illinois and teaches students of all ages and levels. An associate editor for *Keyboard Companion,* now *Clavier Companion,* he has presented workshops throughout the U.S. and is a prominent clinician, editor, and author.

E-I	§	At the Seashore, Vols. I, II	FJH
		Character pieces written in a variety of styles.	
I		Barcarolle Impromptu	Hal Leonard
		This is a beautiful intermediate solo reminiscent of Mendelssohn's three *Venetian Boat Songs.* Berr also has numerous Hal Leonard publications devoted to Christmas and Chanukah music.	

Blok, Vladimir (1932-1996) Russia (b. and d. Moscow, Russia)

Blok was a Russian arranger and composer particularly known for his work with orchestrating selected compositions by Prokofieff.

E-I	§	Twelve Pieces in Folk Modes	Frederick Harris
		Based on Russian folk melodies and modes.	
I		Vignettes	Frederick Harris

Bober, Melody USA

A teacher, composer and clinician with piano degrees from the University of Illinois (B.M.E. and M.M.), Bober is well known as a pedagogical composer. She maintains a thriving private studio in Minnesota and is a widely traveled clinician and presenter.

E		Just for Fun, Bk. II	FJH
		The technical focus is on playing major and minor five-finger patterns.	
E		Melody's Choice, Bk. 2	FJH
E		Solos in Style, Bk. 2 (includes optional teacher accompaniments)	FJH
E-I	§	Best of Melody Bober, The, Bks. 1, 2	FJH
		Many of Bober's pedagogical compositions are sheet music solos at various levels. These two volumes serve to highlight some of her most popular solos.	
I		Cyclone!	FJH
		A suite with titles depicting stormy weather.	
I		***Intermediate Level Collections***	FJH
		Folk Fantasies; Jazzy Rags; Standing Ovations; From the Emerald Isle; Tunes in Transit.	

Brown, Timothy USA

After graduate work (M.M.) at the University of North Texas, Brown studied composition with Brian Lock in London, England. With over 100 compositions in print, Brown has numerous professional credits and currently is a fine arts specialist for the Dallas Public Schools.

E		From Far Away Places (8 descriptive piano solos)	FJH
E-I		Can You Imagine, Bks. 1, 2	FJH
E-I		Lyric Expressions	FJH
I	§	Silhouettes for Piano, Vol. 1	FJH
		Silhouettes is a suite of four contrasting pieces imitating 19th and 20th century styles.	

E (Early Intermediate)   I (Intermediate)   A (Advanced Intermediate to Advanced)

Brubeck, Dave [David Warren] (b. 1920) USA (b. Concord, CA)

Brubeck, an icon of American jazz piano, is perhaps most famous for his original composition, *Take Five*. Although he is primarily considered a jazz composer, Brubeck studied composition with Milhaud and has written works for classical piano. In 2009, he received one of America's greatest honors by being recognized as a recipient of the excellence in Performing Arts Award bestowed by the Kennedy Center in Washington, D.C.

I	§	Nocturnes	Alfred

A delightful and accessible collection of nocturnes in romantic and emotive style, these original pieces, many only one page in length, are not reductions or simplifications and according to the composer were written to bridge classical and jazz performance.

I-A		Dave Brubeck Anthology, The	Alfred
I-A		Seriously Brubeck	Alfred
A		Dave Brubeck at the Piano (Salmon, ed.)	Alfred
A		Dave Brubeck, Vols. I, II	Shawnee/Hal Leonard

Caramia, Tony (b. 1950) USA

One of America's foremost piano pedagogues and composers of original jazz teaching pieces, Tony Caramia is Professor of Music (piano and piano pedagogy) at the Eastman School of Music. He is widely traveled as a recitalist and clinician and internationally known for his many recordings, recitals and lectures on jazz and ragtime music. Many of Caramia's intermediate level sheet music solos such as *Ballad, Carefree Song, Swaying Song,* and *Dreaming,* are available from Hal Leonard in their *Showcase Solos* series.

E	§	Folksongs Revisited	Alfred

This tasteful collection presents nine familiar folk melodies (five solos and four duets), imaginatively arranged with appealing harmonies and clever rhythms. Titles include: *Aura Lee, MacDonald's Farm, Yankee Doodle, When Johnny Comes Marching Home* and *Michael, Row the Boat Ashore.*

E-I	§	Sounds of Jazz, Vols. 1, II	Alfred

Includes blues, rags and other jazz styles.

I		Adventures in Jazz, Vols. I, II	Bärenreiter

Adventures in Jazz Piano is a most attractive collection that includes a wide variety of styles for the intermediate student including blues, boogie-woogie, and ragtime.

I		Jazz Moods	Hal Leonard
I		Six Sketches	Alfred
I		Suite Dreams (4 solos)	Hal Leonard
I-A	§	Fascinating Rhythms (6 jazz etudes)	Kjos

Chagy, John USA

An independent piano teacher and composer, he studied at Julliard and has taught in New Jersey and Atlanta. He has many works for intermediate level piano students and several sheet music solos published by Hal Leonard.

I		Etude Baroque	Carl Fischer
I		Razz-Ma-Jazz	Kjos

Contemporary Literature: Pedagogical Composers *continued*

Chatman, Stephen (b. 1950) Canada (b. Minneapolis-St. Paul, MN)

With degrees from Oberlin Conservatory and the University of Michigan where he studied with Finney, Bassett, and Bolcom, Stephen Chatman currently is Professor and Head of Composition at the University of British Columbia. A former Fulbright scholar, he has received many commissions from organizations such as the Canada Council, the Canadian Broadcasting Corporation, and the National Endowment for the Arts.

E-I	§	Amusements, Bks. 2, 3	Frederick Harris

Similar in purpose to Ross Lee Finney's earlier *32 Piano Games* (Peters), the landmark *Amusements* volumes expose the younger student to contemporary composition through alternate notational systems and symbols. The pieces are very attractive and provide interesting and contrasting recital material. Levels 2 and 3 correspond to two to four years of study and include familiar titles such as *Freak Out* and *Broken Music Box*. Chatman states about the series, "It is hoped that *Amusements* will encourage creative thinking and active participation by the teacher and student, and also help to instill an open and positive attitude toward contemporary music."

E-I	§	Escapades, Bk. 2	Frederick Harris

Attractive play-along accompaniments are provided on MIDI files.

I	Preludes, Bk. 3	Frederick Harris
I-A	Fantasies (11 contemporary pieces in various styles)	Frederick Harris

Collins, Ann USA

A pianist, educator, jazz musician and author, Western Illinois University professor *emeritus* Collins is active as a clinician and instructor of jazz piano throughout the United States. Her background includes public school and independent studio piano teaching, university group piano and piano pedagogy teaching, and music administration. She is well known for her expertise in pre-school piano teaching and as author of *Sing and Play* (Stipes Publishing). She serves as a member of the current IAJE (International Association for Jazz Education) Resource Team representing studio teachers.

E	Jazz Piano Projects	FJH
I	Jazz Works, Book & CD	Alfred

This volume includes play-along CDs and GM Disks, and is designed to help bridge the gap between traditional piano study and jazz instruction.

I	Lead Lines and Chord Changes	Alfred

Subtitled *A Practical How-to Approach for Keyboardists,* this text stresses how to fill out harmonies to achieve improved jazz-like accompaniments for unadorned melodic lines with chord symbols above.

Corea, Chick (b. 1941) USA

Corea is a prominent American jazz pianist, well known for his early recordings with Miles Davis and Gary Burton. He also has composed in the classical vein—piano concerto, string quartet—and recorded selected Mozart piano concerti including the two piano *Concerto in E-flat Major, K 365*.

E-I	§	Children's Songs	Schott

This volume contains twenty pieces for solo piano or keyboard. Numbered but untitled (No. 1, No. 2, etc.) these pieces are very attractive and have been recorded by the composer. They date back to 1971 when the first song was written in the words of the composer, "to convey simplicity as beauty, as represented in the spirit of a child." Corea had the sound of a Fender Rhodes (an early electronic keyboard) in mind with numbers 1-15 and an acoustic piano for 16-20. As with Dave Brubeck's *Nocturnes,* these are wonderful miniatures for a secondary student interested in contemporary jazz sounds. Within the collection Corea composes jazz waltzes, uses Latin rhythms and syncopations, *ostinato* patterns, pentatonic colors, and a great variety of musical textures.

A	Essential Chick Corea, The	Litha Music

  With exception of one solo, Corea provides 14 solo piano transcriptions of his own original compositions.

Coulthard, Jean (1908-2000) Canada (b. & d. North Vancouver)

A pianist and respected Canadian composer, Coulthard studied with Vaughan Williams at the Royal Conservatory of Music in London. She also studied with Copland, Milhaud, Schönberg and Bartók. She taught at the University of British Columbia. Several of her compositions appear in the contemporary anthology, *Music of our Time* as well as in the Frederick Harris *Celebration Series*. She composed works for all genres of music.

I	§	Early Pieces for Piano (twenty pieces)	Canadian Music Centre
I		Four Piano Pieces	Canadian Music Centre
I-A		Pieces for the Present (in impressionistic style)	Canadian Music Centre
A		Sonata for piano	Canadian Music Centre

Crawley, Clifford (b. 1930) Canada (b. Dagenham, England)

Educated in England, Crawley holds degrees/diplomas from the University of Durham, and Trinity College, London. With over eighty published compositions, he presently is Professor *Emeritus* at Queen's University.

E	Exchanges (12 pieces)	Frederick Harris

  For early intermediate students, the challenges include playing dotted rhythms correctly and voicing left-hand melodies above surrounding textures.

Crosby, Anne (b. 1968) Canada

Crosby is a graduate (M.M.) of the University of Michigan where she received the D. H. Baldwin award for excellence in teaching. Her professional base is near Halifax, Nova Scotia where she continues to teach and compose.

E	§	In My Dreams	Frederick Harris
E		In the Mermaid's Garden	Frederick Harris

Diemer, Emma Lou (b. 1927) USA (b. Kansas City, MO)

With degrees in composition from Yale University and the Eastman School of Music, Diemer is one of the leading female composers of her generation. Her intermediate volumes were among the first to explore 20th century compositional techniques for less advanced students. She has written for many genres including voice, chamber, instrumental, choral ensembles, and electronics.

E		Time Pictures	Boosey & Hawkes
I	§	Reaching Out, for Solo Piano	FJH

  Includes: *Slow, Sad Waltz*; *Minor Serenade*; *Drumming It Up*; *Icicles*; *Teasing*. These pieces use a variety of sounds, pedal effects, articulations and non-traditional techniques.

I	Sound Pictures for Piano	Boosey & Hawkes
I-A	Three Pieces for Piano	Plymouth
A	Toccata for Piano	Sisra

Contemporary Literature: Pedagogical Composers *continued*

Donkin, Christine (b. 1976) Canada (b. Grand Prairie, Alberta)

A pianist, violinist, teacher and composer, Donkin studied at the University of Alberta and the University of British Columbia (with Stephen Chatman). She has won national and international awards for her piano, choral and instrumental compositions, such as the 2009 International Music Prizes for Excellence in Composition (Thessaloniki, Greece). She is active as a composer, lecturer, clinician and adjudicator in Canada.

E		Comics & Card Tricks	Frederick Harris
E		Legends & Lore	Frederick Harris
I	§	Imprints	Frederick Harris

With titles like *Snow Falling in the Lamplight* and *Farewell to an Old Friend*, this volume of seven stylish pieces presents musical images to which students can relate.

I	In the Neighbourhood (six pieces)	Red Leaf Pianoworks
A	Peace Country (five pieces)	Red Leaf Pianoworks

Dutkiewicz, Andrzej (b. 1942) Poland (b. Staszów, Poland)

Dutkiewicz studied composition and piano at the Eastman School of Music on a Fulbright Fellowship in the early 1970s. Since 1993, he has served as Professor of Music at the Fryderyk Chopin Academy of Music in Warsaw and is currently the Head of Contemporary Music Studies. Dutkiewicz has recorded his own solo piano works. Some of his excellent early works, such as the *Suite* and *Toccatina*, are currently out of print.

E	§	Puppet Suite, The (16 contemporary pieces)	Kjos

Primarily two-part writing with hints of Kabalevsky, Prokofiev, and Bartók, this is a very attractive collection suitable for less experienced pianists.

I	3 Sketches In Retrospect	Presser
	(*Hymnus, Mazurka, Pastorale*)	

Eurina, Ludmila (Ukraine)

A pianist and composer, she graduated from the National Music Academy of Ukraine in 1990 and took postgraduate composition courses with Yevhen Stankovych. She currently teaches at the National Music Academy of Ukraine. Her works have been published by "Muzychna Ukrajina" and Frederick Harris (Toronto, Canada) and have been performed internationally. Eurina was a prizewinner at the *Torneo Internazionale di Musica* (2000, Italy) and received the Borys Lyatoshynsky award in 2008. She is founder and chair of the Ukrainian Association "Women in Music" and Kiev Branch of ISCM (International Society for Contemporary Music).

E		Town and Country	Frederick Harris

Also includes pieces by Ludmila Eurina, Bohdana Filtz, and Oleksandr Levytsky.

E-A § *	Jazz Fiesta (Blues "Mignon")	Frederick Harris

This volume is part of the *Souvenirs for Piano* series that highlights contemporary composers from Eastern Europe including Russia, Ukraine, and the Czech Republic. Compositions in this series are composed in the spirit of Kabalevsky, Rebikov, and Shostakovich. *Jazz Fiesta* includes 12 pieces with jazz elements such as blue notes, swing rhythms, *ostinato* bass lines, written improvisation, and ragtime.

Evans, Bill G. USA

A jazz and pedagogical composer, Bill G. Evans should not be confused with the jazz great, Bill Evans.

E	Music for the Beach (written for small hands)	Kjos
I	Jazz Sweets (5 jazz solos)	Kjos

E (Early Intermediate)   I (Intermediate)   A (Advanced Intermediate to Advanced)

I-A	Bill G. Evans – Mixed Bag	Kjos
I-A	Bill G. Evans – Ostinato Preludes	Kjos
	Includes *Camel Walk, Low Wind, Punchinella, Rock-A-Bye Boogies, Rondo Vigorous, Slow Dance,* and *Strolling.*	
I-A	Red River Suite	Kjos

Evans, Lee USA

A native of New York City, with music degrees from New York University (B.A.) and Columbia University (M.A. and Ed.D.), Evans has over 80 publications to support the study of jazz. One of the most prolific jazz piano arrangers, his materials are used throughout North America and abroad, particularly Japan and Russia. He is in high demand as a workshop clinician for music teachers associations and national conference meetings.

E		China: Suite for Piano	Hal Leonard
E	§	Jazzmatazz	Hal Leonard
E	§	Tickle the Ivories	Hal Leonard
E-I		Color Me Jazz, Book 2	FJH
I		***Intermediate Level Collections***	Hal Leonard
		Razzle Dazzle, The Elements of Jazz, Watercolors, Jazz Suite for Piano, and ¡Olé!.	
I-A		Celestial Odyssey	Hal Leonard
I-A	§	Easy Jazz Standards (Here's That Rainy Day)	Hal Leonard
		This is an excellent volume to explore jazz sounds and to study jazz voicings. The fourteen "standards" include arrangements such as *Angel Eyes* and *There's A Small Hotel.* The equally successful sequel to this volume is *More Easy Jazz Standards* (12 arrangements).	
I-A		Enchanted Ocean	Hal Leonard
I-A		Lee Evans Arranges: Cole Porter	Hal Leonard
		Additional volumes in this series include volumes devoted to George Gershwin, Jerome Kern, Stephen Sondheim, Duke Ellington, and others.	
I-A		Lee Evans Arranges Jazz Giants and Jazz Greats (2 vols.)	Hal Leonard
I-A		Three 12-Tone Waltzes	Hal Leonard

Faith, Richard (b. 1926) USA (b. Evansville, IN)

A composer and pianist, Faith received his Bachelor and Master degrees from Chicago Musical college and was awarded a Fulbright grant to study composition at the *Accademia Nazionale di Santa Cecilia* in Rome. He was Professor of Piano at the University of Arizona Tucson until his retirement in 1988. Faith has composed four operas, piano works, concerti, choral and chamber works and is recognized nationally for his classical song literature.

I	Finger Paintings (1968)	Shawnee
I	Three Sonatinas (1971)	Schirmer
I	Sonata, no. 1, for piano	Shawnee

Frid, Grigori (Samuilovich) (b. 1915) Russia (b. St. Petersburg, Russia)

Frid is a prolific composer and painter. He studied and later taught at the Moscow Conservatory and has written music in many different genres with styles ranging from traditional to twelve-tone. His output includes symphonies, operas, vocal and chamber music, and music for theater and cinema. He organized the *Moscow Music Club for Young People* in 1965.

Contemporary Literature: Pedagogical Composers *continued*

I § *   A Day in the Country (The Little Shepherd)   Frederick Harris
This volume is part of the *Souvenirs for Piano* series that highlights contemporary composers from Eastern Europe including Russia, Ukraine, and the Czech Republic. Compositions in *A Day in the Country* are composed in the spirit of Kabalevsky, Rebikov, and Shostakovich

Gallant, Pierre (b. 1950) Canada (b. Pembroke, Ontario)

A pianist, teacher, composer and accompanist, Gallant studied piano and composition at The Royal Conservatory of Music. He has served as an RCM examiner and teaches at The Glenn Gould School and The Royal Conservatory of Music in Toronto. His compositions include works for chamber ensembles, orchestra and piano as well as music for theatre, dance, and film. His works have been performed in Europe, Canada, and the United States and reflect a distinctive character and a variety of influences and contemporary elements.

E §   Imitations and Inventions   Frederick Harris
The thirteen imitative and canonical pieces in this album help prepare early intermediate students to play Bach *Inventions* and imitative pieces. Students will experience the challenge of contrapuntal playing while strengthening hand independence.

Ganz, Rudolph (1877–1972) USA (b. Zurich, Switzerland; d. Chicago, IL)

A cellist, concert pianist, conductor, teacher and composer, Ganz studied at the Lausanne Conservatory and later studied piano with Ferruccio Busoni in Berlin. In 1901, he was appointed to the faculty of the Chicago Musical College where he taught for nearly three decades.

E-I §   Animal Pictures   Carl Fischer
Though currently out of print, this is the attractive solo piano version of the set composed for orchestra of the same title, which was premiered with the Detroit Symphony in 1933.

George, Jon (1944–1982) USA

A respected pianist and composer, George is well known for his "Kaleidoscope" volumes for both solo and piano duet and for his many compositions for elementary and intermediate piano students.

E-I § Kaleidoscope Solos, Vols. IV, V   Alfred
The latter two volumes of this landmark series (five volumes total) are superb material for students transitioning from an elementary method to intermediate level compositions.

Gillock, William (1917–1993) USA (b. LaRussell, MO; d. Dallas, TX)

Gillock was a gifted composer, who combined lyricism and rhythmic vitality in a personal style that appeals to students and teachers worldwide. He was an independent music teacher in New Orleans for many years but eventually moved to Dallas, Texas to focus solely on his composing. He presented hundreds of workshops nationally and internationally and received many professional recognitions for his outstanding work as a music educator and composer. His compositions appear on festival and contest lists internationally.

E-I   Accent on Analytical Sonatinas   Willis
E-I   Accent on Gillock, Vols. V-VIII   Willis
The upper level volumes of this series contain many of Gillock's most popular intermediate sheet music solos.
E   Accent on Solos, Vol. III   Willis

E-I § *		New Orleans Jazz Styles (New Orleans Nightfall, Constant Bass)	Willis

One of the first published jazz collections of short jazz compositions, this highly acclaimed series also includes *More New Orleans Jazz Styles* and *Still More New Orleans Jazz Styles*. The titles in the first volume are: *New Orleans Nightfall, The Constant Bass, Mardi Gras, Dixieland Combo,* and *Frankie and Johnny*.

I		Fanfare and Other Courtly Scenes in Baroque Style	Alfred
I		Flamenco	Willis
I		Gillock's Festival of Favorites	Alfred

This collection contains twenty-one Gillock pieces in style imitation, Baroque to Modern.

I		Nocturne	Willis
I		Polynesian Nocturne	Willis
I	§	Sonatina in Classic Style	Willis
I		Three Jazz Preludes	Willis
I-A	§	Lyric Preludes in Romantic Style	Alfred

Subtitled *24 Short Piano Pieces in All Keys*, this set is simply required as preparation for the easier compositions of Heller, Burgmüller, and Grieg. The music has a direct emotional appeal without requiring excessive musical finesse. The use of damper pedal, descriptive titles, and the multi-key variety are excellent preparation for the genre of Romantic preludes. There is no better set of character pieces written by a contemporary composer.

Glover, David Carr (1925–1988) USA

I	§	The Great Smoky Mountains	Alfred
I		Glover's Festival of Favorites	Alfred
I-A		David Carr Glover's Favorite Solos, Bk. 3	Alfred

Goldston, Chris USA (b. 1972) USA (b. Thomasville, NC)

A pianist, teacher, clinician and composer, Chris Goldston is the son of respected composer Margaret Goldston. With degrees from the University of North Carolina Greensboro (B.M.) and Northwestern University (M.M.), he lives in Chicago, Illinois and teaches at the University of Illinois-Chicago, Columbia College, and Sherwood Community Music School. He received the National Federation of Music Clubs *Lynn Freeman Olson Composition Award* in 1991 and was the winner of the 1993 North Carolina State Music Teachers Association Collegiate Composition Contest. Goldston currently serves as National Composition Competition Chair for the Music Teachers National Association.

E	Imprints	Alfred
E-I	Fantastic Fingers, Books 3, 4, 5	FJH

Goldston, Margaret USA (1932-2003) (b. Havana, Cuba; d. Franklin, NC)

A graduate of Louisiana State University, Goldston received the LSU School of Music, *Alumnus of the Year* award in 1991. For years she maintained a thriving piano studio in Franklin, NC and was recipient of the NCMTA *Composer of the Year Award* in both 1983 and 1994. She is the composer of numerous elementary and intermediate collections and sheet solos (not listed below).

E	Windows	Galaxy
E	***Early Intermediate Level Collections***	Alfred

Carnival Capers, Simply Jazzy (Book 2); Romances (Book 1); The Best of Margaret Goldston (Book 2); Travelin' Fingers (Book 2); The Virtuosic Performer (Book 1).

Contemporary Literature: Pedagogical Composers *continued*

I		**Intermediate Level Collections**	Alfred
		Moods (Book 1); The Virtuosic Performer (Book 2); Romances (Book 2); Seasons.	
I-A		**Intermediate to Advanced Level Collections**	Alfred
		Moods (Book 2); Romances (Book 3)	

Grill, Joyce USA

Grill is a pianist, teacher, clinician and educational composer. A former piano faculty member at the University of Wisconsin-La Crosse, her training includes degrees from the University of Wisconsin and additional study in France with Nadia Boulanger (composition) and Robert and Jean Casadesus (piano). She is particularly well known for her piano ensemble publications. She holds the prestigious title of *MTNA Foundation Fellow*. Her versatile approach to music making is reflected in her authorship of the widely used text, *Accompanying Basics* (Kjos, 1987).

E		Character Pieces (seven original pieces in Romantic style)	Alfred
E		Movin' On!	Alfred
E-I		In Style (Bks. I, II)	Alfred
I	§	Down the Road	Alfred
		Through style imitation, the pieces in this volume familiarize students with forms such as etudes, preludes, nocturnes, ballades, passacaglias, barcarolles, and bagatelles.	
I	§	Left Alone–Right On!	Alfred
		This unique book is for a student who can only play (or practice) with one hand temporarily because of an incapacitation. The solos may be played with either hand. The sequel volume is *More Left Alone-Right On!*.	
I		**Intermediate Level Collections**	Alfred
		Changing Moods; In Character; Just for Fun; From Many Lands (nine original pieces in Romantic style); Random Thoughts; Remembering; § Preludes (ten original pieces in Romantic style).	

Hartsell, Randall (b. 1949) USA

Known for his lyrical compositions, Hartsell graduated from East Carolina University and began composing during his pre-collegiate years. Lynn Freeman Olson was influential in encouraging Hartsell to submit his compositions to publishers which has led to a productive career as a composer, teacher, and clinician/adjudicator.

E		New Beginnings	Alfred
E-I		Moments to Remember, Bks. 1, 2	Alfred
E	§	Romantic Etudes (6 original solos)	Willis
I		**Intermediate level collections**	Willis
		Ocean Scenes (6 original solos); Portraits of the Sky; Romantic Impressions; More Romantic Impressions; The Best of Dreams (6 solos).	
I		**Intermediate level collections**	Alfred
		Something Special (Bks. 1-3); Caribbean Dreams; Keyboard Jewels (Bk. 1); Lasting Impressions.	

Karp, David (b. 1940) USA

David Karp is Professor of Music and Director of the National Piano Institute for Teachers and Young Artists at the Meadows School of the Art at Southern Methodist University in Dallas. A nationally known composer, teacher, performer, and pedagogue, his compositions number over 300.

E		Adventures in Sound (an introduction to 20th century composing)	Willis
E		Karp's Festival of Favorites (18 solos) (Flatau, ed.)	Alfred
E	§	Solo Souvenirs and More Solo Souvenirs (Bks. 1, 2)	FJH
E		Spotlights	Shawnee
E-I		Cornucopia (nine pieces for the intermediate pianist)	Carl Fischer
E-I		Jubilant Sounds (eight early intermediate solos)	Alfred
E-I	§	Lady Margaret's Suite (Baroque imitative suite)	Alfred

    This landmark style imitation suite is excellent preparation for music of the Baroque period. Written in the style of J. S. Bach, the movements include a *Prelude, Gavotte, Allemande, Sarabande* and *Gigue*.

E-I		Let's Go Solo (Bks. 1, 2, 3)	FJH
E-I		Sonatina no. 2 for Piano	Carl Fischer
I		A Day at the Zoo	Willis
I		Chanukah, Folk, and Festivals (David and Renee Karp, arr.)	Alfred
I	§	Shades of Time	Alfred

    Titles include *Evening in Montana, Florida Sunrise, Full Moon, Moonlight in Maine, Morning Mist, Nocturne in D,* and *Virginia Sunset*.

I		Sketches in Jazz (6 original solos)	Alfred
I	§	Sonatina for Piano	Willis
I-A		Solo-ettes	FJH

Kocour, Mike USA

Mike Kocour is Associate Professor of Music and Director of Jazz Studies at Arizona State University and was formerly a faculty member at the University of Illinois. Kocour has been a guest of Marian McPartland on her famous syndicated NPR (National Public Radio) program "Piano Jazz" and has appeared with many jazz artists including Dizzy Gillespie. At ASU, Kocour was awarded the Herberger College of Fine Arts *Distinguished Teacher Award* for 2004-2005.

I	Sophisticated Jazz	Noteworthy Publications
A	Jazz Performer—New Perspective	Alfred

    This volume includes solo transcriptions of some of Kocour's favorite jazz standards including *Love Walked In* (Gershwin), *Poor Butterfly* (Hubbell), *Stardust* (Carmichael), and *Sweet Lorraine* (Burwell).

Konowitz, Bert USA

An internationally known jazz educator, Konowitz is Professor of Music Education at Teachers College-Columbia University in New York where he followed John Mehegan. Konowitz is an American icon in jazz education. His *Jazz/Rock* piano course (Alfred) has been a significant contribution in the area of beginning jazz piano instruction. His many honors include a National Endowment for the Arts Award, *Distinguished Alumnus of the Year* at Columbia Teachers College, and multiple Leonard Bernstein *Education Through the Arts* awards.

E		EZ Jazz (7 original jazz solos)	Hal Leonard

    This collection is from the Robert Pace piano education materials.

I		Blues and Jazz Complete	Alfred
I	§	From Hanon to Jazz (with companion CD)	FJH

    A volume that includes original jazz pieces as well as traditional jazz standards.

I		Jazz for Piano (Pace, ed.)	Lee Roberts
I		Jazz Gems, Bks. I, II	Alfred
I		Nothing but the Blues	Alfred

Contemporary Literature: Pedagogical Composers *continued*

Kraehenbuehl, David (1932–1997) USA (b. Urbana, IL; d. Trempealeau, WI)

Composer, pianist, and educator, Kraehenbuehl studied with Paul Hindemith at Yale and also served on the Yale music theory faculty in the early 1950s. He later joined with Richard Chronister (co-founder of the National Conference on Piano Pedagogy) and Thomas McBeth to develop the music publishing firm, *Keyboard Arts Associates*. Kraenhenbuehl was one of many piano educators influenced pedagogically by Frances Clark when he was a composer-in-residence at the Clark non-profit *New School for Music Study* in Kingston, NJ. Many of his excellent solo piano compositions such as *Elegy*, *Patterns in Blue*, and *Spanish Waltz* are now out of print, however, selected solos are still published in the volumes of the *Contemporary Piano Literature* series, Bks. I-VI (Frances Clark Piano Library) published by Alfred.

I-A	Random Walks: The Collected Solo Piano Works	Martha Braden
	Contains *Diptych* (1951), *Five Toccatas for Keyboard* (1955), *A Formal Triad*, (1958), *Toccata Sopra B-A-C-H*, *Tombeau de Bach* (1985), *Random Walks* (1962-1966), and *Looking Back* (1954).	

Kubik, Gail Thompson (1914–1984) USA (b. South Coffeyville, OK; d. Claremont, CA)

A composition student of Walter Piston and Nadia Boulanger, Kubik studied at the Eastman School of Music, the American Conservatory in Chicago, and Harvard University. Thompson taught at Monmouth College and Columbia University. As a composer, he is best known for his music film scores and his Pulitzer Prize in music in 1952 for his *Symphony Concertante*.

I	Dance Soliloquy	Presser/Mercury
I-A §	Celebrations and Epilogue (10 contemporary pieces)	Presser
	Written over a period of several years, these are refreshing contemporary pieces with clever titles. The set opens with two slower pieces and closes with the *Epilogue*, interspersed by seven celebratory titles such as *Birthday Piece* and *Wedded Bliss*.	
A	Sonatina (1941, four movements)	Presser/Mercury

Last, Joan (b. 1908) England

Last was a highly respected piano professor and pedagogue at the Royal Conservatory of Music in London, England. She has numerous pedagogical publications to her credit such as *The Young Pianist: A New Approach for Teachers and Students* (Oxford University Press) and *Interpretation for the Piano Student* (also Oxford).

E	Joan Last: By Land and Sea	Stainer & Bell
E-I	Freedom Technique, Bks. I-III	Oxford
I	Gymnastics	Boosey & Hawkes
I	Petites Images (five solos)	Boosey & Hawkes
I	7 Short Piano Pieces	Boosey & Hawkes
I	Time for Leisure: Six Holiday Sketches for Piano	Novello
I	Tree Pictures	Braydeston Press
I	Two Bagatelles and Valse Gaie	Braydeston Press

Lauer, Elizabeth USA

With degrees in composition from Bennington College (B.A.) and Columbia University (M.A.), Lauer's compositions are primarily in the vocal and instrumental genres. A member of the American Composers Alliance, B.M.I., American Composers Forum, and the International Alliance for Women in Music, she taught composition at the University of Bridgeport, Connecticut.

E §	Soundings	Carl Fischer
I	Magnolia (a Concert Rag)	A.C.A. Pub.
I	Sonata	A.C.A. Pub.

E (Early Intermediate)   I (Intermediate)   A (Advanced Intermediate to Advanced)

Lebeda, Miroslav USA (b. Czechoslovakia)

A graduate of the Conservatory of Music in Prague and the Prague Academy of Music, he immigrated to the United States in 1969.

I	§ *	Music for Young Pianists (Scherzo)	Frederick Harris

This volume is part of the *Souvenirs for Piano* series that highlights contemporary composers from Eastern Europe including Russia, Ukraine, and the Czech Republic. Compositions in *Music for Young Pianists* are composed in the spirit of Kabalevsky, Rebikov, and Shostakovich

Linn, Jennifer (b. 1960) USA

With performance degrees from the Conservatory at the University of Missouri, Kansas City, Linn, is an independent music teacher who currently resides in St. Louis. She holds the title of *Manager-Educational Piano* for the Hal Leonard Corporation and is well known for her national presentations and attractive compositions.

E		Don't Bug Me!	Music Sales America/Hal Leonard
E-I	§	Les Petites Impressions (6 solos)	Hal Leonard

This is a beautifully prepared edition that helps meet the need for more pre-impressionistic preparatory repertoire. Linn's sounds are a perfect match for the style and the titles include, *The Cat and the Gnat, Evening Tide, Moonshadows on the Mountain, Butterflies in the Sunlight, A Lighthouse in the Fog,* and *Marcella's Doll.* This is an excellent volume for pre-impressionistic study.

I	American Impressions (6 solos)	Hal Leonard
I	Yellowstone Suite	Music Sales America/Hal Leonard

Yellowstone Suite features pieces about bears, canyons, and Old Faithful. The set includes technical gestures such as *glissandi* and "roll left arm from elbow to fingertips on black keys," gestures frequently not found in material at this level, but that students will enjoy.

I-A	Reflections (2010)

Pieces include *Aspen Gold, Black Canyon, By the Waterfall, Emerald Lake,* and *Midnight Prayer.*

Louie, Alexina (Diane) (b. 1949) Canada (b. Vancouver, British Columbia, Canada)

Composer-in-residence at the Canadian Opera Company, Alexina Louie's distinct compositional style blends East with West. A major Canadian composer, commissions include the Vancouver, Montreal, Toronto, St. Louis, and BBC Symphony Orchestras.

I	§ *	Star Light, Star Bright (O Moon)	Frederick Harris

This exceptional contemporary set includes 9 pieces: *Distant Star, Blue Sky I, Star-Gazing, Rings of Saturn, Moonlight Toccata, O Moon, Shooting Stars, Blue Sky II,* and *Into Forever.* Techniques include non-standard notation and cluster writing.

McLean, Edwin USA

A graduate of Yale University and current resident of Chapel Hill, NC, McLean is a recipient of several composing awards and a senior keyboard editor for FJH publishing.

E	Miniatures, Bk. 2	FJH
I	Impressions on Rock, Bone, Wood, Earth	FJH

Contemporary Literature: Pedagogical Composers *continued*

A	§	Jazz Nocturnes, Bks. I, II	FJH

Excellent lyrical pieces written in a variety of keys, textures and colors. Effective for both the acoustic and digital piano.

Mehegan, John (1916–1984) USA (b. Hartford, CT)

Mehegan was an influential jazz educator who taught at Juilliard and Yale and played regularly at clubs in New York City. His circle of friends included Art Tatum, Dave Brubeck, and Leonard Bernstein, the latter who dedicated one of his *Anniversary* compositions (see annotation under Leonard Bernstein in contemporary solo section) to Mehegan.

I-A	Improvising Jazz Piano	Music Sales

This is a valuable volume for any pianist who seeks to improve and build their keyboard improvisational skills. It surveys all jazz styles in the modern era.

A	Jazz Improvisation: Tonal and Rhythmic Principles	Music Sales

Mier, Martha (b. 1936) USA

A graduate of Florida State University, Mier is a recognized composer of pedagogical compositions. She is a widely traveled clinician (U.S., Australia, New Zealand) and teaches in her Lake City, FL independent studio.

E		Holiday Treats	Alfred
E-I		Jazz, Rags and Blues, Bks. 2, 3	Alfred
E-I	§	Romantic Impressions, Bks. 3, 4	Alfred
I		Celebrate America!	Alfred

Miller, Beatrice (Bea) USA (b. Detroit, MI)

After earning a M.M. degree in composition from Northwestern University, Miller was a teacher, organist and choir director in Corvallis, Oregon. Her initial focus was teaching and church music, but she gradually devoted more time to composing and won the 1997 Oregon MTA's *Composer of the Year* award.

E		Daytime Adventures	Alfred
I		Concerto in A Minor	Alfred
I	§	Night Songs	Alfred

Excellent pre-romantic style preparation pieces which include *Nocturne in F Minor, Night Song, Dreaming, Reflections, The Gently Rolling Sea, Danny Boy, Impromptu in D Minor,* and *Remembering*.

I	Nostalgic Moments	Alfred

Miller, Carolyn USA

A pianist, accompanist and composer with degrees from the University of Cincinnati and Xavier University, Miller presently teaches group piano in a high school curriculum.

E	§	Student Favorites, Bks. 1-3	FJH
I		Student Hits	FJH

The pieces in this collection are the most successful pieces composed by Miller for students in her studio.

Nakada, Yoshinao (1923-2000) Japan (b. Tokyo)

Nakada was an important Japanese musician. Maurice Hinson notes in his *Guide to the Pianists Repertoire* (3rd ed., Indiana University Press) that Nakada served as Director of the Japanese Society of Rights of Authors and Composers. Nakada's primary publisher is Ongaku-No-Tomo-Sha with Theodore Presser being the U.S. agent.

E	§ *	Japanese Festival (seventeen pieces) (Song of Twilight)	MCA

This is a significant collection which has garnered much respect in North America and has been the inspiration for doctoral research by Tomoko Kanamar. Some of the compositions in the collection (e.g., *Song of Twilight*) have been excerpted for comprehensive piano anthologies such as the *Celebration Series* (Frederick Harris). Because of its varied and interesting music, *Japanese Festival* is an exceptional set for which we include the titles: *Butterfly fluttering, Alone, A green caterpillar and a butterfly, Lively children, A short story, The song of twilight, The ballet by the little flower, The sad waltz, The gear-wheels of a watch, Children's song, Etude moderato, Dance of the aborigines, Japanese festival, A story in my dream, The speedy car, Etude allegro,* and *Children in the mountain.*

E	Piano Pieces for Little Hands	Ongaku /Theodore Presser
I	Suite	Ongaku /Theodore Presser

Niamath, Linda (b. 1939) Canada (b. Vancouver, British Columbia, Canada)

Linda Niamath received her ARCT (Associate, Royal Conservatory Toronto) in piano performance from the Royal Conservatory of Music and her B.M.E. from the University of British Columbia. She is one of Canada's leading educational composers and private teachers. She maintains a private studio in Vancouver and is recognized for her desire to provide effective musical compositions for elementary students to learn. She also has composed for ballet and animated films.

E-I		All Year Round	Frederick Harris
E-I		Fancy Free	Frederick Harris
I	§ *	A Zoo for You (Kangaroos, Penguins)	Frederick Harris

Ten descriptive animal pieces at the intermediate level written with distinctive contemporary, yet pleasing, sounds. *Penguins* contrasts *legato* and *staccato* touches with parallel tritone chromatic runs. *Kangaroos* uses position leaps and accommodates the small hand with no *legato* interval beyond a 6th.

Norton, Christopher (b. 1953) England (b. New Zealand)

Norton has established himself as a unique 21st century composer able to merge classical with contemporary sounds. He currently is based in England and in addition to piano music has written stage musicals, ballet scores, and commercially for television and radio.

E-I	§ *	Microjazz Collection, The, Book 1 (3. Jazz Waltz)	Boosey & Hawkes
E-I	§ *	Microjazz Collection, The, Book 2 (2. Sad Song, 5. Dreaming)	Boosey & Hawkes

This series is intended to assist pianists to understand and feel rhythmically-based blues, rock, and jazz styles. Both books emphasize rhythmic precision. Norton writes in an original and appealing contemporary jazz style.

E-I		Microstyles for Keyboard, Bks. 1–4	Boosey & Hawkes
E-A	§	American Popular Piano (Smith, ed.)	Novus Via Music Group

Merging classical with improvisation and popular styles, and organized Preparatory followed by Levels I-X, this appealing series is comprised of Repertoire, Etudes, Skills, and Technic volumes supported by CDs containing instrumental accompaniments.

E-A	Connections for Piano, Vols. 1–8	Frederick Harris

Includes eight levels of repertoire with coordinated Activity volumes.

Contemporary Literature: Pedagogical Composers *continued*

Ogilvy, Susan USA

A pianist, arranger, teacher and composer, Ogilvy owns and operates a music school in Denton, Texas with husband Jim Ogilvy. She is active throughout the United States as a clinician and pianist and as a keyboard specialist for Yamaha. She is a pioneer in the use of both acoustic and electronic instruments in multi-piano and digital ensembles. (See the listing in the multiple piano section of this text.)

E	Petite Rhapsody	Alfred
E	Toccatina	Alfred
I	Distant Star	Alfred
I	Tarantella	Alfred
I-A	Rainbow's End	Alfred

O'Hearn, Arletta J. USA

O'Hearn is a highly successful teacher, composer and jazz artist living in Portland, Oregon. Her jazz compositions are respected and taught frequently.

E § * Love Jazz (Rock with Jazz) — Kjos
   This volume includes six solos and one duet. The writing is quite original. The first piece, *Rock with Jazz*, a favorite of students, is an excellent study in sharp 9 chords. Other titles in this volume are *Waltz for a Little Ballerina, Walking Crooked Blues, Drifting, A Very Gray Day, Nice 'n Easy,* and *Downtown Cakewalk* (duet).

E Sunshine and Blues (9 solos, 1 duet) — Kjos
   Additional intermediate collections by O'Hearn published by Kjos include: *In a Jazz Grove, Jazz Action, Jazz Introspectives,* and *Swing Street.*

I-A § Three Piano Preludes in Jazz Stylings — Kjos

Oldham, Kevin (William) (1960-1993) USA (b. and d. Kansas City, MO)

Best known for his choral works, Oldham was a talented pianist and musician who studied at Northwestern University and Juilliard and was professionally based in New York City until his early passing due to AIDS. Even when he was suffering from this illness, he completed a piano concerto that he performed with the Kansas City Symphony in 1991.

A Ballade for Piano — Kjos
   This work was premiered at Carnegie Hall in 1992 and later recorded by Karin Kushner.

A § Variations on a French Noël (14 variations) — Kjos
   This set of variations is an excellent concert group useful for recitals and competitions.

Olson, Kevin R. (b. 1970) USA (b. Utah)

Kevin Olson is a member of the piano faculty at Utah State University where he teaches piano pedagogy, piano literature and accompanying, and coordinates the Utah State Youth Conservatory. He has been commissioned to compose for the American Piano Quartet and teachers' associations throughout the United States. His output includes over 100 publications.

E Preludes in Patterns — FJH

E-I	§	Best of Kevin Olson, The, Bks. 1, 2	FJH
		Many of Olson's popular sheet music solos (e.g., *Nocturne*) are available in these volumes.	
E-I		In the Key of Jazz, Bks. 1, 2	FJH
E-I		My Kind of Music, Bks. 3, 4	FJH
E-I		Showcase Solos, Bks. 1, 2	FJH
I		American Scenes	FJH
I		River Rhythms	FJH
I		Sonatina in Colors	FJH
		Additional Sonatinas at the late intermediate level include *Sonatina in Flight, Sonatina in Seasons,* and *Sonatina of the Old West.*	
I		What I Did Last Summer	FJH
I-A		Jazzed Up! Classics	FJH
		This is an appealing collection of classical "standards" imbued with contemporary sounds.	
I-A	§	Outside the Box (10 pieces) (Lehrer, ed.)	FJH
		Co-composed with Wynn-Anne Rossi, this set explores contemporary compositional techniques using melodic and harmonic elements to form new sounds.	
A	§	A Seafaring Suite	FJH

Olson, Lynn Freeman (1938–1987) USA (b. Minneapolis, MN; d. New York, NY)

A Minnesota native with degrees from the University of Minnesota, Olson was an early giant among pedagogical composers and is considered one of America's most respected and influential educational composers and teachers. Olson has numerous successful compositions including elementary sheet solos (e.g., *Lazy Bayou Blues, Willows In the Rain,* etc.) and has edited volumes of classical standards. He co-authored two college group piano texts, the *Music Pathways* piano method with Louise Bianchi and Marvin Blickenstaff, and composed music for the popular CBS television children's show *Captain Kangaroo*. (See Olson under all style period anthologies for his many edited repertoire volumes.)

E	§	Adventures in Style	Carl Fischer
		This is a landmark collection because of the wide variety of sounds within the set. *Finger Painting,* uses one finger to "pick" sounds over a long-held damper pedal. Pieces range from traditional to contemporary. This early intermediate volume is superb material for late elementary and middle school students.	
E		Beginning Sonatinas	Alfred
E-I		Audience Pleasers, Vols. II-III	Alfred
E-I		Four Sonatinas in Varying Styles	Alfred
I	§	Finger Progress	Carl Fischer
		The third and most advanced book of a three-volume technique collection (preceded by *Finger Starters* and *Finger Fitness*), this volume has a nice mix of three approaches: rote technique, written exercises, and musical compositions, the latter emphasizing different aspects of technical development.	
I	§	Piano Favorites, Book 2	Carl Fischer

Contemporary Literature: Pedagogical Composers *continued*

Palmer, Willard Aldrich, Jr. (1917–1996) USA (b. McComb, MS; d. Houston, TX)

With Ph.D. degrees in Music Education and Musicology, Palmer was a pioneer in setting high standards for educational piano publications. As senior keyboard editor for Alfred Publishing, he implemented the Alfred Masterworks Edition with over 100 introductory albums on many composers. His works include 789 publications including methods, piano works, solo and choral works and his edited works. Palmer was the co-author of the Palmer-Hughes accordion method and was influential in developing accredited music degrees for accordion performance in the United States.

E		A Contemporary Album for the Young	Alfred
		Contains effective, original short pieces in modern idioms	
E	§	Baroque Folk	Alfred
		(See annotation in Baroque anthologies.)	
E		Variations on Nine Blind Mice	Alfred
I		Nine Blind Mice	Alfred

Paterson, Lorna (b. 1953) Canada (b. London, Ontario, Canada)

With degrees from the University of Victoria and the University of Alberta, Paterson's compositions have earned respect in Canada. She has received numerous commissions and been featured as a composer for various associations including the Alberta Contemporary Showcase in Edmonton, Alberta.

E		Pianimals	Frederick Harris
E	§	Just a Second! (7 contemporary pieces)	Frederick Harris
		These pieces use mixed meters, contemporary sounds and syncopated rhythms.	
E		Safari Suite	Frederick Harris

Pearce, Elvina Truman USA

A pianist, teacher, clinician and composer, Pearce attended the University of Tulsa and studied with Isabelle Vengerova in New York. She was a pedagogy student of Frances Clark and taught in the Preparatory Division at Northwestern University as well as at North Central College in Naperville, IL. She currently is on the Board of Trustees for the Frances Clark Center for Keyboard Pedagogy and is an editor for *Clavier Companion*. Pearce has an outstanding reputation as a creative teacher, thinker, and composer at the elementary (e.g., the highly successful pedal volume, *Solo Flight*) and early intermediate levels. Her "miniatures" appear in anthologies and collections such as *Contemporary Collection* (Revised edition) published by Alfred.

E		Diversions, Bks. I, II (Flatau, ed.)	Alfred
E		Excursions, Bks. I, II (Flatau, ed.)	Alfred
E-I	§	Seven Preludes, Bks. I, II (Flatau)	Alfred
		Book I centers on white key tonalities and book II black key sonorities.	
I		Expressions	Alfred

Piazzolla, Astor (Pantaleón) (1921-1992) Argentina

I		Astor Piazzolla-El Viaje (15 tangos and other pieces)	Boosey & Hawkes
I-A	§	Piazzolla Tangos (Keveren, arr.)	Hal Leonard
		Piazzolla is best known for his tangos. As part of *The Phillip Keveren Series*, Keveren has arranged 15 of the composer's tangos for late intermediate and early advanced students.	
A		Astor Piazzolla for Piano	Hal Leonard

E (Early Intermediate) I (Intermediate) A (Advanced Intermediate to Advanced)

Rahbee, Dianne Goolkasian (b. 1938) USA (b. Somerville, MA)

Born in Massachusetts of Armenian heritage, Goolkasian's music reflects her ethnic background. She studied at Julliard and at the Mozarteum in Salzburg, Austria. She has numerous compositions including orchestra works, instrumental ensembles, piano, vocal and percussion works.

E §	Concertino No. 1 (Olson/Marlais, eds.)	FJH
	Subtitled *"Peasant Folk Dance, op. 82,"* this is an effective concerto which prepares for early Haydn.	
E-A	Preludes, Vols. I, II (Raffaelli/Marlais, eds.)	FJH
I-A	Modern Miniatures for Piano Solo (Marlais, ed.)	FJH
	Written in the style of Bartók and Kabalevsky.	
A	Piano Sonatas, No. 1 - 4	FJH
	Each published separately, these four sonatas have earned recognition. No. 3 (subtitled *Odyssey*) and 4 are labeled op. 83 and 128 respectively.	
A	Phantasie Variations, op. 12	FJH

Renfrow, Kenon D. USA

Formerly Professor of Piano at the University of Miami (FL), Renfrow currently is *Coordinator of Group Piano* at Bob Jones University. He has co-authored widely used college group piano texts with E. L. Lancaster.

E-I §	Repertoire and Ragtime, Bks. I, II	Alfred
	These unique volumes include original intermediate level solos by composers such as Diabelli, Haydn, and Bach (including the well-known *Musette in D* and *Minuet in G*), with each solo followed by a ragtime variation of the composition arranged by the author.	

Reubart, Dale (b. 1926) Canada (b. Kansas City, MO)

A pianist, teacher, author and composer, Reubart taught at the University of Southern California, Western Washington State Collage and the University of British Columbia becoming a naturalized Canadian in 1971. Composing has always been part of his life, from teenage years to present retirement. He is the author of the well-known text, *Anxiety and Musical Performance* (New York: Da Capo Press, 1985).

I	Pantomimes	Frederick Harris
I	Parodies	Frederick Harris
I	Tonescapes	Frederick Harris

Rocherolle, Eugenie R. (b. 1936) USA (b. New Orleans, LA)

A native of New Orleans and graduate of Tulane University, Rocherolle also studied with Nadia Boulanger in Paris. She is currently a Connecticut resident. With over 80 publications to her credit and numerous compositions recorded, Rocherolle is a premiere American woman composer of educational piano music who has won numerous awards for her compositions. She publishes for genres other than solo piano, e.g., *Vignette for Flute and Piano* (Theodore Presser).

E-I	Momentos, Vols. I, II	Alfred
I	***Intermediate Level Collections with Alfred***	Alfred
	American Panorama; Keyboard Collage: Seven Sketches; Touch of Blue.	
I	On the Jazzy Side (6 original solos, Book and CD)	Hal Leonard
I	***Intermediate Level Collections with Hal Leonard***	Kjos
	American Sampler; Bayou Reflections; Blockbuster; Discoveries; Extravaganza; Just for Friends; New Orleans Remembered; Seven Scenes; Keepsakes, and Souvenirs du Chateau, to name a few.	

Contemporary Literature: Pedagogical Composers *continued*

I	§ *	Six Moods for Piano (Downstream)	Kjos

Some of Rocherolle's earliest and most attractive writing, the moods cover a wide range of sounds. For example, *Pastorale* is helpful for deciding on lengths of right-hand phrases, *Downstream* incorporates crossing hands and a left-hand *ostinato*, while *Fiesta* is a tightly-woven syncopated study.

I-A		A Touch of Romance	Alfred
I-A		Blues Concerto (solo version)	Alfred
I-A		Five Scenes	Alfred
I-A		Recuerdos Hispanicos (7 original solos, Book and CD)	Hal Leonard
I-A		Romancing in Style	Kjos
I-A		Sonata No. 2	Kjos

A three-movement composition which hints at Gershwin's style.

I-A	§	Trois Préludes	Alfred

This early advanced collection is excellent preparation for the easier works of Debussy.

I-A		Valses Sentimentales (7 original solos, Book and CD)	Hal Leonard

Rollin, Catherine USA

A graduate of the University of Michigan (B.M.) and the Oakland University School of Performing Arts (M.M.), Rollin is known nationally for her workshops and presentations and is a respected teacher and composer. Rollin has received composition commissions from *Clavier* magazine, the Music Teachers National Association and the Michigan Music Teachers Association to name a few. She also has adjudicated the national finals of the MTNA Student Composition Competition. In 1987, she was voted *Teacher of the Year* by the Detroit Musicians League.

E		Jazz Gems	Alfred
I		Dancing on the Keys, Bks. 1, 2	Alfred
I	§	Lyric Moments, Vols. 2, 3	Alfred

These are excellent for developing flowing, *legato* style and singing melodic line. They are particularly useful with pre-adolescent students and teens.

I	§	Preludes for Piano, Vols. I, II	Alfred

These preludes, much like those of Robert Vandall's, have claimed a prominent position in the teaching literature and prepare students for the pedaling, hand balance, reading in more complex keys, and voicing skills needed in the ensuing study of more difficult Romantic pieces by period composers such as Heller, Grieg, and Burgmüller. Each volume contains 7 solos.

I	Romantic Gems	Alfred
I	Sounds of Spain, Vols. 2, 3	Alfred

These are very descriptive pieces, with strong melodic and rhythmic character. Students enjoy the "showy" aspects of the music.

I	Spotlight on Style series	Alfred

The *Spotlight on Style* volumes include *Baroque, Classical, Jazz, Ragtime,* and *Romantic*. These are excellent for style preparation. For example, the book devoted to Classical style focuses on the forms used during the period and includes two sonatinas, one theme and variations, and one minuet.

I-A	The New Virtuoso (collection of original etudes)	Alfred

Rubenstein, Beryl (1898–1952) USA (b. Athens, GA; Cleveland, OH)

Beryl Rubenstein taught for many years as a member of the piano performance faculty at the Cleveland Institute of Music. Author of the book, *An Outline of Piano Pedagogy* (Carl Fischer), his compositions are not as well known to the general teaching public and are worth investigating.

E	§	A Day in the Country (five impromptus for piano)	Carl Fischer
		This beautiful set of compositions is a programmatic collection depicting a fox hunt from the initial *Tally-ho* movement to the final *Homeward Bound*. Though temporarily out of print, this set can be found through on-line searching and it is well worth the effort to obtain.	
I		Thirty-Two Piano Studies	Carl Fischer
I		Twelve Definitions	Schirmer

Sanucci, Frank (1901-1991) USA (b. Buenos Aires, Argentina, d. Vista, CA)

Born in Buenos Aires, Sanucci is a graduate of the Eastman School of Music and spent most of his life in California freelancing as a composer and teacher. He wrote music for films (Universal and Republica) and well over 200 compositions for student-pianists. Together with his wife, he operated a joint piano school and children's theater. His piano music consists mainly of sheet music solos though the following collections are still available.

E		Sonatina	Willis
E-I	§	Ghosts (10 mid-intermediate solos)	Willis
A		Three Preludes	Willis

Sheftel, Paul (b. 1933) USA (b. Italy)

Currently based in New York City, Sheftel has performed, lectured, and conducted workshops throughout the U.S. His published piano compositions and supporting software are widely used. Sheftel grew up in Los Angeles, studying composition with Tedesco and later with Tansman in Paris. He trained at Juilliard (B.M. and M.M) and later formed the Rollino and Sheftel piano duo while on a Fulbright grant in Europe which led to performances with such prestigious orchestras as the Berlin Philharmonic and the Chicago Symphony to name only a few. He has performed in important venues in New York City and has served on the faculties of the Manhattan School of Music, the Juilliard School, and Hunter College. He maintains a vibrant private teaching studio in New York City.

E		Merry and Mellow (14 solos)	Alfred
E	§	Patterns for Fun, Bks. 1, 2	Alfred
E-I		"I Haven't Practiced..." (6 solos)	Alfred
E-I		In Perfect Accord (eleven chordal pieces)	Carl Fischer
E-I		No-part Inventions	Carl Fischer
I		Blues and All That Jazz	Alfred
I		Blues for Fun	Alfred
I	§	Declarations of Independence	Carl Fischer
		Original technique pieces designed to develop independence between fingers within the hand, as well as coordination between the hands. Pieces fall into six categories: Positions, Warm-ups, Pedal studies, Rhythm studies, Snippets (short fragments), and Add-a-note (literally).	
I	§	Etudes Brutus	Alfred
		These deceptively difficult but musically entertaining exercises include interesting Czerny-like musical parodies and parodies of other composers as well (i.e., Debussy's first etude).	

Contemporary Literature: Pedagogical Composers *continued*

I		Folk Songs from Around the World	Alfred
I	§	Interludes, Vols. I, II	Carl Fischer

    Subtitled *Mood Studies for Piano*, these very attractive pieces, the majority of which use the damper pedal, utilize technical patterns that easily can be mastered.

I	Paul's Practical Piano Pieces	Carl Fischer
I	Piano Patterns	Carl Fischer
I-A	Blues for Fun	Alfred

Siegmeister, Elie (1909–1991) USA (b. New York, NY; d. Manhasset, NY)

Siegmeister was an influential American composer, one of several Americans who studied with Nadia Boulanger. Performances of his works by major orchestras (including commissions), are too numerous to mention in this short space. Many of Siegmeister's shorter piano compositions are contained in volumes 1, 2, 5, and 6 of the Frances Clark *Contemporary Piano Literature* series (Alfred). Siegmeister developed a unique musical vocabulary which merged various elements of American culture.

E	§	American Kaleidoscope	Alfred

    This is an iconic early intermediate collection. The set contains 19 contemporary miniatures with descriptive titles and music that contains great variety. The set is a must for early intermediate students.

E		Children's Day, The (six pieces)	MCA
E	§	Our Cat (miniature suite for piano in three movements)	Carl Fischer

    A distant cousin to Copland's *Scherzo Humoristique* (The Cat and Mouse), but easier.

E-I	Folk Ways, USA, Vols. 1–5	Presser

Starer, Robert (1924-2001) USA (b. Vienna, Austria; d. Kingston, NY)

An Austrian-born, American composer and pianist, Starer left Nazi Europe at the outset of WWII eventually settling in the United States and studying composition with Copland at Juilliard. Later, Starer taught at Juilliard and the City University of New York. He composed in virtually every genre, especially vocal and opera.

E			Seven Vignettes	Leeds
E-I	§	*	Sketches in Color, Vol. I (2. Shades of Blue), Vol. II	Hal Leonard

    The *Sketches in Color* are well-known if not famous teaching collections, and within each set, employ different compositional techniques including polytonality, jazz syncopation, pentatonic, twelve tone and tonal writing. The second set is slightly more difficult. Probably Starer's most famous piano collection, various sketches have been excerpted for piano solo anthologies. The "colors" in Book I are *Black and White, Bright Orange, Crimson, Grey, Pink, Purple,* and *Shades of Blue*. Set two: *Aluminum, Aquamarine, Chrome Yellow, Khaki, Maroon, Pepper and Salt,* and *Silver and Gold.*

E-A	Album for Piano (complete piano works)	Hal Leonard

    Now back in print, this collection contains works that are otherwise difficult to find including the elementary set, *Even and Odds*, as well as *Four Seasonal Pieces* (1985), *Three Israeli Sketches* (*Pastorale, Little White Sheep, Dance*), and *At Home Alone* (12 short pieces; 1980).

I	The Contemporary Virtuoso (7 pianistic studies)	Alfred
I-A	Excursions for a Pianist	MCA

E (Early Intermediate)   I (Intermediate)   A (Advanced Intermediate to Advanced)

Strommen, Carl (b. 1940) USA

Carl Strommen is best known for his hundreds of arrangements of band, orchestra, jazz band and vocal music. His music is heard in film and on television. A resident of Glen Head, New York, Strommen is currently on the music faculty of the C.W. Post Campus of Long Island University, where he teaches graduate orchestration, composition and arranging.

E	§	Piano a la . . . Jazz, Easy	Alfred
I	§	And all that jazz, Vols. I-III (each with CD)	Carl Fischer
		Basic elements of jazz piano playing are presented in this series that evolves from pieces written for beginners (Book I) through the intermediate (Book 3) level.	
I		Piano a la . . . Jazz, Intermediate	Alfred

Tan, Chee-Hwa (b. 1965) USA (b. Johore, Malaysia)

Educated at Oral Roberts University and Southern Methodist University (M.M. performance), Tan served on the Oberlin Conservatory faculty as their specialist in group piano and piano pedagogy. As an independent teacher in Colorado, Tan brings years of teaching experience to her highly creative and expressive compositions. She is active as a clinician in workshops throughout the United States and Canada.

E	§ *	A Child's Garden of Verses (8 pieces) (The Land of Nod)	Frederick Harris
		In this critically acclaimed volume, illustrations and prose excerpted from Robert Louis Stevenson's *A Child's Garden of Verses* accompany each of the eight pieces. This volume creatively ties poetry to music.	
E	§	Circus Sonatinas	Frederick Harris
		This collection features two attractive sonatinas, *Circus Sonatina* and *Big-Top Sonatina,* each with three movements cleverly subtitled (e.g., Black Bear Boogie, Ferocious Lions, etc.). The writing includes a mixture of hand-crossings, reading both hands in one clef, and *8va* markings to explore wide registers. The *Big-Top Sonatina* is slightly easier than the *Circus Sonatina*.	
E		Through the Windowpane	Frederick Harris

Telfer, Nancy (Ellen) (b. 1950) Canada (b. Brampton, Ontario, Canada)

A prominent Canadian composer with significant premieres to her credit, Telfer received her formal music education at the University of Western Ontario. Her compositions range from elementary piano pieces to concert works for the stage. She is active as a workshop clinician, lecturer and composer with over 300 works for chamber music, orchestra and choir.

E	§	I'm Not Scared (10 pieces)	Frederick Harris
		This volume uses innovative contemporary sounds. Commentary by the composer accompanies each piece. Titles include *Crocodile Teeth, Witch's Flight,* and *Skeleton Dance.*	
E		Planets and Stars	Frederick Harris
E		Wild and Free	Kjos
E-I	§	Land of the Silver Birch (original settings of 10 folk tunes)	Frederick Harris
I		Put On Your Dancing Shoes (9 pieces)	Alfred
		Originally from the Frances Clark Library, this excellent collection uses a variety of rhythms, harmonies and dissonances.	
I		She's Like the Swallow (settings of 8 Canadian melodies)	Frederick Harris
I		Space Travel (9 pieces)	Frederick Harris

Contemporary Literature: Pedagogical Composers *continued*

Tsitsaros, Christos (b. 1961) (resides USA) (b. Cyprus)

A native of Cyprus, with advanced degrees from Indiana University (artist diploma) and the University of Illinois (D.M.A.), Tsitsaros writes in a highly original and creative style and has established himself as a first rate composer of piano compositions for students at all levels. He is Professor of Music (Piano and Piano Pedagogy) at the University of Illinois at Urbana-Champaign. With Hal Leonard Music Publishing, he has made numerous contributions to their *Showcase Solos* series such as the late intermediate, *Bike Ride* (a prize winning composition for the National Conference on Piano Pedagogy) and *Nocturne*.

I	*	Poetic Moments (Blues Valsette, Butterfly Rag))	Hal Leonard
I-A	§ *	Cinderella Suite (Cinderella's Sorrow, Cinderella)	Frederick Harris

Cinderella Suite contains eight late intermediate programmatic pieces. Students musically can follow the fairy tale's story line by playing titles such as *The Dance of the Mice* and *At the Prince's Ball*. The titles are well suited for pre-collegiate recital programs. The lyrical *Cinderella's Sorrow* best introduces the collection.

I-A	§ *	Dances from Around the World (Gypsy Dance, Norwegian Dance)	Hal Leonard
I-A		Songs Without Words (9 character pieces)	Hal Leonard

Sounds of the Rain and *Arabesque* are particularly attractive from this set.

A	Autumn Sketches (five pieces, temporarily out-of-print)	Hal Leonard
A	Nine Tales	Frederick Harris
A	Sonatina Humoresque	Hal Leonard

The composer's expertise in both piano pedagogy and composition shows through in this appealing three-movement contemporary sonatina. In the spirit of Kabalevsky (especially the first movement), it is pianistically perfect for students who wish to build their technique.

Vandall, Robert D. (b. 1944) USA

Currently an independent music teacher in New Philadelphia, Ohio, Robert Vandall is one of the most respected composers of educational music in North America and is widely traveled as an artist clinician and presenter. As a former graduate of the University of Illinois (M.M.), he has been recognized with that institution's second prestigious School of Music *Alumni Achievement Award*, the first of which went to George Crumb.

E		American Folk Songs	Alfred
E		Short Suite	Alfred
E	§	Vandall Stylings U.S.A.	Alfred

This set of intermediate pieces includes *Swinging Musette* which can be taught in conjunction with J. S. Bach's *Musette in D Major, BWV Anhang 126*.

E-I		Bagatelles, Vols. I, II	Alfred
E-I		Modes and Moods	Alfred
E-I		Sampler, Bks. 1-II	Alfred
E-I	§	Vandall Sonatinas (four original sonatinas)	Alfred

Each *Sonatina* is in the standard three movement classical form and the following keys are used beginning with no. 1: C Major, G Major, D Major, and A minor.

I	Contrasts (six solos)	Alfred
I	Etude Suite	Alfred
I	Jazz Sonatina	Alfred

The movements for this popular sonatina are *Rhythmic, Lightly,* and *Driving*.

E (Early Intermediate)   I (Intermediate)   A (Advanced Intermediate to Advanced)

I		*Intermediate Level Collections*	Alfred

Many of Vandall's intermediate solos, such as *Daydream, Movin', Evening Shadows,* etc. are now available in these collections: Romantic Inspirations; Celebrated Piano Solos (Bks. 2-5), Celebrated Lyrical Solos (Bks. 2-5), Celebrated Jazzy Solos (Bks. 2-5), Celebrated Virtuosic Solos (Bks. 2-5), and Take Note (Bks. 2-3).

I-A § Preludes, Vols. I, II — Alfred

Vandall's *Preludes* are well known and can be considered core educational intermediate repertoire. The first two prelude volumes cover 17 major and minor keys of the 24 possibilities and hint at a variety of styles, ranging from Bach (Vol. I, no. 5) to Khatchaturian (Vol. II, no. 8). Without exception, students enjoy the music, and within each volume can master most, if not all of the content.

A § Preludes, Vol. III — Alfred

Volume III covers the remaining seven keys to reach 24. This volume is more advanced technically and musically than the first two. Overall, it represents Vandall's most advanced compositions and is compelling study material for late intermediate/early advanced students. It should be noted that volumes I-III are now available in one book with companion CD, on which the preludes are performed by Scott Price.

Watson Henderson, Ruth (Louise) (b. 1932) Canada (b. Toronto, Canada)

A pianist, accompanist and composer, Ruth Watson Henderson was educated at the Royal Conservatory of Toronto and the Mannes College of Music in New York. She is known and respected for her role as accompanist for the Toronto Children's Chorus and is particularly known for her choral works.

I Six Miniatures for Piano — Frederick Harris

Yeager, Jeanine (Nellis) USA (b. Dayton, Ohio)

A pianist, teacher, arranger and composer, Yeager received her B.M. degree from Capital University and her M.M. degree in theory and composition from The Ohio State University. She is active as a clinician and performer and has received national recognition for her appealing compositions.

E *Early Intermediate Collections* — Kjos

Especially for You, Just for Fun, Roundup Ranch, Solitudes, Technique Teasers.

I § *Intermediate Level Collections* — Kjos

Quiet Moods, Around the Sundial, Classic Inspirations, Déjà Vu, Elegance in Style, Mostly Mellow, Personal Touches, Smart Moves, Strike It Rich (Vols. I, II), Too Hot to Handle.

I-A Sincerely Yours — Kjos

Contemporary and Jazz/Ragtime Collections and Anthologies

SOLO LITERATURE

	Title	**Publisher**
§	Album of American Piano Music (Dubal, ed.)	International

(from the Civil War through World War I)

    Dubal's volume includes representative works from well-known composers such as MacDowell, Griffes, and Gottschalk as well as lesser-known composers such as Amy Beach. A detailed *Preface* includes biographies on eighteen composers with historical notes.

Anthology of 20th Century Piano Music (Hinson, ed.) — Alfred

    This important Anthology is paired with a DVD on early 20th century performance practices. Hinson performs music from the volume and relates valuable information about composers and their music such as Bartók, Debussy, Joplin, Grainger, Hindemith, MacDowell, Coleridge-Taylor, Satie and Schönberg.

§ Black Women Composers: A Century of Piano Music (Walker-Hill, ed.) — Presser

§ Bravo Brazil! Vols. I, II (Appleby, ed.) — Kjos

    This is a unique collection of early intermediate to late intermediate compositions by Brazilian composers assembled by the foremost scholar on Brazilian music, David P. Appleby. The set includes music by composers such as Ernst Mahle, Marlos Nobre, Heitor Villa-Lobos, and Camargo Guarnieri.

§ The Century of Invention, Piano Music of the 20th Century (Hinson, ed.) — Schott

    From the title, the reader might think this volume is a compilation of invention-like textures. Rather, it is a remarkable sampling of 20th-century composers within one volume, divided into two sections: I: Intermediate Level and II: Moderately Difficult Level. A partial list of composers includes Berg, Lutoslawski, Milhaud, Poot, Schönberg, Turina, Bartók, Copland, Hindemith, and Poulenc.

Contemporary Album for the Young, A (Palmer, ed.) — Alfred

    Contains original short pieces in modern idioms.

Contemporary Masters, The (Lew, ed.) — Alfred

    An intermediate collection which includes: *Bagatelle, op. 6, no. 6* (Bartók), *Le petit nègre* (Debussy), *Prelude no. 2* (Gershwin), *Waltz, op. 123, no. 6* (Gretchaninoff), *Toccatina* (Kabalevsky), *The Bagpipes and Lullaby* (Menotti), *Gymnopedie no. 1* (Satie), and *The Mechanical Doll* (Shostakovich).

§ Contemporary Piano Literature, Vols. I–VI (F. Clark, ed.) — Alfred

    This landmark series is one of the first published 20th-century collections of carefully graded contemporary teaching pieces. Since the original publication, it has been updated and revised. The first printing helped introduce many Eastern European names to American piano teachers, composers such as Bartók, Kabalevsky, Prokofiev, and Shostakovich. Other names in these volumes include Finney, Scott, Siegmeister, Stravinsky, and Tcherepnin to name only a few. Short composer biographies are provided.

51 Piano Pieces from the Modern Repertoire — Schirmer

Four Early 20th-Century Piano Suites by Black Composers (Smith, ed.) — Schirmer

    This volume includes intermediate to advanced compositions by Samuel Coleridge-Taylor, Harry T. Burleigh, R. Nathaniel Dett, and Artie Matthews.

E (Early Intermediate)   I (Intermediate)   A (Advanced Intermediate to Advanced)

§	Harris Piano Classics: Romantic and 20th-Century Repertoire	Frederick Harris

(Vols. 1b-7b) These seven books progress in difficulty and include a wide range of Romantic and Contemporary composers. Each volume contains between 16 to 24 pages, and includes 9 to 12 piano compositions.

Masters of American Piano Music (Hinson, ed.) — Alfred

Masters of Impressionism (Hinson, ed.) — Alfred

Masters of Spanish Piano Music (Hinson, ed.) — Alfred
Sixteen piano works by Isaac Albéniz, Mateo Albéniz, Manuel de Falla, Enrique Granados, Padre Felipe Rodriguez and Padre Antonio Soler.

Masters of the Early Contemporary Period (Hinson, ed.) — Alfred
Selected compositions from the late 19th and early 20th centuries.

§ Music of Our Time, Vols. 1–8 — Waterloo
A landmark collection that includes early intermediate and intermediate compositions by composers such as Jean Coulthard, David Duke, and Joan Hansen. The series consists of eight graded volumes that demonstrate 20th-century compositional techniques.

New Direction (Anson, ed.) — Willis
Sixteen Original Examples of Contemporary Idioms

Pianist's Book of Early Contemporary Treasures, The (Banowetz, ed.) — Kjos
Includes original works by Bartók, Debussy, Kabalevsky, Kodály, Nielsen, Prokofiev, Rachmaninoff, Ravel, Satie, Scriabin, Shostakovitch, Strauss, and Tchérépnin.

§ Souvenirs for Piano — Frederick Harris
This seven volume series features little-known eastern European contemporary composers from Russia, Ukraine, and the Czech Republic. Writing varies from early intermediate to early advanced, and features composers such as Grigori Frid, Vladimir Blok, Ludmila Eurina, and Miroslav Lebeda. *Jazz Fiesta* (Ludmila Eurina) and *A Day in the Country* (Grigori Frid) are favorite volumes from this innovative series. Other volumes are: *Twelve Pieces in Folk Modes* (Blok), *Vignettes* (Blok), *Town and Country* (Eurina, Filtz, Levytsky), *Ukranian Echoes* (Eurina, Filtz, Ishchenko), *Music for Young Pianists* (Lebeda).

§ Supplementary Solos, Vols. I–IV (F. Clark, ed.) — Summy-Birchard
This series consists of a graded collection of contemporary jazz-sounding solos by educational composers such as David Kraehenbuehl, Lynn Freeman Olson, and Jon George. Includes well-known titles such as *Broken Record Boogie* and *Chattanooga Cha-Cha*. Excellent material for students exiting a piano method. Books III and IV are early intermediate.

36 Twentieth Century [original] Pieces — Schirmer

Twentieth Century, The Vol. IV (Agay, ed.) — Music Sales
Exploration of the language, attitude, dissonance, and drama of contemporary piano music in the works of Debussy, Bartók, Stravinsky, Piston, Ives, Ravel, Hindemith, and 35 other contemporary composers.

§ 12 x 11 Piano Music in 20th Century America (Hinson, ed.) — Alfred
Twelve original compositions written by eleven highly respected contemporary composers such as George Crumb, Milton Babbitt and Halsey Stevens.

Contemporary and Jazz/Ragtime Collections and Anthologies *continued*

§ 20th-Century Piano Collection, from 1945 (York, ed.) — Boosey & Hawkes
This is a unique collection with original intermediate level solos by composers such as L. Bernstein, B. Lees, Kadosa, and Dello Joio, to name a few.

§ Young Pianist's Repertoire Series, The — Frederick Harris
This is an on-going series of original compositions by contemporary American and Canadian composers. Each volume is devoted to the works of one composer. The series includes educational composers such as Susan Alcon, Stephen Chatman, Linda Niamath, Christopher Norton, Lorna Paterson, Dale Reubart, Nancy Telfer, and Christos Tsitsaros.

Jazz and Ragtime Collections

§ Art Tatum Solo Book — Artist Transcriptions
For advanced pianists who want to tackle original transcriptions from Tatum, this advanced collection contains six well-known solos including *In a Sentimental Mood, Stormy Weather,* and *Tenderly.* This publisher also has volumes devoted to advanced solo transcriptions by jazz greats Bill Evans, Oscar Peterson, and George Shearing, to name a few.

§ Best of Ragtime, The (Morath, ed.) — Music Sales
Ragtime scholar Morath has assembled an excellent collection of original rags by composers such as Scott Joplin and Joseph Lamb.

Classic Piano Rags (Blesh, ed.) — Dover
This volume contains 81 rags by important composers of the genre. Many of the lesser-known rags are difficult to find in print publications.

Fifty [original] Classic Piano Rags (Blesh, ed.) — Dover

Joy of Boogie and Blues, The (Agay/Martin, arr.) — Yorktown

Joy of Ragtime, The (Agay, ed.) — Yorktown

Max Morath's Original Rags for Piano (2008) — Hal Leonard
Seventeen of Morath's compositions dating from 1954-1994.

Ragtime Gems (Jasen, ed.) — Dover

Ragtime Rarities (Tichenor, ed.) — Dover

§ Ragtime Rediscoveries (Tichenor, ed.) — Dover
As the title suggests, this volume contains a unique assortment of sixty-four original works by lesser-known ragtime composers dating from 1897 to 1921. An extensive introduction provides excellent background information on the ragtime tradition.

Women Composers of Ragtime (Lindeman, ed.) — Presser
A collection of six rags by Adeline Shepherd, Julia Niebergall, May Aufderheide, and Irene Giblin.

World's Greatest Ragtime Solos for Piano (Hinson, ed.) — Alfred
For the advanced pianist this excellent and large collection (144 pages) features many original rags by Scott Joplin and others, including Irving Berlin, Mark Janza, Eubie Blake, and Joseph Lamb.

E (Early Intermediate)   I (Intermediate)   A (Advanced Intermediate to Advanced)

Multi-period Collections and Anthologies

Multi-period collections and anthologies are volumes that present music from more than one style period, normally all four keyboard periods.

Title (editor) — **Publisher**

§ Applause! Vols. I, II (Olson, ed.) — Alfred

The *Applause!* volumes are a collection of frequently taught and often performed piano solos representing all style periods. Volume II composers include Mussorgsky, Moszkowski, Pieczonka, Paradisi, and Villa-Lobos.

§ At the Piano with Women Composers (Hinson, ed.) — Alfred

Hinson's volume contains fifteen pieces by women composers from thirteen countries. It includes works by 18th- to 20th-century composers such as Clara Schumann, Amy Beach, Fanny Mendelssohn Henselt, and Wanda Landowska. Extensive background information is provided on each composer.

Beethoven to Shostakovich (Anthony, ed.) — Presser

§ Beginning Piano Solos and More Beginning Solos (Sheftel, ed.) — Carl Fischer

Sheftel's repertoire compilation in these two volumes represents a comprehensive anthology of entry-level piano compositions representing over thirty different composers.

Byrd to Beethoven (Anthony, ed.) — Presser

§ Celebration Series Perspectives — Frederick Harris

Preparatory Repertoire Album; Piano Repertoire Albums, Levels 1–10
Piano Studies Albums, Levels 1–10
Student Workbooks, Levels 1-8 (coordinated with Repertoire Albums 1-8)
Handbook for Teachers and Compact Discs

The widely recognized *Celebration Series*, now in the fourth edition, is a carefully graded collection of solo literature ranging from late elementary to early advanced compositions. The term *Perspectives* designates the most recent edition published in 2008. Earlier editions include the *Piano Odyssey* (2000 edition) and *Centennial* in the early 1990s (first U.S. edition). Each repertoire album is a multi-period offering of compositions from contrasting style periods. A strength of this carefully prepared anthology is the wealth of contemporary music from many different publishers and the scholarly editing. The *Piano Studies Albums* emphasize technical studies at each level. The easy-to-use *Student Workbooks* provide learning resource materials coordinated with the repertoire in the *Repertoire Albums*, levels 1–8. Each workbook offers information about the pedagogical and analytical aspects of the piano repertoire, and includes composers' biographies and specific practice suggestions for each piece. Compact discs, which include expertly recorded performances of all Repertoire and Etudes, are available.

The substantial *Handbook for Teachers* provides order of difficulty charts, summarizes keys, meters and forms, and organizes the Repertoire and Studies albums by including individual discussions on each piece and outlining helpful teaching and practice suggestions including score exploration discussions and creative activities. The *Handbook for Teachers* is essential for understanding and teaching any level from the entire *Celebration Series* anthology.

Multi-period Collections and Anthologies *continued*

	Classics Alive! Bks. 1–3 (Magrath, ed.)	Alfred
	Classics, Romantics, Moderns (Sheftel, ed.)	Carl Fischer
§	Classics to Moderns Series (Agay, ed.)	Music Sales

    Easy Classics to Moderns
    More Easy Classics to Moderns
    Classics to Moderns in the Intermediate Grades
    Early Advanced Classics to Moderns

        These landmark volumes, still in print and progressive in difficulty, represent some of the earliest multi-period piano anthologies published in North America.

	More Classics Romantics Moderns (Sheftel, ed.)	Carl Fischer
	The Complete Piano Player Collection, II, III (Zeitlin, ed.)	Music Sales
§	Creme de la Creme (Sheftel, ed.)	Alfred

    Creme de la Creme features thirty frequently performed early intermediate piano pieces representing sixteen composers from Bach to Bartók. These pieces provide an inviting introduction to the Classical repertoire. Compact disc available.

§	The Easiest Sonatina Album (Aubry, ed.)	Frederick Harris

    We often associate sonatinas only with the Classical period. Here is a collection of eleven early intermediate sonatinas from various style periods by composers such as Beethoven, Biehl, Gurlitt, Lichner, Spindler, and Wagner.

	Easy Keyboard Music Ancient to Modern (Palmer, ed.)	Alfred
§	Encore! Vols. I–III (Magrath, ed.)	Alfred

    Each volume contains approximately twenty piano compositions organized chronologically by style period. A suggested order of progressive difficulty is included. Compact discs are available for each volume.

§	Essential Keyboard Repertoire (Olson, ed.)	Alfred

    Olson's edition includes one hundred early-level piano selections (Baroque to Modern) arranged in chronological order. Twelve selections are identified as easier to assign.

	Essential Keyboard Series (Hinson, ed.)	Alfred

    Repertoire Requiring a Hand Span of an Octave or Less

        This repertoire for small hands includes eighty-three intermediate selections in their original form. The pieces are arranged in three levels: Early Intermediate, Intermediate, and Late Intermediate.

	Essential Repertoire to Develop Technique and Musicianship	Alfred

    Hinson's edition includes seventy-five early to late intermediate selections (Baroque to Modern) in their original form. The pieces are arranged in three levels: Early Intermediate, Intermediate, and Late Intermediate. The contents also list ten categories according to basic pianistic techniques.

§	Essential Intermediate Keyboard Repertoire (Hinson, ed.)	Alfred

    An anthology designed specifically for the intermediate piano student. Selection of repertoire was based on interesting melodies and rhythmic patterns, technical accessibility, formal structure, and exceptional aesthetic value. The eighty-five pieces are arranged in three categories: Early Intermediate, Intermediate, and Late Intermediate. Includes lesser-known composers such as Niels Gade, Valentin Rathgeber, and Domenico Zipoli.

E (Early Intermediate) I (Intermediate) A (Advanced Intermediate to Advanced)

	Everybody's Perfect Masterpieces, Vols. I–IV (Bigler/Lloyd-Watts, eds.)	Alfred
§	Exploring Piano Literature (Olson, ed.)	Carl Fischer
§	Exploring More Piano Literature (Olson, ed.)	Carl Fischer

    These two short volumes contain late elementary entry-level solos appropriate for students just completing a piano method. Detailed practice suggestions accompany each composition.

Favorite Classics (Lancaster/Renfrow, eds.)	Alfred
First Steps in Keyboard Literature (Olson, ed.)	Alfred
Four Centuries of Keyboard Music, Vols. II, III	Boston Music
French Piano Music: An Anthology (Philipp, ed.)	Dover
From Bach to Bartók, Vols. 1A, 1B, 1C (Agay, Lew, eds.)	Alfred
Guild Repertoire (Podolsky/Gowe, eds.)	Alfred

    Intermediate A, B, C, Preparatory A

Harris Festival Series, Levels 1-7	Frederick Harris
Humor in Piano Music: Baroque to Modern (Hinson, ed.)	Alfred
Introduction to the Masterworks (Palmer/Lethco, eds.)	Alfred
Introduction to Theme and Variations (Halford, ed.)	Alfred
The Joy of Classics (Agay, ed.)	Music Sales
The Joy of First Classics (Agay, ed.)	Music Sales
The Joy of French Piano Music (Agay, ed.)	Music Sales
The Joy of Recital Time (Agay, ed.)	Music Sales
The Joy of Russian Piano Music (Agay, ed.)	Music Sales
Leichte Klavierstücke, Bands I, II (Georgii/Theopold, eds.)	Henle
Leichte Klaviervariationen	Henle
Mainstreams in Literature: Classical Pianist, Performer, Patterns A, B, C (Noona, Walter and Carol, eds.)	Heritage

    This intermediate level series includes three books at each level. The Pianist books include repertoire and discovery sheets; the Performer books contain additional repertoire at corresponding levels; the Patterns books are workbooks in style, history, form, analysis, composition, and general musicianship.

Mastering Repertoire, Intermediate Level (Vogt, ed.)	Heritage
Masters of French Piano Music (Hinson, ed.)	Alfred
Masters of Spanish Music (Hinson, ed.)	Alfred

    This volume includes representative keyboard works of Albéniz, de Falla, Granados, Rodriquez, and Soler, spanning three centuries and dating from Soler to de Falla.

Masters of the Suite, a Guide to Style and Interpretation (Hinson, ed.)	Alfred
Masterpieces with Flair!, Vols. 1-3 (Magrath, ed.)	Alfred

Multi-period Collections and Anthologies *continued*

§	Music Pathways Repertoire Series: Books 3A, 3B, 4A, 4B, 5A, 5B	Carl Fischer

This intermediate level series, compiled by Bianchi, Olson, and Blickenstaff, includes three books at each level: *Repertoire*, *Musicianship*, and *Technique*. The music ranges from the early intermediate through late intermediate levels. Concepts in the *Technique* and *Musicianship* volumes reinforce the Repertoire books.

95 Early/Late Intermediate Miniatures-Baroque to Modern (Hinson, ed.) — Alfred

The pieces selected are in their original form and are arranged in three levels: Early Intermediate, Intermediate, and Late Intermediate.

Piano Literature, Vols. I–IV (Bastien, ed.) — Kjos

§ Piano Literature, Vols. I–VI (F. Clark, ed.) — Alfred

This collection, covering literature of the 17th, 18th, and 19th centuries, is one of the first published collections of carefully graded teaching pieces focusing on intermediate level solo piano literature. These repertoire books are companion volumes to the *Contemporary Piano Literature* series.

Piano Literature, Vols. I–IV (Glover/Hinson, eds.) — Alfred

Piano Sonatinas, Books 1–4 (Faber and Faber, eds.) — FJH

§ Masterwork Classics (with compact discs), Vols. 1–10 (Magrath, ed.) — Alfred

§ Practice and Performance, Vols. 1–6 (Magrath, ed.) — Alfred

Compositions in the Masterwork series are selected from Alfred piano editions. Each volume contains thirty to forty pieces divided among the four style periods. The Practice and Performance volumes include practice suggestions for repertoire in the Masterwork Classics series. Practice suggestions center on three stages: preparation, playing, and evaluating. Compact discs are available for each volume.

Premier Recital, Vols. I–III — Salabert

Schubert to Shostakovich (Anthony, ed.) — Presser

Selected Piano Examination Pieces — ABRSM
 Books (Grades) 1–8 (Jones, ed.)

For this recently revised series, each book (through grade 7) contains an assortment of nine pieces representing different style periods. Grade 8 contains twelve compositions, including works by composers such as Scarlatti, Haydn, Field, and Poulenc.

§ Sonatina Masterworks, Books 1–3 (Magrath, ed.) — Alfred

This series is a combination of rewarding sonatina favorites and less frequently heard sonatinas for the sonatina "enthusiast." The fresh balance of works is a welcome addition to the teaching literature.

E (Early Intermediate) I (Intermediate) A (Advanced Intermediate to Advanced)

ENSEMBLE LITERATURE

Introduction to Piano Ensemble Music

The study of piano ensemble literature is an important segment of all pianists' training. Exploring this genre of music at each plateau of instruction, from beginning through advanced levels, will lead to a better understanding of balance (what is musically in the foreground and background), the importance of listening, and of course rhythmic and technical security with a pianistic partner. Perhaps most important is the joy of sharing with another musician in what tends to be a lonely discipline, if the focus is solely on solo repertoire. This fifth edition, with expanded literature sections in the areas of piano ensemble music (note numbered topics below), reflects a heightened interest in ensemble performance and an increase in piano ensemble and monster concerts in both independent teaching settings as well as in colleges and universities.

In the area of piano ensemble, three quite useful resources for teachers and students are *The Piano Duet: A Learning Guide* by Dallas Weekly and Nancy Arganbright (Kjos, 1996), *Piano Duet Repertoire: Music Originally Written for One Piano, Four Hands* by Cameron McGraw (Indiana University Press, 1981 and 2001), and *Music for More than One Piano* by Maurice Hinson (3rd edition, Indiana University Press, 2000).

Ensemble literature is presented in the following categories:

1. Music for One Piano–Four Hands
2. Collections and Anthologies: One Piano–Four Hands
3. Music for One Piano–Six Hands
4. Music for Two Pianos–Four Hands
5. Music for Two Pianos–Eight Hands
6. Music for Multiple Pianos–Multiple Performers
7. Music for Five Pianos–Ten Hands
8. Digital Keyboard Ensemble Music
9. Selected Holiday Literature for Solo Piano
10. Selected Holiday Literature for Piano Ensemble
11. Selected Concerti for Young Pianists by James Lyke
12. Selected Advanced Concerti for Skilled High School Students by Reid Alexander

Composer Biographies: In order to streamline the entries in this section, we have not included composer biographies except for a few composers not listed in a previous section. Please see the Solo Piano Literature sections for brief biographical sketches of individual composers. We have included information on the birth and death place of composers in the twentieth century since many composers were born in Europe and immigrated to other countries or to the United States for a major part of their lives. This information gives a more complete picture of the life of recent composers.

Music for One Piano—Four Hands

	Composer	Title	Publisher

Agay, Denes (1911-2007) USA (b. near Budapest, Hungary; d. Los Altos, CA)

A   Ragtime Duets (Agay, arr.) (6 advanced duet arrangements)   Hal Leonard

Akimenko, Fyodor Stepanovich (1876–1945) Ukraine

Akimenko studied with Rimsky-Korsakov and was influenced by French impressionism when he lived in France after 1917.

I	Pieces ukrainiennes, op. 71 (Six pieces)	Salabert
I	Tableaux idylliques, op. 62 (Valse, Pastorale, Élégie, Danse, Romanza)	Salabert

Albéniz, Isaac (Manuel Francisco) (1860–1909) Spain

I	Aragón fantasia	Unión Musical Ediciones
A	Sevilla	Hal Leonard

Alexander, Dennis USA (b. Kansas)

E	Preludium in D Major	Alfred
E-I §	Just for You and Me, Books 1, 2	Alfred
I	Festival in Cordoba	Alfred
I	Festival Overture	Alfred
I	Touch a Rainbow (Alexander, arr.)	Alfred

    An arrangement of his popular solo piece, Alexander has extended the piece and created a new duet arrangement.

I   Valse Caprice   Alfred

Anderson, Leroy (1908-1975)

I-A	Blue Tango (Edwards, arr.)	Alfred
I-A	Fiddle-Faddle (Esposito, arr.)	Alfred
I-A §	Sleigh Ride (See annotation in holiday listing.)	Alfred

André, Johann Anton (1775–1842) Germany

I   Divertimento in A Minor   Peters

    André wrote several sets of *Divertissements* (e.g., opp. 18, 19, 20), many of which are out of print.

I   Six Sonatinas, op. 45 (Hinson, ed.)   Alfred

Archer, Violet (1913-2000) Canada

E-I   Ten folk songs for four hands (in two books)   Berandol

    Book I: *The Dancing Top, Singing Bells, In The Woods, Gay is the Rose, Music Everywhere;*
    Book II: *Pirate Song, Paul Jones, Eskimo Prayer, Cherry Tree Carol, The Frog and the Mouse.*

Arensky, Anton Stepanovich (1861–1906) Russia

The two important duet opus numbers for Arensky are below, opp. 34 and 66. Titles from those collections appear in many duet anthologies. For example, *Essential Keyboard Duets*, Vol. 2 (Alfred) contains two Arensky duets, one each from opp. 34 and 66.

I	Six Children's Pieces, op. 34 (Philipp, ed.)	International
I-A	Fugue on a Russian Theme	Alfred
I–A	Twelve Pieces, op. 66 (in four volumes)	Jürgenson

Ensemble Literature — Music for One Piano–Four Hands

Music for One Piano—Four Hands continued

These are excellent pieces at the late intermediate level (slightly more difficult than op. 34) organized as follows: Vol. I: *Prélude, Gavotte, Ballade*; Vol. II: *Menuetto, Elégie, Consolation*; Vol. III: *Valse, Marche, Romance*; Vol. IV: *Scherzo, Berceuse, Polka*.

Arnell, Richard (Anthony Sayer) (1917-2009) England

A	Sonatina, op. 61 (Four movements: Andante, Allegro, Andante, Presto)	Schott

Auric, Georges (1899–1983) France

Auric was a member of *les Six*. He was influenced by popular music of his time and peers such as Satie and Stravinsky.

I	Adieu New York	Hal Leonard

This is Auric's piano ensemble version of the piano solo of the same title which was subtitled, *fox trot for solo piano*.

I-A	5 Bagatelles (Ouverture, Petite marche, Valse, Rêverie, Retraite)	Durand

Bach, Johann Christian (1735–1782) Germany

I	Three Sonatas (Weismann, ed.) (1778-1780)	Masters

These *Sonatas* [op. 15, no. 6 (C); op. 18, no. 5 (A), no. 6 (F)], each in two movements, represent some of the earliest piano duets composed. With musical material, including themes, equally distributed between the parts, the writing is comparable in difficulty to Clementi's more difficult sonatinas. The C and F major sonatas have an opening *Allegro* with binary repeats followed by a concluding *Rondo*. The A major has a *Minuetto* as the second movement.

Bach, Johann Christoph Friedrich (1732–1795) Germany

I	Sonata in A (Hillemann, ed.)	Heinrichshofen
I	Sonata in C (Hillemann, ed.)	Heinrichshofen

Each is a three-movement sonata in early classical style.

Bach, Johann Sebastian (1685–1750) Germany

J. S. Bach did not write any original keyboard duet works, however, some of his well-known compositions are often arranged for duet performance.

I		Five Two-part Inventions (Riegger, arr.)	Harold Flammer
I		J. S. Bach Chorales for Piano Duet (Bovet, arr.)	Galaxy
I		Sheep May Safely Graze (Howe, arr.)	Oxford
I-A		Bach Suites (Tucker, ed.)	Alfred
I-A		Suites (Reger, arr.)	Kalmus
A	§	Complete Brandenburg Concertos (Reger, arr.)	Dover
A	§	Jesu, Joy of Man's Desiring (Hess, arr.)	Oxford

(See annotation in Christmas ensemble section.)

A		Six Brandenburg Concertos, Vol. 1 (1-3), Vol. 2 (4-6) (Reger, ed.)	International

Barber, Samuel (Osborne) (1910–1981) USA (b. West Chester, PA; d. New York, NY)

A	§	Souvenirs Ballet Suite, op. 28	Schirmer

A work at the core of the four-hand concert repertoire, *Souvenirs* comprises charming writing using ballroom dance forms of the early 1900s: *Waltz, Schottische, Pas de deux, Two-step, Hesitation Tango,* and *Galop*. Barber transcribed the original duet version for solo piano.

E (Early Intermediate)   I (Intermediate)   A (Advanced Intermediate to Advanced)

Beach, Amy (Marcy) [Mrs. H.H.A.] (1867-1944)

E-I §   Summer Dreams, op. 47 (Weekley/Arganbright, eds.)   Kjos
         The op. 47 duets also are available in the comprehensive book, *The Life and Music of Amy Beach: The First Woman Composer of America* published by Mel Bay. (See Beach entry in Romantic Solo Literature.)

I-A   Three Movements for Piano Four Hands (Block, ed.)   Hildegard

Beard, Katherine K. USA

E   American Folk Song Duets, Set 2   Willis

Beethoven, Ludwig van (1770–1827) Germany

E-I   March in C Major (op. 45, no. 1) and Gavotte in F Major (Sonnen, ed.)   Schott
         The first pairing of these two pieces for publication under one cover was by Harold Bauer in 1920 for Schirmer. The *March* is an original work by Beethoven, however, the *Gavotte* is only attributed to Beethoven (WoO Anh. 8) and is of questionable authenticity. Of the two, the *Gavotte* is clearly at an intermediate level while the *March* is more challenging.

I   Turkish March (from *Ruins of Athens, op. 113*) (A. Rubinstein, arr.)   Zen-On Music
         The *Ruins of Athens* was incidental music composed by Beethoven in 1811. The *Turkish March* was the fifth of eleven movements or sections. Beethoven also used this theme for his op. 76 piano variations.

I-A   All Original Compositions (Complete)   International
         Several complete editions of the four-hand repertoire are published including Peters, Kalmus, Henle, and Schott.

I-A   Sonata Facile in D Major, op. 6   Schott; Berben
         Composed during Beethoven's early period (1797), this is a late intermediate work in two relatively short movements, an *Allegro* followed by a *Rondo*.

I-A §   Three Marches, op. 45   International
         Original duet works, Beethoven titled these *Trois Grandes Marches*. Each has a middle trio section and his choice of keys is C, D-flat, and D major.

I-A   Variations in D Major, WoO74 (on *Ich denke dein*)   International
         Six variations on a song set to text by Goethe.

A   Complete String Quartets Transcribed for Four-Hands (Ulrich/Wittman, arr.)   Dover
         Series 1: opp. 18, 59; Series 2: opp. 74, 95, 120, 130–135

A   Grand Fugue (*Grosse Fuge*), op. 134   Henle; Schott
         This is the composer's arrangement of the *Finale* of his string quartet, op. 130. It is not particularly pianistic but does reveal how Beethoven transcribed music between two genres, string quartet to piano duet.

A   Symphonies, Book 1 (1-5); Book 2 (6-9) (Ulrich, arr.)   Dover
         Before the availability of recordings, playing four-hand versions of symphonies was the only way to hear this music without attending a live performance. This genre of four-hand playing deserves greater attention. Note too that Franz Liszt arranged all the Beethoven Symphonies for solo piano.

A   Variations in C Major, WoO69   International
         Composed on a theme by Count Waldstein, these eight variations with *Coda* are more difficult than the variations on the theme, *Ich denke dein*.

Music for One Piano—Four Hands *continued*

Bennett, Richard Rodney (b. 1936) England

A	Capriccio	Universal

A one-movement atonal work that uses mirror compositional techniques and *glissando* writing.

Berens, (Johann Hermann) (1826–1880) Germany

I-A	Melodious Exercises, op. 62	Kalmus; Peters

Berkeley, Lennox (1903–1989) Great Britain

A	Palm Court Waltz, op. 81	Chester; Marks
A	Sonatina in E-Flat Major, op. 39 (in three movements)	Chester; Marks

Berners, Lord (Sir Gerald Tyrwhitt Wilson "Bart") (1883–1950) England

I	Three Pieces (Chinoiserie, Valse Sentimentale, Kasatchok)	Masters
A	Valses Bourgeoises	Chester

Bernstein, Leonard (1918–1990) USA (b. Lawrence, MA; d. New York, NY)

I-A §	10 Selections from Candide (Harmon, arr.)	Hal Leonard

Includes: *Overture, The Best of All Possible Worlds, I Am Easily Assimilated, Make Our Garden Grow* and others. (Leonard Bernstein Music Publishing Co. distributed through Hal Leonard.)

I-A	Selections from West Side Story (Bernstein/Sondheim) (Klose, arr.)	Boosey & Hawkes

Late intermediate piano duets: *America, Cool, I Feel Pretty, Maria, One Hand, One Heart, Something's Coming, Somewhere,* and *Tonight.*

Bizet, Georges (Alexander César Léopold) (1838–1875) France

I-A §	Jeux d'Enfants (Children's Games) op. 22 (*Philipp)	*International; ASE

Consisting of 12 tone pictures with great musical variety, the movements describe children's activities. This work is an essential part of the original piano duet literature. Titles (translated from the French): *The swing, The top, The doll, Merry-go-round, Badminton, Bugler and drummer, Soap bubbles, Puss-in-the-corner, Blindman's bluff, Leap frog, Playing house,* and *The ball.*

A	L'Arlésienne Suites, nos. 1, 2	Kalmus

Bober, Melody USA

I	Grand Duets for Piano, Bks. 5-6	Alfred

In this duet series, the latter books reach the intermediate level. Parts are of equal difficulty and key, meter, and tempo vary.

I	Southwest Landscapes	Alfred

A Duet suite in three movements, *Colorado River Rapids, Sedona Sun,* and *Majestic Grand Canyon.*

Borodin, Alexander Porfir'yevich (1833–1887) Russia

I	Polka in D Major	Leeds

Several of Borodin's four-hands works, including this *Polka*, are in a multiple composer set (Borodin, Cui, Liadov, Rimsky-Korsakov, Shcherbachov, Liszt) titled, *Paraphrases,* for which the scores can be found on-line.

I-A	Tarantella in D Major (1862) (*Yarbrough-Cowan)	*International; Leeds

E (Early Intermediate)   I (Intermediate)   A (Advanced Intermediate to Advanced)

Brahms, Johannes (1833–1897) Germany

I	§	Liebeslieder Waltzes, opp. 52, 65 (*Mandyczewski, ed.)	*Presser; ASE

The *Liebeslieder Waltzes, op. 52*, and *Neue Liebeslieder Waltzes, op. 65* are essential four-hand duet repertoire. Each set was written for vocal quartet (they are more often heard with vocal octet or small choir) with four-hand accompaniment though the accompaniments can stand alone. The musical variety in each set is simply astounding. Opus 52, which contains 18 waltzes was published in 1869 with the notation that the vocal parts were optional, again suggesting that the two piano parts could stand alone in performance. Brahms deleted this indication in a later revision. Opus 65 appeared a few years later in 1875 and contains 15 waltzes.

I-A		Complete Piano Works for Four Hands (Mandyczewski, ed.)	Dover

Contains 81 compositions including *Variations on a Theme by Robert Schumann, op. 23*; *Waltzes, op. 39*; *Liebeslieder Waltzes, op. 52a*; *Neue Liebeslieder Waltzes, op. 65a*; and *Hungarian Dances, nos. 1-21*.

I-A	§ *	Hungarian Dances, Vols. I, II (no. 5 in F-sharp minor)	Hal Leonard; ASE

These original four-hand dances (21 total) are among the composer's most popular works partly because of their orchestrations. Brahms also arranged 10 for solo piano.

I-A		20 Ländler after Schubert, D 366 (1-16); D 814 (17-20)	Doblinger

These are beautiful transcriptions by Brahms of Schubert solo piano *Ländler*. Brahms also arranged Schumann's *Piano Quartet in E-Flat Major, op. 47* for one piano, four hands.

I-A	§	Waltzes, op. 39 (*Weekley/Arganbright, eds.)	*Kjos; ASE

The op. 39 *Waltzes*, in their original four-hand duet setting, represent, together with the *Liebeslieder* and *Neue Liebeslieder Waltzes*, wonderful opportunities to explore Brahms' writing through compact gems. The intricacy between the *secondo* and *primo* parts, and the various cross rhythms, will challenge duet teams. No. 15 (in A major) is well known and often excerpted from the set for separate publication in anthologies. Brahms also arranged op. 39 for solo piano in two versions (simplified and difficult) and selected five waltzes to arrange for two pianos-four hands (nos. 1, 2, 11, 14, 15). For these latter versions, he changed keys for some of the waltzes. For example, no. 15 is presented in the key of A-flat major (instead of A major) in the two-piano, four hand version.

A	Brahms Arrangements for Piano Four Hands of His String Quartets, The (C Minor, op. 51, no. 1; A Minor, op. 51, no. 2; B-Flat Major, op. 67) (Brahms, transcriber) (Derr, ed.)	Dover
A	Souvenir de la Russie (Six Fantasies) (each about 6 pages long)	Baerenreiter Verlag
A	Symphonies	Schirmer
A	Variations on a Theme by Robert Schumann, op. 23	International; Peters

Brown, Rayner (b. 1912) USA

I	Variations for Four Hands	Western International

Brown, Timothy USA

I	Smoky Mountain Reel	FJH
I	Toccata	FJH

Music for One Piano—Four Hands *continued*

Bruch, Max (Christian Friedrich) (1838–1920) Germany

I-A	Swedish Dances, op. 63 (in two books)	Simrock

These are also available in solo and instrumental (violin and piano) versions.

Bruckner, (Joseph) Anton (1829–1896) Austria

E	§ *	Three Little Pieces (Drei Kleine Stücke), WAB 124 (no. 2)	Schott; ASE

These are excellent early intermediate Romantic duets, frequently excerpted for collections.

I	Quadrille, WAB 121 (1854) (Lemacher, ed.)	Heinrichschofen
I-A	Symphony no. 4 in E Flat Major ("Romantic")	Kalmus
A	Symphony no. 7 in E Major (Bruckner, transcriber)	Kalmus

Burney, Charles (1726–1814) England

I-A	Klaviersonaten zu 4 Händen (Minden, ed.)	Karl Heinrich Möseler Musikverlag

Burney was one of the first to compose sets of sonatas for piano duet, which he called *sonatas or duets for two performers on one pianoforte or harpsichord*. This edition has eight sonatas divided in two groups of four. Each sonata possesses two movements with E-Flat Major being the only non-white key tonic. The writing is largely at the intermediate level. Ensemble challenges in the sonatas include exchange of melody between players, both right hands playing in unison, and balancing the musical texture in a variety of registers. In this edition, the composer states about duet playing: "The playing Duets by two persons upon one instrument, is however, attended with nearly as many advantages, without the inconvenience of crowding a room, or of frequent or double tuning." (p. XI)

Busoni, Ferruccio (Dante Michelangelo Benvenuto) (1866–1924) German-Italian

I	Finnish Folk Tunes, op. 27	Peters

Caramia, Tony (b. 1950) USA

E	§	Folksongs Revisited	Alfred

This tasteful collection presents nine familiar folk melodies (four duets and five solos), imaginatively arranged with appealing harmonies and clever rhythms. Titles include *Aura Lee, MacDonald's Farm, Yankee Doodle, When Johnny Comes Marching Home* and *Michael, Row the Boat Ashore*.

Casella, Alfredo (1883–1947) Italy (b. Turin, Italy; d. Rome, Italy)

I-A	§	Pupazzetti, op. 27 (1916)	Chester

A set of five effective pieces (*Marcietta, Berceuse, Serenata, Notturnino, Polka*), written in a slightly dissonant, "wrong-note" approach. They are short in length, not too difficult, and are excellent recital material.

A	Fox-Trot (1920)	Universal
A	Pagine di Guerra, op. 25 (1915)	Ricordi

Chabrier, (Alexis-) Emmanuel (1841–1894) France

I-A	Cortège Burlesque	Billaudot
I-A	Souvenir de Munich (Samazeuilh, trans.)	Jobert

This is based on musical themes from Wagner's *Tristan und Isolde*.

A	Three Romantic Waltzes (Cortot, transcriber)	Alfred
A	Valzer Romantici	Berben

E (Early Intermediate) I (Intermediate) A (Advanced Intermediate to Advanced)

Chatman, Stephen (b. 1950) Canada (b. Minneapolis-St. Paul, MN)

I § Blues and Bells   Frederick Harris
      This duet collection explores a variety of 20th-century sounds including the blues style (*Sweet Baby Blues*), rag (*Shaughnessy Rag*), and folk song (*She's Like the Swallow*). The last title, *Busy Corner*, is fast and brilliant.

Chopin, Frédéric François (Fryderyk Franciszek) (1810–1849) Poland

E   Albumleaf (Whitis, arr.)   Manduca
I-A   Easy Chopin Piano Duets (Kershaw, arr.) Book and CD   Spartan Press
      These four well-known Chopin piano solos are arranged for duets and can be used as an ensemble introduction to Chopin for the intermediate pianist. Includes: *Étude in E Major, op. 10, no 3*; *Prelude in C minor, op. 28, no. 20*; *Prelude in A Major, op. 28, no. 7*; and *Waltz in A-Flat Major, opus 69, no. 1*. Includes both book and CD with practice and performance tracks.
I-A   Variations in D Major, op. posth. P1 No. 6 (BI 12a)   Chopin Institute; Universal
      An original four-hand work by Chopin, these *Variations* are based on a theme by Thomas Moore and were composed when Chopin was still a teenager (1826). Generally, the *primo* is the more active part, however, in terms of reading difficulty, both the *primo* and *secondo* vary in difficulty from intermediate to advanced.

Clementi, Muzio (1752–1832) England (b. Italy)

E   Two Duettinos   Schirmer; ASE
      These are the shortest and easiest of Clementi's four-hand works and were composed with his daughter Cecilia in mind.
I   Sonatinas, op. 36, nos. 1–6   Schirmer
      Note: For the Clementi Sonatinas, op. 36, see the entry for Timm, Henry C. under Music for Two Pianos–Four Hands.
I   Sonatinas, op. 14, nos. 1, 2   Ricordi; ASE
I   Sonatinen, op. 36 (Ruthardt, arr.)   Peters
I § Three Rondos, op. 41 (Townsend, ed.)   Schirmer; ASE
      These Three Rondos are comparable in level to Clementi's sonatinas.
I-A   7 Sonatas, Vols. 1, 2   Ricordi
      Clementi composed seven original sonatas for four-hands which by movement range in difficulty level from intermediate to early advanced. They serve as excellent sight-reading material or serious companion pieces to easier solo sonatas from the Classical period. Ricordi publishes the sonatas in two volumes. Of the seven sonatas, two sonatas contain two movements and the rest three. Clementi assigned opus numbers which are, op. 3, nos. 1-3, op. 6, and op. 14, nos. 1-3 with the key centers C, E-Flat, G, C, C, F, and B-flat respectively.

Cohan, George Michael (1878–1942) USA

I   Give My Regards to Broadway (Lyke, arr.)   Alfred

Compton, Randall (b. 1954) USA

I-A   C.S. Theme and Variations, op. 6   Heritage
      This tongue and cheek piece dedicated to Victor Borge, is a delightful set of variations written on the Chop Sticks theme! The subtitle for the piece is For One Piano, Four Hands (Give or Take a Hand). The parts are approximately

Music for One Piano—Four Hands *continued*

of the same difficulty level with playful variations of the main theme using *glissandi*, a waltz bass, time signature changes, tempo changes, hand crossings between the *primo* and *secondo* parts, double thirds, a surprising seating position exchange for both partners and a dramatic ending. Fasten your proverbial seatbelt for a fun filled piece and an audience favorite—a perfect ensemble encore!

Copland, Aaron (1900–1990) USA (b. New York, NY; d. Tarrytown, NY)

A	Variations on a Shaker Melody from Appalachian Spring (Lerner, ed.)	Boosey & Hawkes

Variations on the Shaker tune "Simple Gifts" from the ballet *Appalachian Spring*.

Corigliano, John Paul (b. 1938) USA

A	Gazebo Dances	Schirmer

This work is known because of the orchestral and band versions, however, this duet version is the first setting of the music that Corigliano composed. A gazebo is a pavilion where a summer band or instrumental ensemble might play. Thus the work is organized into four "outdoor" movements (*Overture*, *Waltz*, *Adagio*, and *Tarantella*), each movement dedicated to individuals the composer knew.

Crawley, Clifford (b. 1930) Canada (b. Dagenham, England)

I-A §	Four Uneasy Pieces	Frederick Harris

Numbers I and III are particularly attractive late intermediate duets. The first, *Intrada*, is jazz-like, and the technically challenging *Scherzo* (III) shares thematic material between the parts.

Cui, César (1835–1918) Russia

E-I	Ten Pieces for Five Keys, op. 74 (two books)	Leeds
I-A	Suite Miniature (6 pieces)	Kalmus

Short duets: *Petite Marche*, *Impromptu a la Schumann*, *Cantabile*, *Souvenir Douloureux*, *Berceuse*, and *Scherzo Rustique*.

Curwin, Clifford

E-I	6 French Nursery Songs for Piano Duet	Chester; Marks

Very attractive settings of tunes such as *La boulangère* and *Do-do, l'enfant, do-do*.

Czerny, Carl (1791–1857) Austria

I	Sonatina, op. 156, no. 2 (Weekley/Arganbright, eds.)	Kjos
I-A	Studies op. 751	Schott
A	Sonatina Brillante, op. 50, no. 1	Berben

Danzi, Franz Ignaz (1763–1826) Germany

A	Sonata	Amadeus

Debussy, (Achille-) Claude (1862–1918) France

There are many four-hand transcriptions of Debussy's solo works by other musicians. A partial listing of such transcriptions would include *Golliwogg's Cake-walk*, both *Arabesques*, *Images* (Vol. 1), not to mention orchestral works like *La Boite a Joujoux* (Ballet for enfants). However, Debussy's *original* works for four-hands are splendid and belong in the core repertoire for duettists.

E (Early Intermediate) I (Intermediate) A (Advanced Intermediate to Advanced)

I-A	March Écossaise (sur un thème populaire) (1891)	Jobert

A commissioned work based on Scottish airs which Debussy later orchestrated.

I-A § Petite Suite (1889) (*Weekley/Arganbright; **Hinson, eds.)   *Kjos; **Alfred

This attractive four-movement suite is an excellent introduction for ensemble teams to study Debussy's early Impressionistic style. Especially beautiful are *En bateau* (I), which features a lyrical melody and undulating accompaniment, and *Ballet* (IV), which contrasts rhythmic and brisk outer sections with a more relaxed waltz section. *Cortege* (II) and *Menuet* (III) complete the set.

I-A   Six Épigraphes Antiques (1914)   Durand; Henle

Debussy based this 1914 publication on his earlier sketches of incidental music from 1901, scored for two flutes, two harps, and celesta. The music is tied to poetry by Pierre Louÿs. In comparison to the second book of *Préludes*, published one year earlier (1913), the score to the *Antiques* is much easier and on two staves, not three. Some technical figurations in no. 6 even resemble his final *prélude* in book II, *Feux d'artifice*. Titles (translated from the French) are: *To invoke Pan, God of the summer wind; For a nameless tomb; That night may be propitious; For the dancing girl with castanets; For the Egyptian girl; To thank the morning rain*.

A   Symphony in B Minor   Henle

The lesser-known *Symphony* is an early one-movement work (*ca* 1882) and possibly a predecessor for an unfinished orchestral work.

A   Works for Piano–Four Hands and Two Pianos, Books 1, 2   Dover

DeCoursey, Ralph

I   The Blue Pagoda   Schirmer

Delius, Frederick [Fritz] (Theodore Albert) (1862–1934) England

I   A Song before Sunrise (Heseltine, ed.)   Augener

Dello Joio, Norman (1913-2008) USA (b. New York, NY; d. East Hampton, NY)

E § * Family Album (Play Time)   Marks

The easiest of Dello Joio's duet compositions, this set was written with his own family in mind. Titles include: *Family Meeting, Play Time, Story Time, Prayer Time,* and *Bed Time*.

I § * Five Images (The Ballerina)   Hal Leonard; Marks

Elegant writing throughout with musical interest nicely distributed between both parts. Titles: *Cortège, Promenade, Day dreams, The Ballerina,* and *The Dancing Sergeant*.

I-A § * Stage Parodies (The Singer)   Hal Leonard

These three volumes collectively provide original and creative writing for three distinct levels of advancement. *Family Album* is appropriate for late elementary school students, *Five Images* for middle school pupils, and *Stage Parodies* during high school. Selected compositions from any set can be paired for study with Dello Joio's solo piano compositions. The most challenging, *Stage Parodies*, contains four movements: 1. *The Actor*, 2. *The Writer*, 3. *The Singer*, and 4. *The Dancer*.

Music for One Piano—Four Hands *continued*

Del Tredici, David (b. 1937) USA

Distinguished Professor of Music at City College of New York City, Del Tredici's compositional style has evolved from the atonal to neo-classic romanticism. After early study with composers such as Roger Sessions, Del Tredici has received numerous awards including a Guggenheim Fellowship and 2007 Grammy nomination for *Best Contemporary Composition*. He was a Pulitzer Prize recipient in 1980 for *In Memory of a Summer Day*. His compositions have been recorded on significant labels and performed with major orchestras.

I-A	Scherzo for Piano	Boosey & Hawkes

Premiered at Princeton University in 1960, the writing is compact, rhapsodic, and uses serial techniques.

Diabelli, Anton (1781–1858) Austria

E §	Jugendfreuden, op. 163 (Pleasures of Youth) (student/teacher)	Peters; Universal

This collection of six four-hand sonatinas on five notes is excellent sight-reading material and supporting duet repertoire to the classical solo sonatina genre. The *primo* student part is often written in unison octaves between the hands. The *Romanze* in the first sonatina is particularly beautiful.

E §	Melodious Pieces on Five Notes, op. 149 (Student/Teacher}	Schirmer; ASE
I	Five Sonatinas, opp. 24, 54, 58, 60	Peters; Schirmer
I	Rondeau Militaire	Kalmus
I	Three Sonatas, opp. 32, 33, 37	Peters; Schirmer
A	Sonatas, opp. 38, 73 (Ruthardt, ed.)	Peters

Diercks, John (b. 1927) USA

E-I §	Suite no. 1 (March, Dance, Song, Finale)	MCA

Donhányi, Ernst von (1877-1960) Hungary (b. Bragislava, Hungary; d. Tallahassee, FL)

I	Walzer, op. 3	Doblinger

Composed in the Viennese waltz style.

Donizetti, (Domenico) Gaetano (Maria) (1797–1848) Italy

I-A	Sonatina in Re Maggiore	Presser
A	Sonatas	E. C. Kerby
A	Three Pieces	Ricordi

Dring, Madeleine (1923–1977) Great Britain

I	Four Duets	Boosey & Hawkes

Includes: *May Morning, Little Waltz, The Evening Star,* and *Morris Dance.*

I	Three for Two	Boosey & Hawkes

Includes: *Country Dance, The Quiet Pool,* and *Hobby horse.*

Dussek, Jan Ladislav (1760–1812) Bohemia

I-A	Sonata in C Major, op. 43	Mercury
A	Three Sonatas, op. 67	Elkan-Vogel

Dvořák, Antonín (Leopold) (1841–1904) Czechoslovakia

I-A	Complete Legends, op. 59	Alfred

The *Legends* are comprised of 10 untitled pieces. They are generally easier than the famous *Slavonic Dances,* and thus serve as an excellent introduction to Dvořák's four-hand writing.

E (Early Intermediate)   I (Intermediate)   A (Advanced Intermediate to Advanced)

I-A	§	Complete Slavonic Dances for Piano Four Hands	Alfred; Dover; ASE

Perhaps inspired by Brahms' *Hungarian Dances*, the *Slavonic Dances* are also at the core of the four-hand literature. They are divided into two opus numbers, 46 and 72, with eight dances in each opus.

I-A	12 Selected Pieces (Lerche, ed.)	Peters

Contains: *Legenden, op. 59, nos. 4, 6, 8, 9,10*; *Waldesruhe, op. 68, no.5*; *Slavonic Dances, op. 72, nos. 2, 4, 8*; and *Slavonic Dances, op. 46, nos. 1, 2, 8*.

A	Bagatelles, op. 47	Simrock

These are four hand arrangements of five chamber bagatelles that the composer scored for two violins, cello and harmonium.

A	§ *	From the Bohemian Forests, op. 68 (Silent woods)	Bärenreiter; Simrock

Six character pieces: *The spinning room, Walpurgisnacht, In wait, By the dark lake, Silent woods,* and *From Troubled times.*

A	Humoresque in G-flat, op. 101, no. 7 (Taubmann, arr.)	Simrock/Boosey & Hawkes

This transcription is based on the seventh piano solo from the set *8 Humoresques, op. 101.*

A	Polonaise in E flat Major (1879)	Peters

Evans, Bill G. USA

Not be confused with the famous jazz pianist Bill Evans, Bill G. Evans is a jazz educator at West Texas State University, where he coordinates the keyboard area.

E		Mixed Bag (6 jazz duets)	Kjos
I	§	Jazz Tributes (9 jazz duets)	Kjos

Each of these nine attractive jazz duets imitates the style of a different jazz pianist, e.g., Horace Silver, Dave Brubeck, Benny Goodman, and Ramsey Lewis.

Fauré, Gabriel (Urbain) (1845–1924) France

I	Masques and Bergamasques, op. 112 (Fauré, transcriber)	Durand

Comprised of an *Overture, Minuet, Gavotte,* and *Pastorale,* this is a relatively easy transcription of the orchestral work by the composer. This transcription can serve as an introduction to the composer's style and overall, as a four-hand work, it is less difficult than Fauré's *Dolly, op. 56.*

I-A	§ *	Dolly (Suite), op. 56 (Berceuse) (*Weekley/Arganbright, eds.)	*Kjos; ASE

The high-quality of the musical writing in this suite, Fauré's only duet-writing for piano, has made it a favorite concert work of the piano-duet repertoire, and of four-hand teams. Dolly, the little girl to whom this work is dedicated, was the daughter of the banker (and music-lover) Sigismond Bardac, and his wife, Emma, who were friends of Fauré. The six movements represent a variety of levels and textures, ranging from the lyrical, intermediate level first movement *Berceuse* to the rhythmically-challenging, quite advanced Spanish-sounding *Le Pas Espagnole* finale. Other movements are: 2. *Mi-a-ou,* 3. *Le Jardin de Dolly,* 4. *Kitty-Valse,* and 5. *Tendresse.* It should be mentioned that the title *Mi-a-ou* is not reminiscent or suggestive of a cat, but, is the nickname Dolly gave to her older brother Raoul.

A	Sicilienne (Carroll, arr.)	Willis

Feldman, Morton (1926–1987) USA

I-A	Piano Four Hands	Peters

Music for One Piano—Four Hands *continued*

Frid, Géza (b. 1904) Holland (b. Hungary)

I-A	Kermesse à Charleroi	Southern

Fuchs, Robert (1847–1927) USA

I-A	Viennese Waltzes, op. 42, Book 1 (nos. 1-10), Book 2 (nos. 11-20)	Schott
A	Dream Vision	Peters

Gade, Niels (Wilhelm) (1817–1890) Denmark

A	Nordiske Tonebillender, op. 4 (Norwegian Tone Pictures)	Augener

Ganz, Rudolph (1877–1972) USA (b. Zurich, Switzerland; d. Chicago, IL)

A	Qui vive (Grand Galop de Concert), op. 12	Music Sales

George, Jon (1944–1982) USA

E § Kaleidoscope Duets (Books 4-5) — Alfred
   This beautifully graded collection of one- or two-page duets works well with pairs of early intermediate students. Book 5 reaches the easy sonatina level. Books 1-3 are for elementary students.

E   Two at One Piano, Book 3 — Alfred
   The *primo* and *secondo* are equally matched in level of difficulty for two students to play. Titles include: *Ancient Procession, On the Hacienda, Village Dance, Forest Flower, Trolley Song, Pastorale,* and *Celebration.*

Gershwin, George (1898–1937) USA (b. Brooklyn, NY; d. Beverly Hills, CA)

E   Gershwin Piano Duets (10 easier transcriptions) — Hal Leonard

I § By Strauss (Lyke/Haydon, arr.) — Alfred
   A delightful duet arrangement of a song by George and Ira Gershwin featuring the Viennese waltz style. A two piano version also exists by the arrangers.

I   George Gershwin Piano Duets (Portnoff, arr.) — Chappell
I   Gershwin: Rialto Ripples (Lyke, arr.) — Alfred
I   We Love a Piano (Lyke, arr.) (includes Gershwin arrangements) — Alfred
   (See detailed annotation under entry for Lyke, James B.)

I-A § Preludes (Stone, transcribed) — Alfred
   These three *Preludes* are very popular, and highly motivating for students. Filled with jazz elements, syncopations, and large hand-stretches, the solo versions are often too difficult for intermediate students. This four-hand version makes these enjoyable preludes more accessible for students.

A   A Gershwin Medley (Lyke/Haydon, arr.) — Alfred
A   Cuban Overture (Original) — Alfred; Schott
A   Rhapsody in Blue (Levine, arr.) — Alfred

Gilbert, Henry Franklin Belknap (1868–1928) USA

I-A	Three American Dances (Ragtime Dances)	Boston Music

Gillock, William (1917–1993) USA (b. LaRussell, MO; d. Dallas, TX)

E § New Orleans Jazz Styles (Austin, arr.) — Willis
   The compositions in the well-known solo volume of the same title along with the sequels (*More NOJS* and *Still More NOJS*), have been arranged for piano duet by Glenda Austin. Each book comes with a CD with both *secondo* and *primo* recorded on separate tracks so that students can rehearse at home.

E (Early Intermediate)   I (Intermediate)   A (Advanced Intermediate to Advanced)

I	§	Accent on Duets (8 duets)	Willis

           Gillock's best-known sheet music duets are included in this album. Titles include *Jazz Prelude* and *Fiesta Mariachi*.

I	Boogie Prelude	Willis
I	Espana Cani	Willis

Gliere, Reinhold (1875–1956) Russia

I	(24) Easy Pieces, op. 38 (in four books) (1908)	Jurgenson
I	Rondo in G Major (Gunther, arr.)	Willis

Glinka, Mikhail Ivanovich (1804–1857) Russia

I-A	Capriccio sur des Thèmes Russes (1834)	Jürgenson; International

Godowsky, Leopold (1870–1938) Poland

I-A	Miniatures Vols. I-III (Banowetz/Chan, eds.) Books and *CDs	Alfred

           Volume I: Three Suites (*primo* part is based on five finger patterns)
           Volume II: (14) Ancient and Modern Dances
           Ancient refers to 7 Baroque-like dances and modern to 7 more recent dance forms (e.g., waltz, tarântella, polka, jig).
           Volume III: Miscellaneous Pieces (*all CD performances are by Banowitz and Chan)

Gottschalk, Louis Moreau (1829–1869) USA

I-A	Music for Piano Four Hands, Books 1, 2 (List, arr.)	Presser

           Eugene List (1918-1985) was a long time member of the Eastman School of Music piano faculty and a specialist in the music of both Gottschalk and Edward MacDowell.

A	La Jota Aragonesa and other Favorites for Piano Four Hands	Dover

           This is an excellent collection that reflects Gottschalk's visits to Cuba, the West Indies, and South America. Includes: *La jota aragonesa*, op. 14; *Ojos criollos*, op. 37; *Réponds-moi* (Cuban dance), op. 50; *La gallina*, op. 53; *Ses yeux* (polka), op. 66; *Grande tarentelle*, op. posth. 67; *Radieuse* (concert waltz), op. 72; and Gottschalk's arrangement of Rossini's *William Tell Overture*. Introduction and Foreword by Joseph Banowetz.

Goud, Stella Canada

I	§ *	Off-Balance Duets (A Mischievous March)	Frederick Harris

           The "off-balance" title refers to the fact that in each piece, one of the parts is easier or less difficult, though not necessarily the *primo*. Titles include *A Bit o' Boogie, Lonely Lullaby, Misty Morning, Toe Tap, A Wobbly Waltz,* and *Practice Pointers*.

Grainger, (George) Percy (Aldridge) (1882–1961) USA
(b. Brighton/Melbourne, Australia; d. White Plains, NY)

I		Children's March	Schott
I	§	Country Gardens	Boston Music; Schott
I		Let's Dance Gay	Faber

Gretchaninoff, (Grechaninov) Alexander Tikhonovich (1864–1956) Russia

E	§ *	On the Green Meadow, op. 99 (2. Mother's Song) (Wolman, ed.)	MCA

Ensemble Literature — Music for One Piano–Four Hands

Music for One Piano—Four Hands *continued*

A landmark collection of ten early intermediate pieces in romantic style. No. 1, *On the Green Meadow*, is one of the best-known, though not the easiest of the set. Includes: *In the Meadows, Mothers Song, Ballade, Lost in the Woods, Walking, Spring Morning, Tale, In the Country, On the Mountains,* and *Serenade*.

Grieg, Edvard (Hagerup) (1843–1907) Norway

I	Grieg's Best Duets (Weekley/Arganbright, eds.)	Kjos
	Includes *Waltz Caprice, op. 37, no. 2, The Last Spring, op. 34, no. 2,* and *Norwegian Dance, op. 35, no. 2.*	
I	Peer Gynt Suites, No. 1, op. 46; no. 2, op. 55 (Ruthardt, arr.)	Peters
I-A §	Norwegian Dances, op. 35 (original)	Peters; Schott

Any student studying Grieg's solo selections from the Lyric Pieces should explore these original piano duets. No. 2 in A Major is well known. With its tuneful opening theme, based on a Norwegian mountain melody, and brilliant B section, it is one of the most appealing dances in the opus.

I-A	Norwegian Dances, Waltz-Caprices, op. 37 and other Works for Piano–Four Hands	Dover
I-A	(Two) Waltz-Caprices, op. 37	Peters

The two *Caprices* are a wonderful alternative to the op. 35 *Norwegian Dances* and are generally at the same level of difficulty. No. 1, in C-Sharp minor (*Tempo di Valse moderato*), moves to the parallel major in the B section. No. 2, in E minor (*Tempo di Valse*), modulates to E major in the trio section which consists of repeating melodic figures that gradually move higher under a *secondo* chordal accompaniment. It is a very suspenseful trio section that eventually returns to the main theme in E minor.

I-A	Wedding-Day At Troldhaugen, op. 65, no. 6 (Ruthardt, arr.)	Peters

Grill, Joyce USA

E	Four-Hand Fun, Book 1	Alfred
I §	Duets from Many Lands	Alfred
I §	Sparklers	Alfred

This sheet music duet was commissioned for the Goshen College Piano Workshop. It is a perfect duet to celebrate the July 4th holiday!

Gurlitt, Cornelius (1820–1901) Germany

E-I §	The Beginner, op. 211 (22 duets in increasing order of difficulty) (Brehl, ed.)	Schott
I	Stray Leaves, op. 202 (6 original duets, late intermediate level)	Kalmus

Handel, George Frideric (1685–1759) England (b. Germany)

E	Largo from the Opera *Xerxes*	Schott
I-A	Arrival of the Queen of Sheba (from the oratorio *Solomon*) (Weismann, arr.)	Peters

Haydn, Franz Joseph (1732–1809) Austria

I-A	12 Deutsche Tänze (Beer, ed.)	Heinrichshofen's Verlag
I §	Divertimento Il maestro e lo scolare, Hob XVIIa:1 (Gerlach, ed.)	Henle

The term *maestro* refers to the teacher and *scolare* to the student. The *maestro* plays the *secondo*. This *Divertimento* is a delightful theme and seven variations in F major that is more late intermediate than advanced. The student *primo* part is easier. As a short variation set it deviates from the norm as there

E (Early Intermediate) I (Intermediate) A (Advanced Intermediate to Advanced)

is no minor variation. Using musical imitation, Haydn humorously has the student musically follow the teacher throughout as the *primo* always enters two bars later than the *secondo*. As Haydn's sole work for four-hands, it is a delightful work worth exploring.

A   Twelve Symphonies, Vols. I, II (*Ulrich, ed.)   Schirmer

Helps, Robert (b. 1928) USA

I   Saccade   Peters

Hindemith, Paul (1895–1963) Germany (b. and d. Frankfurt, Germany)

I   Ragtime (Goebels, ed.)   Schott
A   Six Waltzes, op. 6   Schott
A   Sonata (1938)   Schott

Hovhaness, Alan (Chakmakjian, Alan Hovhaness) (b. 1911) USA (Armenian heritage) (b. Somerville (Boston), MA; d. Seattle, WA)

I §   Child in the Garden, op. 168   Peters
    This short four-page duet is divided into two parts: an opening Impressionistic-sounding *Andante* followed by an *Allegro*.

Hummel, Johann Nepomuk (1778–1837) Austria

A   Nocturne in F Major, op. 99   Peters

Husa, Karel (b. 1921) USA (b. Czechoslovakia)

I   Eight Bohemian Duets (Acht Böhmische duette)   Schott
    Short intermediate level duets, mostly one to four pages in length. The titles include *Chanson mélancolique, Elegie, Der Abend,* and *Slowakischer Tanz* (longest and only advanced duet).

Ibert, Jacques (Jacques-François-Antoine) (1890–1962) France

I-A   Histoires (Ibert, arr.) (Hinson/Nelson, eds.)   Alfred
    Five pieces from the original *Histoires* arranged for four hands by Ibert.

d'Indy, Vincent (Paul Marie Théodore) (1851–1931) France

A   Sept Chants de Terroir   Roicart, Lerolle and Cie.

Ingelbrecht, D.E. (Désiré-Emile) (1880–1965) France

I §   La Nursery, Books 1–6   Salabert

Jacobson, Maurice (1896–1976) Great Britain

I   Mosaic (1949)   J. Curwen

Jarnefelt, Armas (1869–1958) Sweden

I   Praeludium   Chester

Jensen, Adolph (1837–1879) Germany

I-A   Drei Klavierstücke   Universal
I-A   Wedding Music   Schirmer
A   Abendmusik, op. 59   Hainauer

Music for One Piano—Four Hands *continued*

Joplin, Scott (1868–1917) USA (b. Texas; d. Manhattan, NY)

I	§	Five Joplin Rags (Weekley/Arganbright, arr.)	Kjos
I	§	Four Joplin Waltzes (Weekley/Arganbright, arr.)	Kjos
I		Swipesy (M. Clark, arr.)	Alfred
I-A		(14) Selected Ragtimes, Vols. I, II (Kirchgässner/Didion, arr.)	Peters

Vol. I has no. 1-7, vol. II 8-14. Companion CD has *secondo* accompaniments.

Juon, Paul (1872–1940) Germany (b. Russia)

A   Tanzrytmen (seven books)   Schlesinger

Kabalevsky, Dmitri Borisovich (1904–1987) (b. St. Petersburg, Russia; d. Moscow, Russia)

E   12 Easy Variations, op. 40, no. 1 (Johnson, arr.)   Peters

Karp, David (1940) USA

E §   Scenes   Shawnee

Early intermediate writing encompassing six pieces. The titles include *Blues Tune with Two Variations* and *Friendly Ghosts*. Karp has many intermediate level sheet music duets published by Alfred (e.g., *Dakota Sunset, Prayer for Peace*), Willis (e.g., *Dallas Bolero, Dallas Tango, Western Bolero*), and FJH Publishing (e.g., *Phoenix Blues, Waltz in A Minor*).

Khachaturian, Aram Il'yich (1903–1978) Russia (b. Tbilisi, Georgia, Russia; d. Moscow, Russia)

A   Waltz from Masquerade (VAAP Edition)   Schirmer

Khrennikov, Tikhon (Nikolaievich) (1913-2007) Russia

E-I   Two by Two (fifteen pieces for one piano–four hands)   Schirmer

This volume, from the Library of Russian-Soviet Music, includes pieces as short as eight bars and as long as six pages, though the average length of each part is two pages.

Koch, Friedrich (1862–1927) Germany

I   Golliwogg's Dance   Boston Music

Kolinski, Mieczyslaw (1901–1981) Canada (b. Poland)

E-I   First Piano Duets   Schirmer

Krieger, Edino (b. 1928) Brazil (b. Brusque, Santa Catarina, Brazil)

A   Sonata   International

Kuhlau, (Daniel) Friedrich (Rudolph) (1786–1832) Denmark (b. Germany)

I		Sonatina in G Major	Schirmer
I	§	Sonatina, op. 17 (Weekley/Arganbright, eds.)	Kjos

Kurka, Robert (Frank) (1921–1957) USA (b. Cicero, IL; New York, NY)

I   Dance Suite, op. 29   Weintraub

Lambert, (Leonard) Constant (1905–1951) England (b. and d. London, England)

I   Trois Pièces Nègres (1949)   Oxford

La Montaine, John (b. 1920) USA (b. Oak Park, IL)

A	Sonata, op. 25	Elkan-Vogel

Lang, Walter (1896–1966) Switzerland (b. Memphis, TN; d. Palm Springs, CA)

A	Ferientage, op. 64	Amadeus

Lecuona, Ernesto (1895–1963) Cuba
(b. Guanabacoa, Havana, Cuba; d. Santa Cruz de Tenerife, Canary Islands, Spain)

I	Gitanerias	Hal Leonard
A	Andalucia	Hal Leonard
A	Malagueña	Hal Leonard

Liszt, Franz (1811–1886) Hungary

I-A § Christmas Liszt for Two (Weekly/Arganbright, eds.) — Kjos

I-A § Weihnachtsbaum (Christmas Tree) — Dover; Editio Musica Budapest
(See annotation under Christmas solo and ensemble sections.)

A Grand Galopp Chromatique (Hofmeister) [out of print] — Breitkopf and Härtel

A Hungarian Rhapsody no. 2 (Kleinmichel, ed.) — Schirmer

A Les Préludes (Liszt, arr.) — Schirmer

A § Mephisto Waltz (Weekley/Arganbright, eds.) — Kjos
(Dance in the Village Inn from Lenau's "Faust")
> Technically advanced, this is Liszt's stunning setting for four-hands of the famous *Mephisto Waltz*. Liszt's original soft ending to the duet version is remarkably different than the solo version. Weekley and Arganbright offer an alternate version, in this duet setting, which matches the brilliant climax of the solo version.

A Transcriptions of Orchestral Works — Kalmus
> These are original piano duet transcriptions by Liszt which include: *Les Préludes, Orpheus, Prometheus, Ce qu' on entend sur la Montagne,* and *Mazeppa.*

Lybbert, Donald (1923-1981) USA

A	Movement	Peters

Lyke, James B., arr. (b. 1932) USA

With advanced degrees from Northern Colorado University and Columbia Teachers College, where he studied with Robert Pace, Lyke was a long-time Professor of Piano and Piano Pedagogy at the University of Illinois. He co-founded the *National Conference on Piano Pedagogy* (now Keyboard Pedagogy) and has presented throughout the United States and in several countries abroad. His distinguished achievements in the piano pedagogy discipline resulted in his being named a recipient of the prestigious NCKP *Lifetime Achievement Award.*

I By Strauss (Lyke/Haydon, arr.) — Alfred
> A delightful duet arrangement of a song by George and Ira Gershwin featuring the Viennese waltz style.

I § We Love a Piano (Lyke, arr.) (15 Famous Favorites) — Alfred
> Subtitled, *Duets We Love to Play*, and previously published individually under the umbrella title *Sing Along Pop Piano Duets,* this important revision has all of Lyke's one piano duet arrangements of ageless tunes like *Alexander's Ragtime Band* (Berlin), *Give My Regards to Broadway* (Cohan), *I Love a Piano* (Berlin), *It's a Most Unusual* Day (McHugh/Adamson), *Play a Simple Melody* (Berlin), and many more.

Ensemble Literature — Music for One Piano–Four Hands

Music for One Piano—Four Hands continued

These are excellent, accessible arrangements, which adult students, in particular, enjoy. They also are excellent for sight-reading with all students. Words to each tune are included as text, however, the writing is for piano duet, not vocal/piano.

A	A Gershwin Medley (Lyke/Haydon, arr.)	Alfred

These are duet arrangements of selected Gershwin songs. (See annotation under Gershwin under contemporary solo literature.)

MacDowell, Edward (Alexander) (1860–1908) USA

I	Moon pictures, op. 21 (5 descriptive duets; out of print, available on-line)	
I	The Saracens-Aida, op. 30	Breitkopf and Härtel
I	To a Water Lily	Music Sales
I-A §	Three Poems, op. 20 (*Hinson, ed.)	*Alfred; Schirmer

(*Night by the Sea, A Tale from Knightly Times, Ballade*)

Malipiero, Gian Francesco (1882–1973) Italy (b. Venice, Italy; d. Treviso, Italy)

I-A	Armenia	Salabert
I-A	Impressioni Dal Vero Iia Parte	Music Sales

Mason, Daniel Gregory (1873–1953) USA
(b. Brooklyn, MA; d. Greenwich, CT) (Grandson of Lowell Mason)

I-A	Birthday Waltzes, op. 2	Boston Music

Mehegan, John (1916–1984) USA (b. Hartford, CT)

I	Jazz Caper	Sam Fox

Mendelssohn (-Bartholdy), (Jakob Ludwig) Felix (1809–1847) Germany

The three major duet works by Mendelssohn are discussed below: Opp. 83, 92, and his personal transcription of *A Midsummer Night's Dream*.

I-A	Works for Piano Four–Hands	Henle
A §	A Midsummer Night's Dream (Mendelssohn, arr.) (Neiweem/Aebersold, eds.)	Dover

The full title of this edition is: *A midsummer night's dream: for piano four hands: the composer's original transcription*. This edition presents the composer's original transcription for piano duet which was performed by Felix and Fanny Mendelssohn. Contents: *Overture, Scherzo, March of the elves, Song with chorus, Intermezzo, Nocturne, Wedding march, Funeral march, A dance of clowns,* and *Finale*.

A	Mendelssohn, Original Compositions, Op. 83[a] and op. 98	Kalmus; International

Some editions erroneously list op. 83 as op. 83a.

A	Original compositions for Piano, 4 Hands	Schirmer

This edition includes two concert four-hand compositions by Mendelssohn, the *Allegro brilliant in E major, op. 92* (1841) and the *Andante and variations in B-flat Major, op. 83* (1841).

A	7 Songs without Words, op. 62, nos. 1–6, op. 67, no. 1 (Langley, ed.)	Bärenreiter

Mier, Martha USA

I	A Star-Spangled Celebration for Two (5 Patriotic Favorites)	Alfred
I §	Jazz, Rags and Blues for Two, Books 3-4	Alfred

Milhaud, Darius (1892–1974) France (b. Marseilles, France; d. Geneva, Switzerland)

A	Enfantines	Max Eschig

E (Early Intermediate)   I (Intermediate)   A (Advanced Intermediate to Advanced)

A	La Création du Monde, op. 81a	Durand; Max Eschig
A	Le boeuf sur le toit, op. 58	Durand; Max Eschig

Piano Transcription of Milhaud's music for the ballet, *The Ox on the Roof: The Nothing-Doing Bar*.

A	Suite française	Leeds

Moszkowski, Moritz (1854–1925) Poland

E	Five Waltzes, op. 8 (Currie, arr.)	Willis
I	Minuet, op. 17, no. 2	Augener
I	From Foreign Lands and Five Waltzes, op. 8	Schirmer
I-A §	Spanish Dances, opp. 12, 65	Schirmer
I-A	Spanish Dances, op. 12	Alfred; Schirmer
A	German Rondos, op. 25 (Motchane, ed.)	International

Mozart, (Johann Chrysostom) Wolfgang Amadeus (1756–1791) Austria

I	Divertimento, K 213 (M. Clark, arr.)	Alfred
I	German Dances (from K 600 and K 605)	Breitkopf and Härtel
I	Leichte Sonatinen	Peters
I	Presto, K 252 (M. Clark, arr.)	Alfred

This *Presto* is from the *Divertimento K 252*, a work for small wind ensemble. Alfred also publishes Clark's duet arrangements of the *Polonaise*, *Menuetto*, and *Andante* from K 252.

I	Sechs Sonatinas (Volger, ed.)	Peters
I	Viennese Sonatinas (Johnson, arr.)	Peters
I-A	Eine Kleine Nachtmusik K 525 (Singer, ed.)	International
I-A §	Eine Kleine Nachtmusik (A Little Night Music)	Schirmer

This excellent arrangement allows students at the late intermediate to early advanced level to experience the beauty of these movements. Requires the same clarity of performance, dynamic contrasts, and technical skills as a Mozart solo sonata.

I-A	Fantasy for Mechanical Organ (Badura-Skoda, arr.)	Schirmer
I-A	Original Compositions for Four Hands	Kalmus; Schirmer

Includes: *Sonata in D, K 381, Sonata in B-Flat, K 358, Sonata in F, K 497, Sonata in C, K 521, Fantasy no. 1 in F minor, K 594, Fantasy no. 2 in F minor, K 608, Variations in G, K 501*, and *Fugue in G minor, K 401*.

I-A	6 Easy Pieces from the Opera The Magic Flute (Neefe, arr.)	Schott

These arrangements, intended for teaching purposes, were first published in 1793, two years after the premiere of the opera.

I-A	Works for Piano Four-Hands (Zimmermann, ed.)	Henle
A §	Six Sonatas; Variations	Henle; International

The Mozart four-hand sonatas are at the pinnacle of the piano duet literature. The *Sonata in D Major, K 381*, was composed in 1772 for Mozart to play with his talented sister, Nannerl. In three movements (*Allegro; Andante; Allegro molto*), it is an excellent sonata to introduce the Mozart four-hand sonata style. The slow movement is similar in difficulty and texture to the middle movement of the solo piano *Sonata in C Major, K 545*. On a more challenging scale, the *Sonata in C Major, K 521* (1787) is the last duet that Mozart composed and is pianistically the most challenging of the four hand sonatas. The brilliant passagework, evenly exchanged between parts,

Music for One Piano—Four Hands continued

resembles a concerto-like texture. The *Sonata in F Major, K 497* (1786) presents great depth and also represents the mature Mozart.

A		Symphonies and Serenades, Vols. I, II	Peters
A		Five symphonies for piano four hands	Dover

Symphony no. 35 ("Haffner") in D major, K 385; Symphony no. 36 ("Linz") in C major, K 425; Symphony no. 38 ("Prague") in D major, K 504; Symphony no. 40 in G minor, K 550; Symphony no. 41 ("Jupiter") in C major, K 551.

A		Works for Piano Four–Hands	Dover

Mullen, Frederic Great Britain

I-A		A Madrid Festival	John Church

Nakada, Yoshinao (1923-2000) Japan (b. Tokyo)

E-I		One Piano Four Hands	Ongaku /Theodore Presser

(*Twinkle, twinkle little star; Our shoes squeak; Song of cradle; Play with me, Mama; The letter; Polish! Polish!; The school of killies, The train running*)

Niamath, Linda (b. 1939) Canada (b. Vancouver, British Columbia, Canada)

E	§	Outer Limits	Frederick Harris

Contains: *Parade, Witches' Dance, Dreaming, Journey in Space, Tango,* and *Clown Capers.*

Noona, Walter (b. 1932) and Carol (b. 1935) USA

E	§	All American Hometown Band	Heritage

Students love to play this duet, which alternates a "hometown band refrain" with short excerpts based on familiar folk tunes. Students can substitute a section of their own favorite popular or classical piece between each refrain, thus allowing students to showcase their own skills and repertoire. It is enjoyable to perform in a group ensemble with several players.

E		Capriccio Chromatico	Heritage
E		Spanish Tornado	Heritage

Norton, Christopher (b. 1953) USA (b. New Zealand)

E-I	§	Microjazz Duets, Bks. I-III	Boosey & Hawkes
E-I	§	More Microjazz Duets, Bks. I, II	Boosey & Hawkes

These duets explore modern piano styles (blues, rock, jazz) with an emphasis on solving rhythmic difficulties. Norton writes in an original and appealing contemporary jazz style.

Offenbach, Jacques (1819–1880) France (b. Germany)

I		Barcarolle (Tales of Hoffman)	Music Sales

O'Hearn, Arletta USA

I	§	Jazz Together	Kjos

Four delightful pieces exploring different aspects of the jazz style titled, *Lullaby, Waltz, Scherzo,* and *Nothin' but the Blues.*

Olson, Kevin R. (b. 1970) USA (b. Utah)

I		Canon in D (Pachelbel/Olson, arr.)	FJH

E (Early Intermediate)   I (Intermediate)   A (Advanced Intermediate to Advanced)

A	§	Jazz Suite	FJH
A		A Seafaring Suite	FJH

Olson, Lynn Freeman (1938–1987) USA (b. Minneapolis, MN; d. New York NY)

E		A Folk Gathering (includes parts for other instruments)	Carl Fischer
E	§	Round and Round	Carl Fischer

A delightful duet dedicated to the Nacogdoches, TX Music Teachers Association, the *Primo* and *secondo* are of equal difficulty, with a unison melody in the *primo* against a rhythmic broken-chord accompaniment in the *secondo*. In the middle section, the *primo* player stands and crosses behind to become the *secondo* player; the *secondo* player stands and moves to the *primo* position while continuing to play. The piece then continues with players in their new positions. Students love this piece!

Onslow, (André) George (Louis) (1784–1853) France

A		Sonata for Piano–Four Hands, op. 7	Boonin
A		Sonata for Piano–Four Hands, op. 22	Boonin

Orff, Carl (1895–1982) Germany

A		Carmina Burana (excerpts from) (Regner, arr.)	Schott

Pachelbel, Johann (Bachelbel) (1653–1706) Germany

I	§	Canon in D (Weekley/Arganbright, arr.)	Kjos

This is a superior arrangement of this popular work.

A		Canon in D (Schulz, arr.)	Alfred

Palmer, Robert (Moffat) (1915-2010) USA (b. Syracuse, NY; d. Ithaca, NY)

A		Sonata for One Piano–Four Hands	Peer Southern

Papineau-Couture, Jean (1916-2000) Canada (b. and d. Montreal, Canada)

A		Rondo	Peer Southern

Paterson, Lorna (b. 1953) Canada (b. London, Ontario, Canada)

E		Nothing Up My Sleeve	Frederick Harris
I	§	Too Cool	Frederick Harris

Much of the *primo* part is written in unison rhythms between hands. The *secondo* writing tends to be more difficult. Titles include: *Fun and Games, On the Bay, Exotic Voyage,* and *Too Cool* (rock 'n' roll flavor).

Peaslee, Richard Cutts (b. 1930) USA (b. New York, NY)

E		The Last Bandit	Galaxy
E		The Lopsided Grasshopper	Galaxy

Penn, William USA

I	§	American Portraits	Kjos

Persichetti, Vincent (1915–1987) USA (b. and d. Philadelphia, PA)

I	§	Serenade no. 8, op. 62 (four short duets) (1954)	Presser
A	§	Appalachian Christmas Carols	Presser

(See annotation in Holiday Literature for Piano Ensemble.)

Music for One Piano—Four Hands *continued*

A	Concerto for Piano, Four Hands, op. 56 (1952)	Presser
	A single movement, mature and technically demanding work of about 20 minutes.	

Phillips, Burrill (1907-1988) USA (b. Omaha, NE; Berkeley, CA)

A	Serenade for Piano	Peer Southern

Pleyel, Ignace Joseph (1757–1831) Austria

A	Sonata in G Minor	Peters

Poldini, Ede (Eduard) (1869–1957) Hungary

I-A	Poupee Valsante	Ricordi

Poulenc, Francis (Jean Marcel) (1899–1963) France (b. and d. Paris, France)

I-A §	Sonate (1918) (revised 1938)	Chester
	A superb three-movement work for skilled students that ranges from the rhythmic vitality and cluster chords of the first movement to the easier bird-like tunes in the middle movement *Rustique*. The *Final* uses an imitative five-finger C major motive reminiscent of the first Bach two-part *Invention in C major*.	

Pozzoli, Ettore (1873–1957) Italy (b. and d. Seregno, Italy)

E §	Smiles of Childhood (Little Pieces on 5 Notes) (Student/Teacher)	Ricordi
	Remarkably beautiful pieces (23 total) where the student plays octave melodies in unison between the hands while the teacher supplies a full accompaniment. This is excellent sight-reading material for older students or superior duet recital material for younger students.	
E	Sorrisi Infantili (Student/Teacher)	Ricordi
I	10 Piccoli Pezzi Caratteristici	Ricordi

Prokofiev, Sergei (Sergeyevich) (1891–1953) Russia (b. Sontsovka, Ukraine; d. Moscow, Russia)

E	Gavotte, op. 32, no. 3 (Montandon, arr.)	Willis
	This is an easier duet transcription of the well-known *Gavotte* from the composer's solo piano set, *Four Pieces, op. 32*, composed in 1918.	
I-A §	Fragments (Johannesen, ed.)	International
	An interesting and little-known collection of sixteen arrangements by the composer of melodic excerpts from films and plays such as *Ivan the Terrible* and *Boris Godounov*. Each duet is two to four pages in length and the majority are at the intermediate level.	

Quinet, Marcel (Alfred) (1915-1986) Belgium (b. Binche, Belgium)

I-A §	Cinq miniatures (1964)	CeBeDeM
	Without titles, the five textures range from late intermediate to early advanced. Very rhythmic and mildly dissonant, the set provides a nice change of pace. Approximately five minutes in length, *Cinq miniatures* is an excellent set with which to open a four-hand recital.	

Rachmaninoff, Sergey (Vasilyevich) (1873–1943) Russia (Rakhmaninov, Sergey) (b. Oneg, near Semyonovo, Russia; d. Beverly Hills, CA)

I-A § *	Six Pieces (*Six morceaux*), op. 11 (Romance)	Boosey & Hawkes; International

E (Early Intermediate)   I (Intermediate)   A (Advanced Intermediate to Advanced)

Op. 11 is the core of the composer's contribution to piano duet literature. The overall textures are easier than his solo writing. The final movement (*Slava*) borrows thematic material from Mussorgsky's opera, *Boris Godunov*. These six duets are very appealing. Selecting a movement or two would be excellent preparation for a student desiring to play the *Prelude in C-Sharp Minor, op. 3, no. 2*. Titles: *Barcarolle, Scherzo, Thème Russe, Valse, Romance,* and *Slav* (Glory).

I-A   The Piano Works of Rachmaninoff   Alfred
Volume VIII: Works for One Piano/Four Hands and One Piano/Six Hands. Contains 9 original works for piano duet and piano trio: *Italian Polka* (1906), *Six Duets, Op. 11*, 1894 (one piano, four hands); *Valse, Romance*, 1891 (one piano, six hands).

A   Russian Theme, op. 11, no. 3 (Phillip, ed.)   International

Raphling, Sam (1910–1988) USA (b. Fort Worth, TX; d. Manhattan, NY)

I-A   Four–Hand Sonata   General

Ravel, Joseph Maurice (1875–1937) France

I-A §   Ma mere l'Oye (*Weekley/Arganbright, eds.)   *Kjos; ASE
The five movements of this "classic" set must be mentioned: *I. Sleeping Beauty's Pavane, II. Tom Thumb, III. Little Miss Ugly Face, Empress of the Pagodas, IV. Conversations between The Beauty and the Beast,* and *V. The Magic Garden*. For pianists unfamiliar with the set, the first movement is quite easy technically and rhythmically but requires sensitivity to tone color and pedaling to reach an artistic level of performance. Movements three and four involve the most intricate ensemble, and explore both pentatonic colors (III) and wonderful imagery, both musical and poetic (IV). When the work was not in public domain and only published by Durand, its popularity led to various Durand published arrangements: string quartet (Jones), orchestra (Ravel), two-pianos (Choisnel), solo (Charlot), and piano and cello (Ronchini).

I-A §   Mother Goose Suite (Five Children's Pieces)   Schirmer
This particular edition includes both a complete solo transcription by Lawrence Rosin as well as the original duet version by Ravel.

A §   Bolero (Ravel, arr.)   Durand
This four-hand duet arrangement by Ravel is a must for any serious duettists. It is a spectacular rendition which will please any audience.

A   La Valse (Garban, transcriber)   Durand
This duet arrangement was transcribed for duet playing by Lucien Garban (1877–1959). Orchestrated, arranged for solo piano as well as two pianos, *La Valse* followed the composer's much earlier *Valses nobles et sentimentales*. This duet version is very successful and among the more technically challenging works for piano duet, however, it is not as difficult as Liszt's four-hand setting of the *Mephisto Waltz*. In the original score the composer states: "Through rifts in swirling clouds, couples are glimpsed waltzing. As the clouds disperse little by little, one sees an immense hall peopled with a whirling crowd. The scene becomes progressively brighter. The light from chandeliers bursts forth at fortissimo. An Imperial Court, around 1855." (See Ravel entry for this work in the two pianos-four hands section.)

Music for One Piano—Four Hands *continued*

A	Rhapsodie Espagnole	Kalmus

Ravel first worked out the four movements of this orchestral *Rhapsody* in piano duet form. Soon after (1908) he completed the full orchestration. All four movements are present in this original duet setting: *Prélude, Malagueña, Habanera,* and *Feria*.

Rawsthorne, Alan (1905-1971) England (b. Lancashire, England; Cambridge, England)

I-A	The Creel (Suite)	Oxford

Rebikov, Vladimir Ivanovich (1866-1920) Russia

I-A	Petite Suite (5 duets)	Jürgenson

(*Valse, Danse des myosotis, Tarantelle, Danse orientale, Mazurka*)

Reger, Max (Johann Baptist Joseph Maximilian) (1873-1916) Germany

A	Cinq Pieces Pittoresques, op. 34	Universal
A	German Dances, op. 10	Schott
A	Introduction and Passacaglia	Breitkopf and Härtel
A	Selected Works for Piano Four Hands	Breitkopf and Härtel
A	Six Burlesques, op. 58	Peters; Schott
A	Six Pieces, op. 94 (out of print; available on-line)	Peters
A	Variations and Fugue on a Theme of Mozart, op. 132	Peters
A	Waltzes, op. 22	Universal

Reinecke, Carl (Heinrich Carsten) (1824-1910) Germany

I-A	Nutcracker and Mouse King, op. 46 (Hinson, ed.)	Alfred
A	From the Cradle to the Grave, op. 202	Edward Schuberth

Respighi, Ottorino (1879-1936) Italy (b. Bologna, Italy; d. Rome, Italy)

I-A	Six Little Pieces	Associated

Reubart, Dale (b. 1926) Canada (b. Kansas City, MO) naturalized Canadian

I	§	2 × 2: Etudes for Piano Duet (6 imaginative duets)	Frederick Harris

This collection challenges students with hand-crossings, shared pedaling, and unison articulations that require precise ensemble. Titles: *Hoe-Down, Rag-a-Muffin, Drums and Bugles, Galop, A Quiet Place,* and *Polka*.

Riegger, Wallingford (Constantine) (1885-1961) USA (b. Albany, GA; New York, NY)

I	The Cry	Southern
I	Evocation	Southern
I	New Dance	Southern

Rimsky-Korsakov, Nikolai Andreyevich (1844-1908) Russia

I-A	Scheherazade, op. 35	Kalmus
A	Capriccio Espagnole, op. 34 (piano duet)	Kalmus
A	The Flight of the Bumble-bee (from *The Tale of Tsar Saltan*) (Korn, arr.)	Schott

Rocherolle, Eugenie R. (b. 1936) USA (b. New Orleans, LA)

E		Let's Duet	Kjos
E	§ *	Headin' South (Gone Fishin')	Kjos

With her New Orleans background, Rocherolle captures southern sounds in this early intermediate duet collection. The titles are: *Plantation, Rockin' Chair, Cotton Pickin', Spanish Moss,* and *Gone Fishin'*.

E (Early Intermediate)   I (Intermediate)   A (Advanced Intermediate to Advanced)

E	Twice Blessed	Kjos
I-A	The Way We Danced	Alfred

A duet arrangement of her popular two-piano score. Includes: *Tango for Two*, *"Classic" Rock*, *Slow Dancin'*, *A Winsome Waltz*, and *Jitterbug*. These dances can be used individually, or played as a suite.

Rollin, Catherine USA

E-I	Dances for Two, Bks. 1, 2	Alfred
I-A §	The Nutcracker Suite for Two	Alfred

Rossini, Gioacchino (Antonio) (1792-1868) Italy

E-I	Petite Fanfare	Curci
I-A	William Tell Overture (Gottschalk/Weekley/Arganbright, eds.)	Kjos
A	Opera Overtures	Alfred

Rowley, Alec (1892–1958) Great Britain (b. London, England; d. Weybridge, England)

E	Side by Side (Our First Duets)	Ashdown
I	Polka	Boosey & Hawkes

Rubinstein, Anton (Grigor'yevich) (1829-1894) Russia

A	Bal Costumé, op. 103	Jürgenson

Ruthardt, Adolf (1849-1934) Germany

E-I	Teacher and Pupil	Kalmus

Saint-Saéns, (Charles) Camille (1835-1921) France

A	Danse Macabre (Hiscocks, transcriber)	Peters

Satie, Eric (Alfred Leslie) (1866-1925) France

I	Aperçus Désagréables (1908-1912)	Durand; Eschig
I-A	Trois Morceaux en Forme de Poire (1903)	Salabert
A	Cinema	Salabert
A	En Habit de Cheval	Salabert
A	Parade	Durand
A	Trois Petites Piéces Montées	Associated; Durand

Schickele, Peter (Johann) (b. 1935) USA (b. Ames, IA)

I §	Little Suite For Summer (Student/Teacher)	Elkan-Vogel
I-A	The Civilian Barber (Overture)	Carl Fischer; Elkan-Vogel

Schubert, Franz (Peter) (1797-1828) Austria

I §	German Dances and Ecossaises, op. 33 (Weekley/Arganbright, eds.)	Kjos
I	Military March, op. 51, no. 1 (*Oesterle, ed.)	Alfred; *Schirmer
I-A	Easy Original Compositions	Peters
I-A	Franz Schubert Selected Works (Weekly/Arganbright, eds.)	Kjos

This is a wonderful compilation of some of Schubert's most important four-hand works. Includes: *Fantasy in F minor, op. 103, D 940; Allegro in A minor; Andantino varié; Introduction and Variations on an Original Theme, op. 82;* and *Marche caractéristique*.

Music for One Piano—Four Hands *continued*

ENSEMBLE LITERATURE

I-A	Ländler (original)	Schott

It is important that piano students sight-read and study Schubert's four-hand *Ländler*. Stylistically they foreshadow the later Viennese *Waltzes* of composers such as Joseph Lanner and the elder Johann Strauss and mirror the many solo dances that Schubert composed.

I-A	Marches	Peters
I-A	Schubert's Music for Piano Four-Hands (Weekly/Arganbright, eds.)	Kjos
A §	Fantasia in F Minor, op. 103, D 940 (1924)	Henle; Schirmer; ASE

The *Fantasia in F Minor* is a profoundly moving work, requiring a high level of musicianship. The piece is one of the first of the Romantic hybrid sonata forms; while it is in one continuous movement, it is comprised of four sections which roughly correspond to the movements of a standard sonata: an initial *Allegro*, a *Largo* dominated by double-dotted rhythms, a scherzo-like *Allegro vivace*, and a recapitulation of the first *Allegro* which climaxes in a powerful fugue.

A	Original Compositions for Four Hands, Vols. I-IV	Kalmus; Schirmer
A	Works for Piano-Four Hands, Vols. I-III	Henle

Schumann, Robert (Alexander) (1810-1856) Germany

I	Ghost Story (Appel/Draheim, eds.)	Schott
I-A	Ball-Scenes, op. 109 (9 duets)	Peters

(*Préambule, Polonaise, Walzer, Ungarisch, Francaise, Mazurka, Ecossaise, Walzer,* and *Promenade*)

I-A	Four Works (original compositions) complete (Doerffel, ed.)	International

Includes: *Pictures from the East, op. 66; Twelve Pieces, op. 85; Nine Pieces, op. 109;* and *Six Easy Pieces, op. 130.*

I-A	Kinderball, op. 130 (Six Easy Pieces [duets])	Peters
I-A	Original Compositions for Piano Duet (1 volume)	International; Peters
I-A	Pictures from the East, op. 66 (Six Impromptus)	Kalmus; Peters; Schott
I-A	Scenes from Childhood, op. 15 (Kirchner, arr.)	Peters
I-A	Schumann Original Compositions (Vol. II is devoted to four hands)	Kalmus
I-A	Six Etudes in Canon Form, op. 56 (Bizet, arr; Hinson/Nelson eds.)	Alfred
I-A §	Twelve Pieces for Large and Small Children, op. 85 (Oesterle, ed.)	Schirmer

Represents some of Schumann's best four-hand writing. In spirit, this is Schumann's duet version of his *Album for the Young, op. 68*, which was published two years before op. 85 in 1847.

A	Symphonies (Kirchner, arr.)	Schirmer

Schuster, Giora (1915-2006) Israel (b. Hamburg, Germany; d. Rehovot, Germany)

I	Mimos I	Israeli Music Institute

Seydelmann, Franz (1748-1806) Germany

I-A	Six Sonatas for Two Persons at One Keyboard (1781) (Brauchli, ed.)	Harwood

Some of the first published four hand sonatas in the 1700s were by Charles Burney (see Burney entry in this section). As the keyboard expanded to five octaves, more and more composers were attracted to the genre of four-hand music. After Burney, other composers began writing four-hand duets including Seydelmann, J. C. Bach, Clementi, and Mozart. Seydelmann's sonatas each contain three movements. The writing exhibits a similar level of technical difficulty between parts. His style was influenced by both Haydn and C. P. E. Bach.

E (Early Intermediate) I (Intermediate) A (Advanced Intermediate to Advanced)

Sheftel, Paul (b. 1933) USA (b. Italy)

E	§	One Plus One	Alfred

      Thorough practice steps are included for these fourteen duets, each emphasizing different modes and scales. They also can be played as solos.

Shifrin, Seymour (1926-1979) USA (b. Brooklyn, NY; d. Boston, MA)

I	The Modern Temper	Peters

Shostakovich, Dmitri (Dmitriyevich) (1906-1975) Russia (b. St. Petersburg (Leningrad), Russia; d. Moscow, Russia)

I	3 Pieces for One Piano Four Hands	Schirmer
I-A	Waltzes and Polkas	Sikorski

Shott, Michael J. USA

E	Love Song	Alfred
I	Passacaglia	Alfred
I-A	Ostinato	Alfred

Sinding, Christian (August) (1856-1941) Norway

I-A	Rustle of Spring (Johnson, arr.)	Peters

Sousa, John Philip (1854-1932) USA (b. Washington, D.C.; d. Reading, PA)

I	A Star-Spangled Celebration for Two (Mier, arr.)	Alfred
I	Liberty Bell March (M. Clark, arr.)	Alfred

Spiegelman, Joel (Warren) (b. 1933) USA (b. Buffalo, NY)

I-A	Morsels	MCA

Starer, Robert (1924-2001) USA (b. Vienna, Austria; d. Kingston, NY)

E-I		Five Duets for Young Pianists	MCA
I-A	§	Suite of Piano Duets	Alfred

      From the composer of *Sketches in Color,* these duets may be performed separately or together in a suite format.

A	Fantasia Concertante (1959)	MCA

Stevens, Halsey (1908-1988) USA (b. Scott, NY; d. Long Beach, CA)

I	Sonatina for Piano Four Hands	Helios

Strauss, Johann (1825-1899) Austria

I-A	Famous Strauss Waltzes	Schirmer
I-A	Meine Walzer (7 Waltzes)	Schott
A	Overtures	Kalmus

Stravinsky, Igor (Fyodorovich) (1882-1971) (b. Lomonosov, Russia; d. New York, NY)

E	§ *	Five Easy Pieces (1917) Easy *Primo* (Andante)	Chester; ASE

      This is a very established collection with titles *Andante, Espagnola, Napolitana, Balalaika,* and *Galop. Secondo* parts are considerably more difficult than *primo* parts.

Music for One Piano—Four Hands *continued*

E-I		Three Easy Pieces (1915)	Chester; ASE
		Contents: *March; Waltz; Polka*	
A		Petrouchka (revised 1947 version)	Boosey & Hawkes
A		Rite of Spring (Le Sacre du Printemps) (Stravinsky, arr.)	Boosey & Hawkes
A		Three Pieces for String Quartet (Stravinsky, arr.)	Boosey & Hawkes

Stravinsky, Soulima (1910–1994) USA (b. Lausanne, Switzerland; d. Sarasota, FL)

E-I		Musical Alphabet, Vols. I, II	Peters

Szabo, Ferenc (1902-1969) Hungary (b. and d. Budapest, Hungary)

I		Collected Pieces for Piano Duet (Katalin, ed.)	Editio Musica Budapest

Tansman, Alexandre [Aleksander] (1897–1986) France (b. Łódź, Poland; d. Paris, France)

I	§	Cinq Petites Piéces	Max Eschig
A		Les Jeunes au Piano	Max Eschig

Tchaikovsky, Pyotr Il'yich (1840-1893) Russia

E-I	§	Fifty Russian Folk Songs (original)	International

This International edition, *Fifty Russian Folk Songs*, contains the entire original fifty duets in this set with both Russian and English titles.

E-I	§	Russian Folk Songs (Herrmann, ed.)	Kalmus; Peters

An important collection of thirty-six duets (selected by the editor from the original publication of fifty), arranged progressively by difficulty. The *primo* part is generally easier, with predominantly hands alone or unison writing, as well as chordal textures, in the latter duets. They are excellent for sight-reading purposes, and as an introduction to Russian folk music.

I		Sleeping Beauty Suite, op. 66a (Rachmaninov, transcriber)	Peters
I		Sleeping Beauty Waltz (M. Clark, arr.)	Alfred
I-A		The Nutcracker Suite op. 71a (Langer, arr., Hinson, ed.)	Alfred
I-A	§	The Nutcracker Suite op. 71a (Langer arr., Sternberg, ed.) Book and CD	Schirmer
I-A		The Nutcracker Suite for Two (Rollin, arr.)	Alfred
A		Serenade, op. 48 (Langer, transcriber)	Kalmus

This is a transcription of the composer's famous work for strings in four movements: *Pezzo in forma di sonatina, Valse, Élégie, Finale (Tema russo)*.

A		Symphony No. 5 in E Minor, op. 64 (Tanéeff, arr.)	Schirmer

Tcherepnin, Alexander (Nikolayevich) (1899-1977) USA
(b. Saint Petersburg, Russia; d. Paris, France)

E	§	Exploring the Piano (Student/Teacher)	Peters

Twelve duets in which the easier student part moves progressively from no sharps or flats to six sharps and six flats.

I		Suite Georgienne, op. 57 (originally for piano and string orchestra; 4 mvts.)	Durand

Toch, Ernst (1887-1964) Austria (naturalized American)
(b. Vienna, Austria; d. Santa Monica, CA)

A		Sonata, op. 87	Mills

Townsend, Douglas (b. 1921) USA (b. New York, NY)

I-A		Four Fantasies on American Folk Songs	Peters

E (Early Intermediate)   I (Intermediate)   A (Advanced Intermediate to Advanced)

Tsitsaros, Christos USA resident (b. Cyprus)

E	§	Songs and Dances	Frederick Harris

These duets stimulate the student's imagination and offer an opportunity for exploring new sounds based on familiar technical and musical gestures. *Primo* and *secondo* parts are not always of equal difficulty. *Mountain Melody, Echoes of a Fairy Tale*, and *Country Dance* are some of the titles in this collection.

Turina, Joaquín (y Perez Turina) (1882–1949) Spain (b. Seville, Spain; d. Madrid, Spain)

A	La Procession du Rocio, op. 9	Salabert

Türk, Daniel Gottlob (1750-1813) Germany

I-A	Tonstücke für vier Hände, Vols. I, II	Schott

Vandall, Robert D. (b. 1944) USA

Robert Vandall has produced a wealth of ensemble music for students and teachers. These pieces have become student favorites and are regularly selected for contests, festivals and recitals. His many ensemble pieces published as sheet music by Alfred can be found on the publisher's web site. We have included his duet collections below.

E		Emerald Sonatina	Alfred
E		Sacred Music for Piano Duet	Alfred
E-I	§	Celebrated Christmas Duets, Books 4-5	Alfred
E-I	§	Celebrated Piano Duets, Books 2-5	Alfred

These books bring together some of the favorite Vandall ensemble pieces arranged with equal difficulty and interest for both *primo* and *secondo* parts.

I	Sonatina for Two	Alfred
I	Topaz Sonatina	Alfred

Van Slyck, Nicholas (1922-1983) USA

I	Suite for Four Hands	Willis

Wagner, (Wilhelm) Richard (1813-1883) Germany

I-A	Polonaise in D Major	Breitkopf and Härtel; Schott

Walton, Sir William (Turner) (1902-1983) England (b. Oldham, Lancashire; d. Island of Ischia, near Naples)

E-I	Duets for Children (two volumes)	Oxford

Warlock, Peter (pseudonym for Philip Arnold Heseltine) (1894-1930) England (b. London, England; d. Chelsea, England)

I	Capriol Suite (Curwen, ed.)	Schirmer

Weber, Carl Maria (Friedrich Ernst) von (1786-1826) Germany

I	Easy Pieces, opp. 3, 10	Bärenreiter
I	Invitation to the Dance, op. 65	Ricordi; ASE
I-A	Pieces for Piano-Four Hands, opp. 3, 10, 60 (*Ruthardt)	Peters; *International

Weber composed 20 pieces for four hands, organized in these three opus numbers. The titles are *Six pieces, op. 3* (1801), *Six pieces, op. 10* (1809) and

Music for One Piano—Four Hands *continued*

Huit (8) *pieces, op. 60* (1818). In general, the level of difficult increases as one moves through the three opus numbers. The two longer *Rondos* (op. 10, no. 6; op. 60, no. 8) are particularly challenging. In the easier op. 3, the titles are: *Sonatine* (one movement), *Romanze, Menuetto, Andante con Variazioni* (theme and two variations)*, Marcia,* and *Rondo.*

Weekley, Dallas and Arganbright, Nancy USA (arrangers, composers, editors)

(See the ensemble anthology One-Piano, Four-Hands for a listing of collections by Weekley/Arganbright.)

All the works cited here are published by Kjos Music Publishing Company. The husband and wife piano-duet team of Dallas Weekley and Nancy Arganbright has produced a wealth of ensemble music for students and teachers. These works are excellent arrangements prepared with the experience and knowledge this foremost team has accrued from years of performing the piano duet literature. Their arrangements are considered "go to" editions for duo-piano teams and are student and teacher favorites, regularly selected for contests, festivals and recitals. Their publication, *The Piano Duet: A Learning Guide,* is a most valuable resource for ensemble players and teachers.

We consider the collections arranged and edited by Weekley and Arganbright to be indispensable additions to the piano ensemble library. The § marking is intended for the entire ensuing list:

Early Intermediate:
Beach: Summer Dreams, op. 47
Chinese Lullaby (Folk song)

Intermediate:
Classics for Two
Czerny: Sonatina, op. 156, no. 2
Five Joplin Rags
Four Joplin Waltzes
Grieg's Best Duets
Kuhlau: Sonatina, op. 17
Pachelbel: Canon in D (This is a superior arrangement of this popular work.)
Romantic Piano Duets (includes Mendelssohn's *Song Without Words, op. 30, no. 1*, Field's *Nocturne no. 5,* and *Bagatelle, op. 47, no. 1* by Dvořák, and Verdi's *Triumphal March* from *Aida.*)
Schubert: German Dances and Ecossaises, op. 33
Three Baroque Pieces
Three Sonatinas

Late Intermediate to Advanced:
Brahms: Waltzes, op. 39
(See annotation under Brahms in this section.)
Christmas Liszt for Two
(See annotation in Christmas ensemble section.)
Debussy: Petite Suite (1889)
(See annotation under Liszt in this section.)
* Dolly (Suite), op. 56 (Berceuse)
(See annotation under Fauré in this section.)
Franz Schubert: Selected Works
Poulenc: Sonata
(See annotation under Poulenc in this section.)
Ravel: *Ma Mere L'oye* (Mother Goose Suite)
(See annotation under Ravel in this section.)

Rossini: William Tell Overture (Gottschalk/Weekley/Arganbright, eds.)
Rumba Rítmica (original composition by Weekley/Arganbright)
Schubert's Music for Piano Four-Hands

Advanced:
Listz: Mephisto Waltz (Dance in the Village Inn from Lenau's "Faust")
(See annotation under Liszt in this section.)

Weiner, Leo (1885-1960) Hungary

I-A	Fairy's Dance	Editio Musica Budapest
A	Suite: Hungarian Folk Dances, op. 18	Editio Musica Budapest

Wolf, Ernst Wilhelm (1735-1792) Germany

I-A	Sonata in C Major	Schott

Wolf, Georg Friedrich Theodor (1761-1814)

I-A	Sonata in F Me di Guerra, op. 25 (1915)	Ricordi

Wohlfahrt, Heinrich (1833-1884) (b. and d. Leipzig, Germany)

E-I	Easy Four Hand Pieces for Children, op. 87	Kalmus

Woollen, Russell (Charles) (1923-1994) USA (b. Connecticut)

A	Sonata for Piano Duo	Peer Southern

Wourinen, Charles (b. 1938) USA (b. New York, NY)

I	Making Ends Meet	Peters

Yeager, Jeanine USA

I	Have It Your Way (4 duets)	Kjos
I	Times to Remember (4 duets)	Kjos
I	Two Contrasts (Prelude and Rhapsody)	Kjos

Zipp, Friedrich (1914-1997) Germany
(b. Frankfurt, Germany; d. Freiburg im Breisgau, Germany)

I-A	Canzona e Sonata, op. 22	Schott
I-A	Elmauer Bagatelles	Peters

Ensemble Literature — Music for One Piano–Four Hands

Collections and Anthologies for One Piano–Four Hands

		Title (editor or arranger)	Publisher
E		Blue Ribbon Series: Favorite Piano Duets, The, Level 3, Vol. 1 (Flatau, ed.)	Alfred
E	§	Primo Light (Weekley/Arganbright, eds.)	Kjos

Fourteen duets in which the *primo* is based on five-finger patterns.

E		Primo Profiles (Weekley/Arganbright, eds.)	Kjos

Original duets where the *primo* is based on five-finger patterns.

E		Secondo Light (Weekley/Arganbright, arr.)	Kjos

Five arrangements where the *secondo* is based on five-finger patterns.

E-I		Easy Original Piano Duets	Consolidated
E-I	§	Ensemble Music for Group Piano (Lyke/Hayden, eds.)	Stipes

Though originally developed for undergraduate group piano instruction at the college level, this volume is an excellent collection of ensemble repertoire useful in both individual and group teaching situations. It is divided into three parts which include: duets focusing on major and minor five-finger patterns; original and arranged compositions for one-piano, four hands; and finally music for 2, 3, 5, and 6 keyboards (or parts).

E-I		Essential Keyboard Duets, Vols. 1-3 (Kowalchyk/Lancaster, eds.)	Alfred
E-I	§	Music Pathways, Ensemble, Levels 3, 4, 5	Carl Fischer

These three volumes, compiled by Bianchi, Blickenstaff, Olson, were designed to accompany the *Music Pathways Repertoire Series, Levels 3A–5B*, but are equally useful with any intermediate student.

E-I		Piano Duets of the Classical Period	Oliver Ditson
E-I		Piano for Two (Matz, arr.)	FJH

This six-volume series of duets with equal parts for one-piano, four hands, ranges in difficulty from elementary through late intermediate. Includes classics, well-known favorites, and original pieces.

E-I	§	Pleasure of Your Company, The, Vols. 3–5 (Stecher/Horowitz, arr.)	Schirmer

This collection is one of the most popular duet collections because of the variety of pieces and styles which provide an opportunity for truly sensitive and musical duet performance. This series is a real student favorite.

E-I	§	Popular Soviet Songs and Dances, Band II	Ricordi

A collection of thirteen early intermediate duets, most one page in length (each part), by Russian composers less known in the West such as Sciurovskij, Stepanenko, Shurovsky, and Berkovich. (See Berkovich entry in selected Concerti section.)

E-I	§	Twice As Nice, Vols. I–III (Weekley/Arganbright, eds.)	Kjos

A superbly graded collection of original four–hand duets, these volumes are essential in any ensemble library for intermediate students, whether children or adults. Weekley and Arganbright are a well-known duet team, and their experience is reflected in their excellent editing and fingerings. These selections are superb for teaching the essentials of duet performance. One of the landmark and most important teaching collections for piano duet. The three volumes gradually progress in difficulty.

I		American Portraits (Penn, arr.)	Kjos

Collections and Anthologies: One Piano—Four Hands *continued*

ENSEMBLE LITERATURE

Level		Title	Publisher
I		Baroque Era, The (easier baroque duets)	Peters
I		Classical Duets for Piano, Vols. I, II	Boosey & Hawkes
I		Classical Era, The (easier piano duets)	Peters
I		Classics for Two (Weekley/Arganbright, arr.)	Kjos

Weekley and Arganbright have transcribed four popular classics for the piano duet genre. Included are the *Nocturne* from Mendelssohn's *A Midsummer Night's Dream* and the *Largo* from Handel's *Xerxes*.

I		Classical Masters	Peters

Easier original duets by Beethoven, Clementi, Diabelli, Mozart and Weber.

I		Duet Repertoire Series, Levels 5–9 (Weekley/Arganbright, eds.)	Kjos
I		Overtures, Vols. I, II (Kleinmichel, transcriber)	Peters

This volume consists of well-known Beethoven overtures (e.g., *Egmont, Fidelio, Leonora*) transcribed by Kleinmichel for duet playing.

I	§	Perfect Partners, Vols. I–IV (Johnson, arr.)	Fentone
I	§	Sonaten für Liebhaber (Frickert, ed.)	Schott

This is an excellent collection of sonatas for two pianos, four hands. The editor ranks the sonatas in order of difficulty from Wolf through Mozart, Haydn, Hässler, ending with Bach.

I		Sonatina Album	Peters

Easier piano duets by Clementi, Diabelli, Kuhlau and Mozart.

I		Style and Interpretation, Volume 5: Keyboard Duets 17th and 18th Centuries (Ferguson, ed.).	Oxford
I	§	Three Baroque Pieces (Weekley/Arganbright, arr.)	Kjos

This collection includes *Rondeau* by Jean Joseph Mouret from his "First Suite," first movement (The PBS "Masterpiece Theatre" Theme); *Siciliano* by J. S. Bach from his *Sonata in E-Flat Major for Flute and Clavier, BWV 1031*; and *Arioso* by J. S. Bach from the *Concerto in F Minor for Clavier and Orchestra, BWV 1056*.

I		Three Sonatinas (Weekley/Arganbright, arr.)	Kjos

Three sonatinas by Czerny, Spindler, and Weber.

I-A	§	Classical Album (twelve original duets)	Schirmer
I-A		Essential Keyboard Duets, Vol. 4 (Mauro/Beard, eds.)	Alfred
I-A		Four Centuries of Piano Duet Music (McGraw, ed.)	Boston Music
I-A	§	44 Original Piano Duets (from Haydn to Stravinsky) (Eckard, ed.)	Presser

This volume is a timeless collection of easy to intermediate level duets representing 27 composers. Selections include Arensky, *Waltz, op. 34, no. 4*; Brahms, *Waltzes, op. 39, nos. 10, 11*; Debussy, *En Bateau* (from *Petite Suite*); Fauré, *Kitty Valse* (from *Dolly*); and three pieces by Gretchaninoff.

I-A		Romantic Masters	Peters

Original compositions for four hands at one piano by Bizet, Grieg, Moszkowski, Schubert, and Schumann.

I-A	§	Romantic Piano Duets (Weekley/Arganbright, eds.)	Kjos

Three lesser-known piano duets: Mendelssohn's *Song Without Words, Op. 30 No. 1*, Field's *Nocturne No. 5* arranged by Franz Liszt, and *Bagatelle, op. 47, no. 1* by Dvořák.

E (Early Intermediate)   I (Intermediate)   A (Advanced Intermediate to Advanced)

I-A		Twentieth-Century Composers	Peters

Moderately difficult contemporary piano duets by Hovhaness, Luening, Soulima Stravinsky, and Townsend.

A	§	Four Hand Music by 19th Century Masters	Dover

Includes: *Ich denke dein with Six Variations, WoO 74* (Beethoven); *Hungarian divertimento, op. 54* (Schubert); *Andante and Variations, op. 83a* (Mendelssohn); *Bilder aus Osten, op. 66* (Schumann); *Jeux d'enfants* (Bizet); *Petite Suite* (Debussy); and *Dolly Suite* (Faure).

A	§	Great Works for Piano Four Hands (Herder, ed.)	Dover

This volume is a collection of masterworks from nine composers. Includes Beethoven, *Eight Variations on a Theme by Count Waldstein, Sonata in D, Three Marches, op. 45*; Debussy, *Prelude to The Afternoon of a Faun*; Dvořák, *Six Legends,* from *op. 59*; Janáček, *Moravian Dances*; Rachmaninoff, *Barcarolle, op. 11, no. 1, Italian Polka*; Reger, *Three Burlesques* from *op. 58*; Tchaikovsky, *Waltz* from the ballet *The Sleeping Beauty, op. 66*; and Ravel's *Rapsodie Espagnole*.

Music for One Piano—Six Hands

| | | Composer   Title | Publisher |

Bach, Wilhelm Friedrich Ernst (1759-1845) Germany

E § Das Dreyblatt — Manduca
This humorous piece, in classical style, composed by the grandson of J. S. Bach, features the second (*middle*) part with the player's hands intertwined with the hands of the other players causing interesting performance challenges.

Baines, William (1899-1922) England

I   The King's Review, op. 189 (March) (Liftl, arr.) — Presser

Brown, Timothy USA

I   Triana — FJH

Cheadle, William

I-A   Six for Three — Alfred
Includes: *March, Waltz, Lazy Kitty, Mystery, Bahama Breeze, Folk Dance.*

Gautier, Leonard (1561-1641)

I   Le Secret (Cornelius Gurlitt, arr., Waterman, ed.) — Faber

Grill, Joyce USA

E § Chopsticks Rag for Three — Alfred
I   Three's A Crowd — Alfred

Mozart, (Johann Chrysostom) Wolfgang Amadeus (1756–1791) Austria

I   Village Musicians, K 522 (Musical Joke) (M. Clark, arr.) — Alfred
Originally written for six instruments, this charming piece for three intermediate pianists has twining and intertwined passages "imitating birdsong."

Olson, Kevin R. (1970) USA (b. Utah)

A   out…standing — FJH
"A witty jazz swing piece for three: *primo, secondo,* and a 'free-range' pianist who stands behind the bench and contributes low, mid-range, and high passages."

Rachmaninoff, Sergey (Vasilyevich) (1873–1943) Russia (Rakhmaninov, Sergey) (b. Oneg, near Semyonovo, Russia; d. Beverly Hills, CA)

I-A § Valse and Romance (Hinson, ed.) — Belwin
Written when he was only 17 years old, these pieces were dedicated to three of his friends, Natalya, Lyudmila and Vera Skalon. In romantic in style, they have some rhythmic challenges but are especially nice for late intermediate and early advanced students.

A   The Piano Works of Rachmaninoff — Alfred
Volume VIII: Works for One Piano/Four Hands and One Piano/Six Hands

Music for One Piano—Six Hands *continued*

Ristad, Eloise (1925-1985) USA

I	Storm Gods	Alfred
I	Sunlight on Water	Alfred

Schmitt, Manfred (b. 1939) USA

E-I   Mini Jazz: 13 Easy Piano Pieces for Six Hands   Breitkopf and Härtel

Streabbog, Jean-Louis [Jean Louis Gobbaerts] (1835–1886) Belgium

E   Carnival (M. Clark, arr.)   Alfred

Tchaikovsky, Pyotr Il'yich (1840–1893) Russia

I §   March from the Nutcracker Suite (M. Clark, arr.)   Alfred

Vandall, Robert D. (b. 1944) USA

E   Triple Dip   Alfred
       Triple your fun with these boogie-woogie rhythms and the blues harmonies.

I §   Jazz for Three   Alfred
       Two pieces which combine jazz and blues elements. Includes: *Blue Threesome* and *In the Groove*.

I   Three To Get Ready   Alfred
       Features syncopated swing rhythms.

Weekley, Dallas and Arganbright, Nancy (editors/arrangers)

I §   Gurlitt: Six Pieces For Six Hands (Weekley/Arganbright, arr.)   Kjos
       Accessible to intermediate level students, these six pieces are popular with piano ensemble students. Includes *Capriccietta, Serenata,* and *Impromptu*. These ensembles were prepared for the Piano Trio Event with the National Federation of Music Clubs (NFMC) Festivals Bulletin 2008-2009-2010.

I   Sousa: The Stars and Stripes Forever   Kjos

Anthologies for One-Piano, Six-Hands

I-A §   Essential Keyboard Trios (Mauro/Beard, eds.)   Alfred
       Includes: *Das Dreyblatt* (Bach, Wilhelm Friedrich Ernst); *Sonata for Six Hands, op. 10* (Fodor); *Capriccietta, op. 192, no. 3* (Gurlitt); *Gavotta, op. 192, no. 2* (Gurlitt); *Impromptu, op. 192, no. 6* (Gurlitt); *Hallelujah Chorus* from *Messiah* (Handel, arr. Czerny); *Overture* from *The Marriage of Figaro* (Mozart, arr. Czerny); *Valse* and *Romance* (Rachmaninoff); *Bolero* (Ravel, arr. Streabbog).

Music for Two Pianos—Four Hands

For two-piano literature, the goal has been to identify the pedagogical gems in the teaching repertoire, such as William Gillock's *On a Paris Boulevard,* as well as the important concert works by major composers such as Oliver Messiaen's *Visions de l'amen*. In general, we have not included standard piano concerti where the second piano is a reduction of the orchestration. We have focused on music for two-pianos, four-hands that is currently in print and have tried to avoid out-of-print music.

Composer Biographies: In order to streamline the entries in this section, we have not included composer biographies except for a few composers not listed in a previous section. Please see the Solo Piano Literature sections for brief biographical sketches of individual composers. We have included information on the birth and death of composers in the twentieth century since many composers were born in Europe and immigrated to other countries or to the United States for a major part of their lives. This information gives a more complete picture of the life of recent composers.

		Composer Title	Publisher

Adams, John Coolidge (b. 1947) USA (b. Worchester, MA)

A	§	Hallelujah Junction	Boosey & Hawkes

Agay, Denes (1911-2007) USA (b. near Budapest, Hungary; d. Los Altos, CA)

E-I		The Joy of Two Pianos (arrangements by Agay of familiar melodies)	Music Sales

Alexander, Dennis USA (b. Kansas)

I		Flirtatious!	Alfred
I-A	§	Concertante in G major	Alfred

This is a brilliant sounding three-movement *Concertante* which includes impressive passages that are not as difficult as they sound.

I-A		Concertino in D major (with MIDI Disk)	Alfred
I-A		Fanfare Toccata-Rondo	Alfred

Anderson, Greg and Roe, Elizabeth (arrangers) USA

Juilliard graduates Anderson and Rose are a very current two-piano team playing appealing arrangements. Their arrangements are available on-line at their interactive website: www.andersonroe.com.

A	Bizet: Carmen Fantasy	See website
A	Daquin: The Cuckoo in Sussex	
A	Mozart: "Soave sia il vento"	
A	Ragtime alla turca	
A	The Cat's Fugue	

Arensky, Anton Stepanovich (1861–1906) Russia

A		Polonaise, op. 65, no. 8 (Philipp, ed.)	International
A	§	Suite no. 1, op. 15 (Babin, ed.)	International
A		Suite no. 2, op. 23 "Silhouettes"	International
A		Suite, op. 15 (Oesterle, ed.) (Includes the famous Waltz)	Schirmer
A		Waltz from Suite, op. 15	International

Asch, Anna USA

I	§	Concertino (See annotation in Concerto section.)	Hal Leonard
I		Concertino no. 2	Hal Leonard
I		Jubilation	Hal Leonard

Music for Two Pianos—Four Hands *continued*

Babin, Victor (Viktor Genrikhovich Babin) (1908-1972)
(b. Moscow, Russia; d. Cleveland, Ohio)

Victor Babin, with his wife, Vitya Vronsky (1909-1992), formed one of the most brilliant two-piano teams of the 20th century. Born in Russia, Babin and his wife eventually immigrated to the United States where they became known for their performances and recordings of Rachmaninoff's music. They both served on the piano faculty of the Cleveland Institute of Music where he was appointed *Director* in 1961. Victor Babin is known for his many arrangements and transcriptions for two pianos as well as works either dedicated to or commissioned for the Babin duo team to perform.

A		Concerto for Two Pianos (Babin)	Boosey & Hawkes
A		Petrushka (Stravinsky) (Babin, transcriber)	Boosey & Hawkes
A	§	Waltz of the Flowers (Tchaikovsky, op. 17) (Babin, transcriber)	Boosey & Hawkes

Boosey & Hawkes also publishes Babin transcriptions from Tchaikovsky's *Swan Lake* and *Eugene Onegin*.

Bach, Johann Christian (1735-1782) Germany

I-A	§	Sonata in G Major, op. 15, no. 5	Schott

Bach, Johann Sebastian (1685–1750) Germany

E		Ave Maria (Gounod, arr.)	Willis
E		Sheep May Safely Graze (Howe, arr.)	Oxford
I		Air on the G String (Hinman, arr.)	Willis
I	§	Jesu, Joy of Man's Desiring (Hess, arr.)	Oxford

This is a beautiful arrangement for two pianos based on Dame Myra Hess's (1890-1965) original duet arrangement for one-piano, four-hands.

I-A	Eleven Chorale Preludes from The Little Organ Book	Schirmer
I-A	Seven Bach Chorales (Transcriptions for Piano) (Kurtág, arr.)	Editio Musica Budapest

Includes: *Nun komm' der Heiden Heiland* (BWV 599), *Herr Christ, der eincs'ge Gottes-Sohn* (BWV 601), *Aus tiefer Not schrei' ich zu dir* (BWV 687), *Dies sind die heil'gen zehn Gebot'* (BWV 635), *Alle Menschen müssen sterben* (BWV 643), *Gott, durch deine Güte* (BWV 600), *Das alte Jahr vergangen ist* (BWV 614).

I-A	§	Sicilienne (Maier, arr.)	Alfred

This beautiful Guy Maier arrangement is based on the *Sicilienne* from Bach's second flute sonata. Maier (1891-1956) served on the piano faculties of the University of Michigan, the Juilliard School and later UCLA. His early training was at the New England Conservatory with additional private coaching from Arthur Schnabel. Maier was a very well known pianist, teacher, and contributing author (e.g., *Etude Magazine*) during the first half of the 20th century and his teaching legacy continues to the present.

A	Concerto in F minor (Fischer, arr.)	Music Sales

This is a transcription for two pianos (without orchestration) based on the original work for one cembalo and string quintet.

A	Concerto in C minor, BWV 1060 (Bach, transcriber)	International

(*Allegro, Adagio, Allegro*)

A	Concerto in C Major, BWV 1061 (original work)	International

([*Allegro*], *Adagio ovvero largo, Fuga*)

Bach composed both of these concerti for two harpsichords and string accompaniment with continuo. BWV 1060 is possibly a transcription of a

---
E (Early Intermediate) I (Intermediate) A (Advanced Intermediate to Advanced)

lost double concerto for two violins (or violin and oboe). In BWV 1061, the string accompaniment may have been added later. The two keyboards are not accompanied in the *Adagio* movement of BWV 1061.

A   Prelude and Fugue in D (BWV 532) (Philipp, transcriber.)   Durand

The well-known French pianist and pedagogue, Isidor Philipp (1863-1958), has transcribed many Bach solo keyboard works for two pianos, too numerous to mention in this short space.

Bach, Wilhelm Friedemann (1710–1784) Germany

A § Sonata in F Major (for two keyboards)   Breitkopf & Härtel

One of the earliest works composed for two harpsichords, this is a fascinating work to see on the score and play. (It also can easily be found on-line.) Organized in three movements, *Allegro moderato, Andante,* and *Presto,* the first two movements have binary repeats and the last movement is in spirited triple meter with a fair amount of unison writing between the two keyboards. Through canonic imitation, there is a considerable amount of musical conversation between the keyboards and the score is highly ornamented. No phrasing or dynamics are in the score. It is a piece that struggles to escape the high baroque yet reveals elements of the early classical sonata.

Bacon, Ernst (1898–1990) USA (b. Chicago, IL; d. Orinda, CA)

I   Coal Scuttle Blues (Luenin, ed.)   Hal Leonard

Barber, Samuel (Osborne) (1910–1981) USA (b. West Chester, PA; d. New York, NY)

A § Souvenirs "Ballet Suite," op. 28 (Gold/Fizdale, eds.)   Schirmer

This is a well-known and excellent transcription for two pianos of the original work for piano duet. (See annotation in one-piano four-hand section.)

Bartók, Béla (Viktor János) (1881–1945) Hungary (b. Hungary; d. New York, NY)

A   Rhapsody, op. 1 (1904)   Lengnick

This is the composer's reworking for two pianos of the version for piano and orchestra. It is similar in structure to a Liszt Hungarian rhapsody.

A § Seven Pieces from the Mikrokosmos   Boosey & Hawkes

Two piano arrangements by the composer of nos. 69, 113, 123, 127, 135, 145, and 146 from the solo *Mikrokosmos*. The titles Bartók uses for this two piano version are *Bulgarian Rhythm, Chord and trill study, Perpetuum mobile, Short canon and its Inversion, New Hungarian Folksong, Chromatic Invention,* and *Ostinato*.

Beethoven, Ludwig van (1770–1827) Germany

I   Für Elise (Lancaster/Renfrow, arr.)   Alfred
I-A   Für Elise (Rabinof, arr.)   Alfred

Benjamin, Arthur (1893–1960) Great Britain (b. Australia)

Benjamin received his early musical training at the Royal Conservatory of Music in London, England. He had a professional teaching career that vacillated between England and Australia. He wrote for many genres, including orchestral, opera and film, but best known are these two works in which he used native tunes discovered during visits to the West Indies. His most famous film score was the music, *Storm Cloud Cantata,* heard in Alfred Hitchcock's movie, *The Man Who Knew Too Much*. Among

Music for Two Pianos—Four Hands continued

several premieres to his credit, Benjamin performed Herbert Howell's first *Piano Concerto* and the England premiere of Gershwin's *Rhapsody in Blue*.

A	§	Jamaican Rhumba	Boosey & Hawkes
A	§	Two Jamaican Street Songs	Boosey & Hawkes

Both of these works by Benjamin are excellent two piano works, which can be considered part of the standard two piano repertoire. The *Jamaican Rhumba* includes a driving dance rhythm (123-123-12) in the second piano part against a lively and technically challenging first piano. The *Songs* include lovely melodic sections and contrasting styles. Both pieces are delightful audience favorites and a *must* for the two-piano library.

Berkeley, Sir Lennox (Randal Francis) (1903-1989) Great Britain (b. Oxford, England; d. London, England)

I-A	Sonatina For Two Pianos, op. 52, no. 2 (*Moderato, Andante, Allegro con brio*)	Music Sales

Berkovich, Isaac (b. Ukraine)

I	Piano Concerto, op. 44 (See annotation in Concerto section.)	Hal Leonard

Berlin, Irving (1888–1991) USA (b. Tyumen, Russian Empire; d. New York, NY)

I		Alexander's Ragtime Band (Heitler/Lyke, arr.)	Alfred
I		Simple Melody (M. Clark, arr.)	Alfred
I-A	§	When The Midnight Choo-Choo Leaves for Alabam' (Heitler/Lyke, arr.)	Alfred

This arrangement is part of an ensemble series, arranged by Heitler and Lyke, and is excellent for intermediate students from teenagers through adults.

Bernstein, Leonard (1918–1990) USA (b. Lawrence, MA; d. New York, NY)

I-A		Music for Two Pianos	Hal Leonard

Only recently available, this short work was composed when Bernstein was 19.

A		Age of Anxiety (Symphony no. 2)	Boosey & Hawkes
A	§	Symphonic Dances from West Side Story (Musto, ed.)	Boosey & Hawkes

Includes: *Prologue, Somewhere, Scherzo, Mambo, Cha-cha, Meeting Scene, Cool Fugue, Rumble,* and *Finale*.

Bizet, Georges (Alexander César Léopold) (1838–1875) France

A	§	Carmen, A Concert Suite for Two Pianos (Simm, arr.)	Alfred
A	§	Children's Games (Jeux d'enfants)	Kalmus

This set of twelve pieces describing children's activities is part of the standard two-piano repertoire.

Bloch, Ernest (1880–1959) USA (b. Geneva, Switzerland; d. Agate Beach, OR)

A	Scherzo Fantastique	Schirmer

Bolcom, William (Eldon) (b. 1938) USA (b. Seattle, WA)

I-A	Abendmusik	Marks
A	The Garden of Eden: Four Rags for Two Pianos	Marks

Borodin, Alexander Porfir'ievich (1833–1887) Russia

I-A	Polovetsian Dances (Pope, arr.)	Alfred

Boulanger, Lili (1893-1918) France

A	D'un Matin du Printemps (Francaix, ed.)	Schirmer

Braggiotti, Mario (1905-1996) USA (b. Florence, Italy; d. West Palm Beach, FL)

Braggiotti studied at the New England Conservatory and the Paris *Conservatoire*. He had a life long interest in music for two pianos and early on performed much of the repertoire as part of the two piano team of Braggiotti and Fray and later Braggiotti and Andis (his wife). Braggiotti befriended George Gershwin who helped launch his career. Braggiotti was responsible for bringing *Rhapsody in Blue* to the attention of many European audiences and considered it his signature piece.

I-A § Variations on Yankee Doodle — Schirmer
   Also arranged by the composer for solo piano, these delightful variations for two pianos are a crowd-pleasing concert set. The variations are composed in the style of various composers such as Bach, Beethoven, Chopin, and Gershwin.

Brahms, Johannes (1833–1897) Germany

Brahms' original two piano works are at the core of the repertoire for this genre.

I-A § Five Waltzes, op. 39 (Hughes, ed.) — Schirmer
   The composer selected five waltzes (nos. 1, 2, 11, 14, 15) from the op. 39 duets for this two-piano version. In some waltzes (when compared to the original duet version) Brahms changes the key.

A Sonata in F Minor, op. 34b — International
   This is Brahms' early arrangement for two pianos of the famous F minor quintet, op. 34. The *Sonata* can be viewed as an original work by the composer and deserves greater attention from two piano teams.

A § Variations on a Theme of Haydn, op. 56b ("St. Anthony") — Alfred; Schirmer
   One of the romantic masterpieces of the two piano literature, it consists of the original theme and eight variations. Even though the orchestral version is best known, the original setting was for two pianos.

Britten, (Edward) Benjamin (1913–1976) England
(b. Lowestoft, Suffolk, England; d. Aldeburgh, Suffolk, England)

A Introduction and Rondo alla Burlesque, op. 23, no. 1 (1940) — Boosey & Hawkes
A Mazurka Elegiaca op. 23, no. 2 (1941) — Boosey & Hawkes
   This work with its Polish title was written in memory of Paderewski.
A Music for Two Pianos (1937) — Boosey & Hawkes
A Scottish Ballad, op. 26 (Britten, arr.) (1941) — Boosey & Hawkes
   Originally written for two pianos and orchestra.
A Two Lullabys for Two Pianos — Faber/Alfred

Brubeck, Dave (David Warren) (b. 1920) USA (b. Concord, CA)

A Four by Four (1946) — Associated
   The clever title mirrors the fact that the work is in four movements (*Allegro, Largo, Moderato, Moderato*) to be played by four hands. It is an early student work.

Music for Two Pianos—Four Hands *continued*

A	Points On Jazz (Original two-piano score)	Alfred
	An eight-movement ballet by renowned jazz musician, Dave Brubeck. Includes performance notes by the composer.	
A	They All Sang Yankee Doodle	Hal Leonard
	Also for solo piano, this is a set of variations using several folk songs exploring, in Brubeck's words, "pianistic devices".	

Casadesus, Robert (1899–1972) France (b. and d. Paris, France)

A	Concerto for Two Pianos and Orchestra, op. 17	Durand
A	6 Pieces, op. 2 (1920)	Durand

Casella, Alfredo (1883–1947) Italy (b. Turin, Italy; d. Rome, Italy)

I-A §	Pupazzetti (Five Marionette Pieces) (1916)	Durand
	According to the composer the set can be played on either one or two pianos though it is more interesting to hear when played on two pianos. (See annotation in one-piano, four-hand section.)	

Chabrier, Emmanuel (1841-1894) France

A	España Rhapsody (Simm, arr.)	Alfred

Chopin, Frédéric François [Fryderyk Franciszek] (1810–1849) Poland

A §	Rondo in C Major, op. 73 (1828)	Universal
	Composed while a teenager, this rondo is Chopin's only work for two pianos (not counting orchestral reductions of his concerti). The two parts are balanced with melodic material shared and elegant passagework throughout.	

Clementi, Muzio (1752–1832) England (b. Italy)

I	Sonatinas, op. 36, nos. 1–6 (Hulse, arr.) (also published individually)	Willis
I §	Two Sonatas in B-flat Major, opp. 12, 46	Schirmer
	These two sonatas, both composed in B-flat major, are original works for two pianos written in an early Classical style. The individual movements are: Op. 12, *Allegro assai, Larghetto espressivo, Presto*. Op. 46: *Allegro di molto--Allegretto, Tempo di Minuetto*.	

Cohan, George Michael (1878–1942) USA (b. Providence, RI; d. New York, NY)

I	Patriotic Cohan, A Medley (Heitler/Lyke, arr.)	Alfred

Copland, Aaron (1900–1990) USA (b. New York, NY; d. Tarrytown, NY)

These are all superior two piano arrangements of original works from genres other than piano. *Danzón Cubano* is well known from the composer's orchestration and is the only work cited below that was originally written for two pianos.

A	Billy the Kid (Copland, arr.)	Boosey & Hawkes
A	Dance of the Adolescent (Copland, arr.)	Boosey & Hawkes
	An excerpt from the ballet *Grohg*, arranged for two pianos by the composer during his student years in Paris.	
A	Danzón Cubano (originally for two pianos)	Boosey & Hawkes
A	El Salón México (Bernstein, arr.)	Boosey & Hawkes
A §	Hoe Down and Saturday Night Waltz (Gold & Fizdale, arr.)	Boosey & Hawkes

E (Early Intermediate)   I (Intermediate)   A (Advanced Intermediate to Advanced)

Cordero, Roque (1917-2008) USA (b. Panama City, Panama; d. Dayton, OH)

A		Duo (1954)	Peer Southern

Corigliano, John Paul (b. 1938) USA (b. New York, NY)

A		Kaleidoscope (1959)	Schirmer

Davenport, Carolyn USA

A	§	Toccata Española	Alfred

Debussy, (Achille-) Claude (1862–1918) France

I		Clair de lune (Gunther, arr.)	Jobert
I-A	§	Petite suite (Busser, arr.)	Durand
I-A		Three Nocturnes for Orchestra (Ravel, arr.) (Nuages, Fetes, Sirènes)	Jobert

The original orchestral works were inspired by impressionistic paintings by Whistler. The titles translated are Clouds, Festivals, and Sirens.

A		Arabesque no. 1, no. 2	Durand
A	§	En blanc et noir	Durand

This Debussy work is not arranged from another genre but originally composed for two pianos. Written near the end of Debussy's life at the same time as his solo *Études* and subtitled *poetic epigraphs*, this core work of the two-piano repertoire opens with *Avec emportement*, a waltz, perhaps foreshadowing Ravel's later and famous *La valse*. The middle, *Lent, somber*, is translated slow and somber and was dedicated to Lt. Jacques Charlot, a friend of the composer killed in WWI. Religious overtones are touched by use of the German hymn tune, *Ein feste Burg ist unser Gott* (A Mighty fortress in Our God). The final *Scherzando* is dedicated to Igor Stravinsky but sounds more like serious Ravel than Stravinsky.

A		La Mer (Debussy, arr.)	Durand
A	§	Lindaraja	Durand

Lindaraia is a lesser-known work by Debussy because it was not published during his lifetime. It was, however, his first composition for two pianos and with its Spanish habanera rhythm resembles the musical flavor of his later solo prelude, *La puerta del Vino*.

A		Prélude à l'après-midi d'un faune (Debussy, arr.)	Jobert

Diamond, David (1915-2005) USA (b. Rochester, NY; d. Brighton, New York)

A		Concerto for Two Solo Pianos (1942)	Presser

Donhányi, Ernst von (1877-1960) Hungary (b. Bragislava, Hungary; d. Tallahassee, FL)

A		Valse Boiteuse, op. 39A, no. 3	Lengnick
A		Valse de Fête, op. 39A, no. 4	Lengnick

Both of these waltzes are individual movements published from the composer's *Suite en Valse, op. 39a*.

Dukas, Paul (1865-1935) France (b. and d. Paris, France)

A		Sorcerer's Apprentice (Dukas, arr.)	Durand

Enesco, Georges (George Enescu) (1881–1955) Rumania (b. Liveni-Virnav; d. Paris, France)

A	§	Romanian Rhapsody no. 1 in A Major (Simm, arr.)	Bagaduce Music

First published in 1991, this is a stunning two-piano concert transcription of the well-known orchestral score. Every note in the orchestra score is faithfully transcribed for the two pianos.

Ensemble Literature — Music for Two Pianos–Four Hands

Music for Two Pianos—Four Hands *continued*

Feldman, Morton (1926–1987) USA (b. New York, NY; d. Buffalo, NY)

A	Intermission VI (1953) (1 or 2 pianos)	Boosey & Hawkes
A	Two Pianos (1957)	Peters
A	Two Pieces (1954)	Peters
A	Projection III (1951)	Peters

Franck, César (-Auguste-Jean-Guillaume-Hubert) (1822–1890) France (b. Belgium)

A   Prelude, fugue et variation, op. 18 (Franck, arr.)   Durand
        This is Franck's two-piano arrangement of the well-known organ solo.

Gershwin, George (1898–1937) USA (b. Brooklyn, NY; d. Beverly Hills, CA)

I   By Strauss (Haydon and Lyke, arr.)   Alfred
I-A §   A Gershwin Medley (Haydon and Lyke, arr.)   Alfred
I-A §   Preludes (Stone, transcriber)   Alfred
        These three *Preludes* are very popular, and highly motivating for students. Filled with jazz elements, syncopations, and large hand-stretches, the solo versions are often too difficult for intermediate students. Each piano part of this two piano arrangement is slightly easier than the original solo version thus making these enjoyable preludes more accessible for some students.

A   An American in Paris (Original Gershwin score)   Alfred
A   Cuban Overture (Stone, transcriber)   Alfred
A   Four Songs by George Gershwin (Posnak, arr.)   Alfred
        Advanced duo piano arrangements of *But Not for Me, It Ain't Necessarily So, Someone to Watch over Me, 'S Wonderful/Funny Face*. This work was required in the 2008 Murray Dranoff International Piano Competition.

A   Gershwin Plays Gershwin (Litterst, transcriber; Wodehouse, ed./arr.)   Alfred
        Subtitled, *Selections from the Piano Rolls*, some have been arranged for two pianos in this edition.

A   I Got Rhythm Variations (2nd piano is orchestral transcription)   Belwin
A §   Porgy and Bess Fantasy for Two Pianos (Grainger, arr.)   Alfred
        This advanced concert arrangement is popular with two piano teams and includes songs from the original folk opera such as *My Man's Gone Now, It Ain't Necessarily So,* and *Summertime*.

A   Rhapsody in Blue (Original)   Alfred
        If a student desires to learn the *Rhapsody* to perform with orchestra or band, this is the version from which to learn. It contains the original solo piano part separate from the second piano orchestration. This is the version that Gershwin himself prepared for publication.

A   Second Rhapsody (2nd piano orchestral reduction)   Alfred

Gillock, William (1917–1993) USA (b. LaRussell, MO; d. Dallas, TX)

E §   On a Paris Boulevard   Willis
        A gem of a pedagogical duet for two pianos, *Paris Boulevard* is a light and appealing early intermediate composition with a simple melody over a waltz accompaniment. The interplay of the two parts, and the addition of a descant of double thirds, add to the overall "Parisian" flavor and charm of this student and teacher favorite.

E (Early Intermediate)   I (Intermediate)   A (Advanced Intermediate to Advanced)

Goldston, Margaret USA (1932-2003) (b. Havana, Cuba; d. Franklin, NC)

E	Nightsong	Alfred
I-A	Spanish Rhapsody	Alfred

Gottschalk, Louis Moreau (1829–1869) USA

A	Banjo (Moross, ed.)	Schirmer

Gould, Morton (1913-1996) USA (b. Richmond Hill, NY; d. Orlando, FL)

I-A   Pavanne   Alfred
A   § *   Two Pianos (five pieces) (Echos)   Schirmer
        These five pieces are *Chords, Blues, Waltzes, Echos,* and *Triplets* with a total duration of approximately sixteen minutes. The fourth movement, *Echos,* is most attractive, and the least difficult, of the set. This work was premiered at the First National Two Piano Competition in Miami, FL (1987).

Grainger, Percy (George Aldridge) (1882–1961) USA
(b. Brighton/Melbourne, Australia; d. White Plains, NY)

I-A   Country Gardens   Schirmer
I-A   Music for Two Pianos, Vols. 1-5 (Grainger, arr.)   Schott
A   §   Porgy and Bess Fantasy for Two Pianos (Grainger, arr.)   Alfred
        This advanced concert arrangement is popular with pianists and includes songs from the original Gershwin folk opera such as *My Man's Gone Now, It Ain't Necessarily So,* and *Summertime.*

Grieg, Edvard (Hagerup) (1843–1907) Norway

I-A   Peer Gynt, Suite I, op. 46 (Simm, arr.)   Alfred
        This arrangement is very true to the orchestration with both pianos equally sharing musical material.
I-A   Mozart Sonata in C Major, K 545, Second piano part (Grieg, arr.)   Schirmer
        Grieg composed several second piano parts for selected Mozart solo piano sonatas, however, most are now out of print. The arrangement for K 545 is still available.
A   Dance Caprice, op. 28, no. 3 (Blake, arr.)   Willis
A   §   Wedding-Day at Troldhaugen (Emil Kronke [1865-1938], arr.)   Lauren
        This is a reprint of the popular 1916 John Church edition.

Gurlitt, Cornelius (1820–1901) Germany

I   8 Melodious Pieces, op. 174   Schirmer
I   §   Rondo in D, op. 175, no. 1   Schirmer
        This original and attractive two-piano duet, in late Classical style, is only six pages in length.
I   Rondo in E-Flat, op. 175, no. 2   Schirmer

Handel, George Frideric (1685–1759) England (b. Germany)

I   Harmonious Blacksmith (Palmer, arr.)   Willis
A   §   Arrival of the Queen of Sheba (Simm, arr.)   Alfred
A   Suite à deux clavecins (Dart, arr.)   Oxford
        (*Allemande, Courante, Sarabande, Chaconne*)
A   Water Music Suite   Oxford

Music for Two Pianos—Four Hands *continued*

Hartsell, Randall (b. 1949) USA

E	§	Beyond the Horizon	Alfred
I		Appalachian Rhapsody	Alfred
I		Dreams We Share	Alfred
I-A		The Best is Yet to Come	Alfred

Haydn, Franz Joseph (1732–1809) Austria

Appealing two-piano student concerti by Haydn are also discussed in the concerto section.

I		Little Concerto (See annotation in Selected Concerti section.)	Boston Music
I	§	Piano Concerto in C (Wertheim/Andrewes, eds.)	Boosey & Hawkes

(Orchestral reduction for two pianos. Also, see annotation in Selected Concerti section.)
A concerto in three movements which embodies the spirit and style of Haydn. This intermediate work provides an excellent introduction to the concerto style.

Hindemith, Paul (1895–1963) Germany (b. and d. Frankfurt, Germany)

A	Sonata (1942)	Schott

Hovhaness, (Chakmakjian) Alan (b. 1911) USA (Armenian heritage)
(b. Somerville (Boston), MA; d. Seattle, WA)

I	Ko-ola-u, op. 136	Peters
I	Mihr, op. 60	Presser
I	Vijag, op. 37	Peters

Infante, Manuel (1883–1958) Spain (b. Osuna, Spain; d. Paris, France)

A	§ *	Musiques d'Espagne (Sentimento no. 2)	Salabert
		Three Original Pieces in the Popular Style	
A		3 Dances Andalouses (*Ritmo, Sentimiento,* and *Gracia* [*El vito*])	Salabert

Joplin, Scott (1868–1917) USA (b. Texas; d. Manhattan, NY)

I		Rose Leaf Rag (M. Clark, arr.)	Alfred
I-A	§	The Easy Winners (Arpin, arr.)	Alfred

John Arpin has recorded the complete piano works of Joplin. Other attractive Joplin two-piano arrangements by Arpin include *Glacoulus Rag, Pineapple Rag,* and *Solace.*

Kadosa, Pál (1903–1983) Hungary (b. Levice, Czech Republic; d. Budapest, Hungary)

A	Sonata, op. 37 (1946) (*Allegro impetuoso, Andante, Vivace*)	Editio Musica Budapest

Kapustin, Nikolai (Girshevich) (b. 1937) Ukraine (b. Gorlovka, Ukraine)

A	Paraphrase on Dizzy Gillespie's "Manteca", op. 129	MusT

Karp, David (b. 1940) USA

I	Four for Two	Shawnee
I	Modes for Two Piano Duet	Shawnee

Kasschau, Howard (1913-1994) USA

I-A	§	Country Concerto for Young Pianists	Schirmer
		(See annotation in Selected Concerti section.)	

E (Early Intermediate)   I (Intermediate)   A (Advanced Intermediate to Advanced)

Kraehenbuehl, David (1932–1997) USA (b. Urbana, IL; d. Trempealeau, WI)

I-A §   Rhapsody in Rock (A Concerto in One Movement for Two Pianos)   Carl Fischer

Kurtág, György (b. 1926) Romania (b. Lugoj, Romania)

Even though he has spent most of his life behind the former iron curtain, Kurtág has become a well-known contemporary composer in Europe. A student of Kadosa, Messiaen, and Milhaud, he has taught at the Liszt Academy in Budapest (piano and chamber music) and had artist residencies with prominent organizations such as the Berlin Philharmonic.

I-A   Games IV for four hands and two pianos or piano duet   Editio Musica Budapest
         Subtitled, *Pedagogical performance pieces,* these are short contemporary settings for piano duet or two pianos.

I-A   Games for piano duet and two pianos VIII   Editio Musica Budapest
         Six contemporary miniatures which use alternative forms of notation. These duets are like Ross Lee Finney's *32 Piano Games,* but more difficult. Titles are messages as well as tributes to musicians of the past or contemporary friends. Sample titles include 4. *Hommage a J.S.B.,* 5. *Dirge,* and 8. *A quiet farewell to Endre Székely.*

Lecuona, Ernesto (1895–1963) Cuba (b. Guanabacoa, Havana, Cuba; d. Santa Cruz de Tenerife, Canary Islands, Spain)

A §   Malagueña (Nash, arr.)   Marks

Lees, Benjamin (Benjamin George Lisniansky) (1924–2010) USA (b. Harbin, Manchuria, China; d. New York, NY)

A   Etudes for Piano and Orchestra (974) (reduction by composer)   Boosey & Hawkes
A   Sonata (1951)   Boosey & Hawkes

Leighton, Kenneth (1929-1988) Great Britain

A   Prelude, Hymn and Toccata, op. 96 (1987)   Music Sales

Liszt, Franz (1811–1886) Hungary

A   Concerto Pathétique, S 258 (Hughes, ed.)   Schirmer
         An original work by the composer and not a transcription, it is a one-movement form with three sections (*Allegro energico, Andante sostenuto, Allegro trionfante*), much like a symphonic poem. It was first intended as a solo titled *Grosses Konzertsolo.*

A   Grand gallop chromatique, S 219 (Maylath, ed.)   William Pond
A   Hungarian Rhapsody no. 2 (Kleinmichel, ed.)   Schirmer
A   Polonaise (Rattlino, ed.)   Ricordi
A §   Rákóczi March, S 244c (Szegedi, arr.)   Edito Musica Budapest
A   Réminiscences de Don Juan, S 656 (Szegedi, ed.)   Edito Musica Budapest
A   Spanish Rhapsody, S 254 (Busoni, arr.)   Kalmus
A   Totentanz, S. 652 (Sauer, ed.)   Boosey & Hawkes

Lyke, Jim; Haydon, Geoff; and Heitler, Don (arrangers) USA

I   Samuel Ward: America, The Beautiful (Heitler/Lyke, arr.)   Alfred
I   Irving Berlin: Alexander's Ragtime Band (Heitler/Lyke, arr.)   Alfred
I-A §   15 Arrangements of American Classics   Alfred

Ensemble Literature — Music for Two Pianos–Four Hands

Music for Two Pianos—Four Hands *continued*

(Arr. Jim Lyke, Geoff Haydon, Don Heitler, and John Arpin) Includes: *Ain't Misbehavin', Alexander's Ragtime Band, America, The Beautiful, By Strauss, The Easy Winners, Everybody's Doing It Now, Gladiolus Rag, I Want to be Happy, Look for the Silver Lining, Medley: Yankee Doodle Boy; Over There; You're a Grand Old Flag, Nobody But You, Pineapple Rag, Solace, Swanee* and *When the Midnight Choo-Choo Leaves for Alabam'*.

This collection is excellent for intermediate to early advanced students from teenagers through adults. The pieces are enjoyable to hear and the arrangements are well written, accessible, and assist in keeping American music alive and before the public.

I-A	Euday Bowman: 12th Street Rag (Lyke/Haydon, arr.)	Alfred

Lutoslawski, Witold (1913–1994) Poland (b. and d. Warsaw, Poland)

I-A §	Paganini Variations for Two Pianos	Chester

Composed in 1941 in Warsaw and based on the famous caprices by the violinist Paganini which many romantic piano composers paraphrased, Lutoslawski later (1978) arranged the work for piano and orchestra.

Mendelssohn Felix (1809-1847) Germany

A	Two Preludes and Fugues, op. 35	Peters

Messiaen, Olivier (Eugène Prosper Charles) (1908–1992) France (b. Avignon, France; b. Paris, France)

A § *	Visions de l'amen (1943) (Amen du Jugement)	Durand

Completed one year before his solo set, *Vingt Regards sur l'enfant Jésus*, these seven visions are at the heart of the two piano contemporary literature. Messiaen recorded the work with his wife, Yvonne Loriod. The technical and musical challenges cannot be underestimated, however, the second piano part is generally more melodic and easier (slightly) than the first piano part that was composed with Loriod in mind, who was a splendid pianist. As with the *Vingt Regards*, these visions are full of religious symbolism, bird sounds, and wide ranging pianistic colors and sonorities. Rhythmic challenges abound between the two keyboards. The titles and translations are as follows: I. *Amen de la Création* (Amen of Creation); II. *Amen des étoiles, de la planète à l'anneau* (Amen of the stars, of the ringed planet); III. *Amen de l'agonie de Jésus* (Amen of the Agony of Jesus); IV. *Amen du désir* (Amen of Desire); V. *Amen des anges, des saints, du chant des oiseaux* (Amen of the Angels, of the Saints, of Bird Song); VI. *Amen du jugement* (Amen of Judgement); VII. *Amen de la consommation* (Amen of Consummation).

Mier, Martha (b. 1936) USA

E	Gypsy Celebration	Alfred
E §	Carousel Waltz	Alfred

Mier has numerous early intermediate sheet music compositions for two pianos including *Mexican Holiday, Ocean Breezes, Syncopated Sam,* and *Stairway of Dreams*.

I	Concerto in Classical Style (3 movements)	Alfred

Milhaud, Darius (1892–1974) France (b. Marseilles, France; d. Geneva, Switzerland)

A	Kentuckiana (Divertissement On 20 Kentucky Airs)	Carl Fischer; Elkan-Vogel
A §	Scaramouche Suite, op. 165b	Salabert
A	Suite for Piano (from "Bolivar", op. 236a)	Durand

E (Early Intermediate)   I (Intermediate)   A (Advanced Intermediate to Advanced)

Miller, Beatrice (Bea) USA (b. Detroit, MI)

I-A § The Lone Nightingale — Alfred
   Miller has several intermediate individual sheet music works for two-pianos, four-hands including *A Quiet Moment, Concerto no. 1 in A minor, Elegant Hat Dance, The Garden Swing, The Journey of a Mountain Stream, Heartstrings, The Lonely Carousel, Moonlight Stroll,* and *Ocean Breezes.*

Moszkowski, Moritz (1854–1925) Poland

I § 5 Spanish Dances, op. 12 (Wolff, ed.) — Schirmer
A Serenata, op. 15 — Music Sales

Mozart, (Johann Chrysostom) Wolfgang Amadeus (1756–1791) Austria

I-A Sonata in C Major, K 545 (Mozart-Grieg) — Kalmus
   This work includes a Romantic style accompaniment written by Grieg for this well-known Mozart sonata. This second piano accompaniment turns the sonata into an interesting work for two pianos, and can provide some humorous moments. The Grieg 2nd piano part is more difficult than the original sonata.

A § Concerto in E-flat Major, K 365 — International
   Mozart's only concerto for two pianos and orchestra is at the core of the two piano repertoire. Mozart did write *cadenzas* for this work though some editions exclude them. The International edition is recommended because it includes the Mozart *cadenzas*.

A § Eine Kleine Nachtmusik (Simm, arr.) — Alfred
   Known as the *Serenade for Strings in G major, K 525,* it is comprised of four movements, all of which Simm draws upon for this elegant two-piano version.

A Fantasia for Musical clock Work, K 608 (Busoni, ed.) — International
A Overture to The Magic Flute (Busoni, ed.) — Breitkopft and Härtel; International
A § Sonata in D Major, K 448 (375a), and Fugue in C Minor, K 426 (Hughes, ed.) — Schirmer
   Composed in 1781 and written in the standard three-movement format (*Allegro con spirito, Andante, Molto allegro*), this work, composed in the *gallant* style, is one of the truly great sonatas for two pianos from any style period. The choice of key reveals Mozart's preference for mood. He opens with a fanfare-like theme then draws upon different thematic material for both the Exposition and Recapitulation which are interspersed by a short Development. Throughout, the musical dialogue is shared equally and beautifully between the two pianos with both parts of quite similar difficulty. The elegant middle movement, in ABA form, is in the subdominant key of G. The last movement returns to the original key in the form of a spirited gallop and hints at the third movement *Turkish Rondo* of the solo sonata, K 331.

A Works for Two Pianos (Seiffert, ed.) — Henle
   Includes *Sonata in D Major, K 448* [375a], and *Fugue in C Minor, K 426.*

A Works for Piano Four Hands and Two Pianos — Alfred/Dover
   Two-piano works include the *Sonata In D Major, K 448, Theme And Variations in G Major, K 501,* and *Fugue in C Minor, K 426.*

Mussorgsky, Modest Petrovich (1839–1881) Russia

A Pictures at an Exhibition (orchestral reduction for two pianos) — Boosey & Hawkes

Music for Two Pianos—Four Hands *continued*

O'Hearn, Arletta J. USA

I	§	Jazz Theme and Variations	Kjos

A theme and six variations in jazz style, this is an excellent work that challenges the student while remaining a crowd pleaser and student favorite.

I	Suite Talk	Kjos

Olson, Lynn Freeman (1938–1987) USA (b. Minneapolis, MN; d. New York NY)

E	§	Celebration (Youth Concerto)	Alfred

Commissioned by the Wichita Music Teachers Association, this is an early intermediate work for two-pianos fashioned in a concerto format.

Pachelbel, Johann (1653–1706) Germany

I-A	§	Canon in D (Simm, arr.)	Alfred

This is a very beautiful and musically sophisticated two-piano arrangement of this frequently simplified or arranged work.

Paderewski, Ignace (Ignacy) Jan (1860–1941) Poland (b. Kurylowka, Podolia, Poland; d. New York, NY)

A	Polnische Fantasie, op. 19	Bote & Bock

Palmer, Robert (Moffat) (1915-2010) USA (b. Syracuse, NY; d. Ithaca, NY)

A student of Howard Hanson, Roy Harris, and Aaron Copland, Robert Palmer was Professor of Theory and Composition at Cornell University in Ithaca, NY until his retirement in 1980. He was both a Guggenheim and Fulbright Fellow. Numerous groups commissioned him to compose works including CBS and the Minneapolis Orchestra.

A	Sonata	Presser

Pancoast, Howard (b. 1943) USA

I-A	Two Piano Rondos	Alfred
I-A	Variations for Two Pianos	Alfred

Persichetti, Vincent (1915–1987) USA (b. and d. Philadelphia, PA)

A	Sonata, op. 13 (1940)	Presser

Piazzolla, Astor (b. 1921-1992) Argentina (b. Mar del Plata; d. Buenos Aires, Argentina)

A		Le grand tango	Carl Fischer
A	§	Tangos for Two Pianos, Vols. 1, 2	Carl Fischer

Volume 1: *Libertango, Verano portno, Tangata.* Volume 2: *Fuga y misterio, Milonga del angel, La muerte del angel, Soledad, Micelangelo.*

Pinto, Octavio (1890–1950) Brazil (b. and d. Sao Paulo, Brazil)

I	Scenas Infantis (Memories of Childhood)	Schirmer

Includes: *Hobby-Horse, March, Little Soldier!, Ring Around the Rosy, Run, Run!,* and *Sleeping Time.*

Porter, Cole USA (1891-1964) USA (b. Peru, IN; Santa Monica, CA)

A	§	Cole Porter Medley (Kocour, arr.)	Alfred

Kocour beautifully captures the style of the era in this two-piano medley of favorite Porter tunes, *Easy to Love, I Love You,* and *I Get a Kick Out of You.*

E (Early Intermediate)   I (Intermediate)   A (Advanced Intermediate to Advanced)

Poulenc, Francis (Jean Marcel) (1899–1963) France (b. and d. Paris, France)

I	L'Embarquement pour Cythère (1951) (very short rondo)	E. C. Schirmer

This short waltz in rondo form, is based on the Watteau painting of the same title. The reduction for two pianos is based on Poulenc's score to the film *Le Voyage en Amerique*. Though currently out of print, it is available in some academic libraries.

I-A § Sonate (1918, revised 1939) (for one or two pianos) — Chester
(See annotation in one piano, four-hand section.)

A Aubade (1929) — Salabert

A Capriccio (d'après *Le Bal Masqué*) (1952) — Salabert

A § Concerto in D Minor (2 pianos and orchestra) — Salabert

One of the landmark two-piano concertos of the modern era, this 1932 work structured in three movements, contains both the charming melodic and harmonic events one would expect from Poulenc. The neoclassic middle movement hints at Mozart.

A Sonate (1953) — Durand

Not to be confused with the much earlier 1918 *Sonata,* this is a significant four movement (*Prologue: Extremement lent et calme, Allegro molto, Andante lirico, Epilogue: Allegro giocoso*) original work written for two pianos. One of the great two-piano sonatas of the modern era.

Prokofiev, Sergei (Sergeyevich) (1891–1953) Russia (b. Sontsovka, Ukraine; d. Moscow, Russia)

A Waltzes (based on Schubert waltzes) (Prokofiev, transcriber) — Kalmus

Partially at the encouragement of Stravinsky, and to provide programmatic variety for U.S. tours, Prokofiev took various waltzes by Schubert and arranged them into a solo collage-like medley. His later two piano version, which he wrote for ballet, is based on the solo version, though he made harmonic changes which make the music sound less like Schubert and more like Prokofiev.

Rachmaninoff, Sergey (Vasilyevich) (1873–1943) Russia (Rakhmaninov, Sergey) (b. Oneg, near Semyonovo, Russia; d. Beverly Hills, CA)

I-A Prelude in C-Sharp Minor, op. 3, no. 2 (Rachmaninoff, arr.) — Boosey & Hawkes

Any student who studies the solo version should also be introduced to this two piano arrangement by the composer.

A § Eighteenth Variation (from Rhapsodie on a Theme of Paganini, op. 43) — Alfred

This work is based on the original Rachmaninoff reduction of this variation.

A Fantasy (Suite no. 1) op. 5 — International

Includes: Barcarolle: A Night for Love: Tears: and Russian Easter.

A The Piano Works of Rachmaninoff (Rachmaninoff, arr.) — Belwin/Alfred

Volume IX: Works for Two Pianos, Four Hands: 9 pieces including *Prelude in C-sharp Minor, op. 3, no. 2*. Book and CD
Volume X: *Symphonic Dances, op. 45.* Originally written as an orchestral work, but later arranged for piano duo by Rachmaninoff. Book and CD
Volume XV: *Rhapsody on a Theme of Paganini, op. 43.* Book and CD

A Rhapsody on a Theme of Paganini, op. 43 — Belwin

Listed under *The Piano Works of Rachmaninoff,* this edition is based on the Rachmaninoff reduction and is paginated in 4-staff systems for easier perception of both Piano I and II.

Music for Two Pianos—Four Hands *continued*

A		Russian Rhapsody (Hinson, ed.)	Alfred
A		Suite no. 1, op. 5 (Fantaisie-Tableaux)	Boosey & Hawkes
		(*Barcarolle, A Night for Love. Tears,* and *Russian Easter*)	
A		Suite no. 2, op. 17 (*Phillip, ed.)	Boosey & Hawkes; *International
		(*Introduction, Waltz, Romance,* and *Tarantella*)	
A	§	Symphonic Dances, op. 45 (Simm, arr.)	Alfred
		Reproduced from the original 1942 publication.	
A		Symphonic Dances, op. 45 (Threlfall, ed.)	Boosey & Hawkes
		This was the composer's last composition. This is an excellent edition as it corrects errors in previous printed editions.	

Ravel, Joseph Maurice (1875–1937) France

I-A	§	Ma Mère l'Oye (5 Piéces Enfantines) (Choisnel, ed.)	Durand
I A	§	Pavane pour une Infante défunte (Pavane for a Dead Princess) (Simm, arr.)	Belwin
		Richard Simm has provided an excellent two piano arrangement based on the original solo.	
A		Bolero (1928) (Ravel, arr. 1930)	Durant
A	§	La Valse (Poéme choregraphique pour orchestra) (arr. Ravel)	Alfred; Durand
		Arranged by the composer for two pianos, this is one of the premiere works of the two piano repertory. Ravel marks the music: *mouvement de Valse viennoise*. Ravel composed the original orchestral work with the intent that it would be choreographed for ballet, thus the subtitle. In the original score the composer states: "Through rifts in swirling clouds, couples are glimpsed waltzing. As the clouds disperse little by little, one sees an immense hall peopled with a whirling crowd. The scene becomes progressively brighter. The light from chandeliers bursts forth at fortissimo. An Imperial Court, around 1855."	
A		Rapsodie Espagnole (1907) (Ravel, arr.)	Durand
		The two piano transcription adheres closely to the four movement (*Prélude à la nuit, Malagueña, Habanera, Feria*) orchestral version.	
A		Sheherazade (1898) (Ravel, arr.)	Durand
		The two-piano version precedes the orchestral version. It is in the same spirit as Ravel's song cycle of the same name as well as Rimsky-Korsakov's orchestral suite.	

Reich, Steve (b. 1936) USA

A		Piano Phase (1967) (minimalist writing for two pianos)	Presser

Rocherolle, Eugenie R. (b. 1936) USA (b. New Orleans, LA)

I		April in Paris (by Vernon Duke, arr. Rocherolle)	Alfred
I		Rapsodie De Pyrenees	Kjos
I	§	Waltz for Two Pianos	Kjos
I-A	§	Blues Concerto	Alfred
		An effective "jazz" concerto with rhythmic challenges, beautiful, rich melodies and a effective *cadenza*, this piece is enjoyed by pianists of all ages.	
I-A		Jambalaya: A Portrait of Old New Orleans	Hal Leonard
I-A		Romancing in Style, Music of the 21st Century (Seven two-piano pieces)	Kjos
I-A		Suite Talk	Kjos
I-A	§	The Way We Danced 1949-1999	Alfred
		A very popular two-piano work which includes *Tango for Two, "Classic" Rock, Slow Dancin', A Winsome Waltz,* and *Jitterbug*. These dances can be performed individually or as a suite. Rocherolle also has arranged this work for piano duet-one piano.	

Rollin, Catherine USA

I		Christmas for Sharing and Carol of the Bells	Alfred
I	§	Concerto in C Major (See annotation in the Concerto section.)	Alfred
		This work prepares students for easier Haydn concerti.	
I		Concerto Romantique	Alfred
		This is excellent preparation for romantic literature and orchestral parts are available.	

Rorem, Ned (b. 1923) USA (b. Richmond, IN)

I-A	§	Sicilienne	Peermusic
A		Six Variations for Two Pianos	Boosey & Hawkes

Roscoe, B. J. (Jeanie) (b. 1932) USA

Roscoe has received commissions including *Clavier* magazine, Joanna Hodges Summer Piano Seminar, Southwestern Youth Music Festival and Washington State Music Teachers Association (WSMTA). Her *Youth Concerto* was premiered by the Spokane, WA Youth Symphony. *Visions*, for Piano and Orchestra, was performed by the Vancouver Symphony Orchestra. Additionally, WSMTA honored her as the 2004 *Composer of the Year*. Roscoe operates an independent studio in Seattle, WA, where she offers piano, composition, and music theory instruction.

E	Miniature Concerto	Alfred
I	Youth Concerto "A Festival"	Alfred

Rossini, Gioachino (Antonio) (1792–1868) Italy

A	Soirees Musicales: Suite of Five Movements from Rossini	Boosey & Hawkes

Rowley, Alec (1892–1958) Great Britain (b. London, England; d. Weybridge, England)

I-A	§	Miniature Concerto	Boosey & Hawkes
		This work is a "romantic" style concerto. (See annotation in Concerto section.)	

Rubenstein, Beryl (1898–1952) USA (b. Athens, GA; Cleveland, OH)

Rubinstein was a long-time piano faculty member at the Cleveland Institute of Music. He wrote many pedagogical works.

I-A	Suite for Two Pianos	Schirmer
	The *Suite* movements are *Prelude, Canzonetta, Irish Jig,* and *Masks*.	

Saint-Saëns, (Charles) Camille (1835–1921) France

I		Danse macabre (Saint-Saëns, ed.)	Durand
A	§	Le carnival des animaux (Berkowitz, arr.)	Durand
		Carnaval of the Animals (Le carnaval des animaux, grande fantaisie zoologique pour 2 pianos, 2 violons, alto, violoncelle, contrebasse, flûte, clarinette, harmonica et xylophone) is a favorite among audiences everywhere. The original work is for two pianos and chamber orchestra and should be on the list of any two piano team to learn. In this Berkowitz arrangement, the work has been reduced or transcribed for two pianos where both the orchestration and two original piano parts are merged into both piano parts and thus can be performed without orchestra.	
A	§	Polonaise, op. 77	Durand
A		Scherzo, op. 87	Durand
A		Variations on a Theme by Beethoven, op. 35 (Hughes, arr.)	Schirmer

Music for Two Pianos—Four Hands *continued*

Sanucci, Frank (1901-1991) USA (b. Buenos Aires, Argentina, d. Vista, CA)

I	Ave Maria	Willis
	Sanucci has numerous intermediate arrangements for two piano-four hands including titles such as *Ave Maria, Danza Español, Danza Mexicana, Elegy,* and *Rumba*.	
I-A	Argentinean Rhapsody	Willis
I-A	Ballo	Willis
A	Castillian Rhapsody	Willis

Schumann, Robert (Alexander) (1810–1856) Germany

I	§	Bear's Dance (Appel and Draheim, eds.)	Schott
I		Ghost Story (Appel and Draheim, eds.)	Schott
I-A		Andante and Variations, op. 46 (*Hughes)	*Schirmer; Durand

Originally scored for two pianos, two cellos, and horn, the later two piano version by the composer is one of the great two-piano works of the romantic period. In the two-piano version Schumann eliminated two variations and two episodes which were in the original instrumental work. Unlike classical variation sets, these move continuously without interruption and are not numbered. Clara Schumann and Felix Mendelssohn premiered this work.

I-A	The Happy Farmer and His Family (Rabinof, arr.) (set of variations)	Alfred

Shostakovich, Dmitri (1906-1975) Russia (b. St. Petersburg [Leningrad], Russia; d. Moscow, Russia)

I-A	Concertino, op. 94	International
I-A	Suite for Two Pianos, op. 6 (four movements)	Sikorski

Simm, Richard (arranger) (b. 1926) Iceland (b. Potteries, England)

Born in Newcastle-upon-Tyne, England, Simm performed Liszt's first piano concerto at the young age of 16. As a student of Bernard Roberts at Royal College of Music in London and later Erik Then-Bergh at the *Hochschule für Musik* in Munich, Simm received several performance prizes including third place in the Leeds International Piano Competition. Simm first taught at the University of Wales for nine years and then at the University of Illinois for three years as a Visiting Professor of Piano. During the time in the U.S. he began his publishing relationship with Warner Brothers (now Alfred) earning several ASCAP awards. Since settling in Reykjavik, Iceland in 1989, Simm continues to arrange and compose, teaches at the Icelandic Academy of the Arts, and is very active in that country as a teacher and performer. His relationship with Icelandic violinist Rut Ingólfsdóttir has led to performances in Tokyo, Paris, Brussels, Beijing, Lanzhou and Rome.

I-A	5 Classical Favorites Arranged for Two Pianos, Four hands (Simm, arr.)	Alfred
	Includes: *The Arrival of the Queen of Sheba, Canon in D, Eine kleine Nachtmusik, España, Peer Gynt Suite (Morning Mood, The Death of Åsa, Anitra's Dance, In the Hall of the Mountain King)*.	
I-A	Grieg: Peer Gynt, Suite I, op. 46 (Simm, arr.)	Alfred
I-A	Handel: Arrival of the Queen of Sheba (Simm, arr.)	Alfred
I-A	Pachelbel: Canon in D (Simm, arr.)	Alfred
	One of the best arrangements of this popular tune as the melody is shared between the two pianos.	
A	Bizet: Carmen, A Concert Suite for Two Pianos (Simm, arr.)	Alfred

E (Early Intermediate)   I (Intermediate)   A (Advanced Intermediate to Advanced)

A		Chabrier: España Rhapsody (Simm, arr.)	Alfred
A	§	Enesco: Romanian Rhapsody no. 1 in A Major (Simm, arr.)	Bagaduce Music

First published in 1991, this is a stunning two-piano concert transcription of the well-known orchestral score. Every note in the orchestra score is faithfully transcribed for the two pianos.

A		Mozart: Eine Kleine Nachtmusik (Simm, arr.)	Alfred
A	§	Ravel: Pavane pour une Infante défunte (Simm, arr.)	Belwin

Translated *Pavane for a Dead Princess*, Richard Simm has provided an excellent two piano arrangement based on the original piano solo (1899) and later orchestration (1910).

Starer, Robert (1924-2001) USA (b. Vienna, Austria; d. Kingston, NY)

A	§	The Fringes of a Ball (Waltz variations on theme by William Schuman)	Presser
A		Sonata for Two Pianos	Lauren Keiser

Strauss, Johann (1825–1899) Austria

A	Burleske	Kalmus

Stravinsky, Igor (Fyodorovich) (1882–1971) (b. Lomonosov, Russia; d. New York, NY)

I-A		Capriccio (*Soulima Stravinsky, ed.)	Kalmus; *Boosey & Hawkes
I-A		Capriccio (Reduction by Composer)	International
A		Concerto for Two Solo Pianos (1935)	Schott
A		Madrid (Soulima Stravinsky, ed.)	Boosey & Hawkes
A	§	Scherzo à la Russe (Stravinsky, transcriber)	Boosey & Hawkes
A		Sonata for Two Pianos (1943)	Boosey & Hawkes
A		Spanish Rhapsody (Busoni, arr.)	Alfred
A	§	Three Movements from Pétrouchka (Babin, arr.)	Boosey & Hawkes

Contents: *Russian Dance, Petrouchka, The Shrove-Tide Fair*. (See earlier annotation on Victor Babin.)

Tchaikovsky, Pyotr Il'yich (1840–1893) Russia

I		Dance of the Sugar Plum Fairy (Hesselberg, ed.)	Schirmer
A		March Miniature, op. 43	International
A		The Nutcracker Suite (Economou, arr.)	Alfred

This is a transcription based on two piano performances by Martha Argerich and Nicoles Economou.

A	§	The Nutcracker Suite, op. 71a, Book with CD	Schirmer

Includes: *Arab Dance, Chinese Dance, Dance of the Candy Fairy, Dance of the Reed-Flutes, March, Miniature Overture, Russian Dance, Trepak,* and *Waltz of the Flowers*.

Tcherepnin, Alexander (Nikolayevich) (1899–1977) USA (b. Saint Petersburg, Russia; d. Paris, France)

A	Rondo, op. 87a (from Suite, op. 87) (1957)	Peters

Timm, Henry C. (Christian) (1811-1892) USA (b. Hamburg, Germany)

Timm arrived in the U.S. in 1835 and eventually settled in New York City where he became an active musician and teacher. In addition to being a choral conductor, church musician, and trombone player, he was well-known as a piano teacher and composed other second piano arrangements including some for selected Cramer *Études*. He was president of the New York City Philharmonic Society for many years.

Music for Two Pianos—Four Hands *continued*

I	§	Second Piano Parts to Six Sonatinas, op. 36, by M. Clementi	Schirmer
		Book I: op. 36, nos. 1, 2, 4; Book II: op. 36, nos. 3, 5, 6	

Published in 1891, these second-piano parts by Timm are delightful stylistic accompaniments to this set of war-horse sonatinas. Using the second-piano part is musically refreshing, and assists in preparing students for easier classical concerti.

Vandall, Robert D. (b. 1944) USA

E		Concertino in C (See annotation in Selected Concerti section.)	Alfred
I-A		Blues Nocturne	Alfred
I-A	§	Concerto in G Major (See annotation in Selected Concerti section.)	Alfred

Walker, George (Theophilus) (b. 1922) USA (b. Washington, D.C.)

I-A	Music for Two Pianos	MMB
A	Sonata for Two Pianos	MMB

Walton, Sir William (Turner) (1902–1983) England
(b. Oldham, Lancashire; d. Island of Ischia, near Naples)

I	Popular Song from "Façade" (Lambert, arr.)	Oxford

Weber, Carl Maria (Friedrich Ernst) von (1786–1826) Germany

A	Concert piece in F Minor, op. 79 (Webster, ed.)	International
A	Invitation to the Waltz	Bosworth & Co. Ltd.

Two Piano, Four Hand Anthologies

I-A	15 Classical Masterpieces with Added Second Piano Parts (Rabinof, arr.)	Alfred

Sylvia Rabinof has composed accompaniments to 15 commonly taught compositions. An incomplete list of titles includes *Musette* (Bach), *Für Elise* (Beethoven), *The Happy Farmer* (Schumann), *Solfeggietto* (C. P. E. Bach), and *Rondo Alla Turca, K 331* (Mozart), to name a few.

I-A	Essential Two-Piano Repertoire (Mauro/Beard, eds.)	Alfred

Music for Two Pianos—Eight Hands

Composer   **Title**   **Publisher**

American Piano Quartet Series

This series for two pianos-eight hands has been arranged and/or edited by Mark Wilberg and other members of the American Piano Quartet. This successful piano quartet has performed (and recorded) these arrangements throughout the U. S., Canada, Europe, and the Far East which has led the way in reviving interest in the teaching and playing of music for two-pianos, eight-hands. These are excellent arrangements for students of all ages and are a *must* for any piano ensemble library.

I-A §   A Scott Joplin Rag Rhapsody (Olson, arr.)   Kjos
     An exciting and challenging piece which includes themes from *The Entertainer, Maple Leaf Rag, Solace, Easy Winners*, and more. Written for the American Piano Quartet by Kevin Olson, this excellent arrangement is a proven student and audience favorite.

I-A §   Sicilienne (J. S. Bach/Wilberg, arr.)   Kjos
     A beautiful, flowing *Andante* from Bach's *Flute Sonata in E flat, BWV 1031*.

I-A §   Waltz from Faust (Gounod/de Vilback, arr.)   Kjos
     This classical work will appeal to intermediate level pianists. The lyrical melody and waltz accompaniments demand careful musicianship and listening from the performers.

A §   Fantasy on Themes from Bizet's Carmen (Bizet/Wilberg, arr.)   Kjos
     A rousing piano quartet using music from Carmen. This piece provides musical and technical challenges and is much loved by audiences because of the familiar tunes and the showy ending.

A §   Sabre Dance (Khatchaturian) (Tan, arr.)   Piano Ensemble International
     This famous piece from the *Gayaneh Ballet* (Dance of the Kurds) was arranged by N. Jane Tan for the Quartet. One of the most recognized pieces in the orchestral literature, it has been used as background music for everything from novelty acts like the "plate spinners" on the Ed Sullivan Show to the *Blues Brothers 2000* movie or Woody Allen's film *Scoop*, to TV shows like *The Simpsons, Two and a Half Men* and *SpongeBob SquarePants*. This fast-paced dance has driving rhythms, exciting *glissandi*, and percussive effects, all combining to make it a challenging piece. The use of wooden sticks or dowels in the middle make it a rhythmic and coordination challenge as the pianists try to grab the sticks, play the percussive parts, and then discard the sticks in time to return to playing in the ensemble. The work is very enjoyable to perform and is an audience favorite.

A §   The Stars and Stripes Forever (Sousa/Wilberg, arr.)   Kjos
     With challenging runs and "piccolo" passagework this exciting arrangement is a showstopper that demands teamwork, careful listening, and technical clarity from the performers.

Bach, Johann Sebastian (1685–1750) Germany

I-A   Brandenburg Concerto, no. 3 (first movement) (Bardeen, arr.)   Alfred

I-A   Fugues from the Well Tempered Clavier (Frackenpohl and Haché, arr.)   Manduca
     Available as separate 8-hand ensemble arrangements, fugue selections from Book I are: C Major (BWV 846, no. 1), C Minor (BWV 847, no. 2), C-Sharp Major (BWV 848, no. 3), C-Sharp Minor (BWV, 849, no. 4), G Minor (BWV 861, no. 16) and from Book 2, F Minor (BWV 881, no. 12).

Music for Two Pianos—Eight Hands *continued*

Beethoven, Ludwig van (1770–1827) Germany

I	Adieu to the Piano (Sartorio, arr.)	Willis
I	Egmont Overture (Chwatal, arr.)	Peters
I-A	Country Dances (Parlow, ed.)	Alfred
A §	Fidelio Overture, op. 72b (Chwatal, arr.)	Peters

Cheadle, William

A	Skip to My Lou and Others Too (Cheadle, arr.)	Alfred.

**Dahl, Ingolf (Walter Ingolf Marcus) (1912–1970) USA
(b. Hamburg, Germany; d. Frutigen, Switzerland)**

A §	Quodlibet on (6) American Folk Tunes	Peters

Debussy, (Achille-) Claude (1862–1918) France

I-A §	Petite Suite (Busser, ed.)	Durand

Dvořák, Antonín (Leopold) (1841–1904) Czechoslovakia

I	Ecossaises, op. 41 (Kraehenbuehl, arr., Gowe, ed.)	Alfred
I	Serenade, op. 44 (Morrow, arr.)	Carl Fischer

Elgar, Edward (1857–1934) England

I-A	Pomp and Circumstance (Carper, arr.)	Alfred

Gillock, William (1917–1993) USA (b. LaRussell, MO; d. Dallas, TX)

I §	Champagne Toccata	Willis

    A delightful and sparkling intermediate level piece that students enjoy. This work is a *must* for any piano ensemble library.

Gounod, Charles (1818–1893) France

I §	Waltz (from Faust) (de Vilback, arr.)	Kjos

    (See annotation under the American Piano Quartet Series.)

**Grainger, Percy (George Aldridge) (1882–1961) USA (b. Australia)
(b. Brighton/Melbourne, Australia; d. White Plains, NY)**

I-A	Country Gardens	Schott

Grieg, Edvard (Hagerup) (1829–1869) Norway

I	Triumphal March (Carper, arr.)	Alfred

Gurlitt, Cornelius (1820–1901) Germany

I-A	Rustic Pictures, op. 190 (Ländliche Bilder) (Weekly and Arganbright, eds.)	Kjos

    These fine arrangements consist of four piano parts of equal difficulty and include titles such as *The Start, Arrival in the Country, O'er Hill and Dale, Evening at the Inn in the Wood, Playing Games on Horseback, The Chase, Under the Village Lime Tree,* and *Return to the Town.*

Handel, George Frideric (1685–1759) England (b. Germany)

E	Three Pieces (from the Water Music) (Carper, arr.)	Alfred
I	Allegro Deciso (from the Water Music) (Carper, arr.)	Alfred
I	Two Handel Minuets (from the Music for the Royal Fireworks) (Carper, arr.)	Alfred

E (Early Intermediate) I (Intermediate) A (Advanced Intermediate to Advanced)

Haydn, Franz Joseph (1732–1809) Austria

E	Minuetto from String Quartet, op. 1, no. 1 (Kraehenbuehl, arr.)	Alfred

Joplin, Scott (1868–1917) USA (b. Texas; d. New York, NY)

I-A §	A Scott Joplin Rag Rhapsody (Olson, arr.)	Kjos
	(See annotation under the American Piano Quartet Series.)	

Khatchaturian, Aram Il'yich (1903–1978) Russia (b. Tbilisi, Georgia, Russia; d. Moscow, Russia)

A §	Sabre Dance (from *Gayaneh Ballet*) (Tan, arr.)	Piano Ensemble International
	(See annotation under the American Piano Quartet Series.)	

Liszt, Franz (1811–1886) Hungary

I-A	Rákóczy March (Horn, arr.)	Robert Lienau

Miller, Beatrice USA

I	Enchanted Isle	Alfred
I	Holy Night (Miller, arr.)	FJH
I	The Joy of Spring	Alfred

Moszkowski, Moritz (1854–1925) Poland

I	Spanish Dance, op. 12, no. 1 (Flamenca, ed.)	Peters

Mozart, (Johann Chrysostom) Wolfgang Amadeus (1756–1791) Austria

I-A	Wind Serenade, K 375 (Clark, arr.)	Alfred

Mussorgsky, Modeste (1839-1881) Russia

I-A	Pictures at an Exhibition (Haché, arr.)	Manduca
	Three separate works available: *Promenade, Gnomes, The Great Gate of Kiev.*	

Olson, Kevin R. (b. 1970) USA (b. Utah)

I	Four Arkansas Travelers	FJH
I-A	Legend of the Phoenix	FJH
I-A §	Scott Joplin Rag Rhapsody, A (Olson, arr.)	Kjos
	(See annotation under the American Piano Quartet Series.)	
A §	Perpetual Commotion	FJH
	A fast moving, energetic movement that is enjoyable for both performers and audience.	

Purcell, Henry (1659–1695) England

I	Two Trumpet Voluntaries (Carper, arr.)	Alfred
I-A	When I Am Laid in Earth (Air from *Dido's Lament*) (Rabinof, arr.)	Alfred

Rossini, Gioacchino (Antonio) (1792–1868) Italy

A	Overture to William Tell (Wrede, arr.)	Robert Lienau

Saint-Saëns, Camille (1835–1921) France

I-A	Dance Macabre, op. 40 (Poéme symphonique) (Guiraud, ed.)	Durand

Music for Two Pianos—Eight Hands *continued*

Schubert, Franz (Peter) (1797–1828) Austria

I	Children's March (Parlow, arr.)	Alfred
I	Military March no. 1 in D Major, op. 51 (Tucker, ed.)	Alfred

Smetana, Bedrich [Friedrich] (1824–1884) Bohemia

I-A	Rondo in C Major (Herrmann, ed.)	Peters
A	Sonata in One Movement in E minor (original) (Kuhlmann, ed.)	Peters

Strauss, Richard George (1864–1949) Bavaria

A	Ceremonial Entry (Doebber, arr.)	Robert Lienau

Sousa, John Philip (1854-1932) USA (b. Washington, D.C.; d. Reading, PA)

I § The Stars and Stripes Forever (Wilberg, arr.) — Kjos
(See annotation under the American Piano Quartet Series.)

Tchaikovsky, Pyotr Il'yich (1840–1893) Russia

I	Overture to the Nutcracker Suite (Miller, arr.)	Alfred

Weber, Carl Maria von (1786-1826) Germany

A Polacca brillante, op. 72 (Jansen, arr.) — Robert Lienau
This is a concert arrangement that is very challenging for the performers.

Two-Piano, Eight-Hand Anthologies

I-A 7 Classical Favorites Arranged for Two Pianos, Eight Hands (Carper, arr.) — Alfred
Includes: *Allegro Deciso* from *Water Music*, *German Dance* (K 605, no. 3), *Pomp and Circumstance* (Military March No. 1 in D), *St. Anthony Chorale* from Brahms' *Variations on a Theme by Haydn*, *Triumphal March* from Grieg's *Sigurd Jorsalfar*, Two Handel *Minuets* from *Music for the Royal Fireworks* and Two *Trumpet Voluntaries*.

E (Early Intermediate) I (Intermediate) A (Advanced Intermediate to Advanced)

Music for Multiple Pianos—Multiple Performers

E-I Celebrated Keyboard Ensembles (Vandall, arr.) — Alfred
Nine single-line arrangements for 4 or 6 players. Includes: *Down in the Valley*, *Hush-a-Bye* (All the Pretty Little Horses), *Jingle Bells*, *Looby Loo*, *Michael, Row the Boat Ashore*, *Old Joe Clark*, *On the Bridge at Avignon* (*Sur le pont d'Avignon*), *The Riddle Song*, and *When the Saints Go Marching In*.

E-I § Multiple Piano Ensemble Series — Kjos
This series contains excellent musical arrangements that can be used in group lessons or musicianship classes to support strong sight-reading and ensemble skills. Students may be assigned one (a single line) or two parts. Melodic themes move among the players to enhance participation and to promote careful listening. These arrangements are at the late Elementary/Intermediate levels depending on how many parts are assigned to each performer. Note that *Five Will Get Your Four* is rhythmically quite tricky and thus challenging for high school students or undergraduate majors.

Title	Arranger
Amazing Grace (six parts)	Vandall
Cindy (six parts)	Vandall
Five Will Get You Four (five parts)	Vandall
Greensleeves (four parts)	Vandall
Scarborough Fair (six parts)	Vandall
Shenandoah (six parts)	Vandall
Six for Eight (four pianos, eight hands, six parts)	Balkin
Sixteen Pawns (four pianos, eight hands, sixteen parts)	Depue
Sleep, Baby, Sleep (six parts)	Vandall
Theme and Variations on "Skip to My Lou" (six parts)	Vandall

Music for 5 pianos, 10 Hands

The N. Jane Tan Piano Teams Library (arranged by N. Jane Tan unless otherwise indicated)

Title	Composer
Intermediate	
Beautiful Galatea Overture	von Suppé
Bohemian Dance (Carmen Suite no. 1)	Bizet
Flight of the Bumble Bee	Rimsky-Korsakov
Il Signor Bruschino	Rossini
In the Hall of the Mountain King (from *Peer Gynt*)	Grieg
Slavonic Dance, E minor, op. 72, no. 2	Dvořák
Star-Spangled Banner	John Stafford Smith
Waltz from Serenade in C, op. 48	Tchaikovsky
Intermediate to Advanced	
Ave Maria	Gounod/J. S. Bach
Blue Danube Waltz	J. Strauss
Capriccio Italien	Tchaikovsky
Dance of the Hours	Ponchielli
Dance of the Tumblers (from *The Snow Maiden* opera)	Rimsky-Korsakov
España	Chabrier
Gretchen at the Spinning Wheel	Schubert
Sabre Dance (the *Gayaneh* ballet)	Khatchaturian
The Sorcerer's Apprentice	Tchaikovsky (Shumway, arr.)
Waltz of the Flowers (from *The Nutcracker* ballet)	Tchaikovsky

Digital Keyboard Ensemble Music

With the growth of piano ensembles and multiple piano ensembles using digital keyboards, we feel it is appropriate, even essential, to include a new section listing digital keyboard ensemble music. One important resource is the web site for Ogilvy Music Publishing that lists over 200 ensembles for digital keyboards. Susan Ogilvy is a leading pianist, composer and clinician who has presented workshops and piano ensemble recitals throughout the United States and at state and national conferences. The listings below are featured on her web site. (See the web-site at sospace.com for full information and details including Elementary Ensembles.)

These ensembles are for digital instruments with multiple voices as opposed to acoustic pianos.

NOTE: Each ensemble set includes a MIDI Song file, Score and Parts along with permission to make two copies of each part.

Early Intermediate

Anything for Gloria / Anita B Sweet (6 Parts ea) by S. Ogilvy
A Love Once Remembered (6 Parts) by Dennis Mauricio
Arkansas Tripper / Splendid Spider (6 Parts ea) arr. by S. Ogilvy
Bourree / The Horseman (8 Parts ea) arr. by Donna Smith
Cavatina (Brahms) (8 Parts) arr. by S. Ogilvy
Ceili / Electrostatic Blues (6/3 Parts ea) by Beth Chedester
Christmas Day is Here (9 Parts) by Dennis Mauricio
Dance To It! / Voyager (6 Parts ea) by S. Ogilvy
Dona Nobis Pacem (6 Parts) by Dennis Mauricio
Dream On / Rhythm Matters (8 Parts ea) by S. Ogilvy
Fanfare for the Uncommon Piano Teacher (7 Parts) by S. Ogilvy
Flight to Venus (5 Parts) by S. Ogilvy
The Haunted House (8 Parts) by Dennis Mauricio
Jammin' on the Front Porch in the Back Woods / In the Valley of the Smokies with Clementine! (7/5 Parts ea) by S. Ogilvy
Laugh Along Boogie / Schoolhouse Rock (6 Parts ea) by S. Ogilvy
Let's Go Baroque / Golden Threads (6 Parts ea) by S. Ogilvy
The Little Rickshaw / The Sultan (4/5 Parts) by Beth Chedester
Londonderry Air / La Cucaracha (5 Parts) arr. by S. Ogilvy
Mexican Hat Dance / Range Riders (8 Parts) by Donna Smith
Mombasa / Mediterranean Sunset (9 Parts) by Dennis Mauricio
Morning / Song of the Cuckoo (6 Parts) Grieg / Reinecke arr. S. Ogilvy
Mozart Visits Arkansas / Cosmic Love Story (5 Parts) by Beth Chedester
My Little One Disk (11 Parts) by Dennis Mauricio
One Very Foggy Night (9 Parts) by Dennis Mauricio
Pastoral Symphony (Handel) (3 Parts open score) arr. by Larry Keenan
Shenandoah / Rock-a-My Soul (6 Parts) arr. by S. Ogilvy
She's the Greatest / Huey's Good News (7 Parts) by S. & J. Ogilvy
Silk 'N Clouds / For Frederick (6 Parts) by S. Ogilvy
Simple Gifts (6 Parts) arr. by Dennis Mauricio
Walking with Mike / Trees (5 Parts) by Michael Miller

Intermediate Level

Also sprach Zarathustra (Strauss) (6 Parts) arr. by S. Ogilvy
Amazing Grace (8 Parts) arr. by S. Ogilvy
Barberesque (6 Parts) by S. Ogilvy
The Best in Me (8 Parts) by Dennis Mauricio
Brittany's Song (4 Parts) by Dennis Mauricio

Digital Keyboard Ensemble Music *continued*

Bubbles / Hoedown! (6 Parts) by Beth Chedester
Calypso Holiday (11 Parts) by Wayne Wilkinson
Champions Are We! (with unison choir) (8 Parts) by S. Ogilvy
Children's Prayer (Humperdinck) (6 Parts) by S. Ogilvy
Cybernetic Glowworm / Two Guitars (4/6 Parts ea) arr. by Beth Chedester
Dance of the Dawn Children (8 Parts) by Lynn Purse
Dance of the Sugar Plum Fairy (5 Parts) arr. by S. Ogilvy
Determined Drummer / Thoughts (6/5 Parts) by Carleen Graff
DrumLines 1, 2, 3; Set of 3 separate percussion pieces (6 Parts ea) by S. Ogilvy
From a Classical Terrace / Caves of the Lost Village (8 Parts) by S. Ogilvy
Habanera (from Bizet's "Carmen") (8 Parts) arr. by S. Ogilvy
Hi-Way 23 Fame (11 Parts) by S. Ogilvy
Hong Kong Holiday / Amjenla Rag (5/6 Parts ea) by Beth Chedester
Ivory Pirates / Music Box Fantasy (5/7 Parts ea) by Beth Chedester
Jesu, Joy of Man's Desiring (7 Parts) arr. by Dennis Mauricio
Mariachi de Cinco / Bach Rock (5/6 Parts ea) by Beth Chedester
Morning Sun with audience vocal or 2-part choir (6 Parts) by S. Ogilvy
Number 21/ Wachiwi (3/6 Parts ea) by Beth Chedester
Moonlight Sonata/ Pizzicato Polka (7-11/5-6 Parts ea) arr. by Isa Dunaway
Siciliano (Bach) 5 Parts) arr. by S. Ogilvy
Snowflakes in Paris / Jane Bond 009 (5 Parts) by Beth Chedester
Soda Pop Rock (6 Parts) by J. Ogilvy
Squealin' Lucille (6 Parts) by J. Ogilvy
The Star Spangled Banner (Key) (9 Parts) arr. by Dennis Mauricio
Swing Low, Sweet Chariot (8 Parts) arr. by S. Ogilvy
Troika - A Sleigh Ride (Prokofieff) (8 Parts) arr. by S. Ogilvy
When the Train Comes Along / Samurai (5/4 Parts ea) by Beth Chedester
Victory's Moment (9 Parts) Dennis Mauricio

Late Intermediate Ensembles

Afternoon in San Paulo (12 Parts) by S. Ogilvy
America, the Beautiful (with audience vocal) (8 Parts) arr. by S. Ogilvy
Anitra's Dance (6 Parts) arr. by S. Ogilvy
Ave Verum (Mozart) (6 Parts) arr. by S. Ogilvy
Bartokian Dance (6 Parts) by S. Ogilvy
The Brothers Do (8 Parts) by J. Ogilvy
Canon in D Major (Pachelbel) (12 Parts) arr. by Dennis Mauricio
Caribbean Sunday (9 Parts) by Dennis Mauricio
Cell Phone Mania (9 Parts) by S. Ogilvy
The Entertainer (Joplin) (10 Parts) arr. by Dennis Mauricio
Fantasia on Old One Hundredth (6 Parts) arr. by Michael Sharp
Fiesta de la Sonrisa (9 Parts) by Dennis Mauricio
Heroic Fanfare (11 Parts) by Dennis Mauricio
High Tide (9 Parts) by Dennis Mauricio
How Firm a Foundation (7 Parts) arr. S. Ogilvy
How Lovely Is Thy Dwelling Place (Brahms) (9 Parts) arr. by S. Ogilvy
Hungarian Dance No. 5/Waltz in A flat (Brahms) (6/5 Parts ea) arr. by S. Ogilvy
In the Hall of the Mountain King (Grieg) (6 Parts) arr. by S. Ogilvy
In the Hall of the Mountain King (Grieg) (12 Parts) arr. by Dennis Mauricio

E (Early Intermediate)   I (Intermediate)   A (Advanced Intermediate to Advanced)

Intermezzo (Rachmaninoff) (6 Parts) arr. by S. Ogilvy
A Little Razzle Dazzle (5 Parts) by Dennis Mauricio
O Sacred Head, Now Wounded (Bach) (3 Parts open score) arr. by S. Ogilvy
Pavane (from Ravel's Mother Goose Suite) (7 Parts) arr. by S. Ogilvy
Searching the Stars (w /SATB) (8 Parts) by S. Ogilvy
Stephen Foster Overture (w/audience vocal) (8 Parts) arr. by S. Ogilvy

Advanced Ensembles

American Landscape (11 Parts) by Dennis Mauricio
A Mozart Fugue (from his Mass in C Minor) (12 Parts) arr. by S. Ogilvy
Baroque Festival (7 Parts) by S. Ogilvy
Hallelujah Chorus (Handel) (8 Parts) arr. by Dennis Mauricio
Hard Cold Cash (11 Parts) by Jim Ogilvy
Herbie's Hammer (6 Parts) by Jim Ogilvy
Hungarian Rhapsody No. 2 (Liszt) (9 Parts) arr. by Dennis Mauricio
Legends No. 6 (Dvorak) (7 Parts) arr. by S. Ogilvy
Maple Leaf Rag (Joplin) (8 Parts) arr. by Dennis Mauricio
Nightfall on the Amazon (10 Parts) by Dennis Mauricio
Papa Brown's Bag (8 Parts) by J. Ogilvy
Piano Concerto in F Major, K 413 (Mozart (7 Parts) arr. by Carleen Graff
Power Move (8 Parts) by J. Ogilvy
William Tell Overture (Rossini) (10 Parts) arr. by Dennis Mauricio

Digital Duets – Four hands / one digital piano, each playing a separate sound (split keyboard) accompanied by MIDI orchestration

Book One – Elementary – MIDI file & 6 duets (Aquarium Colors, Steppin' Out, Julia's Song, Coconut Beach, My Mozart Friend, Navajo Sunset)
Book Two – Intermediate – MIDI file & 6 duets (March of the Miniatures, Katherine's Song, Mystery No. 88, Rodeo Dance, Gypsy Carnival, My Beethoven Friend)

Two Pianos – (2 hands) & Digital Ensemble

Kentucky Romp (2 acoustic piano parts & 5 digital parts) by S. Ogilvy

Concertos – (includes MIDI file, Score and Parts) arr. by Carleen Graff

Piano Concerto in D Major (Haydn) Allegro movement (7 Parts)
Piano Concerto in F Major (Mozart K 413) Allegro movement (7 Parts)
Piano Concerto in D Major (Beethoven), op. 19, no. 2 in B flat Allegro movement (8 Parts)

Consembles – the intermediate level piano solo in original form with accompanying digital keyboard ensemble—ala Concerto!

Alla Tarantella (MacDowell) (6 Parts) orchestration by S. Ogilvy
Hopak (Mussorgsky) (6 Parts) orchestration by S. Ogilvy
Moonlight Sonata (Beethoven) (5 Parts) orch. by S. Ogilvy
Puck (Grieg) (5 Parts) orch. by Therese Mathews
Scherzo (Mendelssohn) (5 Parts) orch. by S. Ogilvy
Reverie (Debussy) (5 Parts) orch. by S. Ogilvy
Spinning Song (Ellmenreich) (5 Parts) orch. by S. Ogilvy
Tarantella (Beaumont) (8 Parts) orch. by S. Ogilvy
Hungarian (MacDowell) (5 Parts) orch. by S. Ogilvy

OTHER CATEGORIES OF REPERTOIRE

Holiday Literature for Solo Piano

	Title (Arranger)	**Publisher**
E-I	Carols of Christmas in Baroque Style (Kraft; Flatau ed.)	Alfred
E-I	Christmas with Style (Ray)	Alfred
E-I	Dances for Christmas, Books 1-2 (Rollin)	Alfred

A unique approach combining Christmas melodies with dance forms. Book I: *Jolly Old St. Nicholas* (gigue); *The Little Drummer Boy* (bolero); *Silent Night* (waltz); *Twelve Days of Christmas* (gavotte); *What Child is This* (paso doble meaning double-step); *Winter Wonderland* (Salsa).

E-I	From Many Lands at Christmas (J. Grill; Flatau ed.)	Alfred
E-I	We Wish You a Jazz Christmas (Rollin)	Alfred
E-A	Christmas Jazz, Rags & Blues, Books 1-5 (Mier)	Alfred
I §	A Charlie Brown Christmas (Guaraldi)	Hal Leonard

This publication of tunes from the popular television show is a tremendous hit with intermediate piano students, who recognize each of the nine settings immediately. *Christmas Is Coming* and *Linus and Lucy* are student favorites. Interesting syncopations and creative harmonic settings make each arrangement musically attractive. Chord symbols, used throughout, provide a springboard for theory/musicianship activities. The original volume, which was published by Felfar in the early 1970s, since has been reissued by Hal Leonard.

I §	A Christmas Pageant (Waxman)	ECS (Galaxy)

This collection of Christmas carols from around the world contains thirty selections for piano solo, as well as a few four-hand duets. Settings also include instrumental melodies with accompaniments and choral works transcribed for duet. The wealth of material and varying range of difficulty means that this volume can be used for at least three successive holiday seasons before the student outgrows it. The writing is musically subtle and harmonically refreshing to the ear.

I §	Chanukah & Other Hebrew Holiday Songs (Small)	Alfred

This nicely arranged collection of 25 best-known Hebrew and Yiddish Melodies is ideal for all Jewish celebrations and observances including Chanukah, Passover, and Yom Kippur.

I	Celebrations, Books 3, 4 (Shaak)	Moonstone Music Press

This unique series of books presents holiday music for many celebrations that occur throughout the year, including Christmas, Hanukkah, Halloween, Thanksgiving, Easter, and Passover. Some duet arrangements are included, though the majority of writing is for solo piano.

I	Christmas All Jazzed Up (O'Hearn)	Kjos

O'Hearn is a teacher and composer of jazz who was the National Federation of Music Clubs *Award of Merit* recipient for American Music. These seven arrangements of familiar holiday tunes are cleverly arranged and at the upper intermediate level.

Holiday Literature for Solo Piano *continued*

OTHER CATEGORIES OF REPERTOIRE

I	Christmas Anew (Rocherolle)	Kjos
I	Christmas Carols 'n more, Level 4 (Noona)	Heritage
	These six carols have been treated in an improvisatory manner to create interesting sounds to well known melodies.	
I	Christmas Celebrations (Yeager)	Kjos
I	Christmas Impressions (Rollin)	Alfred
I	Christmas Improvisations (Vandall)	Alfred
I	Christmas Joy (Rocherolle)	Kjos
I §	Christmas Seasonings (O'Hearn)	Kjos
	This collection of nine solo settings uses complex jazz chords to achieve colorful harmonizations. Reaches are limited to an octave, but the student should be careful with phrasing and pedaling throughout.	
I	Christmas Silhouettes (Alexander)	Alfred
I	Have Yourself a Swingin' Little Christmas (Rocherolle)	Alfred
I	Rudolph Goes Baroque (Marks, Rabinoff, arr.)	Alfred
	A Baroque suite (Prelude, Allemande, Courante, Sarabande, Gigue) based on *Rudolph the Red Nosed Reindeer.*	
I	Simply Christmas (Ray)	Alfred
I	Spotlight on Christmas (Rollin)	Alfred
I §	Yuletide Cheer (Rocherolle)	Kjos
	This volume of thirteen appealing contemporary settings limits reaches to within a 7th, which makes the book useful for the intermediate student with a small hand.	
I-A	A Christmas Fantasy (Alexander)	Alfred
I-A	A Dave Brubeck Christmas	Alfred
I-A §	Christmas Around the Piano (Rocherolle)	Kjos
	This substantial collection offers thirty-three secular and sacred carols in early advanced settings, each with full text at the page top. The arrangements often employ clever examples of style imitation. For example, *Deck the Halls*, in the manner of Bach, uses the subject from the *Two-part Invention in F Major* (transposed to E major) as part of the left-hand accompaniment.	
I-A	Classical Piano Music for the Christmas Season	Alfred
	Seasonal piano music by classical composers: Bartók, Brahms, Franck, Liszt, Mendelssohn, Schumann, and Tchaikovsky.	
I-A	Jolly Old St. Nicholas/Pachelbel's Canon (Tingley, arr.)	Alfred
	This is an interesting Baroque arrangement of these two familiar tunes using an *ostinato* bass.	
A	Amahl and the Night Visitors, piano selections (Menotti)	Schirmer
	This volume contains mature piano reductions from this well known operetta commissioned for television in 1951.	
A	Christmas (Mannheim Steamroller, Davis, arr.)	Hal Leonard
	This collection reflects the sound of Mannheim Steamroller, in rich but challenging arrangements of the songs from the album and video titled *Christmas*. Also available for two-pianos, eight-hands.	

E (Early Intermediate)   I (Intermediate)   A (Advanced Intermediate to Advanced)

A		Christmas Collection (Renfrow)	Alfred
A	§	Christmas Miniatures (Vandall)	Alfred

      This collection of nineteen beautifully arranged carols is perfect for the late intermediate student. The solos address specific technical goals, such as passagework in *Joy to the World*, and bringing out an alto melody in *What Child Is This?* The varying range of difficulty permits the book to be used for more than one holiday season.

A		Christmas-Modern Piano Impressions (L. Evans)	Hal Leonard
A		Christmas Silhouettes (Alexander)	Alfred
A		Christmas Stylings, Modern and Bright, Vols. I, II (Aaronson)	Alfred
A		Christmas Tree (*Weihnachtsbaum*), Vols. I, II (Liszt)	Hinrichsen-Peters

      From Liszt's late period, this set consists of twelve compositions, published in two volumes (six per volume) including settings of the familiar carols *In dulce jubilo* and *Adeste Fideles*. Liszt also transcribed the solo collection for piano duet. The entire set takes approximately forty-five minutes to perform.

A		Improvisations on 5 Christmas Carols (Norton)	Universal
A		It's Christmas! (Coates)	Alfred

      A collection of twelve sacred and popular Christmas songs in piano arrangements designed for the advanced pianist. Includes *Ave Maria, We Three Kings, Frosty the Snowman,* and *Here Comes Santa Claus.*

A	§	Jazz Up Your Christmas (L. Evans)	Hal Leonard

      These twelve carols, "in a fresh perspective," offer refreshing and challenging settings in a jazz idiom using devices such as swinging, dotted rhythms, and colorful, complex harmonies. Detailed pedaling and jazz phrasing-articulations assist the performer.

A		The Nutcracker Suite (Tchaikovsky; Hinson, ed.)	Alfred
A	§	Sleigh Ride (Anderson)	Alfred

      This classic Christmas solo in the *original* solo version (not simplified) is a quite challenging technical and musical etude for the skilled high school or undergraduate pianist. A jumping ragtime-like bass, wrist *staccato*, and thick texture create many technical and rhythmic challenges for the student.

A		(Six) Christmas Pieces, op. 72	ABRSM

      Written for his wife's family members in the summer 1842 and also titled by Mendelssohn, these beautiful pieces are not based on Christmas melodies, but are original untitled compositions that are similar in style and difficulty to the composer's *Songs without Words*. No. 2 in E-flat major is the most "song-like". The set is also published under the title *Kinderstücke*, or Children's Pieces.

Holiday Literature for Piano Ensemble

One-Piano, Four-Hands

		Title (Arranger)	**Publisher**
E-I	§	A Christmas Gathering (Olson)	Carl Fischer

These twelve carols, arranged for the student pianist with "helpers," employ three piano parts (piano low, piano center, piano high) plus optional rhythm instruments such as triangle, tambourine, and sleigh bells. The "piano center" part (solo piano) is written for the early intermediate level, in three to four voices. The "piano low" part is a single bass line and the "piano high" part is a simple counter-melody above the piano center. These settings are especially appropriate for use in musicianship classes and for (family) group performances. The use of rhythm instruments provides a refreshing variant on usual lesson material.

EI-I   Christmas Duet Fantasies (Vandall, arr.)   Alfred

Includes four duets *Carol of the Bells, Deck the Halls, Jingle Bells,* and *Joy to the World.* The *primo* and *secondo* parts of these extended arrangements are balanced and of equal difficulty.

E-I   Celebrated Christmas Duets, Books 1-5 (Vandall, arr.)   Alfred

E-I   Celebrating Christmas (Sallee, arr.)   Carl Fischer

E-I §   Easy Jazz Christmas (L. Evans)   Marks

Evans based these five piano duets on the previously published volumes *Jazz Up Your Christmas* and *Christmas: Modern Piano Impressions.* Excellent directions help the student (and teacher) understand elements of jazz style.

E-I   Lovely Sounds of Christmas (Kraft; Flatau ed.)   Alfred

E-I   More Lovely Sounds of Christmas (Kraft; Flatau ed.)   Alfred

E-I   Pat-a-Pan (Vandall)   Alfred

E-I   We Wish You a Jazzy Christmas (Rollin)   Alfred

I   Christmas for Two (Rocherolle)   Alfred

I   Christmas Holidays: Medley (Fordell, arr.)   Charles Hansen

I §   Christmas Music from Around the World (Alexander, Tsitsaros)   Frederick Harris

I §   More Christmas Music from Around the World (Alexander, Tsitsaros)

Each volume from the series, *Christmas Music from Around the World,* contains eight imaginatively arranged duet settings: six familiar carols, and two that are lesser known (unfamiliar tunes from Poland, Cyprus, France, Spain). Difficulty levels span late elementary to early advanced to permit use over several seasons.

I §   Christmas Riches (O'Hearn)   Kjos

I §   Christmas Side by Side (Rocherolle)   Kjos

This duet book, published after its predecessor, *Christmas Around the Piano,* contains 12 four-hand settings based on arrangements from the earlier solo volume. The four-hand arrangements are made easier by distributing rhythmic challenges throughout the four hands, without sacrificing the musical character of each setting.

Holiday Literature for Piano Ensemble *continued*

OTHER CATEGORIES OF REPERTOIRE

I	§	Jesu, Joy of Man's Desiring, BWV 147 (J. S. Bach; arr. Myra Hess)	Oxford

This superb transcription for four-hands, one-piano requires the duettists to trace the chorale line through the musical texture, in order to effectively bring out the melody. The *secondo* part is less difficult than the *primo* part, though it does require *legato* fingerings as well as carefully worked-out finger substitutions. Hess also completed a slightly more complex arrangement for two pianos.

I		Off We Go to Bethlehem (Davie)	Alfred
I	§	Sleigh Ride (Anderson; Edwards, arr.)	Alfred

This very popular arrangement of this Christmas Classic is complete with the whip sounds (hand claps) and is much fun for both *primo* and *secondo* players.

I-A		Jingle Bells (Bober, arr.)	FJH
I-A		The Nutcracker Suite for Two (Tchaikovsky; Rollin, arr.)	Alfred
A	§	Appalachian Christmas Carols (Persichetti)	Elkan-Vogel

This refined collection of seven early advanced settings is for mature pianists. Musically sophisticated, the set is intended to be played in its entirety. John Jacob Niles originally arranged four of the seven works, published by G. Schirmer in 1935. Performance time is approximately seven minutes.

A	§	Christmas Liszt for Two (Weekley and Arganbright, eds.)	Kjos

Contains two original settings by Liszt excerpted from his *Weihnachtsbaum* or *Christmas Tree* (see Editio Musica Budapest publication below).

A	§	Christmas Music (Dello Joio)	Marks

These artistic and technically challenging settings of seven carols employ four familiar carols and three original tunes by the composer. Each setting is also available from the publisher for SATB choir with four-hand piano accompaniment. In the choral version, the piano duet parts are the same as in the original piano duet version.

A	§	Christmas Tree (Liszt; Gábor. ed.)	Editio Musica Budapest

From Liszt's late period, this set consists of twelve compositions including settings of the familiar carols *In dulce jubilo* and *Adeste Fideles*. Liszt transcribed the solo collection (published in two volumes, six pieces per volume, by Hinrichsen-Peters) for piano duet. The entire set takes approximately forty-five minutes to perform.

A	§	Duet Fantasy on Jingle Bells (Vandall)	Alfred

This attractive early advanced duet is in ABA form. It is published in sheet music format.

A		The Nutcracker Suite (Tchaikovsky; Langer arr., Hinson, ed.)	Alfred

Two-Pianos, Four-Hands

I	Christmas for Sharing (Rollin)	Alfred
I	Gesu Bambino (Yon-Frost)	Alfred
A	Christmas (Mannheim Steamroller, Davis, arr.)	Hal Leonard

This collection reflects the sound of Mannheim Steamroller, in rich but challenging arrangements of the songs from the album and video titled *Christmas*. Also available for solo piano.

A	The Nutcracker Suite (Tchaikovsky, Economou, arr.)	Alfred

E (Early Intermediate)   I (Intermediate)   A (Advanced Intermediate to Advanced)

Two-Pianos, Eight-Hands

E	Christmas Carols for Multiple Piano (Bastien, arr.)	Kjos
I	Good Christian Men Rejoice (Miller, arr.)	Alfred
I	Joy to the World (Miller, arr.)	Alfred
I	A Special Night (Miller, arr.)	Alfred
I	O Holy Night (Miller, arr.)	FJH
I	Overture to the Nutcracker Suite (Tchaikovsky, Miller, arr.)	Alfred
I-A	March of the Toys (Herbert, Dickey, arr.)	Alfred

Four-Pianos, Eight-Hands

I-A   Ukrainian Bell Choir (Hayes, arr.)   Shawnee
        A high-energy arrangement that is quite challenging if played at the recommended tempo.

A   We Wish You a Merry Christmas (Bennett, Nielson, Young, Hayes, arr.)   Lorenz
        A challenging waltz arrangement that makes a nice encore or recital finale.

Five-Pianos, Ten-Hands

E-I	Christmas Fantasy (Peskanov, arr.)	N. Jane Tan
E-I	Jingle Bells (Rainone, arr.)	N. Jane Tan
E-I	O Come All Ye Faithful (Reading/Tan, arr.)	N. Jane Tan
I-A	Waltz of the Flowers (Tchaikovsky, arr. Tan)	N. Jane Tan

        Tan's publications are available on-line at: www.pianoteams.com/catalogs/pianoteams_order_form.pdf (accessed 12.12.10).

Concerti for Young Pianists by James B. Lyke

Concerto study at the early intermediate and intermediate levels prepares students for intricacies of balance, *cadenza* playing, and performing with instrumentalists (or in some cases, a second piano). Developing technical facility in these works helps lead to more mature, skilled playing and studying introductory concerti and ensemble music prepares younger students for more mature works such as Haydn's *Concerto in D Major for Piano and Orchestra, Hob. XVIII:2*.

Many talented educational composers have written clever and enjoyable concerti. Coupled with works by Classical composers (such as Haydn), these concerti give students training for and experience in more extended works during the high school years. The following selected listing of concerti (presented alphabetically by composer) serves as a starting point for intermediate level students. Middle school and high school students profit from those concerti graded as Intermediate (I) or higher.

Intermediate Concerti for Skilled Middle School and High School Students

	Composer	**Title**	**Publisher**

Alexander, Dennis USA

I		Concertante in G Major (1998)	Alfred

Dennis Alexander's *Concertante in G Major* is scored for two pianos. Its fresh contemporary sounds and interesting rhythms will appeal to the advancing young pianist. The first movement's introduction demands strong chordal technique. This is followed by a tuneful opening theme that calls for articulate fingers and excellent balance between the hands. Broken-chord figures abound, and a *cadenza* leads to an exciting finish. The second movement opens with the solo piano spinning out a lyrical melody accompanied by lush harmonies. The final movement, Rondo, will challenge students to count carefully. Mixed meters are used throughout (4/4, 7/8, 3+2+3/8, 5/8, etc.). The figurations are always pianistic, and suitable for students with a normal hand span.

Asch, Anna USA

I-A		Concertino (1983)	Hal Leonard

This single-movement concerto is ideal for the fast-fingered middle school or early high school student. Loosely structured in an ABA*Coda* format, the A section, in C major, is built around a five-finger position using many open 5ths and parallel triads, and an energetic sixteenth-note secondary theme, also in a five-finger position. A *cadenza*-like rhapsodic figure leads from the A section into a slower B section, in G natural minor, comprised of a right-hand stepwise octave melody over a jumping quarter-note bass. The return of the A section eventually leads to a *coda* in the parallel key of C minor based on the A section secondary theme. The second-piano orchestra reduction often presents melodic material in contrary motion to the solo part, or supporting harmonic textures in unison rhythm with the solo. Orchestral accompaniment parts are available from the publisher. Hal Leonard has released a *Concertino No. 2* by Asch. This one movement intermediate concerto also gives students the opportunity to experience the pleasure of being soloist with either second piano or orchestra.

Berkovich, I. (Ukraine)

E-I		Piano Concerto, op. 44 (1977)	Hal Leonard

Concerti for Young Pianists by James B. Lyke *continued*

This concerto represents one of four in a Russian series written especially for student-teacher performance in competitions. Each of the three movements offers lyric writing based on folk literature. The student will be challenged by interesting rhythmic figures and technical hurdles. The second movement is based upon a hauntingly beautiful Ukrainian folk song. The third movement features chord outlines exchanged between the hands and a waltz-like middle section before a return to the romping folk song theme upon which the movement is based. Scoring is for two pianos only.

Haydn, Franz Joseph (1732–1809) Austria

E-I   Concertino, Hob. XIV:3 (published 1964)   Peters

This small-scale work contains all the challenges of interpreting classical repertoire. Some technical hurdles include a rapid left-hand triplet accompaniment figure and right-hand trills in the first movement. A *cadenza* is supplied; this could be improvised by the performer. The middle movement, Minuet and Trio, exudes charm. A small string ensemble could accompany the performer. If string players are unavailable, the second piano part provides an adequate substitute.

I   Piano Concerto in C, Hob. XVIII:5 (published in 1955)   Boosey & Hawkes

This concerto must be considered a "classic," one of those "must teach" pieces for young piano students. Clean scale playing, rapid execution of ornaments, and smooth left-hand Alberti bass configurations challenge the performer. The second movement, Minuet and Trio, is an absolute gem. The third movement requires rotational skills, as well as perfect balance between the hands when outlining harmonies. The first movement *cadenza* represents a miniature model for study. This work is scored for a small chamber orchestra. The two-piano version serves well if the student does not play with an orchestra.

I   Piano Concerto in F, Hob XVIII:1 (published in 1960)   International

The *Concerto in F Major* in some ways presents fewer problems than the C major. The second movement is especially lovely, and requires the performer to achieve smooth, *cantabile* playing and perfect balance. The third movement abounds in contrasting touches, broken chord configurations, and syncopation. Some beautiful two-part writing highlights secondary-dominant harmonies prior to the closing theme. Orchestral parts may be rented from the publisher. The piano reduction is very serviceable.

I-A   Concerto in D Major, Hob. XVIII:2
(Ganz, ed., published in 1945)   Schirmer
(Teichmüller, ed., published in 1931)   Peters

This *Concerto in D Major*, cited in the introduction, is the most difficult of the Haydn concerti mentioned here, but very accessible to the capable high school pianist. The first movement employs a buoyant attractive principal theme. Both the secondary theme and development section use right-hand broken chord configurations. The middle movement, *Larghetto*, is the most difficult of the three because of the intricate rhythms and *cadenza*-like interludes. The preferred *cadenzas*, by Haydn, are in the Peters edition, whereas the *cadenzas* in the Schirmer edition are heavily romanticized. Orchestral parts are available.

E (Early Intermediate)   I (Intermediate)   A (Advanced Intermediate to Advanced)

Kasschau, Howard (b. 1913) USA

E-I   Country Concerto (1971)   Schirmer

The first movement opens with a *staccato* theme, alternating with a more lyrical theme. The writing is sparse, but effective. The second movement provides the student with a miniature romantic sounding movement, utilizing scale passages, dotted rhythms, and an opportunity for effective pedaling. The third movement's driving tarantella rhythm builds to an effective climax. Orchestra parts are available from the publisher. The piano reduction serves the student well if orchestra players are not available.

Rollin, Catherine USA

E-I   Concerto in C Major (1993)   Alfred

Rollin's three movement *Concerto in C Major* is written in the Classical style and scored for two pianos. This work would serve as an excellent introduction to the Haydn concerti mentioned above. The first movement is straightforward, requiring attention to dotted rhythms and left-hand finger pedal. Passagework abounds, but lies nicely under a small hand. A brief *cadenza* leads to a brilliant ending. A short (two-page) second movement in a slow 3/4 challenges the student to voice a *cantabile* right-hand melody against triplet-figure left-hand broken chords. Students must be prepared for two-against-three playing in this movement. The third movement (in rondo form) requires precise fingers in scale-passage work, and loose wrists for *staccato* 6ths. A *cadenza* gives the soloist an opportunity to present the thematic material once again. Some of these scale figures were used in the first movement. With this concerto, it is easy to teach the elements of Classical form and develop technical facility with Classical style patterns at the same time.

I   Concerto Romantique (1999)   Alfred

Rollin's Chopinesque *Concerto Romantique*, also in three movements, is solidly intermediate, and slightly more difficult than the earlier *Concerto in C*. It has *cadenzas* for the student to play and contains florid melodic lines framed in Rollin's creative musical texture. Unlike the *Concerto in C*, the *Concerto Romantique* has an orchestration completed by David Daniels, who is well known for his guide to orchestral works (*Orchestral Music: A Handbook*; Scarecrowpress). It is a beautiful orchestration that has been used numerous times in the U.S. and is available by writing (or emailing) David Daniels at 1215 Gettysburg Ct., Rochester Hills, MI 48306, daniels@warrensymphony.org.

Rowley, Alec (1892–1958) Great Britain

I-A   Miniature Concerto for Piano and Orchestra (1947)   Boosey & Hawkes

Rowley's concerto paves the way for the study of Romantic concerti at later stages of development. The G major first movement opens with a short introduction consisting of rich chords and arpeggiations. This is immediately followed by a working of themes and sections in a variety of keys, moods, and styles. The movement is full of scale passages (hands alone and together) and broken chord figures. The second movement is set in D major and requires careful pedaling of chord outlines and of the principal theme. The 6/8 final movement, Rondo, requires precise touch control and agile fingers.

The alternating sections provide a relief from the driving rhythm of the Rondo theme. The *cadenza* will teach a student much about *ad libitum* playing. The closing section restates the opening introduction and concludes in a brilliant scale passage prior to the final chords. Orchestra parts are available from the publisher.

Vandall, Robert D. (b. 1944) USA

I   Concerto in G Major for Piano (1985, Flatau, ed.)   Alfred

Vandall possesses a special gift for combining tuneful melodies with modern harmonies into patterns that feel good under children's hands. Moreover, the composer gives young pianists configurations and interesting technical twists that make them sound (and feel) as if they were at a more advanced level. This work begins with a *cantabile* theme accompanied by broken chords that contrasts with a quicker second theme demanding *staccato* left-hand single notes and right-hand broken octaves. A short *cadenza* leads to a brilliant conclusion. The second movement in E aeolian furnishes the student with long expressive lines as well as some interesting passages with right-hand 3rds. The third movement is in the form of a rondo with a toccata-like flavor. The left hand must be accurate with its crosses over the right hand. The accompaniment is especially appealing with its interesting harmonic progression. At the present time, *Concerto in G* is scored for two pianos only.

I   Concertino in C Major (1992)   Alfred

This concerto is scored for two pianos. It contains all the hallmarks of this composer's style: flowing melodies, interesting rhythms, jazz-like harmonies and technical challenges, the latter bound to improve a student's technique. The first movement intermixes a *cantabile* theme with another, more rhythmic idea. There is a nice interplay of scalar material against a slower-moving *legato* theme. The first movement includes a Piano I *cadenza*. The second movement is a *Scherzo* requiring excellent control over a variety of touches. This 6/8 movement becomes a fine study in rapid five-finger passages. The *vivace* third movement is toccata-like and demands excellent rhythmic and touch control. Students will find this movement exciting. Syncopation abounds in *staccato* passages; *legato* passages provide an opportunity for pedal-work, and for careful listening to contrasts in sound color. The third movement is a gem!

Advanced Concerti for Skilled High School Students

Many high school students have opportunities to prepare single movements from concerti for public performance. These performances might be with their high school band or by winning a young artist concerto competition sponsored by an area community orchestra or youth symphony. Such competitions often restrict the amount of music performed to a single movement. The following concerti movements or works are ideal for study by talented, highly skilled secondary pianists who are embarking on their first major concerto experience.

Beethoven, Ludwig van (1770-1827) Germany

A   Concerto in C Major, op. 15 (first movement)   Peters

The *Concerto in C major* is called Beethoven's first piano concerto because it was the first published (not his first endeavor to compose a concerto). Beethoven premiered the concerto in Vienna, in 1800. The first movement (*Allegro con brio*) is a very manageable first movement and most appealing to students. Internet perusal will reveal talented students as young as middle school age performing this opening movement.

After the orchestral exposition, which introduces the two main themes, the tuneful opening in the piano solo develops into broken arpeggios and the entire movement unfolds as a mix of lyrical writing combined with technical challenges. Technical challenges include an assimilation of techniques such as *Alberti* accompanying patterns and broken chord patterns under right hand melody, brilliant arpeggios and octaves, unison passagework between the hands, and cross rhythms in the development. Beethoven's fondness for tertiary key relationships is reflected by the development beginning in E-flat major and moving to C minor. Three Beethoven *cadenzas* of varying lengths exist for the movement.

Gershwin, George (1898-1937) USA

A   Rhapsody in Blue   Alfred

No list of possible concerti for high school students would be complete without Gershwin's *Rhapsody in Blue* originally titled *American Rhapsody* but later changed at the suggestion of Ira Gershwin. A word of caution should be given concerning assigning the *Rhapsody*. It is much more difficult than it looks and requires an exceptional sense of rhythm and music ensemble when performed with orchestra. As with the Grieg concerto, one advantage of learning the *Rhapsody* is that there is an arrangement available with band and in that version the piano solo part is exactly the same as when played with orchestra.

If the goal is to perform the *Rhapsody* with band or orchestra it is imperative to learn the work from the concerto version. In the concerto edition, one can clearly see the difference between the piano solo part and the orchestra. Many students unknowingly purchase the *solo* version in which the pianist plays both the reduced orchestra part and piano solo texture without understanding which is which. When teaching, it is best to learn section by section. The trickiest ensemble sections are the four versus three cross rhythms between the piano and the orchestra (oboe) and the repeated note piano texture against orchestra (brass). The piece is appealing to the listener for its familiar themes and brilliant merging of jazz with the classical concerto idiom. Gershwin's genius shows through in that he sketched the entire work during a short train ride between Boston and New York. Prominent musicians such as Sergei Rachmaninoff were present for the 1924 debut with the Paul Whiteman band.

Advanced Concerti for Skilled High School Students *continued*

Grieg, Edvard (Hagerup) (1843-1907) Norway

A   Concerto in A Minor, op. 16 (first movement)   Schirmer

The first movement (*Allegro moderato*) of the Grieg concerto is a perfect choice for the skilled high school pianist for many reasons. First, there is a "bandstration" prepared from the orchestration by D. F. Bain for this movement that works wonderfully well with symphonic band. Internet perusal will reveal such performances. Whether performed with band or orchestra, the solo piano part remains exactly the same. Symphonic bands are often more readily available than orchestras and as the original orchestration relies heavily on winds, one does not lose that much by hearing the soloist perform with band instead of orchestra.

The first movement falls neatly into a sonata-*allegro* form and can be studied thematically by section. Cluster practice in the two *Animato* dance-like sections will assist learning the quick position shifts. A consistent fingering must be used for the right hand chromatic thirds. Transposition of the lyrical *tranquillo* theme can be especially tricky in the recapitulation because of the chromaticism involved. The *cadenza* to the first movement is not as hard as it looks and is a joy to play once one gets past the notes and rhythms. Premiered in 1869 but revised several times by Grieg, the Percy Grainger-Schirmer edition is highly recommended both for the second piano orchestral reduction for in-lesson rehearsing and the *ossia* sections which outline superior optional fingerings and technical groupings approved by Grieg and so marked by Grainger. Grainger was very influential in bringing this concerto to the American concert stage through his many performances.

Mozart, (Johann Chrysostom) Wolfgang Amadeus (1756-1791) Austria

A   Concerto in A Major, K 488 (first movement)   Peters

Composed in 1786, the opening *Allegro* of this particular concerto is ideal for secondary students because it uses a small orchestra, making a performance of the movement more feasible. It is scored for 2 flutes, 2 clarinets, 2 bassoons, 2 horns and strings. The structure is a standard sonata-*allegro* that includes a double exposition, the first with orchestra alone, and a final *cadenza* (composed by Mozart and available in most editions) for the soloist to play. The lyrical, sunny disposition and graceful themes are appealing as is the new thematic material introduced by the orchestra in the development. This new material is later restated by the piano in the closing *Coda*. Beautiful melodic writing, *Alberti* accompaniments, scales changing direction in a zigzag manner, scales hands together (octave unison and tenths), broken octave technique, and rhythmically challenging figurations in the *cadenza* are just a few of the benefits of mastering this movement. A student who can play an opening *Allegro* from one of Mozart's moderately difficult solo sonatas will be able to handle this concerto movement. For any pianist who studies a Mozart piano concerto for which Mozart did not provide written out *cadenzas*, a highly recommended edition is Soulima Stravinsky's *18 Cadenzas and 4 Fermatas to Mozart's Piano Concerti* published by Peters.

E (Early Intermediate)   I (Intermediate)   A (Advanced Intermediate to Advanced)

Schumann, Robert (Alexander) (1810-1856) Germany

A   Introduction and Allegro Appassionato, op. 92   Kalmus

When one thinks of Schumann and the concerto format, his famous *Concerto in A Minor, op. 54* comes to mind immediately. Another possibility is this beautiful late work in G major which unfortunately has been overshadowed by the concerto but nevertheless is deserving of more performances and is overall slightly less difficult than the concerto. The advantage of learning op. 92 (not to be confused with his *Introduction with Concert Allegro, op. 134)* is that one performs an entire one-movement work (approximately 15 min.) rather than only an excerpted movement from a full concerto.

The piano introduction consists of arpeggiated harmonies under a beautiful melody shared by different orchestral instruments. The following robust *allegro* falls into a standard sonata-*allegro* form with different themes including one in the relative minor, a full development, and final *Coda* featuring brilliant writing for the pianist which sounds more difficult than it is. The most challenging sections technically comprise leaping broken chords presented first in C major (before the Development) and later in G major (before the final *Coda*).

Materials for Adult Instruction

Anderson, Richard. *Ensemble: Keyboard Proficiency for the Music Major.* Long Grove, IL: Waveland Press, 2001.

Bastien, Jane, Lisa, and Lori. *Piano for Adults*, Books I, II. San Diego, California: Neil A. Kjos Music, 1999.

Chauls, Robert. *Piano for Adults: An Aural Approach.* Los Angeles: Crescendo Publishing, 1984.

Clark, Frances. *Keyboard Musician: For the Adult Beginner.* Sherman Oaks, California: Alfred Publishing, 1980.

Collins, Ann. *How to Use a Fake Book, Fakin' Accompaniments from Melodies and Chord Symbols.* Milwaukee: Hal Leonard Music Publishing, 1985.

Dillon, Brenda, *Piano Fun for Adult Beginners.* Milwaukee, WI: Hal Leonard, 2010.

Faber, Nancy, and Randall Faber. *Adult Piano Adventures: A Comprehensive Piano Course,* Books 1, 2. Fort Lauderdale, FL: FJH Music Company, 2001.

Feldstein, Sandy. *Belwin Complete Adult Keyboard Course.* Sherman Oaks, California: Alfred Publishing, 1997.

Frackenpohl, Arthur. *Harmonization at the Piano* (6th edition). Dubuque, IA: Wm. C. Brown, 1991.

Giles, Allen. *Beginning Piano: An Adult Approach*, Volumes 1, 2 (2nd edition). Bryn Mawr, Pennsylvania: Theodore Presser, 1988.

Heerema, Elmer. *Progressive Class Piano* (2nd edition). Sherman Oaks, California: Alfred Publishing, 1984.

Hilley, Martha, and Lynn Freeman Olson. *Piano for Pleasure: A Basic Course for Adults* (4th edition). Belmont, California: Wadsworth Publishing, 2001.

Hilley, Martha, and Lynn Freeman Olson. *Piano for the Developing Musician* (6th edition). Belmont, California: Wadsworth Publishing, 2009.
Early editions of *Piano for the Developing Musician* comprised two volumes. The author team has since combined the two volumes into a larger single volume intended for 3-4 semesters of college group piano for music majors.

Kern, Alice. *Harmonization-Transposition at the Keyboard.* Sherman Oaks, California: Alfred Publishing, 1968.

Kreader, Barbara, Fred Kern, Mona Rejino, and Phillip Keveren. *Adult Piano Method,* Books I, 2. Milwaukee, WI: Hal Leonard.

Lancaster, E. L., and Kenon D. Renfrow. *Group Piano for Adults,* Volumes I, II (2nd edition). Van Nuys, California: Alfred Publishing, 2008.

Lancaster, E. L. and Kenon Renfrow. *Piano 101*, Books 1, 2. Van Nuys, CA: Alfred Publishing, 1999.

Lindeman, Carolyn A. *Piano Lab: An Introduction to Class Piano* (6th edition). Belmont, California: Wadsworth Publishing, 2007.

Lyke, James and Geoffrey Haydon. *Ensemble Music for Group Piano.* Champaign, Illinois: Stipes Publishing, 2002.

Materials for Adult Instruction *continued*

Lyke, James, and Mike Kocour. *Irving Berlin Melodies for Student and Teacher: The Bass Clef Book.* Champaign, Illinois: Stipes Publishing, 1992.

Lyke, James, and Mike Kocour. *Irving Berlin Melodies for Student and Teacher: The Treble Clef Book.* Champaign, Illinois: Stipes Publishing, 1992.

Lyke, James. *Essential Melodic and Harmonic Patterns for Group Piano Students.* Champaign, Illinois: Stipes Publishing, 2003.

Lyke, James, Reid Alexander, Tony Caramia, Geoffrey Haydon, and Ronald Chioldi. *Keyboard Musicianship, Piano for adults,* Books I, II (9th edition). Champaign, Illinois: Stipes Publishing, 2009.
Book I is intended for music majors in the first year of college group piano and book II the second year (third and fourth semesters).

Lyke, James, Denise Edwards, Geoffrey Haydon, and Ronald Chioldi. *Keyboard Fundamentals, Adult Piano,* Books 1, II (5th edition). Champaign, Illinois: Stipes Publishing, 2006.
Earlier editions of *Keyboard Fundamentals* were one volume. The author team has since split the volume into two smaller books, each representing a semester of study (fall and spring).

Lyke, James, and Don Heitler. *First Year Piano Patterns with Rhythm Background,* Cassette Tapes, I, II. Champaign, Illinois: Stipes Publishing, 1991.

Mach, Elyse. *Contemporary Class Piano* (6th edition). Oxford University Press, USA. 2008.

Mach, Elyse. *Learning Piano Piece by Piece.* Oxford University Press, USA. 2005.

Page, Cleveland L. *The Laboratory Piano Course, for Laboratory or Conventional Class Instruction,* Books I, II. Originally published in 1975 by Dodd, Mead & Company (no longer in print). Rereleased in 2008 by the author as a download e-book, pianotextbooks.com/thebooks.html

Page, Cleveland L. *Ensemble Music for Group Piano, A Creative Approach to Musical Insights and Skills.* 2008. Available from the author as a download e-book, http://pianotextbooks.com/thebooks.html

Palmer, Willard A., Morton Manus, Amanda Vick Lethco. *Adult All-in-One Course: Alfred's Basic Adult Piano Course,* Volumes I-III. Sherman Oaks, California: Alfred Publishing, 1987.

Sheftel, Paul. *The Keyboard, Explorations and Discoveries.* New York: Holt, Rinehart and Winston, 1981.

Squire, Russel N., and Timothy P. Shafer. *Class Piano for Adult Beginners* (4th edition). Englewood Cliffs, New Jersey: Prentice-Hall, 1990.

Starr, Constance and William J. *Practical Piano Skills* (5th edition). Dubuque, Iowa: William C. Brown, 1991.

Stecher, Melvin, Norman Horowitz, Clair Gordon, R. Fred Kern, and E.L. Lancaster. *Keyboard Strategies: A Piano Series for Group or Private Instruction Created For the Older Beginner,* Master Texts I, II. New York: G. Schirmer, 1984.

Zimmerman, Alex H., Russell Hayton, and Dorothy Priesing. *Basic Piano for the College Student.* (5th edition). Dubuque, IA: William C. Brown, 1985.

Appendix I: Listing of Publishers

Addison-Wesley Publishing
   75 Arlington Street, Suite 300
   Boston, MA 02116

Advance Music
   V. Gruber GmbH - Maieräckerstraße 18
   D-72108 Rottenburg, N. Germany

Alfred Publishing Co., Inc.
   16380 Roscoe Blvd.
   P.O. Box 10003
   Van Nuys, CA 91410-0003

Alphonse Leduc Éditions Musicales
   175, rue St-Honoré
   F-75040 Paris Cedex DI, France

Amadeus Verlag
   Postfach 473
   CH-8045 Winterthur, Switzerland

Amadeus Press
   512 Newark Pompton Turnpike
   Pompton Plains, NJ 07444

American Composers Alliance (ACA)
   170 West 74th Street
   New York, NY 10023

Anderson & Roe Arrangements
   http://www.andersonroe.com/

Any Standard Edition (ASE)

Arcadia Music Publishing Co.
   P.O. Box 1
   Rickmansworth, Herts WD3 3AZ England

Arcadian Press
   116 Scudder Place
   Northport, NY 11768

Artia
   (Agent: Boosey & Hawkes)

The Associated Board of the Royal Schools of Music (ABRSM)
   14 Bedford Square
   London, WC1B 3JG
   England
   (Agent: Theodore Presser)

Associated Music Publishers, Inc.
   Hal Leonard Corporation
   7777 West Bluemound Road
   Milwaukee, WI 53213

Augener
   (ECS Publishing)
   138 Ipswich Street
   Boston, MA 02215-3534

Augsburg Fortress Publishers
   426 South Fifth Street
   Box 1209
   Minneapolis, MN 55440

Bärenreiter Verlag
   Heinrich Schütz Allee 31 – 37
   D - 34131 Kassel, Germany
   (Agent: European American Music Distributors)

Bärenreiter-Verlag Basel AG
   Neuweilerstr. 15
   CH-4015 Basel, Switzerland
   (Agent: European American Music Distributors)

M. Baron Co.
   1250 Lakeside Drive
   Corolla, NC 27927

Belwin-Mills Publishing Corp.
   15800 N.W. 48th Avenue
   Miami, FL 33014
   (Agent: Warner Brothers)
   Warner was bought by Alfred

Berandol Music, Ltd.
   P.O. Box 45059, 81 Lakeshore Rd. East
   Mississauga, Ontario L5G 2X4, Canada

Boccaccini & Spada Editori
   Via Arezzo, 17
   00040 - Pavona di Albano Laziale - Roma - Italy
   (Agent: Theodore Presser)

Boonin, Joseph
   (Agent: European American Music Corporation)

Appendix I: Listing of Publishers *continued*

Boosey & Hawkes, Inc.
 35 East 21st Street
 New York, NY 10010-6212

The Boston Music Company
 215 Stuart Street
 Boston, MA 02116

Bote & Bock
 Lützowufer 26
 10787 Berlin, Germany
 (Agent: Boosey & Hawkes)

Bradley Publications
 80 8th Avenue
 New York, NY 1001
 (Agent: Warner Brothers)

Braydeston Press
 (No Information Available)

Breitkopf und Härtel
 Walkmuhlstrasse 52
 P.O. Box 1707
 D-65195 Wiesbaden, Germany
 (Agents: Schirmer; Theodore Presser)

Broekmans & Van Poppel B.V.
 van Baerlestraat 92 – 94
 NL - 1071 BB Amsterdam, Netherlands

Broude Brothers Limited
 141 White Oaks Road
 Williamstown, MA 01267

Brown & Benchmark
 PlayRecord.Net
 Green Lane Dyeworks
 Green Lane
 Yeadon
 LS19 7XP, UK
 (Agent: Boosey & Hawkes)

Brown, William C.
 2460 Kerper Boulevard
 Dubuque, IA 52001

Cambria Records and Publishing
 P.O. Box 374
 Lomita, CA 90717

Carl Fischer, LLC
 65 Bleecker Street
 New York, NY 10012
 (Agent: Theodore Presser)

CeBeDeM
 Centre Belge de Documentation Musicale
 rue d'Arlon
 75-77, B-1040 Brussels, Belgium

Chappell Music Co.
 Warner - Chappell Music
 1290 Avenue of the Americas, 23rd Floor
 New York, NY 10019
 (Agent: Alfred)

Charles Hansen Educational Music
 1870 West Avenue
 Miami Beach, FL 33139

Chester Music Limited
 8/9 Frith Street
 London, W1V 5TZ, England

Éditions Choudens
 38 rue Jean Mermoz
 F-75008 Paris, France
 (Agent: Schott)

John Church Company
 (Agent: Theodore Presser)

Franco Colombo
 Purchased by Belwin-Mills in 1969
 (Agent: CPP/Belwin Music/Warner Brothers)

The Composer's Press
 (Agent: OPUS)

Composers Facsimile Edition
 (Agent: AM.COMP.AL.)

Concordia Publishing House
 3558 South Jefferson Ave.
 St. Louis, MO 63118-3968

Consolidated Music Publishing
 (Agent: Music Sales)

CPP/Belwin Music
 (Agent: Alfred)

Éditions Cranz
    30, rue St. – Christophe
    B - 1000 Bruxelles, Belgium

Crescendo Publications, Inc.
    6311 North O'Connor Road - #112
    Irving, TX 75039 - 3112

Edizioni Curci S.r.l.
    Galeria del Corso 4
    20122 Milano, Italy

J. Curwen & Sons Ltd.
    (Agent: Hal Leonard)

Oliver Ditson Company
    (Agent: Theodore Presser)

Doblinger Musikverlag
    Dorotheergasse 10
    P.O. Box 882
    A-1011 Vienna, Austria
    (Agent: Foreign Music Distributors)

Dover Publications, Inc.
    31 East 2nd Street
    Mineola, NY 11501-3582

DSCH
    Musical Publishers House DSCH (Russia)
    Website: http://iscmrussia.ru/eng_dsch.htm
    Email: mcme@rambler.ru
    (Agent: Alfred)

Durand S.A. Éditions Musicale
    5, rue du Helder
    F-75009 Paris, France
    (Agent: Hal Leonard)

Editio Musica Budapest
    Victor Hugo utca 11-15
    H-1132 Budapest HUNGARY
    (Agents: Boosey & Hawkes; Theodore Presser)

Éditions Aug. Zurfluh
    13, avenue du Lycée Lakanal
    92340 Bourg la Reine, France

Edition 49 GmbH
    Lauteri 7
    10145 Tallinn, Estonia

Édition HAS Music Publishing
    P.O. Box 1753
    Maryland Heights, MO 63043
    (Agent: Hal Leonard)

Ekay Music Inc.
    2 Depot Plz Ste 301
    Bedford Hills, NY, 10507-1834
    (Agent: Alfred))

Elkan-Vogel, Inc.
    (Agent: Theodore Presser)

Empire Publishing
    P.O. Box 1344
    Studio City, CA 91614

European American Music Distributors Corporation (EAMC)
    254 West 31st Street, 15th Floor
    New York, NY 10001
    (Agent: Theodore Presser)

Faber Music Ltd.
    3 Queen Square
    London WC1N 3AU, England
    (Agent: Hal Leonard)

Felfar Music
    Fentone Music, Ltd.
    Now De Haske
    4 Fleming Road – Earlstrees
    Corby, Northants, NN17 4SN, England

Ferguson, H.-S & B
    (Agent: Boosey & Hawkes)

The FJH Music Company, Inc.
    Westport Business Park
    2525 Davie Rd., Suite 360
    Fort Lauderdale, FL 33317-7424

Flammer, Harold
    (Agent: Shawnee)

Éditions Foetisch
    2 Grand Pont
    Postf. 2793
    CH-1003 Lausanne, Switzerland

Foreign Music Distributors
    13 Elkay Drive
    Chester, NY 10912

Appendix I

Appendix I: Listing of Publishers *continued*

Sam Fox Publishing Co.
   (Agent: Theodore Presser)

Frank Music Corp.
   (Agent: Hal Leonard)

The Frederick Harris Music Co., Limited
   Unit 1, 5865 McLaughlin Rd.
   Mississauga, Ontario, Canada
   L5R 1B8

Galaxy Music
   (Agent: ECS Publishing)
   138 Ipswich Street
   Boston, MA 02215-3534

General Words and Music Company
   (Agent: Neil A. Kjos Music Publishing)

Julius Hainauer
   www.load.cd
   GmbH
   Rothausstrasse 1
   8280 Kreuzlingen, Switzerland
   Load.CD is a global music platform for online publication and sale of digital sheet music and performance licenses.

Hal Leonard Music Publishing Corporation
   7777 West Bluemound Rd.
   P.O. Box 13819
   Milwaukee, WI 53213

Hamelle et cie.
   175 rue Saint-Honoré
   F-75040 Paris Cedex 01, France
   (Agent: Robert King)

Hansen House
   1820 West Ave.
   Miami Beach, FL 33139

Harcourt
   6277 Sea Harbor Drive
   Orlando, FL 32887

Harwood Academic Publishers
   Amsteldijk 166
   1st Floor
   1079 LH Amsterdam
   The Netherlands

G. Henle USA, Inc.
   1897 Craig Road
   P.O. Box 460127
   St. Louis, MO 63146

Heinrichshofen's Verlag GmbH & Co.
   Liebigstrasse 16
   W-2940 Wilhelmshaven, Germany
   (Agent: C. F. Peters)

Helios Music Edition
   Plymouth Music Company, Inc.
   170 Northeast 33rd St.
   Fort Lauderdale, FL 33334

The Heritage Music Press
   c/o The Lorenz Corporation
   501 East Third Street
   Dayton, OH 45401

Heugel & Cie.
   175 rue Saint-Honoré
   F-75040 Paris Cedex 01, France
   (Agent: Leduc)

Hinrichsen Edition, Ltd.
   Hinrichsen House, 10 - 12 Baches Street
   London N1 6DN, England
   (Agent: C. F. Peters)

Hinshaw Music, Inc.
   P.O. Box 470
   Chapel Hill, NC 27514

Holt, Rinehart and Winston
   1120 South Capitol of Texas Highway
   Austin, TX 78746-6487

Hug & Cie. Musikverlage
   Fusslistrasse 4
   CH-8022 Zurich
   Switzerland

International Music Publications Ltd.
   (Agent: Warner Brothers Publications)

Israeli Music Publications
   The Israel Music Institute (IMI)
   Israel Music Information Centre (IMIC)
   55 Menachem Begin Road
   IL-67138 Tel Aviv Israel
   (Agent: Theodore Presser)

LISTING OF PUBLISHERS

Editions Jobert
    29 boulevard Beaumarchais
    F-75004 Paris, FRANCE
    (Agent: Theodore Presser)

Jürgenson, P.
    Rob. Forberg - P. Jurgenson Musikverlag
    Baumkirchner Str. 53 a
    D-81673 München, Germany

Edwin F. Kalmus, L. C.
    P.O. Box 5011
    Boca Raton, FL 33431
    (Agent: Warner Brothers Publications)

Kendor Music, Inc.
    21 Grove Street
    P.O. Box 278
    Delevan, NY 14042-0278

E. C. Kerby
    c/o Counterpoint Musical Services
    2650 John Street, Unit 24
    Markham, Ontario, Canada
    L3R 2W6
    (Agent: Hal Leonard)

Neil A. Kjos Music Company
    4380 Jutland Drive
    San Diego, CA 92117-3642

Lawson-Gould Music
    (Agent: Warner Brothers)

Leeds Music Corp.
    (Agent: MCA Music Publishing)

Éditions Henry Lemoine
    25 rue Henri Monnier
    75009 Paris, France
    (Agent: Theodore Presser)

Alfred Lengnick & Co., Ltd.
    (Agent: Music Sales)

Lienau, Robert
    Musikverlag Robert Lienau
    Strubbergstraße 80
    60489 Frankfurt am Main, Germany

Litha Music
    (Agent: Music Sales)

Litolff Collection
    (Agent: C. F. Peters)

Edward B. Marks Music Company
    c/o Carlin America, Inc.
    126 East 38th Street
    New York, NY 10016
    (Agent: Hal Leonard)

Karl Heinrich Möseler Musikverlag
    Hoffman - von - Fallersleben - Straße 8
    D-38304 Wolfenbüttel, Germany

Masters Music Publications, Inc.
    P.O. Box 810157
    Boca Raton, FL 33481-0157

Éditions Max Eschig
    5, rue du Helder
    F-75009 Paris, France
    (Agent: Hal Leonard)

Kevin Mayhew Ltd
    Buxhall Stowmarket
    Suffolk IP14 3BW UK
    (Agent: Brodt)

Music Corporation of America
    MCA Music Publishing
    1755 Broadway, 8th Floor
    New York, NY 10019
    (Agent: Hal Leonard)

Mel Bay Publications, Inc.
    #4 Industrial Drive
    Daily Industrial Park
    Pacific, MO 63069-0066

Mercury Music Corporation
    (Agent: Theodore Presser)

Grand Mesa Music Publishers
    1038 Chipeta Ave
    Grand Junction, CO 81501

Irving Mills Music
    P.O. Box 10372
    Sedona, AZ 86339

MMB Music, Inc.
    3526 Washington Ave.
    St. Louis, MO 63103

Appendix 1

Appendix I: Listing of Publishers *continued*

Moonstone Press
  P.O. Box 100614
  Denver, CO 80250-0614
  http://www.shaakpianomusic.com/Events.htm

MorningStar Music Publishers
  5200 Dixie Road
  Mississauga, Ontario, CANADA L4W 1E4

MSM Music Publishers
  Gilbert House
  406 Roding Lane South
  Woodford Grenn, Essex IG8 8EY, UK

Muller, Leopold, GmbH
  Sudenstrasse 43
  P.O. Box 6
  W-8526 Bubenreuth, Germany

Musicalion
  http://www.musicalion.com/en

Music Sales Corporation
  257 Park Avenue South, 20th Floor
  New York, NY 10010

Musicord Publications
  (Agent: CPP/Belwin Music/Warner)
  CPP/Belwin and Warner bought by Alfred

MusT
  http://www.tutti.co.uk/sheet-music/publishers/must
  (for the music of Kapustin Nikolai Kapustin)

Myklas Music Press
  387 Corona Street
  Denver, CO 80218-3939

Theodor Nagel Musikholzer
  P.O. Box 28 02 66
  W-2000 Hamburg 26, Germany

National Keyboard Arts Associates
  (Keyboard Arts)
  University Park, Princeton, NJ

Verlag Neue Musik GmbH
  Grabbeallee 15
  13156 Berlin, Germany

New School for Music Study
  (Agent: Alfred)

New World Music Company, Ltd.
  (Agent: Alfred)

Novello and Company, Ltd.
  8/9 Frith Street
  London W1V 5TZ, England
  (Agent: Schirmer; Music Sales; Shawnee)

Oxford University Press
  198 Madison Ave.
  New York, NY 10016-4314

Pearson Education
  1 Lake Street
  Upper Saddle River, NJ 07458

Peermusic (UK) Ltd.
  8-14 Peer House Verulam Street
  WC1X 8LZ London, UK

Peermusic Classical
  (Peer-Southern Concert Music)
  810 Seventh Avenue
  New York, NY 10019

C. F. Peters Corp.
  373 Park Avenue South
  New York, NY 10016

The Plymouth Music Company, Inc.
  170 Northeast 33rd St.
  Fort Lauderdale, FL 33334

Édition Chopin Institute
  Polskie Wydawnictwo Muzyczne (PWM)
  Al Krasinskiego 11a
  PL - 31 - 111
  Kraków, Poland
  (Agent: Theodore Presser)

Prentice-Hall, Inc.
  Pearson Education
  One Lake Street
  Upper Saddle River, NJ 07458
  (Agent: Pearson Education)

Theodore Presser Company
  1 Presser Place
  Bryn Mawr, PA 19010-3490

LISTING OF PUBLISHERS

Pro Art Publications
(Agent: Warner)
Warner was bought by Alfred

Redleafpiano Publications
www.redleafpianoworks.com

Ricordi Americana S.A.E.C.
Tte. Gral. Juan D. Perón 1558, Piso 1
1037 Buenos Aires – Argentina
(Agent: Hal Leonard)

Musikverlag Ries & Erler Berlin
Wandalenallee 8
D-14052 Berlin Germany
(Agent: Carl Fischer)

Robbins Music Corp.
(Agent: Alfred)

Goodmusic Publishing
Roberton Publications
PO Box 100
Tewkesbury GL20 7YQ UK

Lee Roberts Music Publishers
P.O. Box 225
Katonah, NY 1053
(Agent: Hal Leonard)

Rouart, Lerolle & Cie.
(acquired by Salabert)
(Agent: Salabert)

Éditions Salabert
Éditions Durand-Salabert-Eschig
5, rue du Helder
F-75009 Paris, France
(Agent: Hal Leonard)

Schaum Publications, Inc.
10235 North Port Washington Rd.
Mequon, WI 53092
(Agent: Alfred)

E. C. Schirmer
ECS Publishing
138 Ipswich Street
Boston, MA 02215-3534

G. Schirmer, Inc.
257 Park Avenue South
20th Floor
New York, NY 10010

Schlesinger
(No information available)

C. F. Schmidt Verlag
(No longer in business)

B. Schott Sohne Musikverlag
Weihergarten 5
Postf. 3640
D-6500 Mainz, Germany
(Agent: European American Music Distributors)

Schroeder & Gunther
(No Information Available)
(Agent: Hal Leonard)

Schuberth & Co., Edward
(Agent: Century)

Shawnee Press, Inc.
1221 17th Ave. South
Nashville, TN 37212
(Agent: Hal Leonard)

Internationale Musikverlage Hans Sikorsky
Postf. 130848
Johnsallee 23
2000 Hamburg 13
Germany
(Agent: Augsburg Fortress Publishers)

John Sheppard Music Press
P. O. Box 6784
Denver, CO 8020

Sikorski, Hans
Internationale Musikverlage
Hans Sikorski
Johnsallee 23
D - 20148 Hamburg 13, Germany

Nicholas Simrock Musikverlag
A Division of Anton Benjamin
Werderstraße 44
20144 Hamburg Germany
(Agent: Boosey & Hawkes)

Appendix I

Appendix I: Listing of Publishers continued

Sisra
1719 Bay Street S.E.
Washington, DC 20003
(Agent: Empire Publishing)

Southern Music Company
P.O. Box 329
San Antonio, TX 78292

Stainer & Bell Ltd.
P.O. Box 110, Victoria House
23 Gruneisen Rd.
London N3 IDZ, England
(Agent: ECS Publishing)

Stipes Publishing Co.
204 West University Ave.
Champaign, IL 61820

Summy-Birchard Co.
(Agent: Alfred)

Edizioni Suvini Zerboni
Via M.F. Quintiliano 40
1-20138 Milano, Italy

N. Jane Tan
Tan's publications are available on-line: http://www.pianoteams.com/catalogs/pianoteams_order_form.pdf (accessed 12.12.10)

Theatrix
(No Information Available)

TRO Inc. (The Richmond Organization)
266 West 37th Street, 17th Floor
New York, NY 10018

Unión Musical Ediciones S.L. [Española] (UME)
Unión Musical Española
Marqués de la Ensenada 4, 3
Madrid, E-28004 Spain
(Agent: G. Schirmer)

Universal Edition
Karlsplatz 6
A-1010 Vienna, Austria
(Agent: European American Music)

Universal Edition, Inc.
254 W. 31st St., Floor 15
New York, NY 10001-2813
(Agent: European American Music)

Vivace Press
P.O. Box 210788
St. Louis, MO 63121

Wiener Urtext Edition
Wiener Urtext Edition
Forsthausgasse 9 A-1200
Wien, Austria
(Agent: Theodore Presser)

Wadsworth Publishing
10 Davis Street
Belmont, CA 94002

Wagner, Karl Dieter
(No information available)

Warner Bros. Publications, Inc.
15800 N.W. 48th Ave.
P.O. Box 4340
Miami, FL 33014

Waterloo Music Company Ltd.
3 Regina Street North
Waterloo, Ontario, Canada
N2J 4A5

Watson-Guptill Publications
1515 Broadway
New York, NY 10036

Josef Weinberger Ltd.
12 - 14 Mortimer Street
London W1T 3JJ England
(Agent: Boosey & Hawkes)

Weintraub Music Co.
(Agent: Schirmer)

Werner-Curwen
(No information available)

Western International
3707 65th Avenue
Greeley, CO 80634

LISTING OF PUBLISHERS

Westwood Press, Inc.
   3759 Willow Road
   Schiller Park, IL 60176
   (Agent: World)

Willis Music Co.
   7380 Industrial Rd.
   Florence, KY 41042

Wise Publications
   Robert Wise
   Music Sales Group
   14-15 Berners Street
   London W1T 3LJ, England

Yorktown Music Press, Inc.
   24 East 22nd Street
   New York NY 10010
   (Agent: Music Sales Corporation)

Zen - On Music., Ltd.
   3 - 14 Higashi Gokencho
   Shinjuku – ku
   Tokyo 162, Japan

Appendix II: Composer Catalogue Numbers

Individual works by a number of composers are identified by abbreviations and numbers assigned by a musicologist, bibliographer or music scholar in thematic catalogues. Catalog numbers are used to establish a sequence and numeric order of a composer's works.

The term *Opus* is used with a number (e. g., op. 49) to designate the position of a given piece in the chronological sequence of works by the composer. These numbers, however, were sometimes assigned by a publisher rather than the composer and are often an unreliable guide. Sometimes a single work will have conflicting opus numbers or be placed out of sequence in terms of when the work was actually composed. For example, the two piano sonatas by Beethoven in op. 49 are by the sequence of the opus number placed in his middle period but were actually composed much earlier.

When a scholar creates a thematic catalogue, the scholar's initials are often used to identify the catalogue number, i.e., Hoboken (Hob.) numbers for works by Haydn or Kirkpatrick (K) numbers for Scarlatti's works. Some catalogue numbers include the prefix "Anh." (for example, BWV Anh. 121). "Anh." is an abbreviation for *Anhang*, a German word meaning appendix or supplement. Certain genres, such as operas and other vocal works, were not always assigned opus numbers. Catalogue numbers used in this fifth edition of the *Piano Repertoire Guide* are listed below.

Works by **Carl Philipp Emanuel Bach** are often identified by "Wq" and/or "H" (Helm) numbers (for example, *Morceaux divers pour clavecin, Wq 117/39, H 98*). Alfred Wotquenne (1867-1939) was a Belgian music bibliographer and author of *Thematisches Verzeichnis der Werke von Carl Philipp Emanuel Bach* (Leipzig, 1905, revised 1964). Eugene Helm is an American musicologist and author of *A New Thematic Catalogue of the Works of C.P.E. Bach* (New Haven: Yale University Press, 1989).

Works by **Johann Sebastian Bach** are identified by "BWV" numbers (for example, *Allemande in G Minor, BWV 836*). BWV is the abbreviation for *Bach Werke Verzeichnis*, the short title of the *Thematisch-Systematisches Verzeichnis der musikalischen Werke von Johann Sebastian Bach* (Leipzig, 1950), a monumental thematic catalogue of Bach's complete works compiled by the German music librarian Wolfgang Schmieder. On occasion, musicians substitute "S" for "BWV" on printed programs.

Works by **Béla Bartók** were catalogued by András Szőllősy. Szőllősy is the author of the volume, *Bibliography of Musical Works and Musicological Writings of Béla Bartók* (1957). From this research, "Sz." numbers (for example, *First Term at the Piano, Sz. 53*) are used to place the composer's works in chronological order. Bartók occasionally used opus numbers but over time was inconsistent in their use and did not always assign opus numbers to his compositions. He designated opus numbers between the years of 1890 and 1894 as well as for a few later works, but stopped using opus numbers after 1921.

Works by **Ludwig van Beethoven** are self-catalogued through the composer's use of opus numbers. In the thematic catalogue of Beethoven's works, *Das Werk Beethovens* (Munich and Duisburg, 1955, completed by Hans Halm), compiled by German musicologist Georg Ludwig Kinsky (1882-1951), works which were published posthumously were designated "WoO." WoO is an abbreviation for *Werk ohne Opuszahl* (work without opus number). Similarly, the term, *Kinsky-Halm*, sometimes is used to identify compositions without opus numbers.

Works by **George Frideric Handel** are identified by "HWV" numbers (for example, *Gavotte in G Major, HWV 491*). HWV is an abbreviation for *Handel Werke Verzeichnis*. The full title for this thematic catalogue, compiled by Margaret and Walter Eisen, is *Händel-Handbuch, gleichzeitig Suppl. zu Hallische Händel-Ausgabe* (Kassel: Bärenreiter, 1978-1986).

Works by **Franz Joseph Haydn** are identified by Hoboken numbers (for example, *Sonata in D Major, Hob. XVI:37*). Anthony van Hoboken was a Dutch musicologist. His thematic catalogue, *Joseph Haydn: Thematisch-bibliographisches Werkverzeichnis* (Mainz: B. Schott, 1957-1971) divides Haydn's works into a number of categories. The piano sonatas are in category XVI and the piano variations are in XVII.

Appendix II: Composer Catalogue Numbers *continued*

Works by **Wolfgang Amadeus Mozart** are identified by "KV" numbers (for example, *Sonata in C Major, KV 545*). KV stands for *Köchel Verzeichnis*. Ludwig Ritter von Köchel (1800-1877) was an Austrian professor of botany who devoted his retirement years to collecting all the known works by Mozart. He created a chronological catalogue in which these works are listed and numbered. Now, "KV" is customarily shortened to simply *K*.

Works by **Franz Liszt** normally are identified by Searle numbers (for example, *Sonata in B minor, S. 178*). These are based on Humphrey Searle's 1954 *The Music of Liszt*, republished in 1966 by Dover.

Works by **Domenico Scarlatti** are usually identified by two numbers, one beginning with "L" and one beginning with "K." The L numbers are from *Opere complete per clavicembalo* (Milan: Ricordi, 1906-1908), compiled by Alessandro Longo. K stands for Ralph Kirkpatrick, an American harpsichordist and scholar who provided a revised and more exact chronology and a new numbering system for the sonatas in his book *Domenico Scarlatti* (Princeton: Princeton University Press, 1953, rev. 1968). In 1967, Giorgio Pestelli published the most recent edition of the 555 sonatas using an alternative third system of Pestelli (P) numbers.

Works by **Franz Schubert** are identified by "Deutsch" numbers (for example, *Waltz in A Flat, op. 9, no. 12, D. 365*). These numbers were assigned by Otto Erich Deutsch (1883-1967) in his thematic catalogue of Schubert's works, *Thematisches Verzeichnis seiner Werke in chronologischer Folge* (*Neue Schubert Ausgabe* Serie VIII, Bd. 4, Kassel, 1978).

Works by **Georg Philipp Telemann** are identified by "TWV" numbers (for example, *Fantasia in D Minor, TWV 33:2*). TWV is an abbreviation for *Telemann Werkverzeichnis*. This thematic catalogue, *Thematischer-Systematisches Verzeichnis seiner Werke: Telemann Werkverzeichnis* (Kassel: Bärenreiter, 1984), was compiled by Martin Ruhnke. The number after the TWV indicates the genre of work. For example, keyboard works are identified between 30-39 whereas chamber music is 40-45.

About the Authors

Cathy Albergo is Professor of Music and Chair of the Department of Music at the University of North Carolina at Wilmington. She was previously Professor of Music and Chair of the Music Department at William Rainey Harper College in Palatine, Illinois. Dr. Albergo is a curricular specialist in piano pedagogy and group piano teaching and has contributed numerous articles to professional keyboard journals. She is co-author, with Reid Alexander and Marvin Blickenstaff, of the widely used *Celebration Series Perspectives, Handbook for Teachers* published by Frederick Harris Music Co., Limited of Toronto, Canada. In collaboration with J. Mitzi Kolar and Mark Mrozinksi, she co–authored the piano method *Celebrate Piano!*, also published by Frederick Harris Music. With music degrees from the University of North Carolina Chapel Hill (BM. Ed.), Southern Methodist University in Dallas, Texas (M.M.) and the University of Illinois at Urbana-Champaign (Ed.D.), Professor Albergo is a nationally recognized authority on piano instruction and a frequent lecturer, adjudicator and workshop clinician. Her leadership contributions include past President of the Illinois State Music Teachers Association, Regional Chair of the National Association of Schools of Music, and National Certification Chair of the Music Teachers National Association.

Reid Alexander, Professor of Music at the University of Illinois, is widely recognized as an inspiring teacher, accomplished pianist, and published author. A finalist in the first Gina Bachauer Competition, his early piano study was with Gerald Snyder, Stanley Fletcher, and James Lyke (piano pedagogy). Additional coaching has occurred with Mieczyslaw Horszowski, Jack Radunsky, and Ruth Slenczynska. A doctoral graduate of Vanderbilt University, he has presented workshops and recitals in over 40 states and abroad. Dr. Alexander collaborated with Andrew Hisey, Samuel Holland, and Marc Widner to write the highly regarded 27-volume *Celebrate Composer* series published by Frederick Harris Music Co., Limited. He also co-authored the *Celebration Series Perspectives, Handbook for Teachers* (see Albergo above) and with James Lyke, Tony Caramia, Geoff Haydon, and Ronald Chioldi the *Keyboard Musicianship* series (Stipes Publishing, Champaign, IL). Earlier in his career, Illinois honored Professor Alexander as a faculty recipient of a campus award for teaching excellence. Each academic year he works with a talented class of international and domestic pianists on the Urbana campus. Leadership contributions include past President of the Illinois State Music Teachers Association and the East Central Division of MTNA. During 1999-2000, he served as Professor of Piano and *Director* of Piano Pedagogy at The University of Oklahoma.